M000187566

COMPETITIVE SOLUTIONS

Competitive Solutions

PRINCETON UNIVERSITY PRESS

Princeton and Oxford

Published by Princeton University Press, 41 William Street,
Princeton, New Jersey 08540
In the United Kingdom: Princeton University Press, 3 Market Place,
Woodstock, Oxfordshire OX20 1SY

LIBRARY OF CONGRESS CATALOGING-IN-PUBLICATION DATA

McAfee, R. Preston.
Competitive solutions : the strategist's toolkit / R. Preston McAfee.
p. cm.
Includes bibliographical references and index.
ISBN 0-691-09646-5 (alk. paper)
1. Strategic planning. 2. Business planning. 3. Decision making. 4. Game theory.
5. Pricing. 6. Antitrust law. 7. Industrial management. 8. Competition.
9. Strategic planning—Case studies. I. Title.
HD30.28 .M3815 2002
658.4′012—dc21 2002020102

British Library Cataloging-in-Publication Data is available

This book has been composed in Adobe Garamond

Printed on acid-free paper. ∞

www.pup.princeton.edu

Printed in the United States of America

1 3 5 7 9 10 8 6 4 2

FOR ELLIE AND KRISTIN

Contents

When your only tool is a hammer, every problem looks like a nail.
—**Abraham Maslow**

Preface

PREAMBLE

This book offers conceptual tools of business strategy with descriptions of practical implementations of the theory. It is intended for a general business audience, especially readers with technical training. It is also designed as a text for a course in business strategy that uses examination of cases as the primary teaching method.

Strategy texts tend to be comprehensive, which entails covering much material that is low on useful insights. In contrast, this book focuses on practical strategy—insights that have significant application in real situations. I use actual rather than hypothetical examples when possible.

A first feature of this practical approach is that I cover different material than other strategy books. The selection of material springs from my work in advising companies and evaluating mergers for antitrust purposes. Pricing provides an example. I pay much more attention to pricing than do most traditional texts. Pricing has been neglected in business strategy. Because many business schools devote a separate course to pricing, strategists often ignore it. Marketers tend to focus on increasing demand for one's product, dismissing prices as either a markup on cost or "what the market will bear." Economists tend to think of price as a single variable rather than as a pattern or dynamic array of prices. On the contrary, I believe that pricing ought to be at the core of business strategy rather than an afterthought. In particular, pricing strategies are important determinants of the profitability of R&D, service contracts, warranties, market segmentation, and other strategic choices.

By the same token, I pay greater attention to litigation and antitrust than is common in other books on strategy. The U.S. Department of Justice's suit against Microsoft showed the folly of ignoring the antitrust laws in the design of business strategy. While few companies receive the level of antitrust scrutiny devoted to

Microsoft, even for much smaller enterprises litigation is a common tool for harassing and punishing competitors. I provide an overview of litigation strategies, which is useful if only to defend against unscrupulous competitors.

Another feature of my more practical approach is that I make only a modest effort to describe strategy as a grand, comprehensive, fully integrated plan. Instead I offer a toolkit of strategic concepts adaptable for different purposes in different situations. The problem with grand comprehensive plans is that they need to be designed for specific firms in specific industries. The right business strategy for oil company British Petroleum is very different from the best strategy for chip designer and manufacturer Intel, and both of these differ from the right strategy for retailer Wal-Mart. Even within low-cost retailing, Dollar General has been very successful competing against, or coexisting with, Wal-Mart, in spite of Wal-Mart's reputation for invincibility and destruction of competitors. Dollar General's success is a consequence of its strategy, which is very different from Wal-Mart's. Indeed, a major theme of modern business strategy is that the best strategy for any firm depends on those the firm's rivals adopt, and this best strategy can be very different from the rival's, as imitation is often a guarantee of mediocre profits. Two rival firms such as Wal-Mart and Dollar General, doing very different things, may be following quite distinct optimal strategies.

Vision is critical to the practical formulation of business strategy. Business strategy is a vision of a profitable future and a feasible path to get there. However, profits arise because of the *uniqueness* of the company's vision. A book that promises to provide a single vision, or even three visions, for all firms in all circumstances should be discarded, or should be read only to identify the activities uninspired competitors might choose.

At the very general level, strategy is about complementarity—choices that fit with each other. In contrast to most books about business strategy, this book focuses primarily on the individual elements of strategies. Again, the book is a toolkit, not a bible. My intention is that those reading this book will find valuable insight into the elements of business strategy and how these elements have been used successfully in the past. Combining and applying the elements in new specific situations will often require additional analysis.

A great deal has been written on the merits and problems of using game theory in business strategy.[1] While there are some situations in which other firms can reasonably be viewed as nonstrategic, in most situations several players are strategic—aware of each other and considering how the others will behave, which is precisely the situation that game theory is designed to study. At a general level, game theory involves specifying the actions and returns to all the participants in a situation, and looking for behavior, called equilibrium behavior, which results in each participant maximizing his or her payoff, given the behavior of others. Equilibrium behavior has the advantage that no one can do better, given the behavior of others. Critics of game theory complain that game-theoretic equilibrium concepts are inappropriate and that game theory has no robust predictions. These critics have a point: it is often the case that equilibrium reasoning will be unhelpful to a strategist. Game-theoretic equilibrium reasoning requires that all firms have figured out their own best strategy as well as the best strategy for their opponents, and that these calculations (each firm's beliefs about what a particular firm should do) coincide, so that no firm is surprised when the game is played. Thus, equilibrium reasoning implies that the strategist's job is already accomplished! However, the logic of the "best response"—how a firm should behave, given an expectation of its rivals' behaviors—is an invaluable conceptual tool for the design of strategy. Moreover, the strategic notion of putting oneself in a rival's position is enormously valuable, and comes straight from game-theoretic reasoning.*

An example of the perils of price-cutting illustrates the importance of game-theoretic reasoning. Nonstrategic reasoning (for example, resource-based) suggests that it is valuable to offer a price cut to the customers who purchase from competitors. If it is possible to offer selective price cuts, offer them not to one's own customers but to the customers of rivals, thereby permitting the firm to obtain extra sales without cutting prices to existing customers. While this sounds plausible, in most cases it is a terrible strategy, for it neglects the reaction of rivals. Rivals—losing business—have an incentive to cut prices as well, to try to preserve their customer base. The consequence is fierce price competition, which can easily spill over to the firms' existing customers and decrease prices for all. Instead, consider the strategy of setting an increase in price for a rival's customers, which can be accomplished by making a general price increase combined with a discount to existing customers that leaves the prices to existing customers unchanged. Such a pricing scheme makes the firm less of a competitive threat to its rivals, inducing the rivals to respond with a price increase. All of the firms make more money.[2] In other words, because of strategic effects, a price increase to potential customers who are not current customers can increase the firm's profits by a general softening of price competition. This situation is a powerful example of game-theoretic reasoning getting the right answer where other approaches fail.

I have attempted to avoid mathematics wherever possible, but there are a

*Of course, the Native American aphorism, "Never criticize a man until you've walked a mile in his moccasins," predates game theory but was not employed to deduce behavior but rather to induce empathy. A game theorist's perspective on the subject, in contrast, is, "Before you criticize a man, walk a mile in his shoes. That way, when you do criticize him, you'll be a mile away and have his shoes." This led Robert Byrne to counter, "Until you walk a mile in another man's moccasins, you can't imagine the smell."

couple of topics where moderately sophisticated mathematics is intrinsic to the topic. One such topic is yield management, which is a sophisticated, dynamic pricing scheme. A second example is asset pricing and valuation, and the capital asset pricing model (CAPM) theory. Because both of these examples are quite sophisticated, some mathematics is essential to communicate their functioning and basis. Ultimately, both yield management and CAPM are formulas. These formulas have proved to be extraordinarily valuable—CAPM guides trillions of dollars of investments while yield management has increased airline and hotel revenues by billions of dollars. In addition, I offer a chapter on statistics, another mathematical field. There are many issues associated with uncertainty in strategy—options, competing against a rival with unknown resources, uncertainty about the future—and an understanding of probability and statistics is valuable for a full understanding of these subjects. Moreover, there are some common statistical mistakes associated with seeing patterns that do not actually exist, and an understanding of statistics can mitigate such common errors.

CONTENTS

This book starts with an application—America Online. AOL serves as a multifaceted example of many of the tools developed within the book. Chapter 2 presents a broad overview—as if from an orbital satellite—of industry analysis. I relate characteristics of industries to their profitability and to the appropriate "big picture" strategies for those industries. Appropriate business strategies associated with industry analysis are further explored in chapter 3. These include the well-known value and cost strategies—up-market or mass-market positioning—but also include accommodation and dissuasion, which involve positioning for cooperation or for a price war. An important issue in the development of a firm's strategy involves the way the firm handles mistakes.

One of the key firm-level strategies involves differentiation—the creation of uniqueness—so we take a closer look at differentiation in chapter 4. Basic strategy for differentiation involves creation of synergies and patent strategy. Strategy for dynamic differentiation is developed in chapter 5, on the product life cycle. Many academic strategists have pooh-poohed the product life cycle, thereby missing important insights associated with positioning for changes that are destined to come. For example, durable goods such as computers are generally subject to a much harsher saturation than nondurables such as writable compact discs, hence confirming the continuing importance of the product life cycle.

Chapter 6 explores cooperation, both between firms in different industries and between firms in the same industry. Cooperation is often the difference between profitability and chronic losses. The techniques for sustaining cooperation involve identifying a shared interest, punishing misbehavior, and recovering from mistakes. These techniques are important for setting product standards, lobbying the government for favorable legislation, avoiding negative advertisements, and many other aspects of corporate existence.

Next, I turn to the design and scope of the organization as an element both of strategy and of profitability. For example, vertical integration facilitates surviving price wars by reducing marginal costs. What is within the scope of the organization—for example, whether to make a product or to buy it—is considered in chapter 7, while the methods of how to motivate employees (and nonemployees who provide services for a company) are explored in chapter 8. The major theme of chapter 7 is the costs of internal production, which must be compared to market prices. A major theme of chapter 8 is the unintended consequences of incentives—strong incentives in one aspect of a job can have significant and often undesirable effects on performance of other duties.

Antitrust enforcement has a powerful effect on corporate activity. Not only do federal and state antitrust laws restrict the firm's set of legal activities, often in somewhat mysterious or unpredictable ways, but private antitrust suits are a common and potentially devastating means of harassing competitors. An understanding of antitrust laws is critical for survival in modern business. Chapter 9 sets out some of the principles and concepts of antitrust at a general level. Chapter 9 is not intended to replace the company's general counsel but rather to insure that executives and managers are aware of the law, so that they do not say, "Cut off the competition's air supply," or call up a rival CEO at home and suggest a price increase.

Probability and statistics are often unpopular topics because they are technical and challenging. However, these topics are of increasing importance to business strategy, and thus chapter 10 provides an overview of statistics for business. This chapter presents some basic ideas and then explores major fallacies. Most people consistently see patterns where there are none, and this psychological misunderstanding of basic statistics accounts for errors ranging from chartism in the stock market to belief in the canals of Mars.

Chapter 11 presents the strategy of pricing. The goal is to charge each person what he or she is willing to pay, which is known as price discrimination or value-based pricing. Pricing is at the heart of profitability because prices determine revenue. Moreover, pricing has important effects on competitors and thus is critical to strategy: pricing and business strategy cannot be formulated separately. The branch of pricing involving auctions is increasingly important, and chapter 12 is devoted to bidding strategy and the design of auctions by sellers.

The way companies respond to crises, the nature of their offices, even the style of clothes executives wear, communicate a great deal about the way the company does business. Because people care about the way a company does business—Does it clean up its mistakes? Does it exploit short-term advantages?—a great deal may be read into ostensibly small behaviors. Such signaling is the subject of chapter 13.

Chapter 14 examines a theory of bargaining, and then illustrates how this theory can be used to toughen a bargaining position. An important scenario in bargaining is the war of attrition or "winner take all" competition. The last chapter of the book provides some concluding remarks.

WHAT IS STRATEGY?

Strategy is the way in which decisions are made. The origin of the term is a Greek word for "military commander," which comes from *stratós,* the army, and *egós,* to lead. The use of the word has broadened from its original military usage, where it meant long-range planning and methods for directing military operations. In military usage, strategy is used both in wartime and in peacetime. Having sufficient force to deter an attack is part of peacetime military strategy, for example. In contrast, tactics are used only during wartime. Business strategy involves the same long-range planning designed to achieve desired goals. As in military strategy, opponents are a major focus of business strategy, those who, in the current jargon, would like to "eat your lunch." As in military situations, firms have allies, who share substantial common interests. Finally, there are usually many neutrals in both military and business situations.

Some of the variables that firms can use strategically are provided in the following list.

Some of the Strategic Variables Chosen by Firms

Product Features and Quality
Targeting of Customers
Product Line
Product Standardization
Technological Leadership
Research and Development
Product Marketing and Positioning
Market Development and Education
Provision of Complementary Goods
Brand Identification
Geographic Markets
Distribution Channels
Product Pricing
Vertical Integration
Cost Reduction Focus
Service Provision
Warranties
Input Pricing
Financial Leverage and Debt
Government Relations
Types of Corporate Divisions
Flow of Internal Communications
Accounting System
Delegation of Decision Making
"Build to Order" or Inventory
Inventory Levels

Not all of these entries represent choices for all firms. For example, warranties may be impossible to provide for some services, such as legal services,* and some firms, such as a coal supplier, may have little ability to influence product quality.

Often firms choose a strategy by setting a goal, such as "40% market share in five years," or "technological leadership of the industry." There are two major problems with the goal-oriented approach. First, until the means of reaching goals are considered, the profitability of various strategic choices is unclear. For example, most General Motors divisions produced mediocre cars during the 1980s. These cars embodied little new technology and did not command a premium price. Was this a bad strategy? It did not enhance GM's market share, nor did it establish GM as a technological leader. However, the GM cars were profitable because there was only a modest investment in them. Moreover, massive R&D expenditures do not seem to have been profitable for GM. In an analogous situation, by 1990 it appeared that Nissan/Infiniti had dropped out of a technology race with Toyota/Lexus, ceding the position of "most technologically advanced Japanese car manufacturer" to Toyota (although recently Nissan has shown signs of reentering the race). Dropping out of the race is not necessarily a mistake; sometimes the less glamorous position is the more profitable.

The second problem with the goal-oriented approach to setting firm strategies is that competitors rarely stand still. Predicting the response of competitors is clearly a crucial aspect of the design of a business strategy, and goals should not be formulated in a vacuum.

For businesses, strategy is usually aimed at creating and sustaining high profits. High profits tend to encourage entry into the field by competitors, which erodes the high profits. A necessary requirement for sustaining high profits is some method or reason for blocking entry. Thus, strategic analysis is often focused on means of deterring or deflecting entry of, and expansion by, competitors.

ACKNOWLEDGMENTS

Much of the research for this book was done at the University of Texas at Austin, which has supported my work in ways too numerous to list. The Murray S. Johnson chair provided extensive financial support for this work. The University of Chicago's Graduate School of Business encouraged me to write this book and provided me with the opportunity to benefit from exposure to the school's terrific students. The majority of the writing was accomplished at the University of Chicago.

*The attorney who offers the warranty, "If you are convicted with my representation, I'll appeal for free," is as successful as the parachute manufacturer who offers a money-back guarantee.

I have learned a great deal from existing work. Especially notable are Paul Milgrom and John Roberts's *Economics, Organization and Management,* John McMillan's *Games, Strategies, and Managers,* and Adam Brandenburger and Barry Nalebuff's *Co-opetition.* All three are strongly recommended for students of business strategy, whether in class or in the real world. Thomas Schelling's brilliant 1960 book, *The Strategy of Conflict,* remains an invaluable resource for a strategist. The origins of business strategy can be traced to Schelling's analysis of national strategy, which in turn can be traced to John von Neumann and Oskar Morgenstern's 1944 mathematical treatise, *The Theory of Games and Economic Behavior.* Many of the insights brought together here come from other books and articles, and I have provided extensive references.

A large number of people provided me with thoughtful comments and advice about the manuscript and the project. Murray Frank, Scott Freeman, Brian Gale, Daniel Hamermesh, Vivian Lee, Bill Lucas, John McMillan, Tara Parzuchowski, David Romani, and Daniel Sokol all gave comments that I used and appreciate. Mark Satterthwaite provided especially detailed feedback, and his advice is reflected in many points in the book.

In addition to her thoughtful comments, detailed reading of the book, and incessant pressure to keep the mathematics to a minimum ("What's *this* symbol?"), Kristin McAfee also had to endure the clack of computer keys, even on vacation. Thanks.

Finally, I appreciate the support and encouragement of my editor, Peter Dougherty, who was enthusiastic about this project from day one. I was greatly assisted by Dimitri Karetnikov and Kevin McInturff of Princeton University Press. I thank Joan Hunter for her detailed and thorough reading and correction of the manuscript, and James Curtis for his fine index. Finally, Linny Schenck provided enormous editorial expertise for this project and I thank her for her patience with me.

1

Introduction

America Online is arguably the most successful Internet-based company, and its success provides a number of lessons in business strategy. Perhaps the most important lesson exemplified by AOL is *know your customer.* CEO Steve Case spent many hours visiting AOL's chat rooms regularly.[1] Chat rooms were designed to provide a more friendly, personalized feel to counteract the geek-oriented, technobabble strategy of rival CompuServe. CompuServe thought AOL had little to offer. According to CompuServe's Herb Kahn: "To us, AOL was junk food and CompuServe was nutritional." But there are worse things than being the McDonald's of on-line services. To further personalize the service, AOL employed a welcoming voice—the infamous "You've Got Mail." AOL was also specifically designed for people who were not computer experts, again in contrast to CompuServe, which generally required a high level of programming expertise.

Case was not the only AOL executive with a know-your-customer mentality. Robert Pittman, hired to create and solidify the AOL brand, also had the same mind-set. When placed as head of Time Warner's troubled Six Flags amusement park, Pittman decided to dress as a janitor and get a janitor's-eye view of the park. "I learned more in that day about what was going on than I perhaps learned in my whole time there," Pittman said. "Our people who cleaned the park . . . hated our customers because they thought the job was to keep the park clean. Who makes the park dirty? Visitors." Pittman redefined the mission—to make customers happy—to make the role of cleanliness apparent.

AOL was criticized and derided by many computer users. AOL subscribers, known unaffectionately as "newbies," were banned from some bulletin boards and information groups on the Web, because of the difference in style between early Web users and AOL subscribers. AOL subscribers were friendly and relatively unsophisticated about computers, and they considered the occasional practical joke—such as an incorrect answer to a question—entertaining. This special nature of the AOL subscriber was a consequence of AOL's far-sighted vision of an entire nation communicating electronically. AOL faced the challenges that every innovator faces in building a new market:

- *Educating potential users.* Many AOL subscribers knew little about computers, and less about the Internet, so AOL had to be simple and easy to use in order to reach the mass market.
- *Building infrastructure.* Because the existing network backbone was inadequate for AOL's expanding size, AOL was forced to provide long-distance communications, an operation later spun off to WorldCom.
- *Dealing with government.* Government can be either a hindrance or a help to a new line of business, and the actuality is usually determined by lobbying. AOL found early on that it had to deal with a government that took a suspicious view of the burgeoning Internet, threatened regulation of content to suppress pornography, and might even hold Internet service providers liable for the e-mails of members.

Such problems are common in all new industries, but the way that a firm approaches them often determines the firm's long-run success. Failing to educate potential customers limits an operation to the early adopters and creates room for a mass-market firm to run away with the business, as CompuServe found. In contrast, expenditures on education often leave a firm vulnerable to a rival that provides no education but has lower prices. Early computer sellers offered a great deal of in-store know-how, starting with the basement clone industry and growing to include CompUSA and Computer City. The very success early firms had in teaching customers how to use computers led to an industry that did not need such an educational infrastructure, and the necessary services provided by the earliest entrants sowed the seeds of their own destruction.

IBM exploited the need to build a market in business machines by offering a total solution—bundling equipment, service, and on-site education for a guaranteed successful installation. In this way, IBM exploited the need for customer education to create a recognizable, strong brand, positioning itself for future competition.

AOL has skirted the problem of competing with low-cost rivals by creating a unique service, one that includes a wide variety of content not readily available elsewhere. AOL offers "bells and whistles," such as AOL keywords and AOL-specific instant messaging, that make AOL attractive to its existing subscriber base. Thus, AOL garnered initial consumers by positioning itself for a mass market of consumers who needed a great deal of help, but it kept them by providing unique services not available elsewhere. AOL's success came as a complete surprise to most of Silicon Valley, which expected AOL to become just another Internet service provider, with content provided by the Web. This view involved a dramatic miscalculation, by first ignoring the sense of community that AOL had built among its subscribers, a community that included not only the internal chat rooms but also a great deal of information, education and references, shareware and useful computer programs, news and financial data, and shopping and travel services. Other firms, notably Yahoo! and MSN (Microsoft Network), came to provide such services as the concept of a portal developed, and these services were offered independently of the customer's Internet service provider. Only AOL, however, tied portal services to Internet service. This tying created a unique service that offered customers value they could obtain only by joining AOL, and that created switching costs for any customer leaving AOL. Essentially, AOL positioned itself in its first phase for ease of use, and in its second phase for value tied to Internet service. This strategy embodies an important understanding of market development: continued success requires creating a transition from the introductory phase to the mature phase of the market.

AOL is an exemplar of the importance of complementary goods and services, a theme that runs throughout modern strategy. The strategy of tying information and chat to Internet service creates and provides complementary goods that enhance the value of Internet service. While it is not much of a trick to figure out what these goods should be and to provide them, the difficulty is in charging for them. The problem of charges can be seen in Internet mapping-service companies, such as Yahoo, Rand McNally, and MapQuest. The maps are almost equally good, and no one wants to pay for them. Any attempt by one company to charge for them sends customers to an alternative provider. AOL skirts such problems by providing many services as part of its Internet package—a bundle that includes access to the Internet, a browser, chat, instant messaging, entertainment, shopping, financial data, games, and many other conveniences. Many, perhaps most, of these services are available elsewhere on the Internet, often without charge, but finding them takes a certain modicum of expertise unnecessary with AOL.

Providing complementary goods and services is important because they lock in customers and thus insure continuing superior performance. Sony has used this strategy in the creation of its memory stick—an exchangeable flash-memory product that is used in computers, digital cameras, personal digital assistants (PDA), camcorders, and MP3 music players. The advantage of the proprietary memory stick is that it ties all these devices together. The Sony camcorder buyer gets a memory stick with the camcorder to store snapshots. Since the memory stick can be inserted into a Sony PDA, the Sony brand PDA has higher value to the Sony camcorder buyer. The effect of the memory stick is to create complementarities among Sony products, increasing the value of any one product when others of the same brand are purchased.

AOL exploits complementarities by tying together a plethora of complementary services. If a customer needs any one of them, he or she is lured to AOL. Perhaps the best example of this strategy is the current "AOL anywhere" campaign—AOL content delivered wirelessly to phones or personal digital assistants. Such an offering enhances the value of AOL's proprietary content, and may encourage AOL subscriptions. Moreover, because of the spillover value, AOL can charge less for this wireless service than Yahoo does for its version of the same thing because AOL captures some of the value through Internet service. In this way, complements both increase the overall product value and create switching costs, thereby increasing firm profits beyond those obtainable when such complements are provided by other firms.

When it was not efficient to produce complements internally, AOL obtained complements by creating joint ventures and cooperative agreements. Indeed, AOL's early history was characterized by such cooperative agreements with Apple and Commodore. Many business schools have popularized the "business as war" mentality, which is often a mistake; war should be a last resort, both in diplomacy and in business. There are many companies in the same business or in other businesses that can benefit from mutual cooperation. Initially, AOL provided Internet services for firms that could have provided these services themselves, although perhaps not as well as AOL. Both companies benefited from such joint ventures. Moreover, as AOL grew as an Internet company, it signed cooperative agreements with a large variety of other content providers, including ABC, Amex, *Business Week,* Disney, Fidelity, MTV, Nintendo, Reuters, and Vanguard. Each agreement benefited both companies. AOL benefited by the increased quality and uniqueness of its service, while the content provider was paid and reached a fast-growing audience.

At one time, Prodigy was larger than either AOL or CompuServe. Like AOL, Prodigy was easy to use and focused on its own content, not on the Internet. Moreover, Prodigy was owned by Sears and IBM and had extraordinary financial resources behind it, so that it could afford to run television advertisements to attract customers. Why did Prodigy stumble and fall? The answer is found in the theory of organizations. Prodigy, as one pundit put it, embodied everything Sears knew about computers and everything IBM knew about retailing,[2] but it had the difficulty of serving two masters with significant differences in goals and vision. Moreover, both companies were justifiably afraid of tainting their good name with unwholesome chat and postings. Consequently, Prodigy adopted a heavy-handed approach to administration, cutting off controversial areas and stifling discussion. The company was hobbled by its owners and unable to compete successfully in spite of superior financing and technology. Prodigy was doomed by the same forces that make it difficult for the government of China to resist interfering, and ultimately damaging, the efficient operation of Hong Kong.

At its core, the theory of organizations suggests that when operations are strongly complementary, it is useful to run them inside a single organization in order to coordinate the aspects of the operations efficiently. In bringing two operations inside the same organization, a loss of incentives will arise; large organizations have inherent inefficiencies in diluted incentives, coordination mix-ups, uninspired yes-men, and other problems of hierarchy. Thus, the advantages of coordination need to be strong to overcome the disadvantages of large operations. In Prodigy's case, the complements—to sell Sears products over the Web, to sell IBM machinery and software to run these operations, and to promote IBM computers for customers—are quite weak. Independent companies like Yahoo feature Sears's products, so that the gain to Sears is only a slightly greater focus on Sears's products. IBM equipment sales were barely affected by Prodigy, which was used mainly by individuals, with the ubiquitous IBM clone made by someone other than IBM. As a result, the gains were tiny; the losses—in organizational flexibility and product design—catastrophic.

Long after it had grown into a major corporation, AOL was still run as if it were a family business, and this was most apparent in its approach to problems. AOL's problems with busy signals started when it began distributing free disks with a month's free service, and for several years demand outstripped AOL's ability to provide service. While some of the shortfall can be attributed to fast growth and lack of capital, much has to be attributed to poor forecasting and, specifically, to poor statistics.

The most famous connection problem occurred when AOL changed to unlimited usage. AOL initially provided five hours for $9.95 per month, with additional hours costing $2.95 each. Under pressure from cut-rate internet service providers (ISPs), AOL introduced a "heavy user" plan involving twenty hours for $19.95, and the same $2.95 per month each for additional hours thereafter. With defections growing, AOL caved in and offered unlimited usage for $19.95 per month; consequently, it was swamped with demand that it could not satisfy. Pundits called AOL "America Onhold" or "America Offline." CompuServe ran advertisements featuring a busy signal and the words, "Looking for dependable internet service? CompuServe. Get on with it. 1-888-NOTBUSY." In response, AOL's CEO Steve Case quipped, "It's like people saying they should come to our restaurant because it's empty."

Case's humor aside, AOL's response to the problem—essentially denying there was a problem—exacerbated the difficulty and created poor public relations. It was a major stumble, which AOL survived primarily because it had already begun locking in customers with its service offerings, and no other firm was well positioned to exploit the error. The way that firms respond to adversity is very important to the perception of their brand going forward. Firms are given a choice in such situations, to respond like Johnson and Johnson did in the Tylenol poisonings, expend resources and garner good public relations and actually build brand capital, or point fingers, deny responsibility, drag their feet, and damage the brand. The early reaction to a crisis is often a strong signal of management's attitude, and this signal will be remembered.

AOL's response to the pressure to offer unlimited usage was flawed. Unlimited usage at a fixed price is, overall, a bad plan for firm and customers alike. The problem with unlimited usage is the cost of service, currently averaging $.33 per hour, but more like $.50 per hour in 1996. With unlimited usage, customers buy more hours than they are willing to pay for, in particular using hours that they value at less than $.50. Many customers stayed logged on to avoid reaching a busy signal when they tried to log on again; such connections are akin to bank runs, where the fear of not being able to connect (or withdraw money) causes a surge in demand. Charging marginal prices (in this case, zero) below marginal costs does not serve customers or the firm well. In large part, AOL's failure to impose a marginal charge led to poor pricing by the entire industry. Moreover, the lack of a marginal charge sent average usage from seven hours per month to nineteen hours per month in the space of a few months, requiring a huge increase in modems and lines. (Average usage is now thirty-two hours per month.) A modest marginal charge would have tempered this growth in usage, while still encouraging efficient use of the facilities.

While average costs may have been $.50 cents per hour, not all hours were created equally—the costs primarily reflect peak usage during the early evening. Consequently, AOL could have improved on a marginal charge of $.50 per hour by imposing that charge only during peak hours, when additional demand requires increasing the number of modems. Indeed, a plan that involves a fixed charge, an off-peak marginal charge (which might be zero), and a peak time charge that reflects the cost of increasing the number of modems, would better serve both AOL and its customers. Free off-peak hours would have gone a long way to dealing with the public relations problem of ISPs with unlimited usage, while still economizing on the number of modems required to provide the service, and limiting the busy signals experienced by the customers. Indeed, the modern theory of pricing suggests that menus of pricing, involving fixed charges along with peak and off-peak marginal charges, improve on simpler pricing schemes. Moreover, it is often desirable to offer two classes of service—high and low priority. High-priority service would provide no busy signals, ever. Low-priority customers would be knocked off the service when congestion set in, in return for which they would pay a lower price. The combination of peak and off-peak charges, with multiple classes of service, is known as yield management, and it garners billions of dollars annually for hotels and airlines.

AOL's cavalier reaction to its problems is an example of bad signaling. But AOL did some excellent signaling, especially in its early years. According to Kara Swisher (of AOL.com), you could see from the lobby into Steve Case's office. "It probably made a favorable impression, because it said he was not egotistical," said reporter Walter Mossberg, "but it also said this was no major corporation that was going to blow anyone away." Markets often react strongly to what seem like small things, such as the position of the president's desk. A 2% correction in a company's earning may send its stock tumbling by a third or more. The theory of signaling shows why such a large reaction is reasonable, and how to manage it.

AOL's strategy, which led it to become the leading internet service provider, illustrates many of the concepts discussed in this book. In particular, AOL matched its product to its customers (chapter 3), used strategic product positioning (chapter 4), exploited the product introduction phase to position itself for the growth and maturity phases of the industry (chapter 5), and exploited complementary products to create a unique service with substantial lock-in and customer value (chapter 2). AOL was also a master of the cooperative joint venture, signing some three hundred such contracts (chapter 6). AOL responded poorly to the busy-signal crisis, ignoring the problem of signaling that magnifies the reaction to such a cavalier attitude (chapter 13). Prodigy's organizational form (chapters 7 and 8) led to a well-funded firm, but one that was unable to compete with the more nimble AOL. AOL's consistent inability to forecast demand showed the importance of an understanding of statistics (chapter 10) in formulating strategy, while the unlimited usage plan shows the central importance of pricing as a tool of strategy (chapter 11).

EXECUTIVE SUMMARY—INTRODUCTION

- Know your customers, by meeting your customer.
- Design the product not for early adopters but for the mass market to follow.
- Product introduction challenges include educating customers and government, building infrastructure, and supplying other complementary goods.
- Expenditures on product introduction may be exploited by low-cost rivals, and a transitioning strategy is necessary.
- A necessary feature of a transitioning strategy is to create a unique desirable good or service.
- Complementary goods and services are a critical component to modern business strategy and provide the best route to sustained profitability.
- Joint ventures and cooperation should be a staple of business strategy.
- The theory of organizations suggests that when operations are strongly complementary, it is useful to run them inside a single organization, in order to coordinate the aspects of the operations efficiently.

- In bringing two operations inside the same organization, some incentive losses will arise—large organizations have inherent inefficiencies in diluted incentives, coordination mix-ups, uninspired yes-men, and other problems of hierarchy.
- Thus, the advantages of coordination need to be strong to overcome the disadvantages of large operations.
- The way that firms respond to adversity is very important to the perception of their brand going forward.
- The modern theory of pricing suggests that menus of pricing, involving fixed charges along with peak and off-peak marginal charges, improve on simpler pricing schemes.
- Moreover, it is often desirable to offer two classes of service—high and low priority.
- The theory of signaling is concerned with how to interpret public behavior.

Ready, Fire, Aim
—Alleged motto of former president Jimmy Carter

2

Industry Analysis

Industry analysis is the attempt to assess opportunities in, and the profitability of, an industry and to identify the strategies that are most likely to be profitable over the long term. In addition, industry analysis attempts to forecast the likely behavior of rivals and potential entrants, the development of new products, methods and technology, and the effects of developments in related industries. In short, industry analysis attempts to provide a case study for the future of an industry.

The foundation of industry analysis is efficiency. The perspective of industry analysis is Darwinian—the fit survive, and the unfit do not. Fit means efficient. The efficient provider of goods and services survives over the long haul, and inefficient providers decline and exit, or are taken over and reorganized by fit providers.

Industry analysis only rarely helps a firm directly in formulating strategy. Instead, industry analysis provides the context in which strategy is formulated. Industry analysis identifies the relevant issues facing a firm in its formulation of strategy—what forces will tend to undermine its strategy. For example, an analysis of the airline industry suggests that new entrants will upset any profitable configuration of the industry—entry and the diversion of planes is too easy. This narrows the set of profitable strategies to being a low-cost provider and being in niche markets.

THE ~~FIVE~~ SIX FORCES

If it claims to work miracles, it's a miracle if it works.
—U.S. Post Office advertisement, 1977

With his 1980 book, Michael Porter changed the way business strategy is formulated. Porter identified five forces that jointly determine whether an industry is likely to provide long-run profitability. These forces can be viewed as methods by

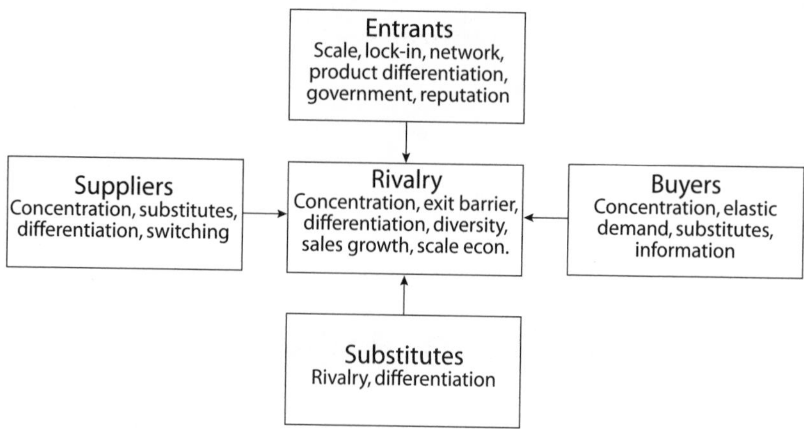

Figure 2.1. The five forces of Michael Porter.

which the profitability of firms in the industry is sapped. Porter's forces, which did not include the sixth force of complements, are

1. New entrants
2. Buyer bargaining power
3. Supplier bargaining power
4. Substitute products
5. Rivalry

All five of these forces have the interpretation that the force is the ability of others to expropriate some or all of a firm's profits. Bargaining power, either by buyers or input suppliers, prevents the firm from charging a high price or obtaining low input prices, respectively. Entrants and firms selling substitute products compete with the firm's products, putting downward pressure on prices. Rivalry summarizes the intensity of competition within the industry. Porter presents the forces in a diagram like figure 2.1.

The industry is located in the center of the diagram, with suppliers to the left, buyers to the right, potential entrants looming above the industry, and sellers of substitute goods located below the industry. One may think of the five forces as aimed at the prices in the industry. Rivalry is the internal force driving down prices and margins, and some of the factors that influence rivalry are listed in rivalry's box. Rivalry can also dissipate profits through the costs for excessive advertising and new product development.

The other four forces are external to the industry. Entrants from outside the industry represent a greater threat when there are low barriers to entry, so various barriers to entry are noted in the entry box. Barriers to entry are a critical component of sustainable profits, and thus are considered in detail below. Buyers can force down prices when they have the bargaining power to do so, because they need the product less than the seller needs the buyer, because the buyer has little ability or willingness to pay, or because the buyer can readily substitute away from the product. In addition, lack of information may constrain some buyers, reducing their bargaining power. Input suppliers can increase the prices charged when the suppliers have market power. Thus, a differentiated input with few sellers is likely to command a higher price, especially when the buyers are dispersed and there are no substitutes. Finally, the more competitively substitutes are priced and the closer they are to the industry's products, the more they matter. Producers of very close substitutes should be included as industry participants.

The utility of Porter's approach lies in the thorough consideration of how structure affects pricing and competition.

Entry

Market power is the ability to increase prices above costs, or above competitive levels, for sustained periods of time. As the term is typically used, market power can be modest, indeed. The stronger term is monopoly power, which generally requires a significant ability to increase prices. The goal of business strategy is often to create, and sustain, market or monopoly power.

Competitive theory suggests that the profits created by market power will attract entrants, who cause erosion of the prices and profits. Ultimately, entry undercuts the profits of the industry, driving profits to the competitive level at which the firms just cover their costs of capital. When entry is prevented or prohibited, an entry barrier exists, and an entry barrier disables the force of new entrants. Consequently, entry barriers are a major focus of business strategy, because entry barriers represent protection against erosion of profits; that is, entry barriers are necessary to achieve sustainable profits over market rates of return. In some cases, it is possible for existing firms in an industry to strategically create or increase entry barriers.

In some industries, entry is simple and easy. Real estate is notorious for ease of entry. Industries characterized by "mom-and-pop" stores, like dry cleaners, local moving companies, diners, or small groceries and delis, have easy entry. At the other end of the spectrum, the production of nuclear submarines and aircraft carriers, computer operating systems, civilian aircraft, and pharmaceutical drugs is quite difficult. Aircraft carriers, submarines, and civilian aircraft have such large economies of scale relative to market size that the industry can support only one profitable firm. Entry into the computer operating system market requires convincing consumers and software writers that there will be a sufficient market in their own operating system to justify the significant switching costs. Pharmaceutical companies' existing products are protected by patents, and the government approval process itself creates something of a barrier to entry.

A large cost to enter is often viewed as an entry barrier, but this is a mistake. It is not the cost per se that is the entry barrier (unless it is in the hundreds of billions of dollars or more), because there are so many firms capable of paying large costs, if the entry is worthwhile. Large costs arise when it is valuable to enter at many geographic points, as in automobile sales, or when the minimum efficient scale is large, as in oil refining or beer brewing. Instead of being entry barriers in their own right, large costs often reinforce other entry barriers, by making the risks larger. Thus, when a solid reputation is necessary to enter an industry, large costs make it difficult or impossible to test the market; instead, the entrant must commit large resources to enter. By reducing the set of firms capable of entering, and by magnifying the risks, a large efficient scale reinforces other entry barriers. The ability to start small and grow through retained earnings is a major advantage for potential entrants. Complying with government regulations, in many cases, increases the minimum efficient scale, reinforcing other entry barriers. A large cost to entering is an entry barrier only if the size of the market is small relative to the efficient scale, as in aircraft manufacturing.

Foreign producers may not face the same barriers as potential domestic entrants. For example, it would be quite difficult to start a new U.S. automobile firm with the intention of reaching the mass market, partly because it would be difficult to bid away the necessary automotive engineers from the existing companies. Foreign producers, however, did not face this problem, and many successfully entered the U.S. market during the 1960s and 1970s.

Exit barriers, which are costs of leaving an industry, can also enhance some entry barriers much the same way that a large entry cost does. Environmental cleanup, pension funding requirements, and other economic obligations that are not eliminated by leaving the industry are exit barriers. Exit barriers increase the downside risks associated with entering an industry. Thus, exit barriers will tend to reinforce existing entry barriers, such as reputation and switching costs.

Some of the factors that create or reinforce entry barriers are:

- Minimum efficient scale large relative to market size
- Differentiated products, product space filled by existing firms
- Consumer switching costs
- Brands and reputation
- Limited access to distribution channels
- Strong learning curve

- Limited access to inputs materials
  - Skilled labor to be bid away from existing firms
  - Best locations taken by incumbents
  - Necessary inputs in hands of incumbents
- Exit barriers and sunk costs
- Government
  - Regulation
  - Agricultural cartels
- Patents

The government creates many entry barriers. It is illegal to deliver first-class mail in competition with the U.S. Postal Service (USPS), and the USPS regularly sues to stop firms from delivering their own bills and engaging in other activities that compete with the Post Office. Moreover, items that are not urgent must be sent by USPS, and USPS has sued to block large firms from sending bills by Federal Express. The USPS has a legally mandated monopoly on first-class mail. This monopoly has been substantially eroded by express mail, facsimile machines, electronic mail, and less expensive telephones, but there is still substantial market power in first-class mail protected by a legal entry barrier.

Many food cooperatives, including those for oranges, peanuts, and hops, have government protection. Local governments often limit the number of taxis, which represents another government-mandated entry barrier. The right to drive a taxi in Boston sold for $95,000 in 1995, a consequence of the limited number of taxis allowed. New York taxi medallions, which confer the right to drive a taxi in New York City, have sold for more than $200,000.

Patents also create a legally protected barrier to entry, although with quite a different purpose, since patents encourage innovation. Once the innovation has occurred, of course, patents protect the innovator from competition for a number of years.

In contrast to patents, trade secrets do not expire, but also they do not have the legal protection afforded patents. A trade secret is also very different from a trademark. Trade secrets have no legal protection except that the firm may contract with the employees not to disclose them. Nevertheless, Coca-Cola has done extraordinarily well since 1886 in protecting its trade-secret formula. The formula for the well-known steak sauce A-1 is also a trade secret. Heinz's attempts to produce a competing product in the 1950s led to Heinz 57 sauce. Whatever you might think about the relative merits of Heinz 57 and A-1, they are hardly similar, which would indicate that A-1's trade secret remains relatively safe.

If one can corner the market on a necessary input—new product or service—one can prevent entry by a competitor. Alcoa used its virtual monopoly on domestically produced bauxite to protect itself from competition until the court found it in violation of the antitrust laws, and the U.S. government promoted the creation of competitors using capacity created for World War II. The De Beers diamond cartel controls about 80% of diamond production. The early entrants into a retail industry may attempt to secure the most favorable locations, providing a modest barrier. Generally, when there is one optimal distribution channel, the ability to secure the channel and prevent access is an entry barrier. Attempts to corner markets are more often legend than reality, however.

A significant economy of scale can create a barrier to entry. By entering at a scale that leads to low average costs, an early entrant can establish a cost position that new entrants cannot achieve. Economies of scale may arise through learning by doing, which permits the early entrant into an industry to get out ahead and remain ahead of later entrants. AT&T is considered by some researchers to have exploited its early size and entry into long-distance telephoning as a means of consolidating the U.S. regional companies into a monopoly. Boeing's strengths and scale economies in producing civilian aircraft insured such a strong position that entry by Airbus required massive subsidies from European governments. For companies involved in the delivery of packages, there are major scale economies, created by the need to have operations all over the country. However, these scale economies are evidently not so strong as to create a monopoly, and several firms, including USPS, offer overnight service.

The learning curve, which represents lowered costs arising from experience in production, can create a barrier to entry, if it produces a serious scale economy. The learning curve represents cost reductions that can be obtained only by experience, which creates a disadvantage for entrants relative to incumbent producers.

Brand names can be a barrier to entry, provided that the costs of creating a new brand rise for subsequent entrants; that is, early entrants obtain an advantage. Such an advantage might occur because customers try the early entrants, whose reputation for quality can be established with minimal advertising. Early manufacturers of mountaineering rope had such an advantage that entry into the mountaineering rope industry has proved difficult, even for skilled manufacturers of other kinds of rope.

Switching costs, which are costs consumers experience for changing brands, create an entry barrier. If consumers are familiar with a given software program, it has an advantage over competing software programs. The first company to market a product may acquire a major advantage in an industry with high switching costs, because consumers are effectively locked in. Typists' familiarity with WordPerfect created some lock-in to that program. The creation of switching costs is a major focus of business strategy, which is explored in chapter 4. Creating switching costs presents a trade-off, because alert consumers will be leery of purchasing a product that it is costly to change from. That is, knowing that they will be locked in, consumers may need a large subsidy to even try the product. In this way, consumers view the product as they might view an addictive drug like nicotine.

A major source of barriers to entry, especially in high-tech products, is a network value. A network value is a value that is greater when there are a large number of users; it represents the flip side of an economy of scale, which is a cost reduction when more, rather than less, is produced. Telephones have a network externality, as does instant messaging for electronic communication. If only one person has a telephone, obviously it is useless. The more people that have phones, the more one can rely on using phones. AOL and Microsoft are currently struggling to promote their style of instant messaging, trying to establish a dominant format. Operating systems have a significant network externality—the more people that use one operating system, the more software that will be available; the more helpers one can get at the office or from lower-cost teenagers, the easier it is to share files. When a network effect is present, a large market share creates an advantage much like an economy of scale—entrants have a difficult time overcoming the value created by the large number of users.

Network values need not be proprietary. Indeed, open-architecture software is intended to enhance network effects by opening the software to many improvers. The success of the video format VHS (Video Home System) over Sony's Beta is generally attributed not to quality but to licensing, which created competition in production of VHS units. Sony kept the Beta format proprietary, and thus did not create the benefit of competition in the product, while VHS was able to be licensed to multiple companies. Ultimately, Beta became extinct as a video format. Similarly, Intel's licensing of the 8086 chip to Advanced Micro Devices (AMD) helped assure customers that the product would continue to be produced at a reasonable price even if it became the industry standard.*

Network values protect a market from entry because an entrant does not offer, at least initially, the network value for the entrant's product. Computers still come with drives for the 1.44MB "floppy" disk (which is solid rather than floppy like the $5\frac{1}{4}$-inch disk it replaced), in spite of the almost absurdly better alternatives such as zip disks or compact discs. Software manufacturers still provide floppy disks for some software, and it is only recently that software manufacturers have begun to assume that the user has a compact-disc drive, which promises to end the reign of the 1.44MB floppy. Floppy drives persisted not because they were good, but because everyone had them and had the equipment for them. Such persistence can be remarkably long-lived—the QWERTY keyboard, which has the letter layout inher-

*Once a network value is created, the firm would like to produce at a higher price and exploit the adopters; this incentive discourages adoption. Consequently, prior to adoption, it is profitable to commit to low prices; creating competition is a means of committing to low prices.

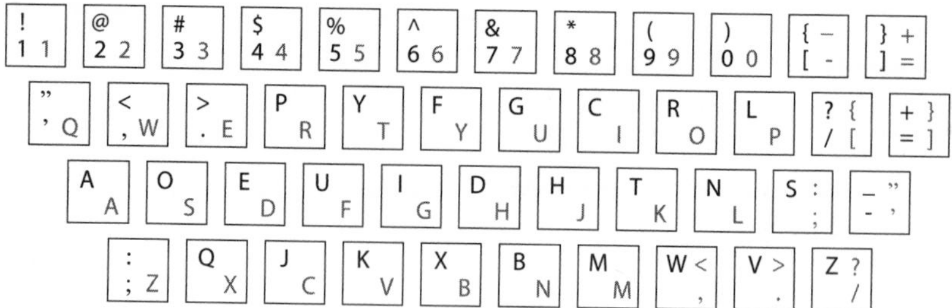

Figure 2.2. The Dvorak keyboard (QWERTY in gray).

ited from typewriters, continues to dominate computer keyboards in spite of experiments performed by the U.S. Navy that show the Dvorak keyboard (see fig. 2.2) is 25–30% faster. That alternative keyboard arrangements are more efficient should not be surprising—the QWERTY keyboard was designed to *slow* typing in order to reduce typewriter jamming. The QWERTY keyboard continues to dominate in spite of the fact that, if everyone switched, we would all be more productive.

Microsoft Windows has a clear network value, created by easily available software and consumers' familiarity with the product. Network values often arise with formats; formats create lock-in. But what barrier to entry protects Amazon from future competition and low profits? Amazon's business plan is easily imitated by competitors, and familiarity with its Web site will hardly deter customers from not seeking significantly lower prices. Another highflier, Yahoo, was differentiated from other search engines by having much more intelligence and thought put into development of a list of searched Web sites rather than using a computer-generated list. Thus, someone looking for a business, other than pornography businesses, preferred to use Yahoo's search engine. As Yahoo has grown, it has added many services, most of them readily imitated. Movie listings, television listings, yellow pages, news and sports, e-mail, Web site hosting, and other conveniences are needed to be a "one-stop" Web site (or "portal"), but they hardly set Yahoo apart. Moreover, oddly, Yahoo has let its unique search service depreciate, failing to remain current and losing the quality set of searched sites that initially was its main distinguishing feature. Neither Amazon nor Yahoo inhabit lines of commerce with substantial barriers to entry, and so they are unlikely to be able to sustain high profits for a significant period of time.

Buyer Bargaining Power

There are two main sources of buyer bargaining power. First, if the buyer can readily switch to alternative suppliers, the buyer can negotiate favorable terms through the threat of switching. This threat is all the more devastating when the firm needs the buyer, because the buyer is a large force relative to the firm's total sales. Buyers can more easily switch when the product is undifferentiated and when switching costs are low. In this case, even if the buyer values the good highly, the buyer can still negotiate favorable terms through the threat to switch to an alternative supplier. A retail grocer that sells bread and milk can readily switch to competing brands, and thus can negotiate low prices. In contrast, when buyers individually are very small relative to total firm sales, buyers can threaten to switch, but such threats are not devastating to the firm. The threat to switch to alternative suppliers, however, is very effective within industries populated by many firms, such as restaurants, dry cleaners, and small law firms.

Second, if the buyer does not value the good highly, the buyer can credibly threaten not to buy the good at all. This is especially true when the buyer needs a large volume of the product to have any use for it—big users gain more from price reductions and thus tend to be more price-sensitive. For example, aluminum smelters require very large amounts of electricity to smelt aluminum. If the price of electricity is too high, it will not pay to smelt aluminum; indeed, aluminum smelters often buy interruptible power, which is cheaper. Electricity is such a large fraction of the cost of aluminum that small price increases render aluminum smelting uneconomic. Consequently, aluminum smelters can negotiate very favorable terms with electric utilities.*

The VISA and MasterCard companies used to charge retailers about 2% for the privilege of accepting credit cards. (Banks, which issue the individual cards, make their revenues from interest and annual charges to the customer.) With thin margins, grocers could not accept credit cards and pay 2%. Consequently, both VISA and MasterCard were forced to cut their fees to extend the business to grocery stores. This is an example of a group of buyers who are not willing to pay a high price negotiating for a low price.

An opposite case from aluminum smelting is beer production. Beer requires hops to be manufactured, but it does not require a large amount of hops. For an average brewer, a pound of hops, which sells for around $3, is sufficient for 6,000 bottles of beer. Not surprisingly, brewers are insensitive to the price of hops—a

*An interesting about-face occurred during the winter (2001–2) electricity crisis in California. Three Columbia River aluminum smelters (Kaiser, Columbia Falls, and Golden Northwest) had deals to buy power for $22.00 per KWH. With prices at that time reaching $405.00 per KWH, it became much more profitable for these companies to shut down the smelting operations and sell the power to California. Kaiser defended its actions, and its unwillingness to donate 25% of the windfall to the power utility, on the basis that it still paid the workers 75% to 100% of their wages. It was estimated that the power input alone was worth over $1.50 per pound for aluminum that sold for $.75 per pound. Source: *Business Week,* 26 February 2001, p. 8.

tripling of the price would have a negligible effect on the demand, because a tripling of the price of hops adds only a tenth of a cent to the cost of a bottle of beer.

Even when a buyer is in an excellent bargaining position, effective use of bargaining power requires knowledge. In order to extract the best price from the firm, a buyer needs to know the firm's cost and the prices offered by others; otherwise, the seller can hide behind the buyer's ignorance and successfully charge a good price. Thus, knowledge itself enhances buyer power. Because of buyer ignorance, small law firms also may command prices well in excess of their opportunity costs.

Supplier Bargaining Power

Suppliers have bargaining power with the firm in the same type of circumstances when the firm has bargaining power over buyers. That is, when there are few suppliers and few substitutes and switching costs are large, suppliers are going to have substantial bargaining power. In this case, the supplier can extract much of the profits of the firm. A shopping mall that sells space for small restaurants and stores has a great deal of bargaining power, because there are typically few substitutes to mall space and no substitute for access to the mall's customers.* Thus, the mall sets prices that leave the pizza or "chicken balls in flaming orange sauce" restaurants with a minimal profit, given the amount of business they do. Similarly, the local shoe store located in a mall has little bargaining power. The cart-type businesses, which sell sunglasses, gold chains, or pagers and are located in the mall's aisles, also have little bargaining power, and the mall charges what the market will bear for the space. The mall—supplier of space—has most of the bargaining power. Indeed, the only real source of bargaining power that a small retailer has is information.

Suppliers can also create bargaining power by the threat of forward integration into the buyer's business. That is, suppliers may be well positioned as entrants, and may deserve special attention as potential entrants, when they control important inputs. For example, when Harlequin, the dominant romance-novel producer, dropped its distributor Simon and Schuster, Simon and Schuster entered the romance-novel business and extracted a substantial portion of Harlequin's profits.

Substitute Products

Most products have substitutes. In some cases, substitutes nearly eliminate existing products. It has become quite difficult to find a manual typewriter. With the advent of handheld calculators, few stores sell slide rules these days. Vacuum tubes

*In contrast, the mall may not have such strong bargaining power with the "anchor" stores, the major department stores that are considered to be the large draw for a mall.

are rare. Beginning in the late 1950s, fiberglass boats decimated the wooden-boat industry.

Other substitutes are not economic—at current prices. Many electrical generation companies switched from oil to natural gas, because natural gas was less expensive. Some of these plants have the capability to burn either fuel. Should natural-gas prices rise sufficiently relative to oil, those with dual capability would switch back immediately. In the face of persistently higher prices, others would acquire dual capability or just switch to oil. In many cases, substitutes for a product restrain price increases that would render the substitutes viable alternatives. As the quality of substitutes increases or their costs fall, substitutes become an increasing threat. For example, as their quality rises and prices fall, plastics play an increasing role in automobiles, diminishing steel's role.

Accounting for substitutes as a threat for the future is often treacherous, because substitutes typically come from outside the industry, and thus management often has little knowledge and experience in the substitute's field. Few wooden-boat builders understood the revolutionary effect of fiberglass at its inception. On the opposite side, many movie-theater owners continue to expect video to stop people from going out to the movies, even after twenty years of coexistence.* People who understand their own business well often have a limited appreciation for the nature of other industries that may have a huge impact on their firm. Thus, the main message of the substitute force is that it is very important to evaluate, and not underestimate, changes in other industries that might lead to dramatic change in one's own industry.

Rivalry

Of the five forces, rivalry generally gets the most attention, perhaps because it is determined fully by factors within the industry. Rivalry is the extent to which firms compete on price. The personal computer industry displays a high degree of rivalry, with firms constantly cutting prices. Airlines often are rivalrous, and price wars have been frequent in the years since deregulation. Pharmaceutical manufacturers, however, are not very rivalrous, emphasizing quality and not price even when the products are similar and rivalry is a serious threat. Similarly, accounting firms and law firms typically are not rivalrous, again focusing their competitive efforts on quality. Gasoline retailers serve as the epitome of rivalry, with the adver-

*The National Association of Theater Owners—the other NATO—still seems to expect technology to destroy its business. What is consistently missing from NATO's analysis is a recognition that people like to get out of their homes. One effect of video, however, was to increase the relative value of movies that benefited from a big screen, and therefore encourage the action-adventure theme.

tised price of regular unleaded gasoline determining their business. Attempts to mitigate rivalry in gasoline, through branding, "full serve," car washes, clean restrooms, and pay-at-the-pump, have had only a small effect—price is still the major competitive battlefield.

The home-hardware industry provides an example of a fairly nonrivalrous industry that was turned into a rivalrous industry through the advent of the superstore. Hardware was primarily a small business that emphasized service and location—people went to their neighborhood hardware store. Price competition was weak. Usually the lumberyard was a separate enterprise from the hardware store. Although lumberyards sold hardware, lumberyards were inconveniently located where land was inexpensive, and their hardware was designed for professionals—barrels of nails sold by the pound, and expensive, high-quality power tools. Home Depot merged the hardware store and the lumberyard concept, brought it into the suburban shopping district, and reduced prices of hardware and service substantially. Home Depot also increased its selection over that of hardware stores and lumberyards by selling bathroom fixtures, kitchen cabinets, tile, carpeting, and bookcases. Home Depot was soon imitated, primarily by Lowe's and Builder's Square, starting an intense rivalry among the superstores, almost to the point of a price war, in the locations where the companies were near each other. Stores devoted just to hardware are going out of business or moving up-market to include such special items as imported espresso makers and those little umbrellas for fruity alcoholic beverages. Because the rivalry of hardware superstores is so intense, two superstores have a difficult time surviving in the same market. Such a situation is an advantage ultimately—the intensity of price competition is an entry discourager, if not an entry barrier.

Office supply is another example of an industry that is very rivalrous, with Staples, Office Depot, and OfficeMax competing strongly when located near each other. Because these companies emphasize low prices over service, and all have a similar selection of the same items, price is the focus of competition.

In principle, an industry could be so rivalrous that the market can support only one firm. Superstores may represent an example of such intense rivalry, although one expects that rather than exit, a superstore could differentiate itself by emphasizing superior service. An office supply store could begin delivering and close the storefront, for example, becoming a virtual supply store, but with same-day delivery because of having a local warehouse. The car rental company Enterprise, which eschews airport locations and tourist travelers in favor of in-town locations, car-repair shops, and those who need a car near home, is an example of such extreme rivalry. Two car rental agencies located in the same car-repair shop are unlikely to both survive.

With the exception of rivalry so cut-throat that it creates a monopoly, rivalry reduces prices and profits. There are six major factors that reduce rivalry.

Few Competitors

A large number of competitors encourage price competition by several means. First, a small firm can increase its sales substantially with a modest effect on the market price. When there are twenty firms, a small firm can double sales with no more than a 5% increase in the market output, and effects on other firms individually are very small. Even if total sales in the market remain constant, when a firm with a 5% share doubles its sales, the other firms experience a 5% decline. Consequently, small firms are encouraged to cut prices to increase sales, and other competitors have too little stake to support cooperation. A large number of competitors encourages strong price competition.

Natural Industry Leadership

In some industries, a natural leader can discourage price competition. Prior to significant entry by the Japanese and European car manufacturers, General Motors served as a natural leader of the U.S. automobile industry by virtue of being the largest firm. De Beers held sway over the diamond industry for sixty years. Leaders can range from large enterprises individually capable of punishing price competition to trade associations or industry organizations.

High, Steeply Increasing Variable Costs

The worst-case scenario for rivalry is to have low marginal costs and high fixed costs. In this case, price competition can easily drive prices below average total cost, since variable costs are still covered. The best case arises when variable costs are steeply increasing in output, so that increasing output is very expensive. Firms will hesitate to attempt to increase sales through a price cut, since the cost of supplying the increased sales is the incremental variable cost. Essentially, when incremental variable costs are much higher than average total costs, the industry must be profitable—prices that cover incremental costs exceed average costs. However, there is a natural tendency for entry to occur in such industries, thereby reducing incremental costs.

Product Differentiation and Switching Costs

Both product differentiation and switching costs directly weaken price competition in two ways. First, they make customers more difficult to steal, so that a price cut produces a smaller increase in sales, and therefore is less profitable. Next, they permit an increase in price to one's existing customers without losing much business to rivals. Thus, product differentiation and switching costs tend to mute rivalry. An interesting feature of these aspects of industry structure is that it is sometimes possible to create switching costs without harming one's customers, as in the case of interchangeable battery systems or frequent flyer miles,* both of which lock in existing customers without tending to steal rivals' customers.

Large Minimum Efficient Scale

The advantage of a large minimum efficient scale is that any attempt to increase output comes in a large step. Suppose the minimum efficient scale is about 10% of the market, and there are five firms, each with two plants. The strategy of cutting price and serving more customers cannot realistically be taken in a small step—it requires building a third plant and increasing industry supply by 10%. This means that expansion requires big steps, and thus has big risks. Consequently, it is unlikely that firms will experiment with price cuts; instead, expansion of output will occur only when it is justified by significant market growth.

There is a significant downside to a large minimum efficient scale when the market is growing rapidly. Each firm would like to wind up holding a large share of industry capacity, and thus it makes sense for firms to build capacity well in advance of the arrival of actual demand, as a way of committing to a high-market-share position. This desire to build in advance creates a costly war of attrition that can absorb the eventual profits. The advantages of a large minimum efficient scale may be squandered through jockeying to be in first place.

Low Exit Barriers

Low exit barriers insure that if the market turns down, firms will exit rather than fight for market share. In declining industries, this ability to exit can be decisive in maintaining adequate prices. In contrast, when it is difficult to exit, firms tend to fight for market share, insuring strong price competition. Moreover, strong exit barriers may matter prior to a declining phase. Once the firms in an industry can see that a decline is coming, price competition tends to break out in advance, as firms try to insure that they are in attractive positions prior to the beginning of the decline.

Low exit barriers have a paradoxical effect of increasing price competition during the growth phase of an industry, by reducing the risk of entering. That is, the reduction in exit costs associated with low exit barriers makes the gamble of

*Frequent "flyer" seems to be the preferred spelling over frequent "flier," with four times as many instances found on Google.

entering a growing industry more attractive, contributing to subsequent overcapacity.

Complements—The Sixth Force

Automobile sales are influenced by the quality of roads and the price and availability of gasoline. Automobile sales are also influenced by credit and insurance costs. Indeed, sales of diesel cars lag behind those of gasoline-powered cars in large part because diesel fuel is often available only at truck stops, while gasoline is ubiquitous. Another illustration of the importance of complementary goods involves radio. Sales of recorded music are promoted by radio stations playing the songs. Radio is traditionally the medium that determines the success of new music, although music videos have an increasing importance. A third-party good—radio—determines the success of music sales. Similarly, Microsoft Windows has a major advantage over Apple's computers and over Linux because much more software is available for Windows. In particular, many games and mathematical programs run only under Windows. Many peripheral devices, including some popular MP3 players, require Windows. In some graphics design applications, Apple computers have an advantage over Windows-based computers, and Apple computers continue to dominate in graphic arts. Apple's advantages, however, have been slipping as programs like Fontographer, a program favored by graphic artists, become available for the Windows-based machine, and other programs become available only for Windows-based machines.

As Adam Brandenburger and Barry Nalebuff emphasize in *Co-opetition*, the five forces analysis omits a force that is often larger than the substitute force included—the force of complementary products. Weakness in complements—video rentals—probably killed the Sony Beta VCR. Microsoft's dominance of the market for computer operating systems was aided by promotion of the provision of complements—software that ran under MS-DOS, and later under Windows. Not only are complements one of the more important forces, but complements often have more implications for strategy than any other force.

Demand for laptop computers and digital cameras is significantly weakened by the presence of a poor complement—batteries. Weak battery performance limits the utility of these devices substantially. Similarly, the development of Internet-based retailing has been hampered by the relatively small number of people with fast Internet connections. As the number of DSL (Digital Subscriber Line), cable modem, and Ethernet connections increases, the use of Internet-based shopping is likely to increase with it. A fast Internet connection is a major complement to Internet-based retailing.

Having failed to establish the Sony Beta as a VCR standard, Sony repeated the same error by overcontrolling the Sony MiniDisc. The Sony MiniDisc is a recordable compact disc with capacity equal to an ordinary CD, but physically it is much smaller. When the Sony MiniDisc first appeared, it offered significantly better technology than recordable CDs, known as CD-Rs, which were not yet in widespread use. Sony might have been able to displace the recordable CD by substantial promotion and licensing of its product. Such a strategy would entail forgoing many of the profits associated with monopoly control. Instead, Sony kept a tight rein on control, and its recordable CD has only a niche market in portable stereo. In this case, the complementary goods are readers and players in computers, stereos, and automobiles. These needed to be ubiquitous and inexpensive for the Sony product to become the standard over the CD-R. As the technology of the standard recordable CD advanced, the prospects for the Sony product dimmed.

The Brandenburger-Nalebuff Value Net

Brandenburger and Nalebuff provide a graphical description, which they call the *value net,* of the influences affecting an industry. The value net for a firm, which represents an alternative to the five forces diagram, is illustrated in figure 2.3. In this description, I have reversed their location of customer and supplier to accord with the common use of upstream and downstream for the location of supplier and customer, respectively. The firm is located in a net. Products flow downward—the firm buys from suppliers, adds value, and sells to customers downstream. These transactions are influenced by competitors, who may try to divert the flow of goods away from the firm toward the competitors. Transactions are also influenced by complementors*—the producers of complements—who increase the value of transactions by the provision of complementary goods.

In terms of the five forces, the value net includes both substitutes and potential entrants in the category of competitors. Competitors, sellers of substitutes, and potential entrants all restrain prices in a similar way—they threaten to take market share, and put downward pressure on prices. Thus, three of the forces are rolled into a single force representing competition, but the new force of complementation is introduced.

There are two advantages of the value net over the five forces analysis. First, complements are specifically included. Second, the graphical representation of the value net diagram has some meaning, in contrast to the five forces diagram. In par-

*Brandenburger and Nalebuff coin this term to represent the firms that provide complementary goods, the opposite of a competitor, who provides a substitute good.

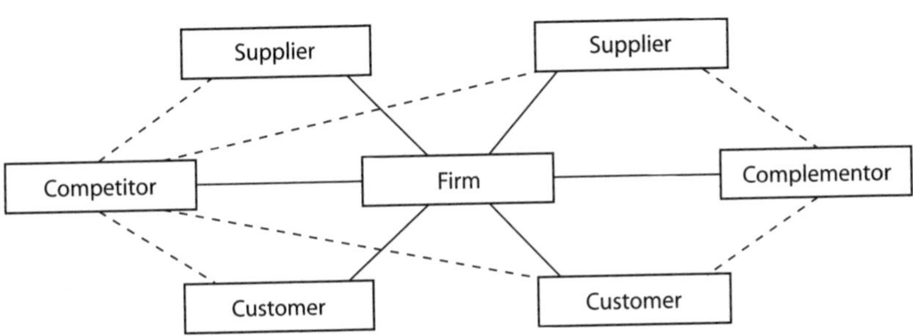

Figure 2.3. The Brandenburg-Nalebuff Value Net. Relationships with the firm are denoted with solid lines, other relationships with dashed lines.

ticular, a value net reveals a certain amount of symmetry in relationships, a symmetry concealed by the five forces diagram. Competitors typically have the same type of relationship with a firm's customers and suppliers—a transaction relationship. Similarly, complementors can have relationships with either customers or suppliers. From the firm's perspective, customers and suppliers play the same roles, while competitors and complementors play roles that are mirror images of each other. Brandenburger and Nalebuff exploit the symmetry to draw a useful insight: the customer is not always right. Indeed, suppliers should be right as often as customers—the firm that neglects its suppliers but treats its customers well risks major problems with suppliers. Instead, the firm should be engaged in the business of maximizing the value to customers minus the cost of suppliers—the net take of the firm. Such a maximization exercise requires not giving all the proceeds to the buyers.

This insight sounds trite, but it is quite powerful in applications. Indeed, many businesses do not consider that they have the same kind of relationship with their suppliers, especially their employees, as they do with their customers. Efforts that lead to suppliers being willing to supply at lower cost are just as valuable as efforts that lead to customers being willing to pay a higher price. Poor working conditions are going to increase the labor costs, which is the parallel to a low-quality good selling for a low price. Morale-boosting efforts that make the workplace a more pleasant place for employees are the counterparts of advertisements that promote the lifestyle aspects of a product, advertisements that boost the morale of the product's consumers.

Both the value net and the five forces are primarily useful for identifying the relevant participants in the market and assessing their influence on the market outcome. The five forces and the value net both provide a structure for performing an industry analysis.

Strategies for Complements

Complementary goods generally offer a great potential for strategy, because a firm and the producers of complementary goods have interests that are aligned. Automobile manufacturers, tire manufacturers, and gasoline companies would like people to drive more, and thus they have a major basis for cooperation. Gasoline companies used to give away free maps as an encouragement to driving. The Michelin tire company produces an excellent series of guides and maps. British Petroleum (BP) has a sophisticated Web site that recommends routes between European locations interactively. These examples represent instances of companies providing complementary goods. However, they do not represent cooperation to provide complementary goods.*

There are four basic strategies with respect to complements:

- Provide the complements individually.
- Subsidize the provision of complements by others.
- Be subsidized to produce complements.
- Form a jointly funded complement provider.

Individual provision of complements will generally result in too few complements being provided. Some of the benefits of a gasoline station providing maps to customers accrues to tire companies; it may be economically worthwhile to provide free maps given the value to the gasoline and tire industries as a whole, but not in any one firm's individual interest. An important aspect of the provision of complements is that an otherwise competitive industry has an incentive to cooperate on the provision of complements.

Tobacco firms all benefit from the kinds of studies that fail to discover a link between smoking and cancer, and these studies are complements to the production and sale of tobacco. The tobacco companies could provide such studies individually, but they are clearly better off forming a research institute. Collectively, they can hire more shoddy scientists and produce more supportive studies. While it is unlikely that one company will directly subsidize the production of such junk science by another company, the joint subsidization of a research institute is a very useful strategy. It is often the case that the production of some real science may enhance the value of the junk science by increasing the reputation of the institute. That is, real science may be a complement to junk science.

In other cases, firms may usefully subsidize another firm to encourage the pro-

*An example of cooperating to provide a complement to this industry was the cooperation by GM, Mack, Firestone, Phillips, and Standard Oil to shut down trolley companies. In this case, the complement was the absence of trolleys.

vision of complementary goods. Alternatively, a firm considering the provision of such goods should seek support from other firms with similar interests. Because the desires to provide the goods are aligned, it should be possible to agree on the provision, although of course each firm will seek to minimize its payment for the complementary goods.

For chip manufacturer Intel, major complements are products that fully exploit the capabilities of its most recent generation of processors. Thus, Intel benefits as Microsoft Windows gets more sophisticated and larger. Similarly, Intel benefits from three-dimensional games. Intel also benefits from desktop video editing, a program that heavily taxes state-of-the-art personal computers at the time of this writing. Video editing, in turn, requires large, fast hard drives, because digital video requires 13 gigabytes per hour.

INDUSTRY STRUCTURES

There are four broad industry structures, based on the size and number of competitors.

- Fragmented
- Dominant firm
- Tight oligopoly
- Loose oligopoly

Fragmented industries like dry cleaning and jewelery making involve many small firms, usually owner-operated ones with a small number of employees. Dominant firm industries are the opposite, with a single large firm and, perhaps, a fringe of small competitors. In between these cases is the tight oligopoly, with two or three players, and the loose oligopoly, with five or more major firms. Coke and Pepsi are examples of a tight oligopoly, and in most cities there are only two major grocery store chains, although the identity of the two varies by city. Boeing and Airbus are the only relevant manufacturers of large passenger aircraft for most of the world. There are four major producers of breakfast cereal—Kellogg's, General Mills, Philip Morris (Kraft/General Foods/Post), and Quaker Oats—and, at present, four major U.S. television networks—ABC, CBS, Fox, NBC. For many years, General Motors, Ford, and Chrysler dominated the U.S. automobile market. The original "seven sisters" oil companies, which are now incorporated into four major oil companies, are members of a loose oligopoly. Today, the big firms are Exxon-Mobil, BP-Amoco-Arco, Royal Dutch Shell, and Total Fina Elf. Similarly, the "big eight" accounting firms have tightened to the big five (Arthur Anderson, Deloitte & Touche, Ernst & Young, KPMG [Klynveld, Peat, Marwick, and Goerdeler], and PriceWaterhouseCoopers). There are loose oligopolies in pulp and paper, cardboard, cigarettes, televisions, stereo electronics, video electronics, and many other items.

The nature of strategy is qualitatively different in fragmented, dominant firm, and loose and tight oligopolies. In fragmented industries, firms can generally consider the behavior of competitors as independent of their own actions, and cooperation on any matter, including the provision of complementary goods, is extremely difficult. A dominant firm can ignore other firms for most purposes, although it must be concerned about being displaced either by entry or substitutes. Tight oligopolies have tight interconnections—the strategy of each firm affects the behavior of other firms. Consequently, the chance for cooperation, either on complements and other market-enhancing expenditures or on prices, is highest in a tight oligopoly. Loose oligopolies fall somewhere between tight oligopolies and fragmented industries. Certainly the tobacco firms have cooperated successfully, while other loose oligopolies have been unsuccessful even at avoiding mud-slinging and disparagement of competitors.

Fragmented Industry

A fragmented industry generally refers to one consisting of a large number of small firms. These may be owner-operated firms like neighborhood hardware stores, taxicabs, and dry cleaners. Ace and True Value hardware stores are members of buying cooperatives, but the individual stores are still typically owner-operated. In some cases, franchised stores act like a fragmented industry. In gasoline retailing, there are company-owned stores, but also branded, affiliated stations that agree to buy gasoline from a particular company in exchange for concessions, including loans, signs, and marketing. The independence of these stations varies with the arrangement with the oil company, but often they are quite independent. Fast-food franchisees of major brands like McDonald's often have little independence, and thus probably should not be viewed as fragmented firms. Other chains, like Big Boy or Dairy Queen, provide a greater degree of autonomy and hence may be viewed as independent owner-operated firms. The restaurant industry is very fragmented, with many independents and chains of two or three. Other fragmented industries include hair cutting and dressing, maid service, legal services, plumbing, and home repair. Microsoft aside, a great amount of software is produced by small operations. Indeed, one company is named One Man and a Cat.

There are some industries that have a small number of very large firms and a large number of smaller firms. Accounting services are an extreme example of this phenomenon, with a big five and thousands of small firms nationwide. Bookstores are another example, with a few big chains and many independents. Usually, such an arrangement is either two industries viewed as one, or a sign of an industry in transition. In the case of accounting firms, there are two industries—five firms that provide high-level accounting services for large corporate and business clients, and other accounting firms that specialize in smaller businesses and individuals, an industry that is fragmented. Bookselling and hardware have aspects of transition; the superstores like Barnes & Noble and Home Depot have captured a larger share of the industry, but the independents, which offer higher levels of knowledge and convenience, and more accurately reflect local conditions and demand, are not disappearing. Like the accounting industry, the major chains may coexist with the smaller firms by offering different products.

In contrast to these examples, video retailing and IBM-clone personal computer retailing were fragmented between 1980 and 1985, with corner stores offering personalized service and assistance. These firms mostly disappeared in the face of superstores like CompUSA and Blockbuster; their coexistence for a time was a sign of transition rather than evidence of two markets.

Fragmented industries usually exist because of the importance of providing incentives at the store level. It is difficult to motivate a manager in a chain store to perform as well as the owner of a store will perform. Yardstick compensation and large bonuses motivate managers, but it is the ability to keep *all* the proceeds that keeps the owner in the store until two in the morning working hard. When such strong incentives are very important, it is typical to find fragmented industries. For example, buyers of computers needed personalized service in order to make the machines useful in 1980; computers required a great deal of knowledge on the part of the customer to be valuable. As a consequence, an important method of sales to individuals was the owner-operator clone builder, who would answer the phone and give knowledgeable advice even after the purchase. Once the knowledge was disseminated among the customer base, the reason for such an expensive method of selling vanished, and computers became more of a commodity. Hence, the fragmented industry gave way to an oligopoly.

The fragmentation of the video rental market at its inception might seem mysterious, but the explanation lies in the pricing of videos. Initially, videos supplied for the rental market were quite expensive—about $50 to $100 each. Consequently, it was important for a video rental company to know what the local market demanded, and to match the local demand with the stock of videos. In order to conserve on inventory, a motivated manager was required. As the price of videos for the rental market fell, the strategy of having a large supply of everything became economical, and the industry ceased to be fragmented. At sales of $80 per video, a knowledgeable owner with a good feel for local conditions and a specialized stock outperforms a less informed manager, who can be hired inexpensively, with a large inventory. At $20 or less per video, the reverse is true.

Home Depot entered the very fragmented hardware market with a different model for sales. In particular, Home Depot sold not only typical hardware supplies but also lumber and kitchen and bath supplies such as cabinets and tile, thereby offering a much greater selection than competitors. Moreover, using Home Depot's competitors for do-it-yourself projects and general construction required the buyer to visit two or three distinct stores; Home Depot offered one-stop shopping. Do-it-yourselfers generally wanted information from a hardware store. Home Depot attracts knowledgeable individuals from the construction trade to work part-time in the store; the advantage for these knowledgeable people is that they can troll for business inside Home Depot. In addition, Home Depot pays a premium for a more stable, full-time workforce.

Home Depot grew by redefining the industry and by recognizing a shift in the nature of customers, who were increasingly involved in larger do-it-yourself projects. The hardware delivery process worked best as a fragmented industry with personalized service; indeed, Snap-On tools operated a fleet of trucks that delivered tools to businesses. The market for supplies for contractors and do-it-yourselfers doing large projects works better with large stores, low costs, and one-stop shopping. Home Depot prospered by redefining the industry from three or four separate industries that catered to different aspects of home remodeling and repair to a single industry catering to all aspects of home repair.

Personalized service usually is provided most successfully by owner operators, because service involves intangibles and is hard to monitor. Consequently, jewelers, lawyers, small-enterprise accountants, dry cleaners, and others that depend on difficult-to-monitor high-quality service and on repeat business are organized as small firms. Businesses that generally rely on the performance of one individual or a family, like taxicabs and variety stores, are also often fragmented, because a chain has difficulty competing with highly motivated individuals. In such cases, the advantages of a large enterprise are small, especially when a buying co-op like Ace Hardware is available to provide most of the advantages of size. Similarly, franchises provide the advantages of size and reputation while still offering incentives for strong individual performance.

Dominant Firm

The main challenge for a dominant firm is the desire of other firms to displace the dominant firm and reap the profits. IBM, a dominant firm in computers in the 1960s and early 1970s, faced several attempts to displace its dominance in business computing, notably from the Digital Equipment Corporation (DEC). Today, IBM remains a leader in database management, although it is no longer dominant. The regional Bell operating companies, or RBOCs, are facing similar challenges in local telephony. Local telephone service is relatively profitable, and Congress has ordered the local markets opened to competition. Cable companies have dominated the markets providing local television signals, although they now face competition from satellite-based companies. Air travel to and from many smaller cities is dominated by a single carrier.

The reason that an industry has a dominant firm matters greatly to the formulation of strategy. When the industry can only support one firm, either because of scale economies or because of a network effect, the preservation of dominance is a matter of behaving in a way that makes entry infeasible. Microsoft charges moderate to low prices for its operating system, which lowers the value of any attempt to displace Windows, because there is little demand for a product that would be lower priced but run fewer applications. Indeed, most computer owners will not switch to Linux at a price of zero for Linux.

Dominant firms are often displaced by new technologies. Competition from satellite-based television is the major threat to the profitability of the local cable company. Microsoft is often accused of responding slowly to the threat that the Internet and the programming language Java represented to its operating system. The Internet did, and still does, represent a threat, because someone with a computer could reach applications stored on another computer. This means that instead of running programs on one's own computer, a user could run them on a server at the office or at an Internet service provider. As a consequence, an operating system on one's own computer becomes little more than a browser. This is an example of a threat from an improved substitute.

The main focus in the press concerning the preservation of monopoly power has been on tying the browser to the operating system and to having contracts with Internet service providers and computer manufacturers to discourage the use of Netscape. Separately, Microsoft worked on improving its browser; by 1999 Microsoft's browser was better than Netscape's browser in two ways: it performed better, and it supported features that Netscape did not support. These features often were conveniences for programmers. For example, making a link light up when the cursor passes over the link is easy for Microsoft's Internet Explorer, but difficult for Netscape. Many programmers wound up inserting commands that Internet Explorer could interpret but Netscape could not. These functions were conveniences rather than necessities, so while Netscape would function on the Web sites using these features, Netscape would not perform as well as Internet Explorer. In the end, enhanced feature support led many users to favor Internet Explorer over Netscape.

Microsoft's strategy in enhancing the appeal of the browser to programmers was very clever, because the design of Internet Explorer emphasized an otherwise minor network effect—it helped if everyone used the same browser, so long as that browser was Internet Explorer. The network effect operates via programmers, who are induced to employ Internet Explorer exclusives because of their power and convenience. This is precisely the tactic used in the establishment of the MS-DOS operating system: encouraging the use of third-party software to increase the value of the operating system. With Internet Explorer, Microsoft encouraged third-party Web site designers to use features available only in Internet Explorer. These features would eventually become available in Netscape, but after a substantial time lag. Moreover, Microsoft created Web site design tools that automatically incorporated such features; an HTML document created in Microsoft Word will often incorporate features not supported by Netscape.

Microsoft's dominance of the operating system market is based on network effects rather than cost. Provided that Microsoft's products are reasonably priced, attempts at entry will fail to win many customers. There were several attempts at entry—IBM's OS/2 attracted a modest following but failed to catch on with the wider population. Novell's Dr. Dos attracted almost no customers. Maintaining a network effect primarily requires not abusing the customers too much, and watching out for substitutes that come from distant technologies.

Interestingly, Microsoft has embraced the Web-based threat to Windows with its new .NET model strategy, through which Microsoft effectively rents software, much of which would not reside on a customer's computer. The .NET strategy encompasses other Internet integration technologies, including bill paying and Web site maintenance as well.

In contrast to Microsoft, a cable company has a local monopoly because of decreasing average costs. In such cases, monopoly power rests on the threat that entry will spark a ruinous price war, and that the market cannot support two or more firms. In this case, the key to preventing entry is to insure that price is the main vehicle for competition, and that there is no less threatening entry posture. For the potential entrant, the optimal circumstance is entry with a substantially differentiated product, so that the incumbent is encouraged to coexist rather than wage a ruinous war. In particular, entry with a high marginal cost and low fixed cost, so that the entrant will not find it profitable to fight a price war, is preferred to entering with a comparably low marginal cost and a high fixed cost. In the low marginal cost case, the outcome is much more likely to be a price war.* Thus, satellite television, with its relatively high marginal costs (which are on a per customer basis rather than a per neighborhood basis like cable), makes a better entrant to the cable TV industry than a duplicative cable system. Cable TV companies are differentiated by cable modems and the number of channels they offer, and hence are less likely to declare a war against satellite competition than against another cable system entering the market.

*If the entrant can enter with such a low marginal cost that it wins a price war, then it might make sense to enter with the low marginal cost.

Tight Oligopoly

Tight oligopolies provide a wealth of strategic choices and present the best case for cooperation, because each firm reaps a sizable fraction of the benefits of cooperation. Moreover, the likelihood of cooperation being spoiled is reduced. Finally, punishment-type strategies—cooperate or face a strong reaction—work best when there are only a few firms involved.

A tight oligopoly has the enhancement of the market as a basis for cooperation. Thus, while Coke and Pepsi may spend a large amount of money on advertising the superiority of their respective brands of cola, they do not engage in saying negative things about each other. If both should engage in criticizing the other, consumers would be likely to conclude that cola itself is unpleasant, and the market overall would be injured. Moreover, Coke and Pepsi have many common interests. For example, they value the removal of the sugar quota, which props up the U.S. price of sugar above world levels.

There can be relatively subtle forms of cooperation that are unimaginable even in a loose oligopoly. For example, Coke and Pepsi often sign exclusive contracts with movie theaters and fast-food restaurants. Competition to become the exclusive provider is costly to the firms, and the companies pay significant sums for such rights. Moreover, consumers are often induced to try the competing brand because it is the only brand available, and the brand of cola is not sufficient to dictate the customer's choice of movie. From Coke and Pepsi's perspectives, it would be better to avoid this competition, which encourages the firms to compete on the price paid to the theater, and also encourages consumers to switch back and forth from day to day, perhaps making them more price-sensitive. That is, an agreement to always compete in every venue and to never sign exclusive contracts with distributors might soften price competition for the two companies.* As a practical matter, the companies fail to achieve this subtle cooperation.

Tight oligopolies must be much more sensitive than loose oligopolies to the reaction of their rivals to strategy. A useful strategic question is: "If my rival adopts my exact strategy, will we both be better off?" In the case of frequent flyer programs, the answer is yes. In the case of product differentiation, again the answer is usually yes. Under such a hypothetical case, an attempt to steal a rival's business is usually unprofitable; it only pays when the stealer has a very significant advantage.

*As a practical matter, it seems unlikely that Pepsi is going to sell Coke in Pepsi's Taco Bell subsidiary. There is also the issue of the theater that will handle only one brand. Nevertheless, an implicit agreement never to pay to be the chosen brand could benefit both companies.

Loose Oligopoly

In a loose oligopoly, the potential for cooperation is muted relative to that of a tight oligopoly. Usually several firms perceive their interests to be at odds with the remainder of the industry and serve as spoilers to any cooperative agenda. There are two main strategies for achieving profits in a loose oligopoly. First, differentiation may work well. Airlines differentiate on routes and services. Large accounting firms differentiate on consulting services and expertise. Tobacco companies are masters of differentiation. Nevertheless, differentiation does not always work: the major oil companies have found little basis for differentiating at the retail level, although some differentiated their gasoline with additives ("Put a tiger in your tank"). However, consumers generally fail to perceive any advantage to one set of additives over another, and there is actually little difference now that the product is substantially regulated by the EPA. Gasoline retailers are judged more often by the cleanliness of their restrooms than by the quality of their gasoline. The second main strategy is to change the nature of the industry, perhaps by redefining the product. For example, check-printing companies attempt to incorporate service, such as direct customer ordering, check personalization, and expedited handling, into the provision of the physical good, differentiating their offerings and increasing entry barriers.

A loose oligopoly usually has few entry barriers, for otherwise there would not be so many firms. Consequently, unless the level of entry barriers is increasing, or the nature of the product and competition is changing, the prospects for substantial profitability are remote. The difficulty is that even if a firm finds a means of achieving profitability, such profitability attracts entry and imitation. Increasing entry barriers benefits the entire industry but often requires cooperation that is difficult to sustain, given the number of firms.

EXECUTIVE SUMMARY—INDUSTRY ANALYSIS

- Six forces govern the profitability of industries:
  - New entrants
  - Buyer bargaining power
  - Supplier bargaining power
  - Substitute products
  - Rivalry (price competition)
  - Complementary product producers
- Barriers to entry are critical to the long-term profitability of an industry. In the absence of entry barriers, profits are dissipated by competition.
- Barriers to entry include:
  - Government restrictions and patents

Trade secrets
Sufficient scale economies
Learning
Brand names
Customer switching cost
Network values

- Scale economies enhance other barriers like reputation and brand names.
- Bargaining power on the part of buyers and suppliers limits the amount of the value of production captured by an industry.
- Substitute products create a threat that is often neglected, especially when substitutes are not currently economic.
- Price competition by incumbent suppliers often eliminates industry profitability. Factors that limit rivalry include:
  Few competitors
  Natural industry price leader
  Differentiation and switching costs
  Large minimum efficient scale
  No exit barriers
  Steeply increasing variable costs
- Complementary products offer interesting strategic opportunities, creating
  A natural basis for cooperation,
  A means of locking in customers, and
  A means of predicting and influencing industry evolution.
- There are four basic strategies for providing complementary products:
  Provide the products directly.
  Subsidize the provision of complements by others.
  Be subsidized to provide complements.
  Form a joint venture to provide complements.
- Customers and suppliers have similar and equally important relationships with the firm. Efforts to enhance the value proposition for suppliers are as important as efforts to market to buyers.
- There are four basic industry structures:
  Fragmented industry (many small firms)
  Dominant firm
  Tight oligopoly
  Loose oligopoly
- Usually there is a structural reason for the industry to be composed the way it is, often because it is efficient to provide goods and services that way.
- In some cases, an industry's structure can be reformed by a new means of providing the goods or services.

3

Firm Strategies

Southwest Airlines, Enterprise Rent-A-Car, and Wal-Mart are all firms that have coherent strategies—each element of the strategy serves a single vision of the positioning of the firm. These visions guide decision making at every level, informing everyone from an assistant to the CEO to a management trainee how to make decisions. These companies are successful because the overall vision is well adapted to the environment in which the companies operate, and the vision involves the provision of a desirable set of goods and services at an attractive price. How do these companies consistently remain more profitable than their rivals?

VALUE / COST STRATEGIES

Michael Porter introduced two main strategies, which he named generic strategies, for firms to pursue—the value strategy and the cost strategy. Broadly speaking, the cost strategy represents the pursuit of minimum cost, while the value strategy represents staking out a high-quality position.* For some products, Porter's classification is sensible. Consider the market for rental cars. A large fraction of the customers are very price-sensitive, and so there are firms to serve this group—Alamo, Budget, Dollar, and others that usually require a bus ride from the airport to pick up the car. Other companies, such as Hertz and Avis, pursue the upscale tourist and business travel customer and offer quick pickup, locations in the terminal, satellite guidance positioning systems (GPS) in the cars, and other features. Two separate strategies—one serving price-sensitive consumers, the other serving higher-end consumers—survive in the marketplace. Because of the absence of serious entry barriers, the firms at the airport do not make a significant profit.

*In addition, Porter describes the differentiation strategy, which requires pursuing either a value strategy or a cost strategy for a niche or market segment.

For most industries, value and cost strategies do not represent extremes—firms are located on a value spectrum, and minimize cost *for the moderate value provided,* not the overall cost. For example, Southwest Airlines clearly follows a cost strategy; Southwest has low costs and low prices, and this makes it profitable. Moreover, low costs protect the profits; other airlines with higher costs cannot erode Southwest's profits without incurring substantial losses. However, Southwest does not literally minimize cost—it could pack even more people into its airplanes and stop giving out peanuts—but instead it minimizes cost for a modest level of value. A better terminology is that Southwest follows a mass-market strategy, offering the best value/cost proposition for a large number of tourist travelers. Similarly, American, Delta, and United do not specialize in high-value customers. In the airline business, specializing in high-value customers (i.e., the business traveler) fails. Business travelers place a high premium on flexibility in their schedule. Consequently, serving business travelers well requires frequent flights, and offering frequent flights essentially requires accommodating tourist travelers as well, for there are not enough business travelers to justify the needed frequency of flights.

The plan for this chapter is first to consider quality choice without competition, then to consider at a very general level how to think about quality choice with competition, by introducing some basic game theory and, in particular, the concept of how to give a best response. We then return to quality choice to use the best response tool to understand the positioning of two firms, and how one firm can strategically locate and affect its rival firm. A key insight is that there is an advantage to being the first mover—the first entrant can strategically locate itself in a more profitable position, leaving a less desirable position for the rival.

Quality Choice without Competition

To begin thinking about the location a firm should choose in value/cost space, consider first a firm that does not face competition. Should the firm produce more than, equal to, or less than the quality that suits the typical or average customer? An increase in quality permits the firm to charge more for the product, but the price increase will cause the loss of some customers at the low end who do not value quality as highly as others. The surprising answer is that the product should be optimized for the *lowest* type of customer demand that will purchase the good.[1] The reason is that if the product is designed for a lower type than actually buys the good, all the customers buying the good are willing to pay for the cost increase of higher quality. When the quality is higher than is optimal for the marginal customer, only a fraction of the customers will be willing to pay the cost increase required for higher quality, and thus the cost of a quality increase cannot be fully recovered.

In contrast to the intuition that the product should be designed for approximately the middle customer, in a wide variety of circumstances the product should be designed for the marginal or lowest customer. There are two main circumstances when this logic is incorrect—when the firm sells multiple products of different qualities, and when the firm faces competition for the product. When the firm sells multiple products, the price of the low-quality product has an impact on the price of the higher-quality products, a subject considered more thoroughly in chapter 4. With competition, a firm may use the quality to injure a rival, or move further away from a rival's quality, an issue that will be considered below. Nevertheless, the insight that a monopoly with one product should design the product for the lowest purchasing customer is a remarkably general and occasionally valuable insight. Unfortunately, the insight does not reveal whether the product should be designed to serve most of the potential customers or not—that depends on the nature of costs. The insight instead suggests that whatever group is served, the product should be designed to be the most preferred product of the lowest type of customer. In particular, the decision to add a feature to a product can be assessed by answering the question of whether the feature improves the value proposition for the lowest type of customer. If it does not, then either the lowest type of customer should not be served or the feature should be optional—offering a model that does not contain it.

When a firm can sell two products, it will typically want to position one above, and one below, the single-product choice. The higher-quality product should be designed for the marginal customer who purchases it, as in the single-product case. However, this customer type will usually be a higher customer type than was chosen in the one-product case. The lower-quality product should be further reduced in quality—it should have a lower quality than is optimal for any of its buyers, as an encouragement for customers to buy the higher quality. Thus, relative to the single-product case, the firm should offer both a higher quality and a substantially lower quality.[2]

The analysis of competition requires some background on game theory, and that is provided in the next section.

Games and Best Responses

> The guy was all over the road. I had to swerve a number of times before hitting him.
>
> **—Statement on an automobile accident report**

A "best response," as its name suggests, is the optimal action given the expected play of other players. It is the major tool for the analysis of competitive strategies, so it is worth a few general remarks on best-response reasoning.

The game of matching pennies is a game with two players. Each player has a penny, and can choose either heads or tails. One of the players gets both pennies if the pennies match (either both heads or both tails), and the other player gets both pennies in the event that the pennies do not match. For the player who gets both pennies when they match, the best response is to do the same thing as the other player is expected to do—choose heads if the other player is expected to choose heads, and choose tails when the other player is expected to choose tails. If the other player is randomizing—picking heads or tails at random, the best response depends on the likelihood of heads.

Consider the game of chicken, played by teenagers in automobiles. In this game, two drivers head toward each other down the middle of a road. The first one to swerve and avoid a collision is considered to lose the game. If both swerve, the game is a draw. If neither player swerves and a head-on collision results, the worst outcome arises. Each player's best response is to do the opposite of the other player. If the other player is expected to swerve, the best response is to not swerve, while if the other player is expected not to swerve, the best response is to swerve.

Consider two florists, Ann and Bob, who sell bunches of flowers at the weekly farmer's market. This example, which considers quantity competition, will illustrate the logic of the best response, logic that is useful in its own right and that will be useful when we return to the discussion of quality competition. Each florist chooses the number of flowers to bring to market. Once at the market, the two compete fiercely to sell their flowers, which results in a uniform price, determined by the demand for flowers. To provide a concrete illustration, suppose that the demand is indicated by a straight line such that one bunch of flowers could sell for $10, but to sell one hundred bunches would require a price of zero. The demand is illustrated in figure 3.1. It has the feature that each extra bunch made available to the market reduces the market price by a dime. The two florists buy their flowers for $2 a bunch, and this cost is illustrated by the dashed horizontal line.

How many bunches of flowers should Ann bring to the farmers' market? If she thinks Bob will bring twenty bunches, the prices Ann faces are illustrated in figure 3.2. If Ann brings thirty, her thirty are added to Bob's twenty for a total of fifty, which yields a price of $5 a bunch. The demand for Ann is as if the dotted vertical line was the axis; that line accounts for Bob's twenty units. From Ann's perspective, it is as if Bob sells to the highest-value buyers and Ann sells the rest of the units, even though they both sell to all the buyers.

It turns out that, to maximize profits, Ann wants the total amount sold to be the midpoint between Bob's quantity and eighty, the break-even point. This amount maximizes Ann's profit, which is the price minus $2 times Ann's quantity. Ann's desired quantity, when Bob is selling twenty, is thirty, which produces a profit of $90 ($3 per bunch times Ann's thirty bunches). If Ann sells twenty-nine units, she drives the price up to $5.10, making a profit of $3.10 times twenty-nine, or

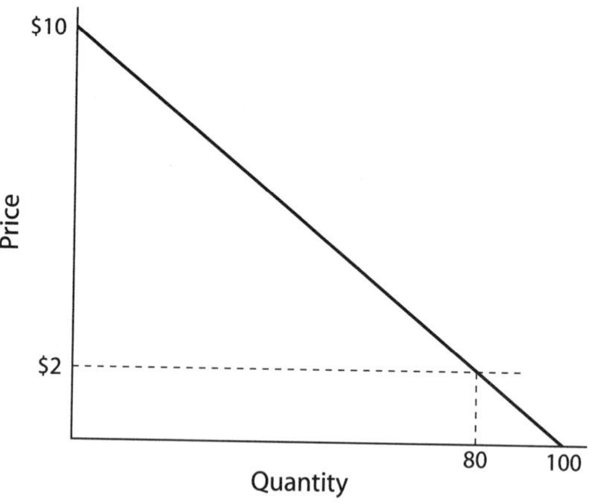

Figure 3.1. The demand for flowers in the farmer's market.

$89.90. Similarly, if she sells thirty-one bunches, she makes a profit of $2.90 times thirty-one, or $89.90. Her maximum profit arises at thirty units, and hence her best response to Bob's choice of twenty is thirty.

In general, Ann's best response is a quantity that is $\frac{1}{2}(80 - Q_{\text{Bob}})$, where Q_{Bob} is Bob's quantity. This is the quantity that maximizes Ann's profits, given Bob's quantity. If Bob brings no bunches of flowers to the market, Ann would like to bring forty, which is the monopoly quantity. When Bob brings eighty bunches, there is no room for Ann to sell profitably—Bob has driven the price to $2, the marginal cost, single-handedly. Ann's best response, given Bob's quantity, connects these two extremes where Bob brings zero, in which case Ann wants to bring forty, and Bob brings eighty, in which case Ann brings zero.

The best response can be used by Ann to calculate what she should do, given the way Bob behaves, but that is hardly the end of the usefulness of the best response. Consider, for example, a situation where Bob buys flowers first, and Ann gets to see how many bunches Bob bought prior to choosing her quantity. This situation arises frequently, when one firm builds a factory with an observable capacity, and then an entrant decides how much capacity to build. How many bunches should Bob buy, knowing that Ann will react to his purchase?

We can solve this problem by considering the demand curve facing Bob, when Ann's sales are taken into account. Recall that Ann's best response is $\frac{1}{2}(80 - Q_{\text{Bob}})$. Thus, if Bob buys Q_{Bob} for resale, the total number of bunches brought will be

$$\tfrac{1}{2}(80 - Q_{\text{Bob}}) + Q_{\text{Bob}} = \tfrac{1}{2}(80 + Q_{\text{Bob}}).$$

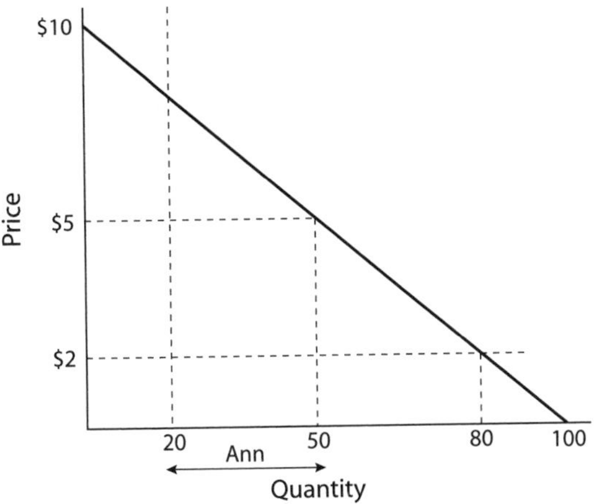

Figure 3.2. The demand remaining for Ann if Bob brings 20.

This is illustrated in figure 3.3. This quantity leads to a price of \$10 – \$0.10 ($\frac{1}{2}(80 + Q_{Bob})$), which equals \$6 – \$0.05 × Q_{Bob}. It is now a simple mathematical exercise to deduce the profit maximizing quantity for Bob, which turns out to be forty.* Ann responds to Bob's choice with twenty. In this case, Bob's first-mover advantage is dramatic, with Bob earning twice what Ann earns. Moreover, Bob sells as many units as he would sell even if Ann were not present. The reason is that Ann subsidizes Bob's sales by 50%; for every extra sale Bob makes, Ann makes half a sale less. This compensation encourages Bob to increase his production, since he gets all the benefits of his increased production, and Ann is paying half the costs.

In addition to understanding moves made in sequence, the best response can be used to help estimate what a player may do. Suppose that Bob has been producing alone in the market for a while, selling forty units each period. Ann is about to enter. How much should she expect Bob to sell? This will depend on several factors. However, the concept of a best response is still quite useful. If Bob is very naive, he may continue to produce forty. If Bob is a bit more sophisticated, he may reason that Ann will likely optimize against his output of forty, and thus Ann would produce twenty. Consequently, Bob should optimize against Ann's output of twenty, which gives thirty for Bob. Ann can use the logic of best responses to identify scenarios for Bob's likely response to Ann's behavior. Such an analysis is presented in table 3.1.[3] With the naive conjecture, Bob does what he did in the

*Bob's profits, subtracting the cost of \$2/bunch are (\$4 − \$0.05 × Q_{Bob}) Q_{Bob}, which is maximized at $Q_{Bob} = 40$.

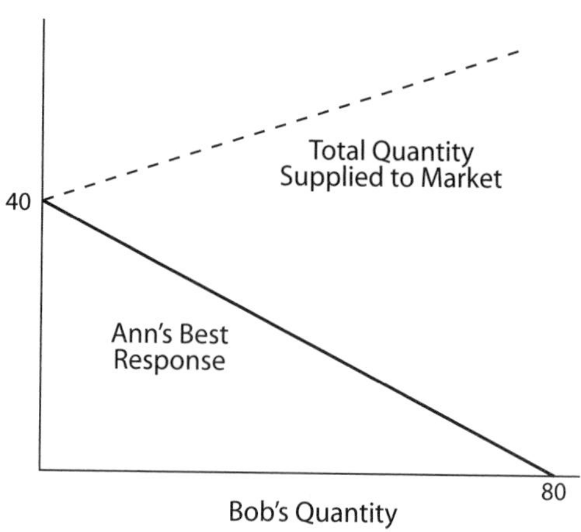

Figure 3.3. Ann's best response.

past, and Ann reacts to this. When Bob is a bit more sophisticated, he understands that Ann will enter, and thinks that she will enter responding to his previous quantity of forty, and hence she would produce twenty. Bob's best response to twenty is thirty. Ann, responding to thirty, produces twenty-five.

This process can be continued; if Bob figures out that Ann will produce 25, he should produce $27\frac{1}{2}$, and Ann's best response to this production is $26\frac{1}{4}$. This process can be continued without end, and results in what might be termed ultrasophisticated conjectures, because they involve both parties understanding the conjecturing process and conjecturing correctly what the other party will do. In this case, both produce $26\frac{2}{3}$. The two parties produce this level because $26\frac{2}{3}$ is a best response to itself—if Bob produces $26\frac{2}{3}$, Ann should too, and vice versa.[4]

The logic of best responses is very helpful at identifying the likely actions of competitors. In addition, the logic of best responses permeates the analysis of business strategy, which focuses on the actions, and reactions, of rivals.

The Effects of Competition on Quality Choice

Two firms with very similar product qualities face a serious pricing problem—the firms are likely to be quite rivalrous, for customers can easily substitute one for the other. Consequently, in choosing the value/cost offering, the most important consideration is to be different. In particular, it is usually more profitable to offer a lower quality than the same, higher quality as a major rival. The reaction of the rival to the quality choice is the important determinant of profitability—locate too close, and the firm encourages intense price-cutting.

TABLE 3.1
Four Scenarios for Bob's Reasoning

Scenario	Description	Bob's conjecture	Q_{Bob}	Q_{Ann}
Naive	Ignores Ann	none	40	20
Primitive	Reasons that Ann reacts to Bob's previous output	$Q_{Ann} = 20$	30	25
Sophisticated	Reasons that Ann will deduce that Bob considers Ann's reaction to Bob's monopoly output	$Q_{Ann} = 25$	$27\frac{1}{2}$	$26\frac{1}{4}$
Ultrasophisticated	Both Bob and Ann believe that the other understands best response logic	$Q_{Ann} = \frac{1}{2}(80 - Q_{Bob})$	$26\frac{2}{3}$	$26\frac{2}{3}$

Consequently, two firms will tend to position themselves at very different points of the quality spectrum. In considering the ideal point of a middle customer, there will tend to be one firm above, and one firm below, this middle point. Either position can be the more profitable—the low-quality position when there are many more price-sensitive customers than customers with a high willingness to pay for quality, or the high-quality position when there are about as many at the upper end. (Usually the higher-quality firm earns more per customer.)

Because the high and low positions do not entail the same profits, it matters who moves first; the first mover or leader in the industry can stake out the more profitable position. When the high-quality position is the most profitable, as has arisen with elevators, the leader in the industry has an opportunity to recognize this and position itself for the profitable position, insuring that later entrants choose to locate in the less profitable position.

Moreover, the leader has a unique opportunity to distort the follower's positioning. Suppose, for example, that the high-value position is the most profitable. By positioning at the high end, but a little closer to the middle, the leader can drive the follower into a slightly less advantageous position. As the leader positions itself a bit closer to the middle, the follower is forced to adopt an even lower quality, an advantage to the leader. This attempt to force the follower farther down carries several risks:

- If pushed too far, the follower will choose a high-quality position instead, eliminating the advantage of the leader.
- The move toward the middle makes a third entry, at an even higher quality, more likely to arise.

Generally, the leader should locate near the ideal point of the larger revenue-adjusted customer segment, and in this way grab the best position for itself. However, the largest customer segment depends on a forecast of the ultimate size of the market, forecasts that are notoriously unreliable. Nevertheless, the general insight that leaders should be aware of the effects of their positioning on subsequent entry is an important and powerful one.

Accommodation and Dissuasion

Consider a leader that expects a second firm to enter an industry. Relative to the monopoly position, the leader chooses a quality level that accommodates the entrant. If, for example, the entrant enters with a low-quality product, the leader should move upscale somewhat, to reduce price competition. When a pharmaceutical manufacturer is presented with entry of generic equivalents, the manufacturer tends to increase price and aim the marketing at the upper-end segment, rather than trying to confront the generics head on. This "live and let live" strategy involves accommodating the entrant. Accommodation has two elements—making room for an entrant, and weakening price competition. Thus, by leaving a valuable portion of the customer base poorly served, or not served at all, room is left for entry. By moving products even farther away from this portion of the customers, price competition is weakened. The overall effect is to encourage a rival to enter a niche that minimizes competition. Both firms prosper in the accommodation strategy, but the incumbent prospers less than without the entry.

A riskier strategy is to try to block a potential entrant by product positioning, to dissuade the entrant from entering the market at all. With a single quality, this means locating at or near the spot that minimizes the entrant's maximum profit, which entails moving toward the middle.

The dissuasion strategy is constructed by enhancing price competition. That is, the dissuasion strategy should imply that entry induces a price war. At its essence, the dissuasion strategy is the doomsday device of Dr. Strangelove—positioning the firm so that any attempt at entry into the market induces a ruinous price war. There are two major components to the dissuasion strategy. First, products must be positioned so that there is no available niche; the product space must be filled out sufficiently that any entrant confronts an existing product head-on. Second, the product design must involve low marginal (variable) costs, so that margins are high. High margins insure that the incumbent firm will fight to keep the customer base; that is, high margins insure that the price war will actually erupt following entry.

There are several means of lowering marginal costs. First, vertical integration tends to lower marginal costs. When an input is bought, the entire purchase price of the input is a marginal cost to the firm. Although the input supplier has fixed costs, the supplier's fixed costs are variable to the buyer. When producing the input in-house, the fixed-cost portion of the supplier's costs becomes part of the firm's fixed costs and is not in the marginal cost component. Vertical integration increases the portion of overall costs that are fixed, and reduces marginal costs.

Second, the design of production facilities can be tilted to reduce marginal costs. A larger scale often reduces marginal costs with an increase in fixed costs. Although personnel are usually variable costs—people can be laid off—robots are fixed costs. Thus, labor-saving devices reduce the marginal cost, with a corresponding increase in fixed costs. Union contracts, which reduce the employer's flexibility with respect to layoffs, have the effect of converting labor from a variable cost to a partially fixed cost.

In sum, there are two broad product-design strategies. First, there is the accommodation strategy, which involves making room for rivals, minimizes price competition, and insures all firms obtain a satisfactory profit. The accommodation strategy is enhanced by high variable costs and low fixed costs, reducing the threat of a price war and allowing separate niches for each firm in the product space. Second, there is the dissuasion strategy, which entails triggering a price war in the event that a rival encroaches on the firm's customers. Following a dissuasion strategy requires filling the product space so that an incursion by a rival encounters an existing product. The dissuasion strategy works best when the firm has very low variable costs and high fixed costs. Dissuasion is riskier than accommodation because the downside of dissuasion is a ruinous price war.

Low-Cost Strategy

The concepts of accommodation and dissuasion suggest a very different interpretation of the low-cost strategy than that discussed by Michael Porter. In particular, a low-cost strategy is not just about reducing costs as a way of creating an advantage over other firms. Instead, a low-cost strategy is aimed at creating a situation in which a firm can fight and win a price war. Thus, a low-cost, mass-market strategy is aimed at creating a situation in which the firm not only will fight a price war in the event of entry but can win a price war. The key to victory in a price war is low *variable* costs, so that it is possible to price below the rival's variable costs and yet still cover the firm's variable costs. The low-cost strategy generally involves choosing the products that suit the largest numbers of customers. Moreover, the design of individual products needs to permit the exploitation of scale economies. Thus, there are a limited number of product variants, and the variants have many components in common. Additional variants are added when the addition reduces average variable costs still farther. For example, a high-end VCR that shares many components with the mass-market VCRs may permit a reduction in the average cost of the mass-market VCRs through the exploitation of scale economies in the components.

The advantages of the low-cost strategy are:

- High volume
- Solid profit margin
- Dissuasion of competitors
- Ability to survive a price war

A major problem with the low-cost strategy is that expensive, high-technology factories that currently create low costs will become obsolete in the future. Ford's enormous Rouge River Center, begun in 1917 and finished in 1925, employed over 100,000 workers and was a marvel of vertical integration and factory design. Iron ore, coal, and other raw materials came in through docks on the Rouge River, and finished automobiles—one every forty-nine seconds—came out. Rouge River Center provided Ford with a massive cost advantage over rival GM through the late 1930s. Ford's marvel, however, gradually became a dinosaur. The plant was designed to produce only one model of automobile and was ill-suited to increasing demand for variety. New developments in steelmaking rendered Rouge's steel mill obsolete. Today, only 7,000 workers report to Rouge, and only one model is produced—the Ford Mustang.

Thus, the problem with the low-cost strategy is that the firm may become locked in to an obsolete production technology. It is very difficult to stay current with the technology—often staying current requires junking expensive machines that still work quite well. Imagine attempting to stay current with one's personal computer. Buying a new computer every month would insure that no real work actually gets done, and would involve a full-time employee just to transfer files. The low-cost strategy, with its large fixed costs, contains the seeds of its own destruction. The large fixed costs become a barrier to updating the technology to stay current, making it possible for an entrant to nibble at the edges of the firm's strategy (see cream-skimming, below) or even conduct an assault on the main customer base. Much as the large steel mills gave way to smaller, more efficient steel mills in the 1960s, a large, efficiently scaled plant will eventually become obsolete. The firm is faced with the choice of harvesting the plant and permitting a rival to eventually replace the firm as low-cost leader, or junking the plant and building a new plant incorporating recent technological developments. Which choice is most profitable depends primarily on the speed at which the new production technologies will supplant the existing technologies. If the new technology is coming slowly, harvesting is most profitable. When the new technology will supplant quickly, harvesting has low value and it pays the firm to build a new facility, rather than let a rival build the facility. Thus, the major problems facing a firm adopting the low-cost, mass-market strategy are:

- Obsolescence of technology
- Loss of high-end customers to specialized firms

Cream-Skimming

A major problem for a low-cost strategy is the need to serve a very large market as part of minimizing costs, and yet avoid the problem of including many expensive variants. This leaves the firm vulnerable to firms that design their products to suit the most profitable market segments. Usually these are high-end customers, who are willing to pay more for higher quality and appreciate design and service not compatible with a low-cost production technology. The U.S. Post Office's delivery inefficiencies create opportunities for several firms—speedy firms and low-cost, exclusively local firms. (The latter type of enterprise is ruled out by statute.) European and Japanese automakers have taken over many car buyers, at both the very low end and the high end. However, the cream can be the low end—Enterprise found the low end of car renters, those with car problems, much more lucrative than the mass market of airport rentals.

Cream-skimming refers to designing a product to suit high-end customers who are willing to pay a premium price for a better product, or offering low prices to customers who are inexpensive to serve. The $15,000 plasma flat-screen television created by Royal Philips Electronics of the Netherlands—essentially a 42-inch laptop screen—is a recent example of cream-skimming in the television market, siphoning off the highest-end users. Internet appliances, in contrast, attempt to serve computer users with very low values at an attractively low price, by stripping out much of the functionality and cost of computers. Internet appliances, so far, have been unsuccessful. The failing Iridium satellite-based telephone system was an attempt to supply telephone services to business travelers anywhere in the world, a market now sought by Globalstar. In cellular telephones, Nextel specializes in the business user, attempting to skim off the customers with steady demand and a higher willingness to pay for convenience and mobility.

The strategy of cream-skimming can provide a defensible niche. The goal is to find a product that serves a group of customers so well that no other company will find it worthwhile to enter the business. United Parcel Service serves a market—for packages larger than an express envelope—so well and at such a reasonable price that no firm has seriously fought for UPS's market. Other firms have, however, skimmed the cream off UPS's business with overnight envelopes and two-day air. There are other freight companies that carry packages larger than

UPS. Nevertheless, UPS's core business remains uncontested, except by the U.S. Post Office.

COHERENT STRATEGIES

A business strategy is, at its root, a vision of the company in the future. Craig McCaw's vision of cellular communications was more accurate than many of his rivals', and his company, McCaw Cellular, created significant value by assembling licenses for cellular communications. Whether McCaw's subsequent vision of telepathic communications via brain implants becomes a reality is anyone's guess.* However, visions are not just about predicting the future but also about an organizational system that will be consistently profitable. Anyone who can consistently predict the future can make lots of money, but a coherent strategy will help even when the future is unpredictable.

Southwest Airlines is consistently profitable, weathering bad economic times with aplomb and expanding during good times. There are several elements to Southwest's business strategy.

- Primarily short-haul routes, less than 750 miles
- Smaller markets
- Avoiding competition with the majors†
- Very low costs
  - One class of service
  - Rapid 20-minute turnarounds
  - One kind of plane (Boeing 737)
  - No assigned seating
  - Minimal food
  - No in-flight entertainment
- Point-to-point transit
- "Underdog corporate culture"
- Decentralized operations and authority
- Everyday low pricing

*According to Andrew Kuper ("AT&T's $12 Billion Dream," *Fortune,* 12 December 1994, p. 2), "Craig McCaw is the kind of man who once suggested in all apparent seriousness—as the color drained from the face of a (corporate) PR man in attendance—that the Federal Communications Commission should reserve spectrum for telepathic communications to be made possible by brain implants he thinks will exist some day."

†Ironically, Southwest is often not considered one of the major airlines, in spite of the fact that Southwest's market capitalization exceeds the combined levels of American, Delta, and United at the time of this writing.

Southwest Airlines has been extraordinarily successful in large part because of the *coherence* of its business strategy. The major elements of Southwest's strategy involve its low costs, which permit it to enter markets that the majors cannot profitably serve. To promote low costs, it relies on high morale of employees, produced in part by a relatively high degree of decentralized authority; but it also profits by corporate gimmicks, including unusually painted airplanes and CEO Herbert Kelleher's antics. Morale is essential to the twenty-minute turnaround organizational method; pilots must be cooperative, even enthusiastic, to make fast turnarounds occur. Low costs are also encouraged by the no-frills flights. Low costs make reprisals by major airlines very costly for the majors, and Southwest has successfully "flown below their radar screens," unlike Vanguard and other smaller carriers. The point-to-point route structure also make it difficult for the majors, whose flights are primarily hub-based, to engage Southwest in a price war. All of these factors contributes to creating an airline that is insulated against fare wars with major airlines, in spite of its profitability. A key aspect of Southwest's strategy is that the individual elements of Southwest's strategy reinforce each other. This coherency of Southwest's strategy provides three major benefits:

- Each element of the strategy is made more effective by the choice of other elements, which increases the profitability of the overall strategy.
- The overall strategy is difficult to imitate by entrants or competitors because it represents an interactive system of choices.
- Value creation is a natural by-product of a coherent strategy, with each element of the strategy producing more because of the other elements.

In contrast to Southwest's, the strategy of the Coors beer company in the 1980s combined two disparate elements—an appeal to those who desired superior water, hops, other high-quality inputs and lengthy brewing techniques leading to the attempt to market the beer as a premium beer, combined with low costs in the West and commensurately low prices. Upscale positioning requires the kind of added expenditures that conflict with low costs. The elements of Coors's strategy lacked coherence, and indeed, actively conflicted with each other. It was a recipe for poor performance.

Similarly, Sears has not been able to create a coherent retail strategy, and has lurched from centralized to decentralized organizational forms and back again. Sears's strategy to have retail stores was initially designed as a complement to its mail-order business, which was entirely centralized and used a single enormous warehouse. Operating stores across the United States with a single warehouse does not work very well, and Sears has oscillated between centralized and decentralized operations, trying to find a workable organizational form. Sears's stores not only did not reinforce the mail-order business, but each reduced the value of the other.

A coherent strategy is one in which the individual elements of the strategy reinforce the other elements. For example, Paul Milgrom and John Roberts's description of modern manufacturing (discussed in chapter 7, boxes 7.1 and 7.2) emphasizes the complementarities in the elements of manufacturing. Such complementarities create reinforcement—each element enhances the productivity of the other elements.

Strategic coherence begins with product definition. General Electric redefined its military goods operations to emphasize services. Providing services is generally more profitable than selling hardware, because services are more differentiated across firms and exhibit weaker price competition. GE exploits complementarities among services and has produced a coherent strategy that appears to succeed in quite different fields, including medical systems, power generation, rail transport, and aircraft engines.[5] GE devised a strategy of manufacturing to provide services; manufacturing is an element in creating the expertise and demand for service provision.

Illinois Tool Works is a firm that specializes in improving the processes of other businesses. It buys firms that produce intermediate goods (those not sold to final consumers) and reorganizes the subsidiary, generally by splitting out the part of the business with the highest return and closing or selling the other components, depending on their viability. ITW makes everything from welding equipment to the plastic rings that hold six-packs together. ITW's main strategy, like the strategies of Cooper Industries in tools and GE in services, is not concerned with its own production and distribution of goods so much as applying organizational skills to other organizations. In the cases of ITW, Cooper, and GE, the good produced is organization itself. Network company Tivoli Systems is so successful at hiring employees that it hires for other companies as well as for itself; one of the "goods" Tivoli produces is employee selection and assignment.

The Three-Layer Model

Standard models of firm activities, such as the value chain or the supply chain, often seem to obscure the coherency of an organization. The standard approach fails to incorporate the relations of various activities very well. For example, the human resources department is treated as a secondary activity, or a support activity, of the firm. However, such a view neglects the multiple roles that the human resources department plays in the firm. HR departments generally are involved in hiring, which puts HR in the input supply or inbound logistics portion of the company. HR, however, also handles unusual problems with employees and other employee-relations matters, which is traditionally classified as a support activity. Indeed, there are two major forms of secondary or support activities—handling problems and issues outside of normal operations, and redesigning or improving operations. For example, HR not only has to deal with the crazy employee threatening to burn down a factory or an office, but it also formulates family-leave policies. In the former, HR fixes problems and errors on an incident-by-incident basis, while the latter example is part of a system self-correction or improvement function. Indeed, all activities of the firm naturally divide into three categories or *layers:*

Layer 1. *Processing.* These activities are the activities required to bring a good to market, and include inbound logistics such as purchasing, transportation, and warehousing of inputs (including labor), and processing inputs into outputs, and outbound logistics such as pricing and distribution of outputs. Each firm involves multiple processing streams, often including the provision of complementary goods such as marketing. Operations is often the largest component of processing.

Layer 2. *Error correction.* This layer handles all problems and mistakes that arise in processing. Systems for handling input failures and shortages, weather-related problems, strikes, lawsuits, and most inquiries by government regulators would all be handled by the error-correction layer of the organization. Many lower-level managers are part of error correction. In addition, service functions may be part of error correction, or part of processing, depending on the nature of the services.

Layer 3. *System enhancement.* This layer of the organization is aimed at improving the operation of the two levels below it, and includes top management. It includes most R&D functions, which improve products or production processes, except in firms where R&D is itself the output. Measurement activities usually operate as part of system enhancement. Accounting serves both an error correction function—finding and identifying theft, for example—and a system enhancement function, providing information on the health of the organization.

Processing

Processing is probably the best understood activity of firms, and a variety of useful models exists for this layer. Porter's (1985) value chain model, for example, provides a standard model of firm processing. In this five-step model, inputs are purchased, transported, and warehoused in an "inbound logistics" function. These inputs are operated upon, to produce outputs, in the "operations" function. The outputs are transported and distributed by an "outbound logistics" function. These outputs are sold by a marketing and sales function, and, finally, the sold products are supported by a services function. Porter's model is finished by including four

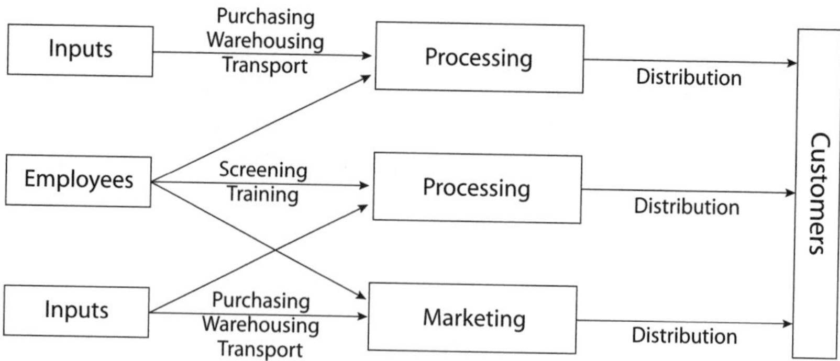

Figure 3.4. The Processing Layer. Inputs, including labor, are acquired, moved, and processed, leading to an output that is delivered to customers. Marketing produces a separate product, complementary to the firms' other products.

support functions: procurement, human resources, research and development, and infrastructure.

Figure 3.4 presents an illustration of the processing layer of the organization. Inputs are acquired, transported, and processed into products. Employees are inputs, similar to other inputs, although the inbound logistics for employees can be substantially different than those for material inputs. Processing of inputs creates salable goods, which are then distributed to customers.

In most organizations, marketing involves the provision of complementary products and serves only a modest role in the processing chain for the product. Marketing involves producing advertisements and handling customer relations, which enhance the value of the primary product. The production of advertisements is the production of a separate product that has its own logistics issues. Moreover, services can also be a separate product; note GE's focus on services as the more profitable segment of military and aircraft supply. In other organizations, services are part of the error-correction function of the organization and not a product per se, which is more in accord with the Porter model.

Error Correction

Error-correction functions of organizations include the mechanisms that permit the organization to deal with adversity, mistakes, and problems. While systems are put in place to handle problems that arise, each incident is handled individually. For example, inventories of inputs are kept as a means of handling late deliveries or an unusually high failure rate. When these problems arise, inventories are tapped and later replenished. Procedures to deal with disgruntled customers and litigious

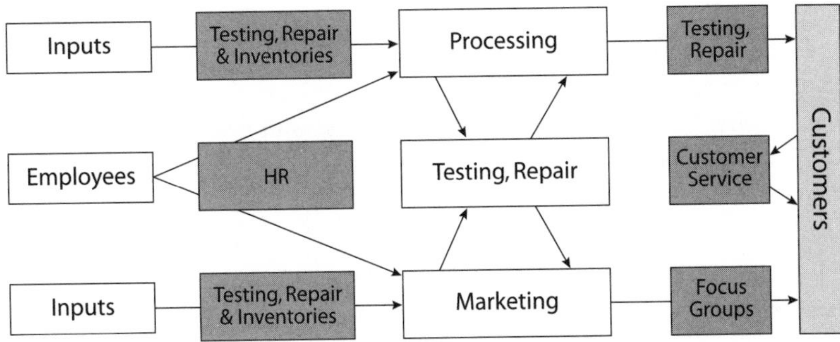

Figure 3.5. The Error Correction Layer. This layer intercedes to solve problems, repair defective machinery, replace incompetent workers, and solve customer problems.

employees are part of error correction; these issues are handled on a case-by-case basis, using procedures designed to handle such problems.

Figure 3.5 adds an error-correction layer to the processing layer. Error correction may require additional steps in the processing, such as testing in inputs and outputs for quality. Alternatively, error correction may involve responses to problems, such as having Human Resources deal with a problem employee, or Customer Service handle complaints. That is, error correction may be like a police officer patrolling a given route, examining whatever passes by, or a fire department that waits for a telephone call. The optimal organization of error-correction functions depends on the particulars of the situation.

American Airlines recently announced a massive restructuring of its largest error-correction function. Typically, adverse weather conditions at Dallas or Chicago have had major systemic effects throughout American's entire system, because so many flights went through these hubs. Thus, flights out of Miami were hampered when Chicago's O'Hare Airport closed, because American flights that went through Chicago to other cities eventually landed in Miami. American used a complex rescheduling system to deal with weather-related problems. Recently, American announced a plan to replace that system with a system that relies on "there and back" flights. Most flights out of American's major hubs would fly to a city and then return to the hub. This procedure isolates the hubs from each other—when O'Hare shuts down, the only flights to Miami that are affected are the O'Hare to Miami flights. In essence, American's new plan disconnects various flights from each other, thereby reducing the propagation of problems throughout the network.

The explicit recognition of error-correction functions is important because so many innovations to organizational design require modification of error processing. For example, just-in-time production techniques replace inventories with coordination of processes, essentially changing the means by which errors and hazards of the production process are mitigated. Toyota's modern manufacturing system involves hiring workers who are able to deal with machinery breakdowns, thus changing the employees who are responsible for equipment problems. Such changes require substantial increases in the training and skill levels of workers on the factory floor. Organizational design changes affect not just the typical outcome but also the variance of the outcomes, just as American's route structure affects not only its cost of flights but also its on-time arrival probability. Moreover, the variance of the outcomes has important effects on other operations. Many manufacturing processes possess "tolerances," which are essentially the degree of error in manufacturing that is consistent with product functioning. Tolerances operate not just with nuts and bolts but also with the sales force, transportation, information technology, and other aspects of the firm. Indeed, IBM's IMS database, a 1960s technology, remains in use by many firms primarily because of its low variance.

There are a variety of error correction functions and methods in an organization. These include:

- Inventories
- Excess production capacity
- Flexible manufacturing
- Skilled employees
- Human resources
- Legal department

Smart Signal offers an interesting example of a company that specializes in error correction:

> It's the perfect time for our technology. Devices are getting smarter and wireless sensors are churning out more data. The world's awash in data, and we're the only ones who can make sense of it.
>
> **—Gary Conkright, CEO of Smart Signal**[6]

Smart Signal is a privately held company that sells technology to predict when airplanes will need maintenance. It costs Delta Airline nearly ten times as much to replace an engine in Japan as it does to replace the engine in Atlanta. Thus, if Delta can better predict when engines will need replacement, it can save by doing preventative maintenance when costs are lower.

Smart Signal's detection strategy involves detecting normal versus slightly abnormal levels of mechanical vibration. When those levels drift outside the normal range, Delta can be alerted to perform maintenance at the first convenient time, essentially providing advance warning of potential problems.

Smart Signal offers cutting-edge software to accomplish a job for aircraft that holds lessons for organizations. By thinking about an airplane as a system, Smart Signal integrates the information from a wide variety of sensors to detect and predict problems. A corporate organization, like an aircraft, has normal abnormalities and problems, and should be designed to detect and compensate for these problems.

System Enhancement

While error-correction functions often involve systems, the operation of these systems tends to be on an item-by-item basis. Error correction resides in the value chain; figure 3.5 illustrates error correction operating in conjunction with processing. In contrast, system enhancement tends to operate on a cycle, with a longer horizon. A subsystem of the firm that has not been examined and optimized recently is a candidate for an examination and overhaul, as are systems whose performance is deteriorating. Some firms use an annual evaluation cycle. System enhancement tends to be proactive, while error correction is reactive.

Both the processing layer and the error-correction layer of an organization can be modeled as a group of processes operating together, as figure 3.5 illustrates. Inputs enter, are operated upon, and ejected (sold). While using two layers is important conceptually—the layers are present for distinct reasons—the two layers could be modeled as a single layer. System enhancement involves the improvement of the processing and error-correction layers. Improvements come from three broad sources:

- External technological changes
- Internal technological developments
- Responses to environmental changes

External technological changes include the incorporation of new technology in the organization. Automakers increasingly use plastics to replace steel as the technology of plastics improves. Changing the product and introducing new products—to increase value or reduce cost or both—as the available technologies evolve is a major role of the system-enhancement function of the firm. Internal technological developments require different consideration, because it may be possible to keep such changes proprietary. For both the internal and external cases, management technology is a relevant technology. Information technology has changed the means and methods of management by expanding the information available at all levels of the firm.

Changing external circumstances also requires altering the way an organization operates. For example, changes in relative prices can change the desirable production techniques. Just-in-time production methods minimize inventories. Such an approach is useful when inventories are expensive, either because real interest rates are very high or because storage is expensive. Thus, just-in-time concepts made sense in Japan, with its relatively high land values, and in the 1980s, when real interest rates exceeded 7%, but they make less sense in, say, a Tennessee automobile factory. The 1973 oil price increases put an end to the technology that killed weeds with flamethrowers.* As the costs of peripherals like laser printers have fallen, firms have substituted personal printers for networked printers. Business travelers carry more equipment, and have more information at their disposal. Changing circumstances generally require changes in the operation of the firm.

The behavior of other firms also changes the optimal firm design. United and Delta needed to respond to American Airlines's recent four-inch increase in coach legroom. United and Delta were significant competitors to American, offering extensive networks, frequent flights, and a relatively high level of service. American's increase in quality required a response from its rivals, to protect their market share and customer satisfaction. United's partial response—some seats increase in legroom and some do not—aids in price discrimination (chapter 10) but muddies the distinction between premium and economy airlines.

Changes in production methods can also change the competitive landscape in a beneficial way for the firm. In chapter 7, we will examine divisionalization, which involves creating multiple competing divisions. Divisionalization is beneficial partly because of the reaction of competitors, who rationally contract in response to an increase in apparent competition. Frequent flyer programs and interchangeable batteries are also techniques that are beneficial, even when copied. Both create complementarities among the firm's offerings. Moreover, their adoption changes the behavior of rivals in a useful way.

Stuck in the Middle

One of the primary features of coherent strategies is that distinct choices reinforce each other. As Paul Milgrom and John Roberts, as well as Michael Porter, emphasize in their work, this means that intermediate choices are often bad choices. The restaurant with high ambiance and poor food is unlikely to survive, and will be

*Killing weeds with flamethrowers was taken sufficiently seriously in the 1960s that fire-resistant corn varieties were bred. Even the low oil prices of the late 1990s did not bring back that vision, perhaps because of environmental concerns.

less profitable than a high ambiance, high-quality-food establishment or a low-quality, low-ambiance, inexpensive restaurant. A natural feature of complementary choices is that "all high" or "all low" dominate "some high, some low." A firm that tries to steer a middle course between two extremes will often fail to find a profitable niche.

Changing circumstances often require one to change from one kind of strategy to another. For example, a restaurant that tries to move upscale by improving only its ambiance will likely not be profitable—it is generally necessary to change all of the characteristics simultaneously, and advertise improvements. Changing only a few characteristics fails to exploit the reinforcement and synergies available only with wholesale changes. In examining a change in the organization, it is important to follow the effects of changes throughout the organization, and not just to examine the effect in isolation. For example, changes in database management might require changes in the way records are kept, and make it profitable to use scanners for warehouse management and inventory control, which requires an increase in the technical sophistication of employees, which permits an increase in employee responsibility, which requires retraining lower management. What seems like a small change on the surface—a change in database management—winds up implying the retraining of lower management. Exploiting complementarities requires a rethinking of all related choices when some are changed.

DEALING WITH COMPETITORS

In the fight between you and the world, back the world.

—Frank Zappa

Probably the number-one mistake made by business people is to underestimate the competition. It is a natural mistake, because successful executives tend to have substantially more managerial ability than most of the people, including subordinates, encountered on a day-to-day basis. However, that does not make an executive better than his or her counterpart at a competing firm. The best guide to what a competitor will do is to figure out what you would do in the competitor's shoes. This is a valuable exercise, especially when combined with scenarios to deal with uncertainty about the competitors. Indeed, the process of war-gaming, with a team playing the role of each competitor, can be very illuminating about the likely actions taken by rivals.*

*In my experience, war-gaming requires a substantial investment of time that few firms seem willing to make. However, it is a very useful approach to understanding the competition, and worth the investment in many circumstances. What is perhaps the most difficult aspect of war-gaming is the chal-

When taking major actions, it is important to consider the likely responses of rivals. What are the effects on the rival, and what options do the rivals have? The best guide to rivals' likely actions is the long-term interest of the rival. For example, the introduction of color devices for Windows CE, the handheld Windows operating system, was sure to evoke a response from Palm Computing. And so it did, although that response was surprisingly slow in coming.

Some companies will start a price war rather than lose substantial market share. This is important because such a policy on the part of a rival renders a business-stealing strategy unprofitable. More frequently, it is necessary to evaluate the incentive of rivals to figure out a likely response to any significant move. Will they find it in their interests to match a major marketing campaign, to blunt its effectiveness? Will a rival file a spurious patent-infringement suit to delay introduction of a new product?

It often seems desirable to try to take market share from rivals, even if such business stealing requires a price war, but rarely is it desirable. Firms with similar cost structures rarely benefit from price wars. There is little to be gained from fighting with an equal; both firms are injured, and neither wins the price war. Unless a firm enjoys a substantial quality-adjusted cost advantage or unless the market can support only one firm, winning a price war is unusual. This logic suggests there are three main circumstances when a price war makes sense. First, if a firm can literally win a price war and eliminate a competitor, it can make sense to start a price war, although the antitrust risk from such an action can easily render it unprofitable. Second, it may be necessary to fight a price war periodically, as a means of policing cooperation, to keep competitors in line and establish a commitment to toughness, a topic explored extensively in chapter 6. Third, it is necessary to fight a price war when another firm starts one.

If there are substantial barriers to entry, and the firms in an industry have similar quality-adjusted cost structures, it makes sense instead to avoid price wars. Chapter 6 discusses many of the issues involved in such a "live and let live" approach to business. Unfortunately, the line between being too greedy and being a pushover can be a very fine line, indeed.

EXECUTIVE SUMMARY—FIRM STRATEGIES

- Without competition, products should be designed to suit the *lowest,* rather than the average buyer.

---

lenge of playing a rival who is somewhat ignorant about one's own firm. Thus, the Southwestern Bell Corporation (SBC) employee who plays Bell Atlantic in a war game has difficulty forgetting inside knowledge of SBC.

- In forecasting the reaction of a rival firm to a strategy, the concept of a *best response* is valuable. What is in the firm's interest, given your behavior?
- Best responses can be used to maximize profit against rival actions.
- With competition, there is a significant first-mover advantage in locating near the ideal point of the best-customer segment.
- Leaders can also shift subsequent firms by their product positioning.
- There are two main strategies for a leader:
  Accommodation
  Dissuasion
- The accommodation strategy involves making room for an entrant and insures that it shares the market profitably as well.
- The dissuasion strategy involves positioning to minimize entrant profits, thereby deterring entry.
- A key element to dissuasion is to maximize price competition—locating in the positions where head-on price competition, a price war, is unavoidable.
- The key to winning a price war, and hence maximizing the credibility of the dissuasion strategy, is to have low marginal costs.
- Vertical integration provides a method of lowering marginal costs.
- A low-cost strategy involves producing few standardized varieties, with a high volume. The advantage of such a strategy is the ability to survive a price war and consequent dissuasion.
- The disadvantage of the low-cost strategy is the risk of obsolescence and the loss of high-end and niche customers—death of a thousand cuts.
- Cream-skimming involves identifying profitable niches and fitting them perfectly.
- Coherent strategies involve making all of the elements of the strategy complementary.
- A firm can be usefully viewed as having three layers:
  The standard processing layer
  An error correction layer
  A system enhancement and repair layer
- Error correction involves the methods of handling mistakes and adversity, and includes human resources, customer service, and inventories.
- Skills, flexible manufacturing, and the organization of the production process affect not only the average cost of production but also the efforts needed for repair and error correction.
- System enhancement involves reorganization of the firm in response to changing circumstances.
- The presence of complementarities often means that extreme choices are

preferable to being in the middle. This leads to situations in which firms, unable to choose, become "stuck in the middle."

- Competitors are often very smart individuals with similar training and ability. It is useful to place oneself in a competitor's shoes to predict his or her likely response.
- How is your competitor thinking about your thought process?

Build a better mousetrap and the world will beat a path to your door.*

—**Ralph Waldo Emerson**

Differentiation

Lee Iacocca was a remarkably successful automobile executive, so successful that there was considerable talk of his running for president of the United States. Iacocca is credited as being the driving force for both the Ford Mustang and the minivan. The minivan caught the Japanese automobile companies by surprise and left them scrambling to catch up, and the minivan was a major component in the perceived revitalization of the U.S. automotive industry. One of Iacocca's less celebrated, but extraordinarily important, initiatives at Chrysler was to compel the executives to drive cars. When Iacocca joined Chrysler, top executives rode to work in limousines. Iacocca set up a rotating schedule through which executives drove both Chrysler cars and the competition's offerings. In this way, Iacocca insured that the top management was familiar with both the company's products and the competitors' products. Iacocca understood that knowledge of both customers and competitors is an essential ingredient of strategy, one that is all the more important when the products are differentiated.

A key business strategy involves differentiating one's product from competitors' offerings. The simple advantage of differentiation is uniqueness—offering a product that no one else sells. Uniqueness confers a degree of market power, although sometimes only a small degree. A new color may be preferred by some consumers, as Apple Computer recently illustrated with the introduction of iridescent colors for its computers. In some cases, modest improvements may dominate the market. The soft rubber grips of OXO's Good Grips kitchen tools helped the company penetrate the kitchen-tool market and left competitors behind. The little spring-loaded retractable ball on a socket wrench, which fits in a depression in the socket

*According to the *Lubbock Avalanche-Journal,* 27 October 1997, the U.S. patent office has granted about 350 patents on new mousetrap designs in the past two centuries. Marie Woodruff was granted a patent on 1 April 1997 for her mousetrap design, a tube, closed at one end, with a spring that snaps shut when a mouse enters. A gel capsule attracts a mouse into the tube. The mouse is unharmed by the trap.

and holds the socket on snugly, yet is removable without tools, netted Sears as much as $100 million during the life of the patent, because it was such a useful improvement on the existing socket wrenches, whose sockets tended to fall off in use. In other cases, differentiation carves out a niche market. Most new breakfast cereals, such as Ancient Grains or Bunuelitos, garner a tiny fraction of the market. Many new breakfast cereals, such as Apple Cinnamon Cheerios, are variations of existing cereals. Some cereals are transitory in nature, such as those aimed at children and based on a recent children's movie. Differentiation is the key strategy to reducing rivalry, and thus is worth a much closer look.

There are two major forms of product differentiation: quality and variety. Quality, as the term suggests, refers to characteristics about which there is general agreement on desirability. In automobiles, the gas mileage, acceleration, braking, interior space, and CD player are based on quality—people uniformly want better gas mileage, acceleration, and braking, more interior space, and a CD player. In contrast, color and shape do not have such widespread agreement. There is no uniform preference for a blue car over a green car, or rectangular taillights over round ones. Similarly, energy efficiency is a quality attribute of appliances, while color is a varietal aspect. Quality and variety are often referred to as vertical and horizontal differentiation, respectively.

Quality differentiators include reliability, durability, features, and performance. Service and product support generally increase the quality of the product. In contrast, aesthetic characteristics including color, shape, and appearance tend to be varietal or horizontal differentiators. Brand identification can provide either quality—insuring that the product meets standards, for instance, or variety. A very significant horizontal differentiator is location. Identical stores in distinct locations will attract different clienteles, and there is no uniform preference over location, although obviously consumers prefer stores close to their home or office.

The profitability of entry is critically dependent on the prices of rivals, which are likely to change as a consequence of entry. Thus, room for an entrant at existing prices is hardly sufficient to guarantee a successful entry; rivals will likely lower their prices to maintain existing customers. The further away the rivals are in product space, the more likely entry will be successful; the lower rivals' costs are relative to the entrant's cost, the less likely that an entry will be profitable. Figure 4.1 summarizes the likely success of entry in a "location/cost" space. With low costs relative to those of the competition, it is possible to survive price reductions by competitors after entry. With a good cost position relative to the competition, and no close competitors, entry is likely to be successful; even if a price war arises, the entrant will likely survive thanks to the superior cost position. Moreover, a price war is unlikely, because the incumbents are some distance away from the entrant, and therefore the incumbent's profits are not seriously threatened by the entry. In

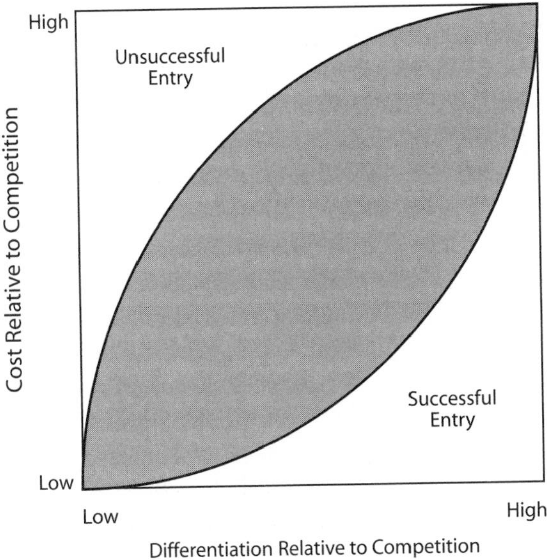

Figure 4.1. The prospects for successful entry are higher with greater differentiation, lower with greater costs.

contrast, with a high cost and many close competitors, entry is unlikely to succeed. Incumbents have a strong incentive to cut prices to maintain their customer base, and such price competition is likely to be fatal to the entrant.

There is a large grey area, shaded in figure 4.1, where the success of entry is uncertain. In this area, more information is necessary to estimate the likelihood of success.

COMPETITION IN DIFFERENTIATED PRODUCTS

Consider the pretzel vendor on the streets of New York City. The vendor can locate in midtown, say across from the Museum of Modern Art, where many people will gladly purchase a pretzel. However, the vendor faces substantial competition—good locations often have two or more vendors. Alternatively, the vendor can move half a block away and be alone—but have fewer customers. Where should the vendor locate?

This problem was first analyzed by Harold Hotelling.[1] He considered the location of two businesses on a line segment, which could be Main Street in a town or the transcontinental railway. In Hotelling's mathematical model, customers are located uniformly across the line segment. The first are denoted L and R, for left

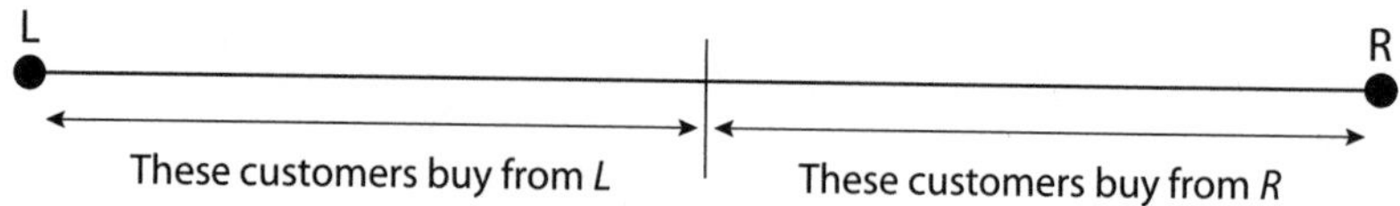

Figure 4.2. The Hotelling Line. Customers on the left buy from firm *L*, the remainder buy from firm *R*. The crossover point is determined by the price difference.

and right. Customers are thought to walk to a store to purchase products, and walking expends time and effort. Other things equal, customers would prefer to shop at the nearest store.

The line introduced by Hotelling, and illustrated in figure 4.2, is a fundamental tool for the analysis of product differentiation, because many types of differentiation can be analyzed using line segments. For example, breakfast cereals can be rated by their sweetness, ranging from sugar-free high-fiber cereal that tastes like sawdust with a sprinkling of bark chips to Count Chocula. Similarly, potato chips range from low-fat chips that substitute for drink coasters to greasy kettle chips that taste great and harden arteries in seconds. Color ranges from white to yellow to orange to red to green to blue to purple to black, following the rainbow. Alternatively, a color scale might also range from dull earth tones to bright Hawaiian-shirt colors. Geography is a major form of differentiation. Laptop computers range from compact, lower performance three-pound machines to twelve-pound behemoths that rival desktops in performance. Movies can be usefully described based on the age of the target audience—five-year-olds prefer different movies than ten-year-olds, who prefer different movies than teenagers, and so on. Typically, a movie aimed at fifteen-year-olds will appeal to some twelve- and eighteen-year-olds, fewer ten- and twenty-year-olds.* Time during the day for airline flights connecting two cities is also a form of differentiation that is naturally thought of as a line segment.

On a physical line like a road, it is easy to understand what it means for a consumer to be located at a particular point—that is, where they live, or where they work. The same line is used to represent the locations of the firms. When the differentiator is not physical space but some characteristic of the product, the line is used both to represent the product characteristic and to represent consumer preferences. To use a line to represent cereal differentiation in sweetness, a consumer who likes one sweet cereal is presumed to prefer other sweet cereals over unsweetened cereal. When the scale is bright versus dull colors, consumers who like bright colors are presumed to prefer fairly bright colors to fairly dull colors. That is, when

*Movies designed for young adults can be put on a line of their own. They range from romantic comedies, known as "chick flicks," to action-adventure shoot-em-ups. Interestingly, horror movies represent a compromise, appealing equally to both males and females.

the line is used for a metaphor for differentiation more generally, a consumer's location represents the consumer's most desired point in the spectrum; consumers are also assumed to prefer closer locations over more distant locations.

Consider a customer located at a point that is the fraction x of the way from L to R, and suppose the cost of moving from L to R is c. This customer pays the price at L, which will be named p_L, plus xc, the total transport cost for moving the distance x, for buying at L. Similarly, a purchase at R has the total cost of $p_R + (1 - x)c$. Taking into account both the purchase price and the cost of transportation, the customer would like to choose the location that has the smaller of $p_L + xc$ or $p_R + (1 - x)c$. This desire to minimize the total cost of the purchase determines a marginal customer, x^*, who is indifferent to choosing between going to L or going to R. That marginal customer is located where these total costs are equal, $p_L = x^*c = p_R + (1 - x^*)c$, which solves for the location of the marginal customer, x^*:

$$x^* = \frac{1}{2} + \frac{p_R - p_L}{2c}.$$

If the firms have the same prices, the marginal customer is in the middle, halfway between the locations of the firms. If the firm L has a higher price than firm R, $p_R - p_L$ is less than zero; the marginal customer will be to the left of the midpoint between the two firms, and firm L will have fewer customers than firm R. When firm L decreases its price, it increases its sales at a rate proportional to $1/c$. Thus, when c is very close to zero, a small price change results in a large change in sales—business stealing is relatively easy. In contrast, when c is large, a small change in prices results in a small change in sales. When c is small, most consumers go to the lower-priced firm. The products of the two firms are hardly differentiated. When c is large, in contrast, the products are very different, and few customers respond to a price change. The transportation cost c measures the differentiation of the products of the firms.

What prices emerge? The share of the market that firm L obtains is x^*. Setting aside the issue of production costs, firm L would like to maximize p_L times x. It turns out that firm L's best price, the price that maximizes $p_L x^*$, is the average of c and p_R. An increase in either c, which isolates firm L from firm R, or in p_R, which reduces the business lost to R, will result in an increase in L's price. The Hotelling line model illustrates a general feature of differentiation: desired prices increase in both the amount of differentiation and the level of competitors' prices. Moreover, there is less than full pass-through: the firm responds partially to an increase in the competitor's price.

The logic for firm R's choice of p_R is analogous; only firm R wishes to maximize p_R times R's market share, $1 - x^*$. If both firms play their best strategy against

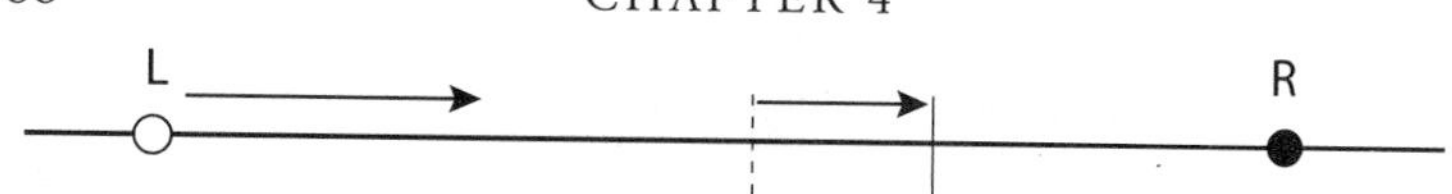

Figure 4.3. As firm *L* moves to the right, firm *L*'s market grows.

the other, it turns out that they will both price at *c*, the consumer's cost of transportation from *L* to *R*. Here, firm profits increase in the total differentiation; indeed, they increase proportionally to the differentiation. This is a feature of most differentiated products theories. Maximal differentiation would be desirable, were it not for a desire of both firms to locate where most consumers are located. It does little good to have a monopoly over a market with no customers. Thus, as the New York pretzel vender found, location represents a tradeoff—moving closer to the customers generally entails moving closer to the competition.

Endogenous Location

> Hustle. That's us. It's what we do. In financial services, where if anyone in town comes out with a new product everyone else has it five seconds later, what really matters is daily execution.
>
> **—George Schaefer Jr., CEO of Fifth Third Bancorp**

Where should a firm locate? Let us first consider this question apart from the question of pricing, and thus hold the prices constant. What is clear from figure 4.2 is that, with equal prices, the marginal consumer is in the middle, halfway between the two firms' locations, for this consumer has an equal cost of buying from either firm. As a consequence, we can see that if the firm on the left moves toward the center, it increases its market share; moving toward the center pushes the marginal consumer toward the right (fig. 4.3). Similarly, the firm on the right would like to move left, and thereby push the marginal consumer to the left. Without consideration of prices, both firms wind up next to each other. It is not uncommon to see two pretzel vendors in Manhattan located next to each other, in spite of the fact that both have wheeled carts that could be moved to a more separated spot.[2] Hotelling had the insight that when prices are fixed, the firms will choose to locate next to each other, and in the middle.

Hotelling's location observation is often applied to political parties; there is a tendency for the candidates to try to seek the middle, with the Democratic candidate locating just to the left of the Republican. When one locates too far to one side of given voter preferences, as happened with Goldwater in 1964, the other candidate tends to win by a large margin. Usually, however, candidates excel at finding the middle.

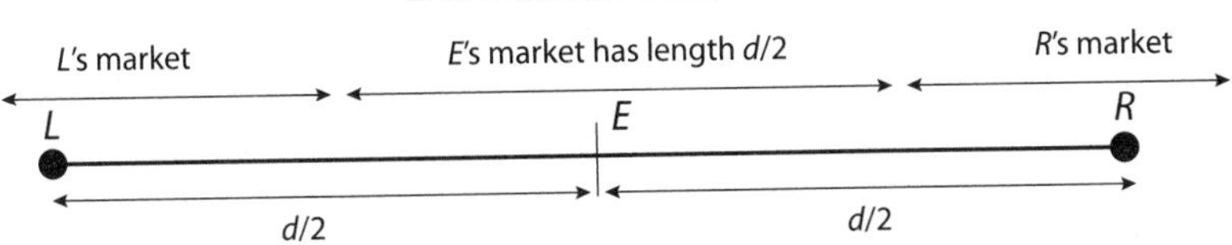

Figure 4.4. Effect of *E*'s entry into the market between *L* and *R*.

Hotelling's insight is helpful in understanding product design only in situations where prices are not adjustable. In the more common case of flexible prices, it pays to be distant from one's competitors. Consider again the analysis of prices given above. When both firms use their best responses, the price came out to c, the transport cost between the two locations. The farther apart the firms are, the higher this cost is, and the more profitable the firms tend to be. Indeed, the only restriction that arises on maximum differentiation is moving so far away from customer tastes that demand begins to fall off.

An important aspect of location is the effect it has on the other firm's price. By moving farther away from one's competitors, a firm increases its own desirable price, an effect that actually helps one's competitor. The competitor benefits in two ways: the competition is farther away, and it has a higher price. However, the firm that moved away receives a second benefit as well—competitors raise their prices in response.

Recently, for example, American Airlines increased the legroom in economy class by a substantial margin. United and a few other major airlines mostly copied this move. Southwest, ATA, and other low-priced firms did not copy the majors. What is the effect? First, by offering higher quality service, the majors can get a higher price from existing customers without losing these customers to Southwest. Southwest's optimal response to the higher price, higher quality service of American is to increase its prices; there is less competition for Southwest's now more differentiated market niche. American's optimal response to Southwest's increased prices is a further increase, an effect that should reverberate, increasing prices by successively smaller margins until a stable point is reached. For example, in the simple example analyzed above, each firm's optimal response was the average of the transportation cost and the rival's price—so each increase in price by a firm induces the rival to increase price by half the increase, spurring an increase by a quarter by the initial firm, then by an eighth, and so on. In this case, the reverberation is as large as the initial price increase, which is to say, half of the full effect of increased differentiation comes from rivals' responses.

Generally, increasing differentiation creates a trade-off in that locating close to customers means also locating close to competitors. For example, the busiest corners have the most pretzel vendors. The choice of location—in geography or in product characteristics—involves trading off an increase in demand by an increase in competition. Simply put, the locations with the most customers also tend to have the most competitors.

In some cases, the locations with the most competitors are the only places where there are a substantial number of customers. Rug and carpet dealers tend to be located close to each other, in both the United States and Istanbul. Often automobile dealers are located on the same stretch of highway outside a city. Customers usually go where the aggregation of sellers are located, and a store by itself will typically get very few buyers—the buyers are attracted to the larger market. In such instances, a firm that locates itself away from the group will often be unprofitable. Moreover, in instances where many firms are selling similar products in locations close to each other, it is important to differentiate in other characteristics. Shoe stores in malls each carry distinct lines of shoes to avoid direct competition. Customers are attracted by the number of stores and the variety they offer, but the stores avoid strong price competition by differentiation in other respects. In the Third World, price competition is reduced by price discrimination; extracting a good price quote from an Istanbul rug merchant can require hours of consumption of Turkish coffee. Thus, most buyers will find the rug that seems best, then start laborious negotiations, which are unlikely to involve the use of competing price quotes.

Broadway shows compete within New York City, but they complement each other by increasing the total size of the market; visitors come to New York just to go to Broadway shows. In the case of Broadway, and off-Broadway, theaters compete on a day-to-day basis, but complement each other on a year-to-year basis. The long-term complementarity forms a useful basis for cooperation, in the form of joint advertising, hotel and theater bundle discounts, and the like, cooperation that benefits all of the theaters.

Spatial Preemption

Often, firms can operate more than one store, or sell more than one product. In this way, a firm can attempt to fill the product space by offering such a rich set of products that there is no room for entry. Consider, for example, the Hotelling line segment model studied above. The optimal prices were c, the transport cost between the two locations. Suppose there is a fixed cost, F, for creating a new location. How far apart must two products be to prevent admission of an entrant?

If the transport cost per unit of distance is t, and the distance between the two existing outlets is d, then the outlets price at $c = td$, the transport costs between the outlets. An entrant would choose to locate exactly in between (to maximize the differential) and would be located $\frac{1}{2}d$ from competitors on each side. This would create transportation costs of $c = \frac{1}{2}dt$. Moreover, the number of consumers would be proportional to the size of the market, which would be $\frac{1}{2}d$. These calculations are illustrated in figure 4.4. The effect is that the entrant's profits are price times quantity, which is $\frac{1}{4}d^2 t$. Thus, it is profitable for the entrant to enter whenever $F < \frac{1}{4}d^2 t$, or

$$d > 2\sqrt{F/t}.$$

This is an interesting formula for several reasons. The market could accommodate firms that are much closer together than the level at which preemption occurs. Indeed, at the distance $\sqrt{F/t}$, the firms just break even. We know this because when the distance is exactly twice that level, the firms break even from entering and reducing the distance to $\sqrt{F/t}$. Second, one can preempt with substantially fewer products than would be sold in competitive conditions. The reason is that the number of products need not be packed as close together as the competitive outcome, but merely as close as it takes so that, *after entry*, a situation worse than the competitive outcome arises. This can involve as few as half as many products as prevail under competitive conditions. Third, as fixed costs grow, the distance which preempts entry also grows, but at a decreasing rate, so that increasing the fixed costs, as a means of preempting, may not be a cost-effective strategy. Fixed costs can be increased by encouraging government safety and environmental regulation, which would increase the burden on an entrant, especially when existing firms are grandfathered. However, fixed costs need to be increased by a relatively large amount to preempt and maintain high profits.

In contrast to increasing fixed costs, filling the product space can be a useful strategy for deterring entry, especially if entry tends to be at a relatively small scale. The reason is that when the product space is filled with products from the same firm, that firm can selectively cut prices to injure entrants and attempt to establish a reputation for a strong response to entry. It has been alleged that established gasoline retailers selectively cut prices to contain, and deter entry of, firms that build large ten- or twelve-pump stations centered around a convenience store and use low gasoline prices as an inducement to bring business in to the store. An advantage of a full line of products is the ability to selectively cut prices as a means of competing, using the price cuts to maximal effectiveness. An important aspect of spatial preemption is that the density need not mirror the competitive outcome but may involve fewer outlets. The goal is to fill the space sufficiently so that, were an entrant to enter, the decision to enter is rendered unprofitable by the ensuing price competition.

When Hewlett-Packard introduced its very successful HP IIP laser printer that printed at five pages per minute (5 ppm), IBM quickly followed with a unit that offered almost identical performance at a slightly higher price. Does that make sense as a business strategy? Prior to IBM's response, IBM held the high ground with a 10-ppm printer. IBM's 5-ppm printer had little differentiation from the HP unit, and thus competition was fierce, forcing prices lower very quickly. The lower prices on the 5-ppm units forced IBM's prices on its higher-end printer to fall. Overall, prices were much lower than they had to be. Was this strategy optimal for IBM? Perhaps, but IBM's strategy is not sensible in the context of laser printers alone. Exact imitation of a product, with minimal differentiation, encourages fierce price-cutting. Reducing the price at one location tends to induce prices to fall across the entire spectrum of products. Instead, IBM's strategy in laser printers makes sense as part of a larger strategy to offer one-stop shopping for business machine customers, who might otherwise be induced to buy some of the modestly priced HP units. Even in light of the larger strategy, IBM could have differentiated the product more by offering six pages per minute, a larger paper tray, and other enhancements with a higher price, or the reverse and a lower price, to reduce the incentive of HP to cut its price. More likely, IBM thought it could preempt HP's entry into the laser printer market altogether, in which case an identical product, with its fierce price competition, makes sense.

When does it make sense to copy a rival's product? In some cases, there is room for two or more firms. Many airline markets support multiple firms. Occasionally, there are as many as four gasoline stations at a particular street corner. It can make good sense to imitate a successful product. Generally, it does not make sense to imitate a rival product when price competition is fierce. For example, it can make sense to imitate successful movies because price competition is weakened by the method by which movies are distributed, which discourages direct competition on price. Similarly, as music compact discs are typically sold in price categories, price competition is muted, which makes imitating a product more successful. In the context of the simple theory presented here, one can think of the price as being nearly fixed in these markets, which means that location next to one's competitors tends to be the optimal strategy. In contrast, when price competition is fierce, as in the airline industry, offering a similar product can be disastrous, encouraging price competition so severe that fixed costs are not covered.

Creating Synergies

The Sony memory stick is a flash-memory device that competes with compact flash memory and smartmedia. The memory stick is similar to these technologies but probably inferior to compact flash, which enjoyed a greater development time and strong competition in production. However, Sony enjoys an advantage that compact flash does not enjoy—Sony can incorporate memory sticks in the wide range of Sony electronic products, and that is precisely what Sony is doing. Sony digital cameras, camcorders, MP3 players, palm devices, and laptop computers all use memory sticks for portable, transferable memory. Consequently, the owner of a Sony camcorder or digital camera can take digital still pictures, eject the memory stick and insert it into a Sony laptop computer, and store the pictures on the computer for uploading to the Internet or e-mailing to friends and family. The same actions are possible with the compact flash memory and competing devices. However, one can take the memory stick in the computer, copy music files in the MP3 format onto the memory stick, and play the music in a Sony MP3 player. Essentially, Sony is exploiting its strength in the camcorder and other markets to encourage adoption of a proprietary technology that would increase the value of other Sony products.

One sees a more modest version of Sony's memory stick strategy with electronic components such as televisions, VCRs, and stereo equipment. If a customer buys electronic equipment from the same manufacturer, typically one can use a single remote to control many devices. As the proliferation of remote controls is a major annoyance for the target consumers of this type of equipment, the advantage of a single remote can be a significant selling point. In addition, many manufacturers have enabled the equipment to communicate, so that the command to play a compact disc switches the stereo receiver to the right input. Like the Sony memory stick, it has the valuable advantage of lock-in. Once a customer has a system with a single remote and wires connecting all the pieces, there is a good reason to replace any obsolete or failed component with a product from the same manufacturer.

The strategy of creating synergies is not limited to electronic components. Microsoft attempts to exploit it by making PowerPoint, Word, and Excel work together. In principle, one can drop Word tables and Excel charts right into a PowerPoint document. For a PowerPoint user, this portability is a major reason to use Word over WordPerfect, and Excel over Lotus. The business software giant BMC has the motto "1 + 1 = 3." The meaning of this motto is that BMC backup and reorganization utilities enhance each other; if you own one, it will make others by BMC perform better. Such synergies in product design encourage customers to continue to buy one company's products even when one product is inferior when taken in isolation.

Synergies create what is known as a scope economy—producing multiple products together has higher value, or lower cost, than producing the products in separate firms. Scope economies provide a basis for integrating the design of the products, in order to better exploit the scope economy.

The tool manufacturer DeWalt offers a line of cordless hand tools—electric drills, screwdrivers, jigsaws, and the like—all of which use the same interchangeable batteries. The advantage of this system to the customer is that by having, say, three batteries, they are likely to have sufficient battery capacity to perform whatever job they are doing at the time. On days when the drill is being used heavily, typically the jigsaw is not being used at all, so three batteries will cover the job. In contrast, if the customer buys cordless tools from several manufacturers or a single manufacturer without the interchangeable batteries, the customer has to own two or three batteries *per tool* to have a similar reserve capacity. The interchangeable battery system reduces the customer's costs of using the power tools, which has a direct translation into willingness to pay for the products. Moreover, the interchangeable batteries encourage additional tool purchases from the same company. The system of interchangeable batteries locks in the customer with a particular manufacturer, even if all manufacturers offer such systems. In that regard, interchangeable batteries work like frequent flyer programs, encouraging the customer to stay with the same company. Interchangeable batteries soften price competition, even when similar systems are adopted by all companies, provided that each company offers a proprietary system.* Indeed, Black & Decker (which owns DeWalt) offers a similar system, without harming DeWalt's lock-in.

Other companies could exploit the idea of the interchangeable battery system. No major producers of consumer electronics and computers use a uniform system of batteries and chargers for their products. A camcorder owner who can use the same batteries in his or her laptop computer is encouraged to buy more batteries, which become a stock of batteries, which can encourage the purchase of still more electronic components from the same company. Chargers, too, offer a similar functionality. Most business travelers find themselves carrying separate chargers for their laptop computer and cellular phone, and, in some cases, for their digital camera, CD player, mini-DVD player, and camcorder, each requiring a separate charger. Creating a uniform charging system for a set of products is a modest encouragement to concentrate purchases on a single manufacturer.†

Many new products are risky from a customer's perspective. Buyers of early Intel chips were very concerned about being locked in to Intel technology, and hence in a weak bargaining position. Intel took the bold and costly move of li-

*While offering a nonproprietary, open system may create a temporary advantage, it is likely to be copied by rivals, resulting in a convergence of the technologies and a reduction in differentiation. Consequently, it is not a move to take lightly, as it is often tantamount to the first salvo in a price war. Nevertheless, an open system is sometimes necessary because customers can forecast the disadvantage of lock-in.

†The failure to exploit this kind of advantage often seems to be a result of a failure of the product designers to talk with customers, or to use the products themselves. In that way, it seems related to the problem of automotive executives who do not drive, or Prodigy executives who did not frequent chat rooms.

censing the technology to Advanced Micro Devices (AMD) as a means of alleviating these holdup fears. Similarly, buyers of computer technology are concerned about being locked in to obsolete technology. Such concerns can be alleviated by an early-adopter upgrade program. The motivation for such a program is twofold. First, early adopters are justifiably the most concerned about a new technology failing to catch on, because at its introduction little is known about its eventual success. Moreover, early adopters are often a company's best customers. Early adopters of consumer electronics are generally the wealthiest and most technologically savvy customers, and thus are very desirable. Therefore, locking in these customers has the highest value of all customer groups. A means of locking them in is to upgrade them at relatively modest cost when technology changes. Thus, if new versions of camcorders offer connectivity to computers that early versions failed to offer, upgrading the equipment of early buyers will help deter these buyers from going to competitors. Cellular phone companies should offer reduced prices for equipment purchases to their highest-volume customers. At a minimum, companies should offer their best customers what they offer their new customers, because otherwise their best customers are likely to become new customers at the competition. While a few companies keep track of their best customers, many more can profitably do so.

Good offers to your best customers are not just about price but are about products as well. Offering better products, or product improvements, to existing customers has the advantage of weakening price competition. In contrast, offering the better products only to potential customers strengthens price competition, because it encourages defection by your rival's customers, and hence a stronger reaction from rivals to keep their customers. The cellular phone company that offers a free new phone to new customers but not to its best current customers risks having the best customers go to the competition. In contrast, the cellular company that offers a new phone and other perks annually to top spenders, perks not offered to new customers, encourages rivals to do the same, weakening price competition to the benefit of all.

Cellular companies tend to get this issue—to whom to make offers—exactly backward, offering new phones and technology upgrades only to noncustomers. Such offers encourage price-cutting responses by rivals, and reduce or eliminate lock-in. The failure to anticipate the response of rivals to a strategic move can often have disastrous effects on profits.

A major advantage of offering products in preference to a discount to the best customers is that discounts are comparable, while products are differentiated. Thus, offering a new Motorola phone or a new Ericsson phone is not valued in the same way by different customers. The goal is to offer products that are valued highly by one's own best customers, and less highly by a rival's best customers. This is advantageous, relative to a 10% discount, because a discount is valued the same by customers, while the phones are not. By offering a perk that one's own customers tend to value (e.g., a Motorola phone), which a rival's customers value less (because they like Ericsson), the threat to the rival of the perk is reduced. Consequently, the reaction of the rival is muted, tending to reduce price competition.

United Airlines has been known to offer their Premier Executive status to fliers who have Platinum status on American Airlines, when the American customer calls to request it. The problem with such an offer is that it encourages a strong counterattack by American. Instead, it is better to lock in existing customers and, at a minimum, only engage in stealing the competitor's best customers as a punishment for the same behavior by rivals, or only when the customer has a particularly understandable reason—for instance, when a customer has moved from an American hub such as Dallas to a United hub like Denver. The risk that business-stealing behavior might set off a war of the "double coupons" variety, with each firm honoring the status granted by the rivals in the way that grocery stores honor rivals' coupons, is sufficiently high that it may pay never to engage in it. Business stealing is like deciding whether or not to use nuclear weapons, in the sense that zero is often the only verifiable level of activity. Permitting a higher level of business stealing risks an all-out war.

QUALITY COMPLEMENTARITIES

For many products, various aspects of the overall quality will be complementary; that is, a higher quality in one dimension will increase the value of quality in other dimensions. As automobiles are made more durable, the value of increased quality in plastics, fabrics, and design is enhanced, for the increased durability insures that these other aspects of the car are used longer. An improvement in the ambiance of a restaurant will often increase the value of an improved meal, by moving the restaurant into the top tier. A major failure in any aspect of the overall dining experience prevents the restaurant from attracting the customers who will pay extra for the best possible dining experience.[3] Increases in the processor speed of computers enhance the value of faster communication buses, larger hard drives, and higher resolution monitors, as well as increase the value of adding peripherals.

When various aspects of quality are complementary, the best strategy is to correlate the qualities of any product design. For example, putting a high-quality computer in a cheap, easily broken case is bad business, as is putting poor-quality components in a beautifully machined, durable titanium case. Complementarities guarantee that increased quality in one dimension increases the value of increased quality in other dimensions. Complementarities work like the weakest link of a chain; increasing the strength of some links increases the value of improving the weaker links. Strategic product design requires identifying the quality aspects that do not fit—those too good, or too poor, for the overall product quality—and adjusting them appropriately to offer the best value for the cost and to maximize the value produced.

Quality complementarities can provide designs that are difficult for competitors to replicate, because to replicate the overall value generated, competitors must get most or all of the quality aspects right. The problem facing competitors is compounded by complementarities, because they must imitate or engineer around a large set of characteristics; failing in any one dimension significantly lowers the value of the overall product. For example, the ease of use of a handheld computer operating system (such as Palm), the ease of synchronizing with Microsoft Outlook, and the quality of the hardware are complementary. The proprietary operating system protected Palm from entry even by firms with superior hardware technology, until Palm licensed the operating system to others. Once the operating system was available, fierce competitors in hardware came into existence. Licensing may have been profitable given the licensing fees earned, but it also illustrates the difficulty of entering when quality is complementary.

NETWORKS

DOS isn't done until Lotus won't run.

—Slogan attributed to Microsoft

A network good is a good that has higher value the more customers that use it. For example, a telephone network has higher value the more people that are on the network; if only one person has a phone, there is no one to call. If a thousand people worldwide have telephones, what are the odds that they would want to call someone else with a phone? The more people that are connected, the more valuable the phone, because there are more people who can be reached. Microsoft's operating system is a network good, because the more people that use it, the more likely users can get help from their neighbors, the more software that will be written for it, and the more portable applications and data become. Videotape standards proved to be a network good through the intermediation of video stores. A Sony Beta VCR has little value, because there are no tapes to rent for that format, because so few people own Beta VCRs. Similarly, the compact disc has become a network good, both in music and in computers. The value of CDs has increased because almost everyone has them—manufacturers can offer a single format for both software and music.

Ownership of a network good can be incredibly valuable, because entry against an established incumbent is so difficult. Once the market has settled on a standard or a network has been created, entrants must enter at a massive scale to challenge the value created by the incumbent's large network. Moreover, the entrant faces the difficult problem of convincing customers that its network will prevail over the entrenched incumbent. Both problems create an entry barrier, and this barrier permits sustainable profits for the incumbent.

The promise of profits, and of a single eventual winner, typically makes the competition to become the network quite intense. Indeed, a fight to be a monopoly network creates a classic war of attrition in which most or all of the present value of the profits is expended in the competition to own the network. Customers care who will eventually win the war, so as not to be stuck with obsolete technology, as happened to the owners of Beta VCRs. Consequently, the presence of the war tends to slow purchases, a phenomenon observed in the battle between Sky Television and British Satellite Broadcasting (BSB) for the satellite TV market in Britain, discussed in chapter 14. Potential customers look to market share to forecast the winner, and so the battle tends to be for market share. The principle that the firm with the larger market share is more likely to win the war of attrition creates an advantage for the larger share. Indeed, a large market share may be a self-fulfilling prophecy of ultimate success in the market.

Amazon and Barnes & Noble have fought such a war of attrition for market share, and Internet retailers struggled for market share by pricing below their average costs. What makes the Internet retailers difficult to understand is that network effects and other sources of lock-in are minimal in retailing. The only significant network effects in book retailing is the advice one can provide, based on the purchases and reviews of other customers; this is such a small effect that the only sustainable profits will be modest, and will not nearly justify the 1999 market value of Amazon stock. It is mysterious why the stock market took years to understand the difference between Amazon, with its modest potential for long-run profits, and Microsoft or eBay, companies where network effects permit enormous profits without serious threat of entry.

A major network war is being fought by Microsoft, with its Windows CE (also called Pocket PC) operating system, and Palm Computing, maker of the Palm devices, over the standard for handheld computing devices. Customers like a common technology in palm computing devices for the same reasons that they prefer a common operating system—more help and more software are available. Corporate customers, especially, prefer to deal with a single operating system, given the requirement that the handheld device synchronizes with company computers. Both Palm and Microsoft have advantages—Microsoft's CE offers a greater number of potential applications and more computing prowess, as well as the Microsoft name (which promises straightforward synchronization with Windows), while Palm offers simplicity, user-friendliness, and a commanding market share, as well as more existing applications. Microsoft supported color screens well before Palm, but Palm dominates in third-party software. Palm has attracted more business users. Which will come to dominate the handheld market?*

An important strategic question in the competition to be a provider for a network good is the openness of the network. Intel helped establish the 8086 processor as the standard for personal computers by creating a competitor through licensing to AMD. Similarly, Sony's decision to preserve monopoly production of the Beta VCR is often credited as being the cause of the failure of the Beta to become the standard, while the VHS standard was licensed to several firms. By opening a product to multiple producers, a firm increases the chance that the product becomes the standard through two means. First, competition itself tends to improve the product quality and to lower costs. Second, and usually more important, the presence of competition serves as a commitment to low prices. Because there are multiple manufacturers of VHS, the benefits of competition will make VHS more attractive in the future, and thus VHS is more likely to win the battle with Beta. Since the forecast of likely dominance is a major component of value to customers, licensing dramatically improves the likelihood of victory by changing consumer expectations about the future. Unfortunately, licensing improves the likelihood of victory by a means that reduces long-run profits, because of increased competition. That is, licensing a technology increases the chance of a victory, but at the expense of losing long-run profits from the technology competed away.

A very important means of competing for network goods is through complementary goods. In some cases, complements are the major battlefield. Customers of VCRs generally cared about the complementary good—video rentals—much more than any other feature of VCR format. Consequently, a slight dominance of VHS in video rentals was a major source of value. Similarly, Microsoft subsidized the writing of software in the early DOS days as a way of providing an advantage over Apple. This advantage in the provision of complementary goods (third-party software) proved decisive to many consumers. When third-party products are the source of a network effect, encouraging and subsidizing third parties is an important strategy. In the palm computing device war, Microsoft is gaining in the provision of third-party software, by encouraging third parties. However, Palm has a somewhat different vision of palm computing, a vision that does not involve serious computing on the devices; ultimately, the battle will be decided by which vision—the micro-PC vision of Microsoft, providing most of the capabilities of a

*It is possible that both products can survive, given their differences. If so, it is a mistake for Palm to imitate Pocket PC features like multimedia, and focus instead on its core strengths: simple and reliable business applications. Indeed, the biggest threat to Palm may not be Microsoft but smart cellular phones that contain most of the functionality of the Palm devices.

personal computer in a small package, versus the electronic day-timer vision of Palm, offering a calendar, Rolodex, and other means of keeping office records—appeals most to consumers. These visions are sufficiently distinct that it is possible for both to survive. However, the companies are currently pitching the products as if only one can survive.

The firm that is the first to recognize that a product has a significant network effect can obtain first-mover advantages.[4] The firm that is first can position itself to be the incumbent. Perhaps the best example of such behavior is AT&T, which recognized very early that long-distance telephoning would provide a significant network good. AT&T's long-lines division created a network that led to a fifty-year dominance of U.S. telephony. Certainly, Microsoft recognized the network effect of operating systems and acted on that knowledge much more quickly than Apple, and consequently quickly came to dominate the operating system market. Microsoft's position was strengthened by Intel's decision to create competition in the 8086 chip and the openness of the IBM-compatible PC architecture. Apple attempted to control all portions of computer production, essentially adopting the Sony Beta approach. In contrast, Microsoft benefited from competition in hardware—a complementary good—that reduced the cost of the software/hardware bundle. Microsoft enhanced the value of DOS, and later Windows, by encouraging the provision of third party software.

TECHNOLOGICAL RACES

> If the automobile had followed the same development cycle as the computer, a Rolls-Royce would cost $100 today, get one million miles to the gallon, and explode once a year, killing everyone inside.
>
> **—Robert X. Cringely, *InfoWorld***

It is not uncommon for a technological leader to be leapfrogged by an upstart. For example, AT&T was leapfrogged by Intecom in the voice and data PBX (Private Branch Exchange—a small telephone network inside a business) market.[5] The incumbent, with massive technological advantages, was almost blindsided by Intecom. Many analysts believe that Microsoft was quite slow to recognize the value of the Internet, creating significant problems for the company. Sears, once the most successful consumer retailer, was unable to adjust to changes in purchasing patterns in the 1960s and began a forty-year decline. Not so long ago, to describe the most luxurious and best product, say a sofa, one might say "the Cadillac of sofas." Now, few Americans consider Cadillac a top-quality luxury car, and it does not command the price of Mercedes, BMW, Lexus, and Infiniti.

As in the PBX market, the incumbent often seems to be upstaged in a technological race. The reason that this happens is known as "cannibalization." Consider the incentives of AT&T and Intecom to innovate in the PBX market. If AT&T succeeds, it winds up replacing its own products already in customer's hands; the effect is that AT&T makes some money on the new product but loses potential sales of the old product. In contrast, Intecom has no existing product of any significance; it makes sales on the new product without suffering a loss of sales on existing products. Consequently, the incentive to innovate, especially in the short run when a firm has a commanding lead, is muted for the leader, relative to that of a follower or an upstart. In essence, the incumbent cannibalizes its own products with innovation, whereas an entrant suffers no loss of existing business.

Cannibalization mutes the incentives of incumbents to innovate, and it can leave incumbents vulnerable to entrants. For example, Buick, Oldsmobile, and Cadillac were slow to innovate, perhaps because changes risked losing the existing customer base. When it is possible to sell existing technology to a significant number of customers, innovation and further technological development may not have been profitable for these brands, and GM seems to have followed the harvest strategy with respect to several of its brands, innovating with Saturn and harvesting with the Oldsmobile and Buick brands. In its ads, Oldsmobile protested, "It's not your father's Oldsmobile," but in fact the company continued to manufacture cars that appealed primarily to an increasingly elderly customer base. It is difficult to imagine that the decision to cede technological superiority of Cadillac was intentional; this seems to have been a management error. However, cannibalization probably played a role in GM going from a technological leader to a maker of mediocre cars.

While it probably made sense for GM to harvest two or three of its existing brands, given the changes in customer tastes and increasingly intense foreign competition, in many instances a firm's long-run health requires a means of maintaining technological leadership and overcoming the tendency to be satisfied with existing products. The desirability of this technologically superior strategy depends on the nature of technological advance.

The Japanese method of modern manufacturing pioneered by Toyota emphasizes continuous improvement. The organization strategy, discussed in chapter 7, supports continuous improvements in a variety of ways, including producing in small batches so that improvements can be incorporated quickly, and having a more skilled labor force, which permits frequent changes in job tasks to reflect changing technology, but also permits more and better feedback from the workers on the production methods. With a more skilled labor force, it becomes useful for the company to "flatten" the hierarchy, encouraging direct communication rather than communication through channels, a system that characterized large U.S. automakers. Toyota's system is geared toward offering many small improvements, and it encourages the development of small improvements. The flattened approach to hierarchy has been carried to its logical extreme in the United States in some Silicon Valley firms, where all doors are open to all.

In some cases, it is desirable to attempt to create revolutionary improvements, rather than the incremental improvements emphasized by the modern manufacturing approach. In such cases, it is useful to harness the forces of competition within the firm, an approach at odds with the harmonious, flattened-hierarchy design of modern manufacturing. The most successful method was pioneered by General Motors between the world wars, and involves creating competing teams that share some inputs but have autonomy in design. In this way, separate teams within the organization can follow individual team approaches to solving problems and creating new products. Lockheed Martin maintains three major R&D installations within the corporation, and these teams compete vigorously in the design of aircraft and missiles, often taking distinct routes to problems of design and the development of new technology. This strategy, sometimes called divisionalization, can be very useful in harnessing market forces within an organization to foster research and development.

PATENT STRATEGY

Elisha Graves Otis did not invent the elevator. Indeed, steam and hydraulic elevators were in use prior to Otis's first safety elevator. What Otis did invent was an elevator brake, which was demonstrated at the Crystal Palace Exposition in Chicago, in 1853, to gasps from the crowd. Otis ascended in the elevator, and then had the cable cut. The elevator did not plummet to the ground, but instead hung on the toothed guide rail. (The technology is similar to the mechanism that locks seatbelts in place.) When the cable was not engaged, the teeth prevented the elevator from falling. The first Otis passenger elevator was installed in 1857 at 488 Broadway, New York City, and by 1873, over two thousand Otis elevators were in use worldwide. Otis's invention made the skyscraper possible. Figure 4.5 shows the world's tallest buildings, from 1890 to the present. Interestingly, the world's tallest building has the same growth pattern as the product life cycle, which can be seen from figure 4.6 (compare fig. 5.1 below). It appears that the growth phase started around 1900, with an increasing rate of growth, and maturity was induced by the Great Depression in 1933, with the growth rate declining.

Elisha Graves Otis died in 1861, but his sons followed his path. In 1889, they unveiled the first direct-connection geared elevator, which relied on electrically driven gears for motion. In 1899, Otis Elevator introduced the escalator, by hiring its inventor. In 1903, Otis Elevator introduced the gearless traction elevator, which permitted much faster ascents and descents, making very tall buildings pos-

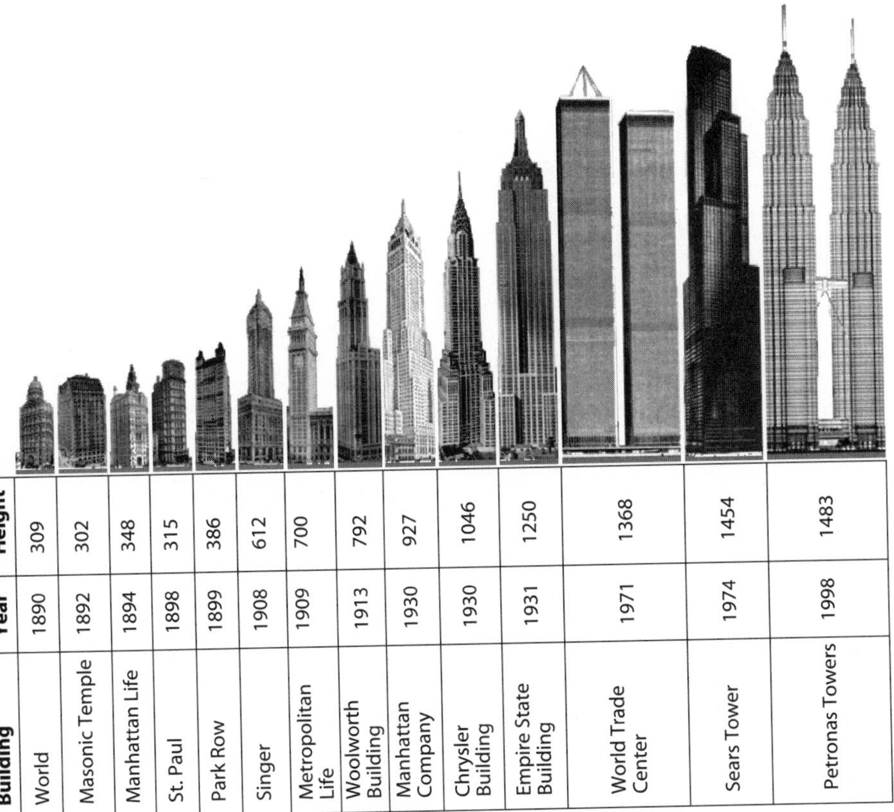

Building	Year	Height
World	1890	309
Masonic Temple	1892	302
Manhattan Life	1894	348
St. Paul	1898	315
Park Row	1899	386
Singer	1908	612
Metropolitan Life	1909	700
Woolworth Building	1913	792
Manhattan Company	1930	927
Chrysler Building	1930	1046
Empire State Building	1931	1250
World Trade Center	1971	1368
Sears Tower	1974	1454
Petronas Towers	1998	1483

Figure 4.5. World's Tallest Skyscrapers. Shorter buildings listed as taller because of having highest occupied floor. *Source:* Skyscraper Museum, New York City; www.skyscraper.org.

sible and perhaps initiating the growth phase of skyscrapers. Since then, Otis has introduced a variety of electrical and electronic controls and communication devices, along with the computer programs that optimize elevator locations to minimize transportation times, which is known as intelligent dispatching.

The Otis Elevator Company is an early example of a company that set out to stay at the state of the art in a fast-changing, technologically sophisticated environment. Indeed, Otis, now a division of United Technologies, recently introduced a replacement for the steel cables that have been in use for 150 years—a coated steel belt, which eliminates the need for a separate machine room, and enhances safety and energy efficiency.

Otis is an exemplar of the patent strategy that seeks to keep a firm at the top of

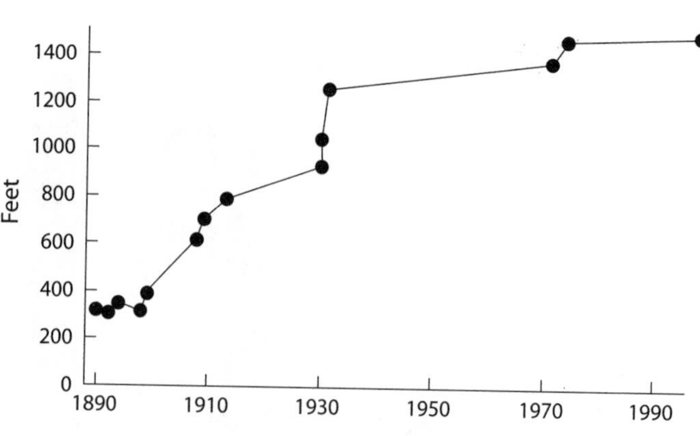

Figure 4.6. Maximum building heights.

the industry for a sustained period of time. Patent strategy is a technology strategy to minimize competition by the use of trade secrets and the patent system. Patent strategy can be summarized by the following questions:

1. Should we seek a patent or a trade secret?
2. When should we patent a group of inventions?
3. How can we minimize the risk of competitors engineering around our patent?
4. How can we use patents to hobble our competitors?
5. Should we license patents to other firms? License from them?

Patent or Trade Secret?

The choice of a patent or trade secret is straightforward in principle, though thorny in application. The trade-off is that a trade secret has minimal legal protection but lasts as long as the trade secret remains secret, while a patent has a fixed expiration, at which point it becomes part of the public domain. The formula for Coca-Cola, which remains a trade secret, has been immensely profitable. Coca-Cola has vigorously defended its trade secret against employees who would reveal it, and has minimized the number of employees with access to the formula. Trade secrets often involve being extremely careful about who has access to the secret, and insuring that those with access are trustworthy. While legal action can be taken against employees who reveal trade secrets, it is difficult to repair the damage that a single disgruntled employee can do.

In addition to its indefinite length, a trade secret has the advantage of not revealing a technology to competitors. It is often difficult to protect a patent against alternative approaches that offer similar functionality. Having seen a patent, others may be inspired to engineer around the patent to produce the same effect. In such situations, the openness of the patent is a major disadvantage. These situations arise frequently with software developed to implement a computerized business. One can patent the implementation of a business model but not the model itself; anyone who can find a substantially different program that implements the same model can copy it. (Renaming the variables will not work.) Patent law is evolving very rapidly in software, so the present situation could change dramatically.

The openness of a patent to others can also be an advantage, especially when the patent holder intends to license the patent. Because others can see the patent, they can improve upon it. The improvements will be patented, but such improvements can enhance the value of the product to licensees, increasing the value of the original patent.

The Timing of Multiple Patents

Pharmaceutical manufacturers attempt to use the patent system to slow the entry of generics and insure that they have a superior product to others. When one company makes two discoveries simultaneously, it can be profitable to hold back one of the patents, introducing it only as the other patent is about to expire. The value of withholding a secondary discovery is especially attractive when the secondary discovery is a substitute for the first, so that introduction of the second would cannibalize the first. There are two major costs to the strategy of delaying a patent. First, if another company develops the unpatented product, not only is the opportunity to patent lost, but a major competitor has been unnecessarily created as well. Second, holding back also means keeping the product off the market, which means discounting the profits and risks of other inventions and discoveries that would render the product obsolete. The strategy of waiting to patent a discovery is rarely a good idea, unless the product is not yet ready for commercialization but needs to wait for enabling technology. In this situation, however, it is sometimes possible to extend a patent.

Protective Patents

Xerox is credited with protecting its copying invention extraordinarily well, by filing a blizzard of patents that shut off alternative routes to producing similar functionality. Protective or blocking patents are patents on inferior technologies that might threaten the important patents. Protective and blocking patents are part of an "offensive patent strategy," which seeks to block alternatives to the main technology in the same way that spatial preemption was intended to deter entry everywhere in the product space. While easy to describe, a successful offensive patent strategy can be very difficult to produce.

Often, the firm that invents a new technology has tried a variety of alternatives, and thus has good knowledge of the likely approaches that other firms might take. The protective patenting approach is to identify important enabling technologies for each of the alternatives, and to patent the technologies. If this is successful, all of the alternative routes will be blocked. The problem that arises, however, is that a research team may have ruled out one approach early on, so that little is known about that approach. Finding a blocking patent for every rejected path is a monumental undertaking. Moreover, even if undertaken, there maybe routes that were not considered, due to lack of expertise or unavailable technologies.

Nevertheless, often it is possible to preempt major avenues to alternative technologies, and such protection may delay entry by others substantially. At a minimum, it is usually worth patenting the discoveries that were not, in the end, useful.

Defensive Patents

Defensive patent strategy is a means of preventing your competitors from producing innovations. One aspect of defensive patent strategy is to defend your innovations against technological developments by rivals. But another aspect is to prevent technological developments by rivals that would give them a competitive advantage. Defensive patent strategy involves analyzing your rivals' patents and finding holes or gaps, and then patenting technology in those gaps. In this way, a firm can either destroy a competitor's advantage or insist on being a partner in a new-product launch.

In reference to a suit filed by Hewlett-Packard against Xerox for patent infringement in user interface technology, HP CEO Lewis Platt said, "HP has invested many billions of dollars in technology R&D. We have a deep and rich patent portfolio, which serves us well in situations like this." The suit was filed on 28 May 1998, just two weeks after Xerox filed suit against HP for inkjet patent infringement. Defensive patents can serve the useful purpose of creating a lawsuit standoff, so that both sides can settle without incurring major costs.

Licensing

A firm that licenses its patent obtains many of the benefits of divisionalization by creating competition, but also by extracting some of the profits in the form of royalties. In particular, cost reduction and technological improvement make the patent more valuable, permitting the firm to capture more revenue than it might capture on its own. Moreover, in the case of network goods, licensing is sometimes necessary to assure customers that they will not be subject to holdup.

Licensing a patent, however, means sharing some of the profits with licensees. Moreover, as Intel found with Advanced Micro Devices (AMD), a licensee may not vanish when a license is revoked. AMD has stayed current with Intel, without the benefit of having a license for Intel's current technology. Not only did Intel create a competitor, but by revoking the license Intel no longer receives revenue on new-product licenses from AMD. Indeed, while the decision to license the technology may have been forced upon Intel, the decision to withdraw the license may have been bad strategy. As Lyndon Johnson said about why he retained J. Edgar Hoover:[6] "It's probably better to have him inside the tent pissing out, than outside the tent pissing in."

Having helped AMD become skilled with the technology, ending its license may have been a worse strategy than being paid by the producer of an exact copy. However, it is difficult to evaluate this decision in retrospect. AMD won rights in court to use some Intel code through the 486 series of chips, and it negotiated access to some code in a settlement, in exchange for certain payments that were not made public. Thus, the unpredictability of the court system may have made Intel's decision seem less profitable than an evaluation at the time would indicate.

Licensing technology to other firms is a way to extend the application of the technology by employing it in other venues and by obtaining access to enhanced distribution, more capital, and other complements.

Licensing technology from other firms is often a cost-effective way to move up the learning curve, or to extend one's reach. Two firms with a partial product line can create a full product line by cross-licensing, without suffering the disadvantages of merger. A problem with licensing, however, is that the firm with the patent has an incentive to license an inferior technology rather than to create a more able competitor.

HEDONIC PRICES

How should differentiated products be valued? What should the introductory price of a new product be? These questions can be answered using the technique known as hedonic regression or hedonic pricing. While simple in concept, hedonic pricing may have substantial difficulties in implementation.[7]

The basic idea of hedonic pricing is that a product's value is the sum of the values of the product's attributes. Hedonic prices are familiar from a significant application of the theory—estimating the price of houses. Appraisers estimate the price of a given house by starting with an average of some similar houses, then adding and subtracting amounts for various features such as a swimming pool, an extra living room, a city view, and so forth.*

Consider the camcorder. Different camcorders use different types of tape, known as their format. Camcorders may have a black-and-white or a color viewfinder, and may or may not have a side-mounted monitor. The value of the camcorder will depend on the monitor's size as well. Image stabilization, light weight, and the ability to export pictures in the industry-standard JPEG format (named for the Joint Photographic Experts Group, which created it) will also increase the value of the camcorder. The hedonic pricing model suggests that the value of any given camcorder is the sum of the values of the attributes the camcorder offers. Thus, for example, if a color monitor adds $60 in value, camcorders with color monitors should sell for $60 more than those without color monitors but with the same other features.

Nicole Shepler of the Bureau of Labor Statistics has performed a hedonic price analysis of camcorders. Some of the results of the study are presented in table 4.1.[8] The base price of a camcorder is $347, which means a VHS-C, her base model, with a black-and-white viewfinder, should sell for that amount. She finds sale prices reduce camcorders by 7.5%. To find the value of a particular camcorder from the analysis, one begins with the base price and performs adjustments to arrive at a final price. For example, a JVC mini-DV camcorder with a three-inch monitor, color viewfinder, image stabilization, low weight, and JPEG format, that is not on sale, is worth $347.26 plus 95.9% for DV, 12.9% three times for the monitor, 9.8% for the color viewfinder, 7.4% for image stabilization, 33.7% for its low weight, and 65.6% for picture format. This gives

$$\text{Value} = \$347.26 \times 1.959 \times 1.129 \times 1.129 \times 1.129 \times 1.098 \times 1.074 \times 1.337 \times 1.656 = \$2556.05.$$

This value is approximately the 1998 price (the time of the article), corroborating Shepler's calculations.

Similarly, a basic VHS camcorder with a black-and-white monitor, a three-inch viewfinder, and no other listed features should sell for $347.26 × 0.916 × 1.129 × 1.129 × 1.129, which is $457.75, and on sale, for $423.42.

The selection of attributes for hedonic pricing is generally an art. Because of

*In Austin, Texas, the value of a view of the University of Texas's notorious tower has been estimated to be worth $25,000 or more. The tower is lit with orange light when a UT team wins a game. As UT's athletic prowess declined, the victories for which the tower is lit was expanded to include academic victories, such as the Law School team's winning of the National Student Trial Advocacy Competition in April 1999. This expansion of the tower lighting events is an example of the ratchet effect discussed in chapter 8.

TABLE 4.1
Camcorder Hedonic Price Regression Results

Variable Name	*Price Effect*
Base Price (VHS-C)	
B&W Viewfinder	$347.26
On Sale	−7.5%
Non-Sony 8mm	−15.3%
VHS	−8.4%
Non-Sony Hi 8mm	8.9%
Sony Hi 8mm	46.2%
Sony Digital 8	79.8%
Non-Sony Mini-DV	95.9%
Sony Mini-DV	141.2%
Monitor size	12.9%/inch
Color Viewfinder	9.8%
Image stabilization	7.4%
Low Weight	33.7%
JPEG Format	65.6%

complementarities between features, often two features will not be observed without each other. For example, only Sony makes digital 8mm tape. Consequently, care must be taken not to confuse the Sony brand with consumer's valuations of other digital 8mm tape. The Sony brand adds significant value in the eyes of consumers—nearly 25% more in the case of mini-DV digital format. Thus, a careless analysis might suggest that consumers value digital 8mm tape more highly than they do, because the observed price of the digital 8mm includes a Sony effect. Similarly, units with a four-inch monitor generally have a color viewfinder. As a consequence, the value of a color viewfinder is commingled with the value of a large monitor, and it is difficult to separate the effects. Stereo audio recording is a feature of all high-end, and no low-end, models, and thus it is nearly impossible statistically to separate the effects of stereo from other high-end indicators. As with the predator theory of tornadoes (discussed in chapter 10), where the supply of mobile homes determines the number of tornadoes, it is possible for calculated statistics to be severely misleading. (The theory is that mobile homes are the food supply of tornadoes, so that an increase in the number of mobile homes causes tornadoes.)

In spite of the problems that may arise in estimating hedonic prices, techniques do exist to mitigate the statistical problems. In particular, when there are complementarities between features, a straight regression will tend to inaccurately estimate the value of the features. However, this value can be correctly estimated by using an "interaction effect," in which the values of the features by themselves are estimated separately from the value when both the features are present. Interaction effects capture the complementarities between features, providing specific estimates of value.

The hedonic pricing model offers a means of forecasting how a new product, with a different mix of features than any existing product, will fare in the market. The cost of the new product can be compared to the predicted hedonic price, and if the cost is substantially less than the price, it should be profitable to introduce the new product. Care must be taken that any complementarities that exist are accounted for in the analysis. For example, image stabilization was estimated to add 7.4% to the value of a camcorder. However, image stabilization is much more valuable in small camcorders, and it is present in all camcorders that weigh less than one pound. Consequently, the average value of 7.4% understates the actual value of image stabilization in palm-sized camcorders, and it likely overstates it in large, "luggable" camcorders. Similarly, a monitor is a substitute for a viewfinder, even though many camcorders come with both. The value of a color viewfinder on a camcorder with a monitor is probably less than the value of a color viewfinder on a camcorder without a monitor.

In spite of the problems, hedonic pricing analysis provides a useful alternative to polling potential buyers to estimate the value of new products, as the polling approach is notoriously unreliable. In addition, hedonic pricing can be useful in guiding product development by suggesting the value of enhanced features. For example, an analysis of refrigerators generates estimates of the value consumers place on energy consumption and noise, which suggests whether further reductions in energy usage and noise will be profitable. Similarly, an analysis of laptop computers will suggest the value that consumers place on screen size, additional battery life, and the like, offering a means of optimizing the design of laptop computers. An analysis of the prices paid for trips on cruise ships could suggest the profit-maximizing set of features for a given type of cruise. That is, the hedonic pricing model can be used not only to suggest the price of a new product but also to determine the features that should be included in the new product. Should an

TABLE 4.2
Laptop Values

Attribute	*Value*
15-Inch Screen	$330
Battery Life/Hr.	$200
Weight/Lb.	−$300

icemaker be included in a new refrigerator? Should a CD player be included in a new SUV? Is it worth an additional $175 in costs, along with a thirty-minute drop in battery life, to use a fifteen-inch screen rather than a fourteen-inch screen? These are precisely the kinds of questions for which hedonic prices are helpful.

For example, an analysis of existing laptop computers might suggest values like those in table 4.2. The base model is a seven-pound laptop with a three-hour battery life and a thirteen-inch screen, which was valued by consumers at $1700. There are several available design technologies. By adding a fifteen-inch screen, the battery life falls by thirty minutes and the weight rises by half a pound. Thus, adding a fifteen-inch screen brings in $330 in extra revenue but costs $250, in the form of $100 for the thirty-minute drop in battery life and another $150 in weight penalty for the half pound in added weight. Thus, adding a fifteen-inch screen is profitable if it costs less than $80 more than the fourteen-inch screen, but is otherwise unprofitable.

Should this new laptop computer include the latest version of Microsoft Word? According to Michael Dertouzos (*New York Times,* 24 June 1997, Section C, p. 1):

> Calling today's machine "user friendly" because of its endless choice of fonts and screen patterns is tantamount to dressing a chimpanzee in a green hospital gown and earnestly parading it as a surgeon.

Like Iacocca making executives drive cars, and Steve Case participating in AOL chatrooms, perhaps Microsoft executives should type a letter now and then.

EXECUTIVE SUMMARY—DIFFERENTIATION

- Quality and variety are the two major forms of differentiation.
- When quality attributes are complements, it is important to offer all or none.
- The firm selling the highest-quality product is rarely the most profitable.
- Positioning a product near the ideal spot for the largest mass of consumers usually entails the most intense competition.

- A key insight for conceptualizing competition in differentiated products is the Hotelling line.
- The Hotelling line plots products and consumers on the same line, using the trick that a given product is associated with the consumer for whom that product is optimal.
- A product's positioning has significant impact on rivals' choices of positioning.
- *Spatial preemption* involves filling the product space so that there is no profitable niche for rivals.
- A key insight for spatial preemption is that entry may be deterred with relatively few, carefully placed, products.
- An important aspect to product design is the creation of synergies with other products, so as to achieve lock-in.
- The best competition is for all the firms to lock in their own customers. This reduces price competition.
- Offer bonuses to your best customers, not to your competitors' best customers. That way, neither company competes vigorously over important customers, and all companies earn profits.
- Networks create lock-in naturally, and hence can be very profitable to own.
- The competition to become the network provider creates a war of attrition that dissipates the profits.
- Incumbent producers often lose technological races by favoring their existing product.
- Patents create a wealth of opportunity for strategic behavior, by creating ownership and by the ability to hobble and harass competitors.
- *Hedonic price estimation* provides a means of valuing complex products by valuing individual characteristics and groups of characteristics.
- Hedonic prices provide a basis for pricing strategy and for product design.

5

Product Life Cycle

To better understand differentiation, it is useful to examine product competition from a market perspective, in what is known as the product life cycle. This traces a product from its inception through mass production to its replacement by other products. Substantial differentiation usually arises twice during the product life cycle. First, products are often improved substantially during their initial evolution, and such improvements are introduced through new variants of the product. In this case, differentiation is primarily vertical, via increases in quality. Second, a mature product may be tailored to specialized customer groups, producing a set of standard variants to the successful basic design.

Historically, the product life cycle theory focused on the emergence of a dominant design. In this view, many firms initially competed with their own designs for a new product, and the research efforts of the firms were devoted to improving the product design. Competitors copied innovations and improvements, and the product design converged on a best product. As a "best" design emerged, the firms most capable of producing the best design, not necessarily the first developers of the best design, grew as a proportion of the market. A shakeout occurred as these firms grew, and the number of producers diminished significantly. After this time, the market size stabilized. A major problem with this description is that many products never have a dominant design, because consumer preferences support a variety of designs. Recent research has enhanced our understanding of the product life cycle, although there is much more to know.

A large number of familiar products appear to have fit the product life cycle framework. Several of these are illustrated in figure 5.1.[1] Most of these products have periods during which the growth *rate* increases, followed by slowing growth. Color television (fig. 5.2) provides an excellent example. Market penetration built slowly in the late 1950s, and took off in the early 1960s. After explosive growth, the market was saturated with televisions, and most sales were replace-

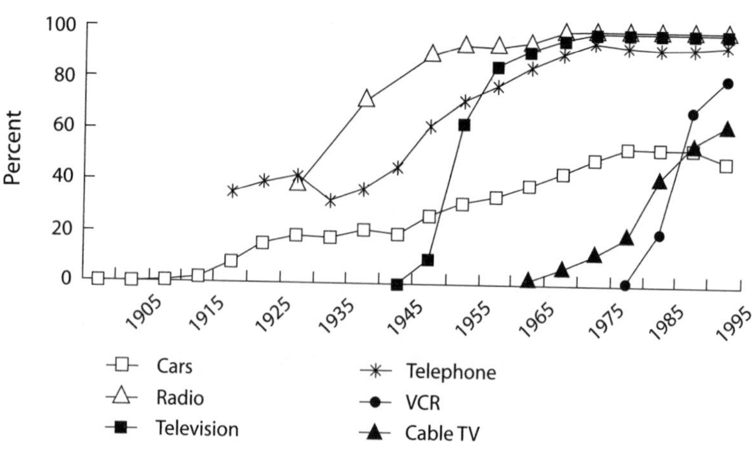

Figure 5.1. Historic market penetration.

ment units, along with modest new sales as the number of televisions per household rose.

There are two major problems confronting a systematic study of the product life cycle. First, there often is disagreement over what constitutes a new product. Are radial tires a new product or simply an enhancement of an existing product, the tire? Are handheld and palm computing devices in the same market as computers, or do they compose a separate market? The market for handheld computers is especially difficult to categorize because the smaller handheld devices require the use of a computer, and thus are complements to rather than substitutes for computers. The larger handheld devices, however, offer most of the functionality of notebook computers, and hence compete with computers. Difficulties in agree-ing on product definitions has hindered a systematic study of the product life cycle.

The second problem with product life cycle research is that it tends to focus on products aimed at final consumers, rather than products aimed at businesses. Prestige and branding play a much larger role, as does the need for early adopters, in the final consumer market. In contrast, business sales are often straightforward economic calculations. For example, the EMC Corporation's dual-disk drives, which integrate backup into their operation, eliminate the need for costly backup software; the economic value of the device is readily calculable. Consequently, EMC's dual disks have penetrated the market in a manner that would be unlikely for a final consumer good embodying new technology. Similarly, a company that repairs CT scanners runs advertisements in magazines aimed at hospital administrators showing that each hour of downtime for CT scanners costs the typical

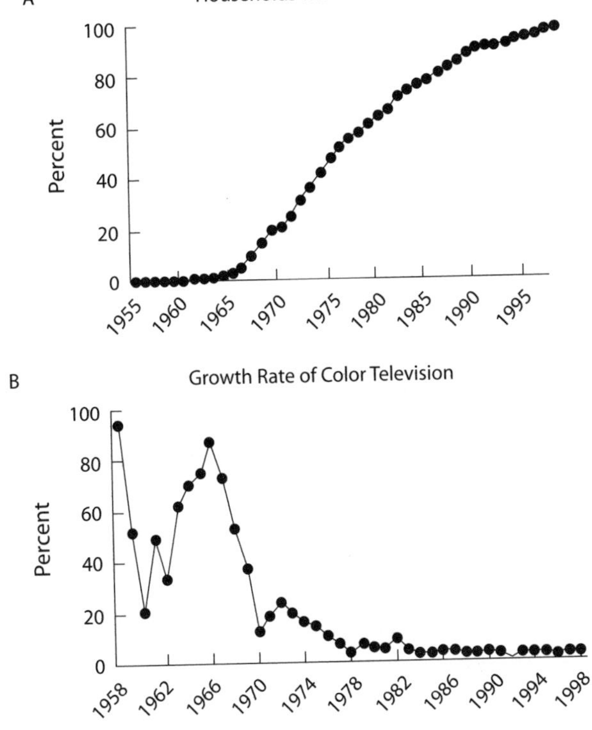

Figure 5.2. (a) Increase in households with color television; and (b) growth rate of color television.

hospital $5000, which makes the company's two-hour response time appear extraordinarily inexpensive. Potential customers can readily assess the value of the service.

In spite of the difficulties, there has been progress in understanding the product life cycle since the theory's formulation in the 1950s. Steven Klepper[2] summarizes recent research with six regularities about new products, some of which are illustrated in figure 5.3.

- The number of entrants either falls consistently or rises and then falls, in either case eventually dwindling to zero.
- The number of producers grows, reaches a peak, and then declines steadily despite growth of the market.
- The market shares of the firms begin to stabilize after the number of producers peaks.
- The variety of product designs peaks before the number of producers peaks.

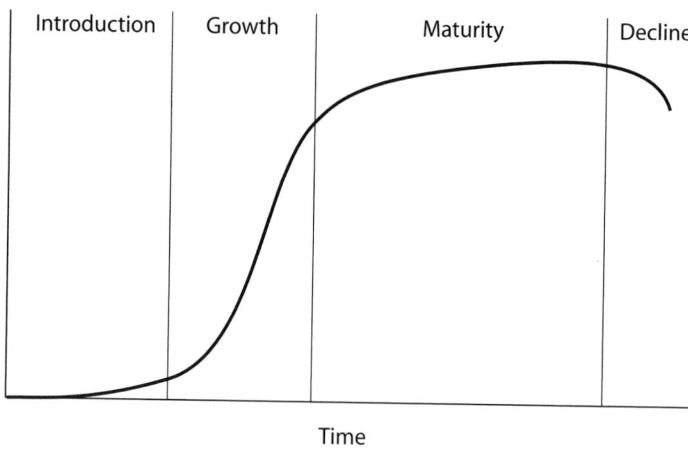

Figure 5.3. Industry demand during the four phases of the product life cycle.

- Prior to the peak in the number of producers, new entrants account for most of the new product designs.
- The share of research effort devoted to process innovation and cost reduction grows over time.

It should be emphasized that there is significant variety across products in the product life cycle. The Apple Newton handheld device failed, and one could view the entire market as a false start. However, the wildly successful Palm Pilot is viewed reasonably as an alternative design in the "handheld-computing" or "pen-based computing" device market, as are the Windows CE (now Pocket PC) devices, some of which have keyboards, and others of which look like Palm Pilots. Was this a case of a market that failed, or the shakeout of a poor design prior to the entrance of the second design? There is often ambiguity about what is a new product and what is an enhanced version of an existing product.

Klepper's regularities ignore some of the strategic aspects of market development. Associated with the beginning of a new market is a need for consumer education—the product needs to be explained, consumers need to be informed, and the product must be promoted to consumers or users. When the buyers are businesses, the buyers need to understand how a new product will save them money or produce more or better output and, in the latter case, how they can pass on the costs of the higher quality, so education downstream may be required. A leading example of such a producer is Intel, which promotes Intel processors directly to consumers to make it possible for PC makers to charge consumers the added cost of an Intel processor.

The product life cycle can usefully be divided into four phases. In the first, the product comes to market, usually sold by a few pioneering firms that offer a complete solution to an identified customer need, or a proliferation of high-service boutique enterprises that offer information and education with the product. This phase is short or nonexistent for some products. As customers become increasingly savvy, the growth phase of the industry arrives, characterized by increasing regularity in the set of product designs (best practices adopted across the industry), and the beginning of mass production and mass distribution. This phase is followed by a maturity phase, in which the shakeout begun in the growth phase is completed, only small improvements to designs occur, R&D focuses on cost reduction, and total output stabilizes. For some products, the mature phase is followed by a decline or replacement stage, when a better alternative arises.

INTRODUCTION

Art is making something out of nothing and selling it.
—Frank Zappa

The nature of the beginning of a market varies significantly across products. Often, production costs are high, and products are priced to appeal to only a small portion of the potential market. Potential customers often need a great deal of education on the reasons for purchase and on the use of the product. For example, the urban legend of the computer customer who used the CD drive as a drink holder reflects a reality of customers who are relatively ignorant about product characteristics. Even with business customers, a certain amount of education is often necessary, although the form of the education usually focuses on the value equation—that the product price is substantially less than the financial returns received from owning the product. In addition, the "total solution" concept pioneered by IBM, which provides a guarantee of performance by including operational assistance at each stage of the product implementation, is often successful with business customers, especially when there is a strong likelihood that an innovation cannot be adopted by the company's employees without such assistance.

While some products need substantial consumer education, others need only small inducements for consumers to try the product. For example, free samples of NutraSweet-based chewing gum helped promote the gum, by permitting risk-free customer trials. Early low prices and money-back guarantees also help reduce customer fears about experimentation.

In consumer products, the need for consumer education leads to proliferation of small, "boutique" firms, which offer personalized expertise, generally in the form of an owner/operator who is knowledgeable about the item. In both personal computers and video rentals, small boutique stores initiated the market growth.

Getting a new product off the ground is often quite difficult. One hundred

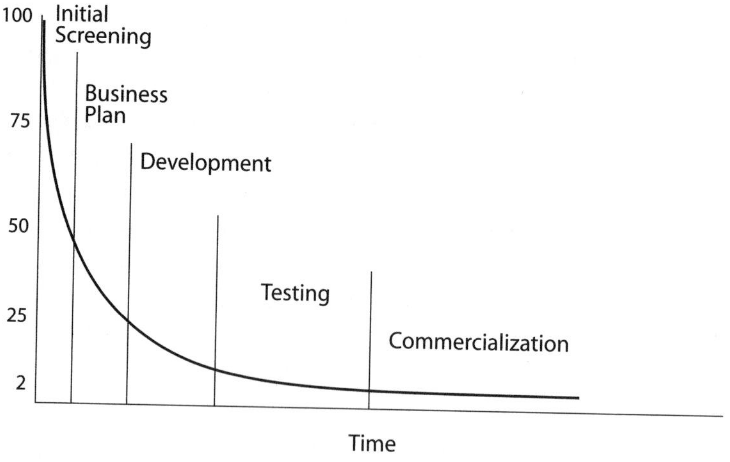

Figure 5.4. The survival of new ideas: one hundred ideas are winnowed to one or two.

seemingly good ideas typically turn into one or two commercial products, by surviving progressively more intense scrutiny. The scrutinizing process is illustrated in figure 5.4. An initial screening or reality check kills a majority of the proposed ideas.* Further analysis reduces the number of projects or ideas passing initial scrutiny, until only one or two in a hundred survive to become products.

The introductory phase for a product begins with one firm or a couple of firms. If the market appears attractive, entry may occur quite rapidly, and the number of firms rises. If technological challenges make entry difficult, entry may occur relatively slowly. The overall market size is small, composed primarily of customers who have a pressing need or who are very sophisticated or both. The leading firm or firms are early entrants who establish a reputation for very high quality, one-stop shopping, problem solving, high-quality customer care, convenience, and service. Firms are typically making low or negative operating profits; that is, little revenue is contributed toward the fixed costs of product development. With a U.S. innovation, imports into the United States are generally nonexistent, and exports out of the United States have not yet begun in earnest.

*Fans of the late senator William Proxmire's Golden Fleece awards, which attempted to identify government projects that should have failed the initial screening, will know many of these. For example, the National Endowment for the Humanities spent $25,000 in 1977 attempting to identify why people cheat, lie, and act rudely on Virginia tennis courts. The National Institute on Alcohol Abuse and Alcoholism spent millions in 1975 attempting to find out if drunken fish act more aggressively than sober ones. The U.S. Army spent $6000 in 1981 preparing a seventeen-page document on how to purchase Worcestershire Sauce. Thanks to $1 million from the EPA, Trenton, New Jersey, preserved a sewer as a historical monument.

During the introductory phase, the activities of the leading firm may involve promoting the product, and indirectly promoting all the firms in the market, more than promoting the firm itself. Thus, early computer sellers educated customers, only to lose markets to mail-order companies like Dell. Nevertheless, educating the customers is often a necessary precondition for market growth to occur. Advertising shared among all the firms to increase the size of the market pays better than advertising by one firm aimed at stealing business from rivals, because there is relatively little business to be stolen.

The first firm into a market faces much higher risk than later entrants face. The history of product introductions is littered with notorious and expensive flops, such as the Apple Newton and quadraphonic music reproduction. A pioneering firm takes two major kinds of risk. First, there is the risk of a flop, a risk that the imitators avoid. Second, the pioneer risks deploying a technology that quickly becomes obsolete. In a few cases, the nature of the market is uncertain, and the pioneer risks choosing an inadequate technology or design, as happened with AT&T in the PBX market. In addition, the pioneer typically suffers major costs of product development that can be minimized by imitators by using such means as observing the pioneer and hiring key employees. The pioneer often must invest in customer education, which benefits later entrants almost as much as it does the pioneer. In some industries, educating government regulators about new technology is quite costly as well. Compensating for these disadvantages of being first, the pioneer starts down the learning curve much more rapidly, and may be able to achieve economies of scale that create a barrier to entry. The pioneer has the ability to obtain loyal customers and build a brand identity without competition. In a few industries, it is possible to lock up inputs like skilled labor, although this advantage is more often a disadvantage. Sometimes, having trained skilled workers at great expense, the industry loses them to competing firms, or the workers leave to start a competing firm.

GROWTH

The growth phase of a product is when much of the profit occurs. During this time, market expansion keeps competition weak, so that there is only modest pressure on prices. The expenses of the introductory phase, especially research and development, are recouped. Market leaders are usually the firms that began with a solid reputation, like IBM in personal computers, or who have developed one during the introductory phase, like Compaq in personal computers. Sales grow very rapidly during this phase. Costs begin to fall rapidly as economies of scale are exploited and improvements in the production process occur. Falling costs, stable prices, and rapidly increasing demand combine to make the growth phase a heady time for a company.

Typically, many new varieties are introduced, but major improvements are incorporated into other firms' products, so that the growth phase ends with a handful of major designs. Little attention is paid to market segmentation during the early part of the growth phase, because the market growth is sufficient. During the growth phase, the cultivation of a brand name is a major focus for firm strategy. This creation of a brand name is often aided by the perception, based on reality, of offering the highest quality product and service.

As the market settles on a limited number of preferred designs, it becomes possible to reduce costs still further by designing production facilities for efficient scale and minimum cost; the flexibility for design changes required early in the period is less important. The reduction in cost, combined with a stabilizing of market demand as the product reaches most potential customers, begins to put downward pressure on prices. This has the effect of reducing the profits of smaller, weaker, and less efficient competitors.

The transition from growth to maturity is often a very turbulent time, one of opportunity and threats. Not all of the firms that entered during the growth phase will survive to maturity; the less efficient firms, firms with a poor reputation, and firms unable to switch to the new demands of the market will fail or be absorbed into market leaders. It is very important during the profitable phase to position the firm for the likely shakeout and intense price competition that will arise when the market growth slows. Cost reduction via standardization of the product is often a useful strategy, and designing efficiently scaled production facilities will also reduce costs. Weaker firms may specialize in hard-to-serve customers, thereby reducing the likelihood of direct price competition.

Distribution methods often change during the growth phase. As the product becomes more familiar to customers, less effort toward customer education is needed, and thus a more "outlet" style distribution method can work. While new mainframe business software often comes with an installation technician to assist a first-time installer, older software comes off the shelf with a terse instruction manual. Simplification of the product itself, combined with a more informed customer base, usually means that there are substantial efficiencies to be obtained through changes in distribution. These changes may range from selling through the superstore to Dell's build-to-order direct sales, a selling method that is eliminating the superstore from the computer business.

The end of the growth phase increases the returns to seeking new markets, and foreign markets often provide a method of sustaining growth for a time.

MATURITY

The mature market has a stable demand. With nondurables, this demand is at a relatively high level—the market has converged to this level from below as the product reaches more and more customers. With durable goods, however, full penetration may involve something of a crash, as occurred with CB radios in 1977. In either case, usually a shakeout occurs, eliminating less efficient firms. There are two major focuses during the mature phase. First, firms minimize cost, which involves building plants that are scaled efficiently. In order to minimize cost, firms adopt a product design and build the plant to fit the product design. The design, however, may incorporate flexibility, as in the modern manufacturing method; indeed, for products that incorporate new technology rapidly, like computer memory, the "design" is more of a construction method than a product design.

Second, the attempt to stop margins from deteriorating will motivate segmentation of the market—specializing the product to maximize the value of a specific customer group. As Michael Porter has observed, these are often opposing forces on the firm—one encouraging a proliferation of product varieties specialized to the needs of particular consumers, the other encouraging a small number of similar varieties produced at very low cost.

The challenge of the transition to maturity of the market is choosing profitable locations for the firm in product space. It is very difficult to survive as a low-cost, low-quality firm when several others adopt the same strategy. Often the market has room for only one low-cost, low-quality firm. Moreover, the low-cost firm that competes with firms offering higher quality may need substantially lower costs to offer consumers more value. Starting in 1908, Ford successfully used the one-variety strategy with its model T ("The public can have any color it wants so long as its black"), producing a majority of the automobiles manufactured in the United States for twenty years. However, General Motors successfully overturned Ford's dominance by producing a large variety of automobiles at only a modest cost disadvantage. In the automobile industry, the low-cost strategy worked only temporarily.

A major, and often neglected, aspect of the mature phase is distribution. Indeed, cost minimization applies not just to the primary product but also to the total cost of using the product. Thus, one sees mass marketers and superstores arise during the mature phase of an industry. Firms that excelled at the introductory stage may have difficulty with the transition. CompuAdd, which retailed its own brand of computers, is an excellent example. The company did well with a trained service staff, who helped early customers understand how to use the product. The staff did a fine job helping the customers feel comfortable with computers and eased fears of problems, because the store was nearby. Once customers were comfortable with the product, however, the trained staff and facilities became albatrosses for the company, representing substantial costs that no longer brought much of a return. While many consumers did not switch to direct-mail sellers at the time of the demise of the CompuAdd stores, they did switch to CompUSA,

Computer City, and other lower-cost retailers, who offered a larger variety of off-the-shelf computers with only a modicum of service and expertise. Now these stores are in turn falling prey to the direct-mail retailers, who have even lower costs and less shopping service.

The mature phase of an industry often sees the standardization of product design. Thus, the entry-level VCR is nearly the same for most sellers. The VCR is an example of a product that went from being a high-technology item to one that was almost a commodity, through a process with the cumbersome name "commoditization." In this process, the product is turned into a black box or single item, rather than being viewed as having multiple replaceable parts. When a VCR fails, it is replaced with a new one, rather than being repaired. Cigarette lighters and disposable pens and razors are examples of products that were successfully commoditized.

The countervailing force to commoditization, however, is the desire to satisfy specific consumer groups very well, and thereby charge more to that specific group. Thus, for example, as the camcorder market matured, new features—better batteries, low light capability, side screens, stabilization technology—were added. During the mature phase, such innovations typically bring only transitory improvements in profits, for the profits are rapidly eroded by imitation.

While exports may offer an extension of the growth phase, competition by foreign suppliers soon creates added downward pressure on prices. When it is feasible to produce the product cheaply with a less-educated labor force, foreign competition may virtually eliminate the domestic industry, as it has in shoes.

An interesting example of a market reaching maturity involves automated teller machines, which dispense cash and allow limited electronic banking. The number of such ATMs in the United States has been consistently growing. Moreover, in examining figure 5.5a, growth shows no sign of slacking off. Thus, the market for ATMs appears to be in the growth phase. However, the proliferation of machines is the result of competition among banks, and the value of the machines shows significant signs of slowing, because transactions per machine peaked around 1993 and have been steadily falling ever since (fig. 5.5b). This decline in usage per machine means the costs of ATM transactions to the banks are rising—banks require more machines per thousand transactions.

Point-of-sale terminals, which are in stores and banks and permit the use of credit and debit cards for transactions, tell a similar if more extreme story. The growth of POS terminals continues strongly (fig. 5.5c). However, usage is falling rather dramatically, from over three thousand transactions per terminal per month to about one thousand (fig. 5.5d). The decrease in usage certainly reflects reduced costs of terminals, but it also reflects impending saturation of the market.

A similar story arises with cellular telephones in the United States (fig. 5.6). While the number of subscribers continues to grow dramatically, saturation is ar-

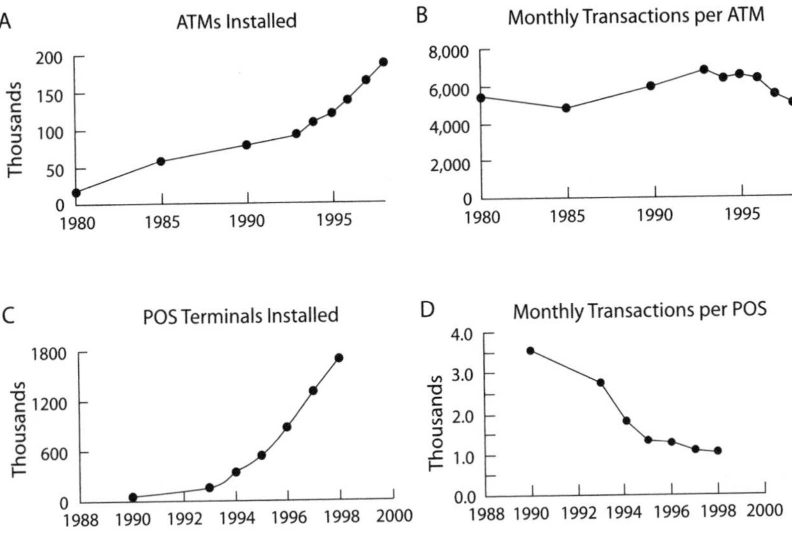

Figure 5.5. (a) ATMs installed and (b) monthly transactions per ATM; (c) POS terminals installed and (d) monthly transactions per POS terminal.

riving in the form of reduced average monthly bills. Customers who have subscribed recently are spending less per month than those who subscribed earlier, and intensified price competition is reducing the bills of customers who use more minutes.

DECLINE AND REPLACEMENT

Most products are eventually replaced with a superior alternative that offers better value. Technological progress in electronics has reduced the window for selling electronics goods to a few years; after that, the goods are obsolete. Technological progress in electronics is so rapid that many electronics goods improve noticeably from year to year. Advances in pharmaceuticals displace many popular drugs. Some products decline because tastes change. Tobacco is an example of a product abandoned by many customers, in spite of a resurgence of cigar smoking. While candy cigarettes have virtually disappeared in the United States, essentially the same candy-stick product is for sale (without the red food coloring to make the candy tip look like an ember) under the name "Monster." Some products are mandated to decline. The government has banned lead-based paint, tetraethyl lead in gasoline, and chlorofluorocarbons (CFCs), the latter being important ingredients in air-conditioning, refrigeration, Styrofoam, pressurized canisters, and some in-

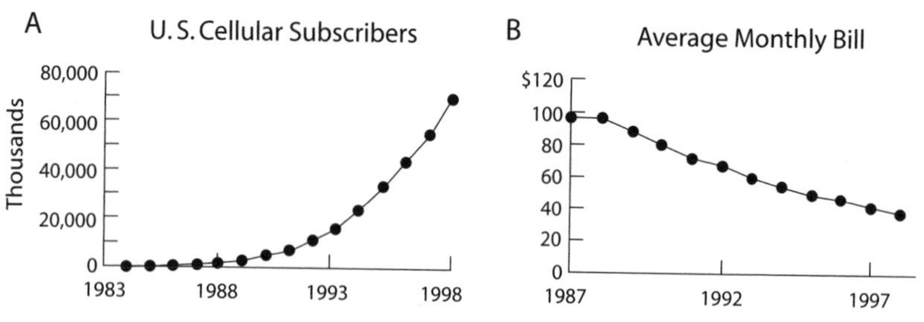

Figure 5.6. (a) U.S. cellular subscribers; and (b) average monthly bill.

halers, because of the damage CFCs do to the ozone layer. Some products are fads, which are briefly popular and then plummet in popularity. Nehru jackets and cabbage patch dolls are relatively difficult to find. Many fashion goods disappear, only to reappear a generation later. Wide ties, hula hoops, platform shoes, and tie-dye garments have all enjoyed a resurgence at one time or another.*

Industries in decline typically do not decline uniformly; some parts of the industry decline faster than others. For example, people with higher incomes are disproportionately less likely to smoke cigarettes, and thus brands appealing to the lower middle class did better than brands aimed at the upper middle class. Even as an industry declines, profitable segments may remain. Thus, one important strategy for dealing with a declining industry is to reposition the product for sales to the profitable segments. For example, black-and-white TVs are rarely purchased for watching television, but are quite common as security monitors and infant monitors. Thus, a niche persists for the black-and-white TV. Security monitors do not require a full tuning system, but usually require a wireless connection. Therefore, repositioning black-and-white TVs also involves a modicum of redesign to take advantage of the particular nature of the demand.

Moreover, often the decline of one industry is caused by the growth of another, closely related industry. For example, the collapse of the vinyl-record industry was brought about by the switch to compact discs, much as the disappearance of the large-size black-and-white television was a consequence of the arrival of color television. Similarly, the radial tire drove out the bias-ply tire, the car eliminated the urban horse, and the Sony Walkman reduced the transistor-radio industry. At the time of this writing, DVD players are replacing CD players in most computers. In

*Interestingly, personal names seem to follow a ninety- to one-hundred-year cycle. Unusual names seem fresh and are adopted by many parents. This makes the name seem very common and not at all unusual. Children with such a name view the formerly unusual name as common, and avoid using it when they name their own children. As their generation ages and dies off, the name returns to "unusual" status. Exceptions include John, William, and Elizabeth.

TABLE 5.1
Major Defense Industry Acquisitions, Second Wave

Date	*Acquisition*	*Price ($Billions)*
1992	Hughes buys General Dynamics missile division	0.45
Mar 1993	Lockheed buys GD aircraft division	1.52
Apr 1993	Northrop buys GE aerospace	3.05
Dec 1993	Loral buys IBM military electronics division	1.57
May 1994	Northrop, Grumman merge	2.17
Dec 1994	Lockheed, Martin Marietta merge	10.0
Apr 1995	Raytheon acquires E-systems	2.3
Mar 1996	Northrop Grumman acquires Westinghouse defense electronics	3.2
Apr 1996	Lockheed acquires most of Loral	9.0
Nov 1996	General Dynamics acquires Lockheed combat vehicles division	0.45
Dec 1996	Boeing acquires Rockwell defense business	3.2
Dec 1996	Boeing, McDonnell Douglas merge	13.3
Jan 1997	Raytheon buys Texas Instruments military electronics	2.95
Jan 1997	Raytheon merges with Hughes electronics	9.5

many cases, the decline of an industry is merely one expression of a need to reorganize the firm to efficiently produce alternative goods.

The most common means of addressing a declining market is the harvest strategy. This strategy requires remaining in the industry as long as the capital equipment remains useful, but not replacing the capital equipment, and exiting when the capital equipment wears out or when the price falls below variable costs. When oil fell below \$20 per barrel in the mid-1980s, drilling operations virtually ceased in Texas and Oklahoma. Existing wells continued to operate, but few new wells were drilled. This is a simple example of harvesting—the existing capital equipment (oil wells) was used but not replaced. Exxon, a large producer on Alaska's North Slope, stopped bidding for new tracts in 1995; it apparently has adopted the harvest strategy of continuing to drill and pump on its existing tracts but not exploring for new oil.

The third major strategy for dealing with decline is consolidation of the industry. The idea of consolidation is that the configuration of the capital stock of the industry is inappropriate for the industry's current demand. A firm can buy a large share of the total industry capital stock, shed the least efficient units, and create an efficiently scaled firm. In this way, sufficient capital is removed from the industry that prices return to a level that covers average costs.

There is a major basis for cooperation in decline, even though few industries succeed in achieving any cooperation but instead devolve into price wars. The basis for cooperation is the requirement that firms coordinate their choices of exit, harvest, and consolidation. For example, if all firms choose to exit or harvest, the consolidation strategy will be profitable; if many, but not all, firms choose to consolidate, the consolidation strategy will not succeed. As a consequence, the strategic choices are interdependent. In particular, consolidation ought to arise in such a way that it will insure that the final industry structure leads to sustainable profits.

The defense contracting industry has experienced both a massive decline—expenditures on major weapons systems fell dramatically from the 1990 level—and an enormous restructuring through consolidation. Overall military procurement fell by half, from $99 billion in 1990 to $48 billion in 1996. In 1990, thirteen firms were capable of making tactical missiles; today, there are four. Similarly, eight U.S. firms in 1990 made fixed-wing aircraft (not helicopters); now there are three. Just two firms—Lockheed Martin and Boeing—make "expendable launch vehicles," which we might call rockets, while there were six firms in 1990 (table 5.1).

The defense consolidation has benefited the industry in two ways. First, capital was withdrawn from the industry in a manner that minimized the overall losses. A major form of capital is actually human capital—teams of engineers and skilled workers. Boeing was able to shift some capacity from its military to its booming civilian aircraft division. A team of Northrop Grumman design engineers allegedly went to Disney. Second, competition for the scarce new projects was reduced, reducing the odds that prices would be ruinously low.

The three major strategies—find a surviving market niche, harvest, and consolidate—all require coordination, in the sense that it is not desirable for all firms to follow the same strategy. A firm that has chosen the harvest or niche strategy is a good candidate for consolidation, for example. If all firms seek niches, there are unlikely to be sufficiently many niches available, and it would pay some to harvest or consolidate. If all firms seek to be consolidators, the prices of target firms will be bid up too high; it is better to be a target. If all firms choose to harvest, eventually all capital would exit the industry; it pays to consolidate.

Because decline generally requires coordination, the sorts of preannouncements and signaling discussed in chapter 13 play a major role. By merging early in the decline, and by rationalizing capacity, a firm can stake out the role of consolidator. An early and significant commitment of resources to the best niches may also deter others from sinking resources into these niches. However, there is a serious risk that the most attractive option will attract too many players, creating a war of attrition. Thus, sometimes it may pay to seek the second best option, rather than compete with several players for the best.

The defense industry consolidations point to another major issue. Raytheon, already strong in military electronics, purchased two firms with strong military electronics—the military electronics division of Texas Instruments and Hughes Electronics, leaving only Northrop Grumman as a major contender in military electronics. Boeing purchased several aircraft manufacturers, including its largest rival, McDonnell Douglas, leaving only Lockheed Martin and Northrop Grumman as major contenders in military aircraft. That is, the mergers were not random across product types but instead represented substantial increases in market power for particular components or subsystems of major weapons systems. When an industry must go from eight firms to three firms, it is best for the industry (and usually worst for the customer) if the three firms have very different skills and advantages, rather than have three firms with similar sets of skills.

SUMMARY OF THE PRODUCT LIFE CYCLE

The product life cycle represents a useful way of guessing the future, and producing scenarios for growth. Many of the attributes of the product life cycle are summarized in table 5.2. However, it is important to realize that some products die without a growth phase, like Apple's Newton handheld device, and that for a given product a particular phase may be very short or nonexistent. Moreover, the product life cycle is intended to provide a typical case. For some products or services, the timing of various aspects of the industry will occur out of phase, unsynchronized with others.

Some products have very long introductions, while others reach the growth phase in a very short period of time. Fashion foods often skip maturity entirely, going from growth to decline much the way Midwest weather goes from winter to summer with an hourlong spring. The decline of a product usually means that another product is in the growth phase; it is sometimes not so obvious whether there are two products or two versions of a single product. An innovation can rejuvenate an existing product, as fiberglass did in the sport-boating industry.

There may be macro-level, larger-scale phenomena in research and development—phenomena that cut across firms, industries, and even nations in a "technology wave." Some consider that there have been four major waves of technology in the past two hundred years. The first centered around steel, which made possible modern guns, woodworking tools, the steam engine, and railroads. There were many subsidiary inventions to the one basic invention, but all share the feature of requiring high-quality steel to be feasible to manufacture.

The second wave centered around 1900–1920, and included devices that har-

TABLE 5.2
Life Cycle Characteristics

	Industry Phase			
	Introduction	*Growth*	*Maturity*	*Decline*
Number of Firms	Small, growing fast	Large	Shakeout, number stabilizes	Small, exiting
Market Size	Small	Large	Large	Declining
Market Growth	Fast	Fast	Slow	Negative
Entry	Large	Medium	Low	Negative
Market Leader Characteristics	Existing reputation innovator, educator, flexible, total solution	Existing reputation marketing, quality production, modular	Reputation for quality, low-cost production and distribution, specialization	Low cost, serving niche market
Profits	Negative	Low, but sharply increasing	High, then declining	Low, then negative
Product Varieties	Few and growing	Increasing, then declining to few dominant designs	Increasing specialization and segmentation	Declining
Distribution	One-stop shopping	Various outlets	Superstores, direct sales	Minimum cost
Investment	High	High	Low	Negative
Average Costs	High, falling	Medium, falling	Low	Low
Foreign Trade (domestic invention)	Low exports	Increasing exports	Initially exporting, then importing	Imports
Customer Name	Innovator /early adopter	Early majority	Late majority	Laggard
Customer Needs	Sophistication, features, fit	Performance	Price /performance	Low price

(*continued*

BLE 5.2 (*contined*)

	Industry Phase			
	Introduction	*Growth*	*Maturity*	*Decline*
stomer Knowledge	Low	Medium	High	High, declining
duct Complexity	High	Simplified	Low: standardization and commoditization	Low
ormation Collection	Demand, customer awareness and satisfaction, repeat buying	Marketing, relative performance, product improvement	Cost reduction, new markets, competitive threats	Capacity reduction, new uses, new features
arketing Strategy	Promotion of brand *and* market	Build brand identity	Segment market, steal business	New promotion; bitter attacks

ness electricity, many of which were invented by Thomas Edison, but the period also included the telephone, the internal combustion engine, refined oil products, aircraft, bridge building, skyscrapers, organized commodity and stock markets, and radio. A third postwar wave in the 1950s and 1960s developed atomic energy, pharmaceuticals, satellites, chemicals, and plastics. The fourth wave, going on today, centers on computers, microchips, and genetic engineering.

The existence or nonexistence of such waves is quite speculative and controversial, but it is important for stock market valuation. If we are in the midst of a significant leap forward today, the massive increase in stock market valuation in the 1990s is comprehensible as a forecast of technological growth, based on innovations of the 1980s and 1990s, including personal computers, fiber optics, satellite technology, the Internet, and biotechnology. Whether or not there are waves or technological advances, it is clear that fundamental inventions such as steel, electricity, and integrated circuits take decades to fully exploit. Other inventions are derived from earlier inventions, either because new developments become possible, or because they are needed. For example, the phonograph and electric light bulb clearly required development and understanding of electricity before such devices could even be contemplated—supply-driven innovations. In contrast, the mid-nineteenth century development of accurate watches was a consequence of need—railroad scheduling demanded more accurate timekeeping to prevent catastrophic crashes. Timekeeping advances are demand-driven advances. Battery technology is demand-driven, but major improvements have been slow in arriving.

Macroscopic waves of technology advance may be akin to the canals of Mars and may not be based on a fundamental reality. Figure 5.7 illustrates the number of U.S. patents, both in absolute numbers and per million of population, from 1800 to the present. There is no strong evidence in favor of major waves of patent filings, beyond the fact that the Great Depression derailed technological advance in this country, an effect that lingers well past World War II. However, there are dips in the per capita patent filings in the 1890s, 1930s and 1940s, and 1970s, suggesting that these periods might represent troughs.[3] Whether technological waves are a real phenomenon, or an attempt to impose order where none exists, is important and unknown.

THE LIFE CYCLE FOR DURABLE GOODS

The product life cycle is substantially different for durable goods than for nondurables. Durable goods can saturate the market, and, as a consequence, maturity may require a *reduction* in production from levels prevailing throughout the growth phase. In contrast, with nondurables such as pharmaceuticals or light beer, there is usually no decline in production from growth to maturity; instead, the growth *rate* falls to a level approximating population or income growth, depending on the nature of the good.

Nondurables tend to have a "soft landing" in the transition from growth to maturity, with no fall in production. This makes the strategy of building capacity to meet current demand appropriate for many nondurables. In contrast, with a durable good, the strategy of building to meet current demand can be catastrophic. At the growth peak, a large fraction of the potential customers may be in the market for the innovation. Investing in the capacity to meet all their demands in a single year will mean that nearly the entire demand is met in that year. The second year's demand will come primarily from new customers (population growth and increased penetration) and replacements. With a good that typically wears out over ten years, there will be little replacement demand for five years, and thus the second year's demand may be only a few percentages of the first year's demand, were the first year's demand fully met. In such cases, it is desirable to build an amount of capacity that will require many years to satiate demand.

There are two major problems with building a low level of capacity. First, if the product has a fad component, like the annual "must have" children's toy such as beanie babies or cabbage patch kids, the fad may pass before market demand is

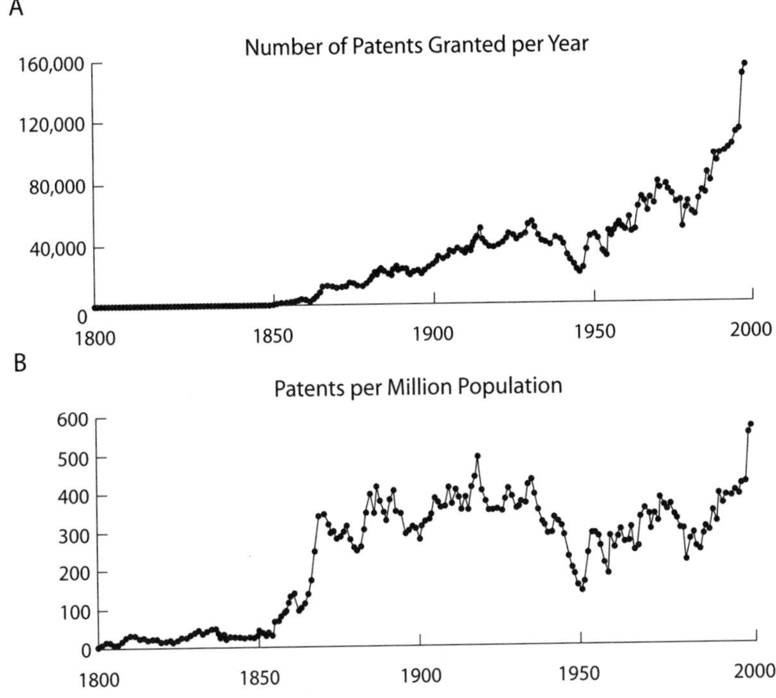

Figure 5.7. (a) Number of patents granted each year; and (b) patents per million population.

met, and a significant number of potential sales may be lost. Second, the longer substantial demand is unfilled, the more likely that serious entry will occur. Letting a significant portion of the customers wait a substantial length of time for the good means that customers will seek alternatives, and potential entrants will try to create a good to satisfy the demand. Thus, often it will be the case that it is sensible to satisfy most of the demand in spite of the "hard landing" that is created. The hard landing is one of the costs of reducing the risk of competitive entry or missing the fad. Nevertheless, a company should prepare for the hard landing by finding alternative uses for the production capacity, or by building replacement demand. For example, saturation in the color television market did not require a fall in sales because of sales of multiple televisions per household.

Some insight in to the desirable capacity for a durable good can be derived from the analysis of the case when there is no risk of entry by another company and the product is not a fad.[4] In this case, a relatively simple formula governs the optimal capacity size. Suppose that c is the cost of capacity per dollar of net variable profit from annual sales. For example, if a factory costs \$50 million to build, and then

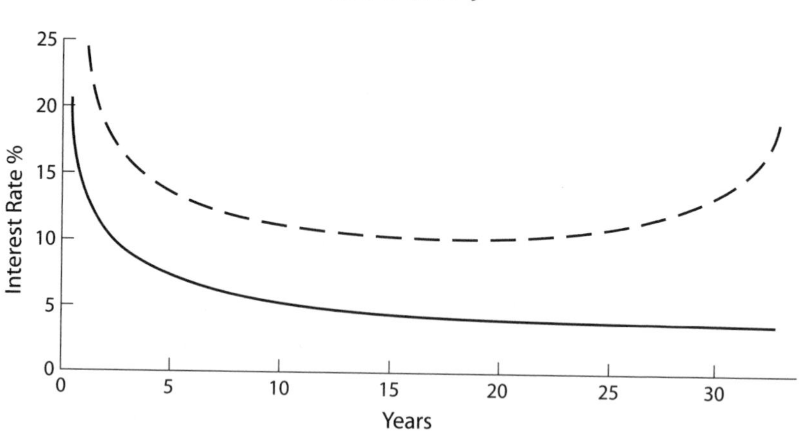

Figure 5.8. The dashed curve represents the number of years before optimal market saturation, as a function of the interest rate expressed in percent, with $c = 3$ and perfect durability. The unbroken curve represents years to optimal market saturation, when $c = 1$.

produces goods whose variable profit (ignoring the fixed cost of the factory) is \$10 million per year, c is 5—the cost of the capacity per dollar of variable profit. Let T be the length of time, in years, before saturation is reached. The depreciation is assumed to be zero—having purchased, consumers are out of the market. Let r be the annual rate of interest.[5] The overall investment determines T—the capacity determines the amount sold each year, which determines how long it takes before the market is saturated. With some elementary mathematics, it is possible to derive the formula for the profit-maximizing level T. This will depend, generally, on the good's depreciation (which generates repeat buyers), the interest rate, and the cost of investment. When depreciation is zero, the following equation determines the optimal time to market saturation, T:

$$1 - rc = e^{-rT}(1 + rT)$$

In this formula, e is Euler's constant, approximately 2.718. This formula gives the length of the optimal growth phase, when there is no depreciation or competition. For example, if a factory costs \$15 million, and the product from that factory, net of labor and materials, produces \$5 million annually, then c is 3. At a 10% interest rate, r is 0.1. The formula can then be solved for T, and it turns out that T is 10.97. That is, the factory should produce about 9% of the annual demand. If, in contrast, c is 1 and r remains 10%, the optimal replacement falls to 5.3 years. These values are plotted in figure 5.8 for the values of c of 1 and 3.

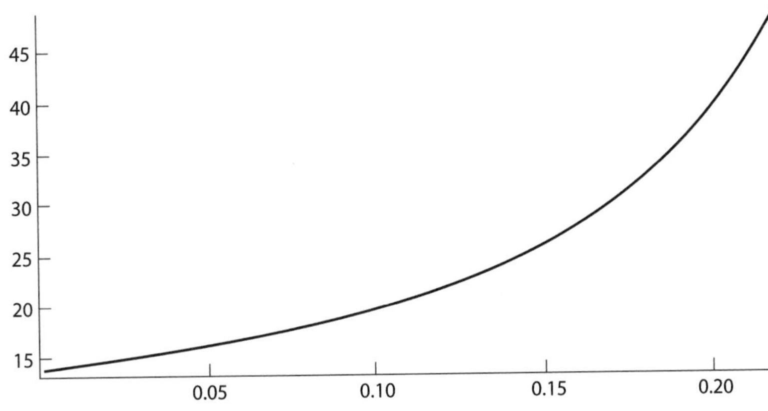

Figure 5.9. The effect of depreciation (in proportion that depreciates each year) on the optimal time T*, with a 5% interest rate and $c = 3$.

An interesting aspect of these formulas is that the optimal time to market saturation is *not* monotonic in the interest rate but is, in fact, U-shaped. When the interest rate is very low, it is optimal to be patient—delayed sales are almost as valuable as quick sales. Thus, the optimal T is high for low interest rates. However, as the interest rate gets very high, the value of the entire enterprise falls, and the optimal time to market saturation converges to infinity. At an interest rate $r = 1/c$, it ceases to be valuable to invest at all.

It is also interesting to know how high the optimal time to market saturation is. A capital cost $c = 3$ is a relatively small capital cost, with payback in a bit more than three years. At a real interest rate of 4%, the time to saturation is almost fifteen years. Such large times-to-saturation are almost never observed, probably because of the threat of entry, and the risk that the demand for the product, if unfilled, will pass. Even when the formula overstates the best strategy, the formula suggests important questions that should be asked about capacity choice: How long before overcapacity is reached? What is the present value of additional investment, which will be underutilized after saturation is reached?

What is the effect of depreciation of the good on the time to saturation? This is a complex relationship. As the depreciation rises, there is an advantage to selling the good quickly, to obtain repeat sales from early buyers. On the other hand, the difficulty of saturating the market increases as the depreciation rises. For the example discussed above, with a 10% interest rate and $c = 3$, the optimal time to saturation is given in figure 5.9. An increase in depreciation increases the speed of market saturation, because the first effect dominates the second. That is, with significant replacement, the optimal time to satiate the market increases.

EXECUTIVE SUMMARY—PRODUCT LIFE CYCLE

- There are four main phases to the product life cycle: introduction, growth, maturity, and decline.
- Early firms experience the most risk and may get caught with obsolete technology but typically obtain a free reputation and can exploit other first-mover advantages.
- Early in a product's life, customer and government education may play a major role, and advertising should be business-expanding rather than business-stealing.
- The growth phase accounts for most of the profits. During this phase, market leaders tend to be firms with solid reputations from the introductory phase. Technology standardizes and costs fall.
- During the maturity phase, less-efficient producers are driven out by falling prices. The market settles on a limited number of designs, but differentiation becomes increasingly important as a means of achieving market power. Distribution becomes more mass market, with a reduced service component.
- There are three main strategies to deal with decline:
  Find a surviving or growing market niche.
  Harvest existing facilities but stop investment.
  Consolidate and rationalize capacity.
- The first mover during decline can often grab the most profitable strategy.
- The life cycle for durable goods may involve a crash, as with CB radios, while the life cycle for nondurables usually has a softer landing.
- The optimal capacity for introducing a new durable not subject to competition is surprisingly low, with up to ten to fifteen years to achieve full market penetration.

Diplomacy is the art of saying "Nice doggie"
until you can find a rock.
—**Will Rogers**

Cooperation

Until relatively recently, the strategic theory of cooperation, also known as the theory of collusion or cartels, focused primarily on price cooperation. The main question concerned the ability of an industry to achieve a better price outcome than the competitive outcome, and to determine what kind of strategies on the part of firms support such an outcome. Why do price wars break out? Why have the agreements of the Organization of Petroleum Exporting Countries (OPEC) frequently broken down?

COOPERATION ON A VARIETY OF ISSUES

As Adam Brandenburger and Barry Nalebuff's 1996 book *Co-opetition* correctly emphasizes, price competition is only a part of the interactions between firms. There are many other aspects of the interactions that form a basis for cooperation. Firms design new products and set standards for the operation of products. Firms establish brand names and promote these brands. Firms advertise their own brand, but also enhance the value of the product in general. Firms produce products that work together with and enhance other firms' products. Firms lobby the government for some regulations and against other regulations. Firms lobby for tariff protection for their output and for the elimination of tariffs on imported inputs. Firms lobby the government for the provision of infrastructure—roads and airports and research—and lobby against taxes. Firms make deals with other firms, concerning inputs, outputs, standards, and product design. Many of these actions have little or nothing to do with price directly, but all of these actions by a given firm or firms will affect other firms.

Advanced Micro Devices (AMD) is headquartered in San Jose, California, but it has a major manufacturing facility in Austin, Texas. AMD lobbied American Airlines to provide nonstop service between these cities and offered to buy a portion of the seats on every flight. The flight was popular with other firms, and quickly grew to four nonstops per day. AMD and American Airlines are not in the same business, and their relationship is, or at least should be, cooperative. Nevertheless, AMD would like American to offer more frequent flights and to charge less for the seats, while American would like AMD to use more seats and pay more for them. While their relationship is primarily cooperative, there is still tension over the number of flights, number of seats, and price. Such a tension exists in most vertical relationships; input suppliers would like more money for fewer, lower-quality, products, while buyers would like to pay less for more, higher-quality inputs.

Firms rarely run negative advertisements about other firms in spite of the potential to grab some business by negative advertisements. The reason is clear. Typically, a negative advertisement begets a negative response, which induces more negative advertisements, and soon the entire industry is bad-mouthing each other. Widespread negative advertisements convince consumers that the industry's products are junk, an outcome that damages all the firms. Firms know, instinctively or through conscious calculation, not to open the door of negative advertising. Politicians often fail to resist the siren call of negative advertisements, because the winner-take-all nature of voting outcomes prohibits sharing of the spoils. That is, the nature of the payoffs to political competition makes cooperation difficult.

Negative advertisements are inhibited by tacit or implicit collusion, which essentially means that the firms have a shared understanding of what is mutually beneficial, enforced by the expectation of retaliation in response to uncooperative behavior. If Coke runs negative advertisements about Pepsi, Pepsi will respond with negative advertisements about Coke, and soon consumers will become convinced that colas are poor products. This threat is reminiscent of "mutually assured destruction," which was designed to deter a nuclear first strike but has the advantage of being self-enforcing: Pepsi's optimal response to Coke's negative advertisements is negative advertisements of its own.

Dr. Strangelove: Punishment Harms the Punisher

In Stanley Kubrick's classic 1964 movie *Dr. Strangelove,* an insane American officer has launched an unprovoked nuclear first strike against the Soviet Union. The American government informs the Soviets of the impending attack and enlists their help in preventing the first strike and the Soviet counterattack. The Russian ambassador explains that the Soviets have built a retaliation machine, which will automatically respond in the event of an attack by the United States:

> When it is detonated, it will produce enough lethal radioactive fallout so that within ten months, the surface of the Earth will be as dead as the moon! When

> they are exploded, they will produce a Doomsday shroud. A lethal cloud of radioactivity which will encircle the earth for ninety-three years! It is not anything a sane man would do. The Doomsday Machine is designed to trigger itself automatically. It is designed to explode if any attempt is ever made to untrigger it.

The ambassador explains the economics of the retaliatory device:

> There were those of us who fought against it. But in the end, we could not keep up with the expense involved in the arms race, the space race, and the peace race. And at the same time, our people grumbled for more nylons and washing machines. Our Doomsday scheme cost us just a small fraction of what we'd been spending on defense in a single year. But the deciding factor was when we learned that your country was working along similar lines, and we were afraid of a Doomsday gap. Our source was the *New York Times.*

The presidential adviser Dr. Strangelove explains the need for commitment, for the automatic detonation, in the Doomsday machine:

> It is not only possible—it is essential. That is the whole idea of this machine, you know. Deterrence is the art of producing in the mind of the enemy the fear to attack. And so, because of the automated and irrevocable decision-making process which rules out human meddling, the Doomsday Machine is terrifying. It's simple to understand. And completely credible and convincing.

Strangelove adds:

> The whole point of the Doomsday Machine is lost if you keep it a secret. Why didn't you tell the world, eh?

The Russian ambassador explains:

> It was to be announced at the Party Congress on Monday. As you know, the Premier loves surprises.

The difficulties in carrying out punishments—punishments harm the punisher as well as the punishee—are illustrated by this entertaining movie. Punishments create a problem of credibility: since punishments harm the punisher, the punisher will have an incentive not to carry out the punishment. Usually some mechanism is needed to insure punishment will be carried out with sufficient force to deter bad behavior. Moreover, the essential need for all parties to understand the punishment that must follow bad behavior is aptly captured by Dr. Strangelove; the whole point is lost if it is kept secret (or misunderstood). This need for the punishment to be understood by the parties creates a problem for illegal cartels—communication is risky.

TACIT COLLUSION

This chapter will focus on tacit collusion; that is, cooperating without explicit agreements or even discussion. Many of the principles for explicit cooperation are the same as the principles for tacit cooperation, although tacit cooperation is much more difficult to implement, primarily because it requires a shared understanding without providing much of a mechanism for reaching a shared understanding. Indeed, a reasonable interpretation of the airline fare wars since deregulation is that Robert Crandall, CEO of American Airlines, was attempting to teach the airline industry how to cooperate, mainly without talking directly to rivals. United and Delta were, and remain, cooperative. Northwest and the carriers in bankruptcy (e.g., Braniff, Eastern) were not.

There are three elements to achieving cooperation. First, there must be a basis for cooperation—a shared interest. Second, there must be punishments to prevent opportunistic behavior. Finally, a mechanism for recovering from mistakes is necessary, because mistakes usually happen.

Shared Interest

Firms producing competing products may still share a mutual interest in improving the basic technology, and joint ventures in research among competitors came into fashion in the 1980s, only to go out of fashion a few years later. In pricing by firms in the same industry, the shared interest tends to be toward higher, less competitive prices. Two firms with no shared interests cannot cooperate; unless there is a basis for improving the welfare of both parties, at least one party will fail to cooperate with any plan.

A shared interest provides a basis for cooperation or agreement. Even with strong competitors, the overall health of the industry, including consumer perception of the firms and products, regulation, production technology, supply assurance, and other features of the industry landscape, is an issue of shared interest. Early in the evolution of an industry, advertising often educates consumers about the product; this advertising is viewed rightly as purely cooperative in nature, because all firms benefit from improved consumer appreciation for the product.

Part of the design of cooperation is to identify issues on which firms have shared interests. Telephone companies who would vie for Personal Communication Services (PCS) spectrum auctioned by the Federal Communications Commission (FCC) had an interest in the efficiency of the auction and the minimization of unnecessary financial risk. While there were several "design an auction that favors me" proposals,* there was also widespread agreement that the auction should be efficient. Efficiency of the process eliminates unnecessary risk and minimizes the amount of resale that will occur after the auction.

The "Big Five" accounting firms share a liability insurance pool. Consequently, a large damage award against any one of the firms would increase the premiums to all of the firms. According to some observers, this shared interest makes the companies hesitant to testify against each other in court. Indeed, it has been alleged in a lawsuit that the companies actually "water down" criticism of each other.†

An essential feature of cooperation is to identify the issues on which firms can agree. In most cases, there will be many issues. Once the basis for agreement is established, a proposal to share the proceeds of cooperation is needed. It is important that every party who can upset the agreement share in the proceeds. Giving too little to one party invites uncooperative behavior. A firm that is going bankrupt anyway has little to lose from running a string of negative advertisements attacking its competitors or pricing below average cost. (This is the reason that American Airlines' CEO Robert Crandall frequently complained about bankrupt carriers like Braniff continuing to fly.)‡ To prevent such bad outcomes, it is important that each party share reasonably in the agreement. (Sometimes a price war, which will finish off a troublesome competitor, is the best outcome—a future cooperative market may be worth a costly battle.)

What is fair? All parties will tend to jockey for position, trying to make it appear that their fair share is large. Each party faces a trade-off—ask for more and risk losing the entire agreement. Such risks are compounded with tacit agreements, because a tacit agreement leaves little scope for negotiation. Consider Pepsi's taste-test advertisements, in which a majority of those sampled in some small towns prefer Pepsi. To Pepsi, these advertisements probably do not seem like negative advertisements about Coke. They do not say that Coke tastes bad but rather that

*In 1994, prior to the first auction, MCI lobbied extensively for a nationwide license that would sell at the sum of the bids on the individual regions. MCI was the only major telephone company eligible to bid on a nationwide license, for cellular holding preempted PCS bidding. This transparent attempt to distort the outcome in its favor was summarily rejected. An important lesson is that there was no shared interest in the MCI proposal, and it flopped.

†An interesting aspect of the lawsuit is that a fraud went undiscovered in part because an embezzler never took a day off in sixteen years, permitting him to cover up his continuing thefts. Mandatory vacations may serve the role of encouraging accountability and reducing embezzlement. *Business Week*, 30 October 2000, pp. 90–92.

‡According to Crandall (27 April 1990 interview with the *Tulsa World*), failing airlines, such as Pan Am, Eastern, and TWA, are still flying but are doomed to go out of business. These carriers are charging prices intended only to recover their cash (marginal) costs. "They're not recovering the costs of buying airplanes for the future because they're not buying any airplanes for the future."

Pepsi tastes better. But they are on the margin of negative advertising, and Pepsi should tread lightly lest retaliation by Coke be provoked. Neither company benefits when both companies run advertisements saying the other company's product tastes bad.

In some instances, there is no basis for agreement because interests are not shared. The U.S. Federal Communications Commission attempts to avoid imposing standards on industry where possible; instead, it prefers that the firms agree on standards. The FCC policy works well when the firms cooperate on setting an efficient standard, which they often do. However, it can work poorly when the firms cannot agree. There were two major finalists in the role of standard for digital PCS transmission—Code Division Multiple Access (CDMA) and Time Division Multiple Access (TDMA). CDMA created higher capacity at higher cost relative to TDMA. Proponents of each allegedly attempted to sabotage the design of the competing standard, with the result that standards for voice communication for both were delayed, and data transmission standards for CDMA were delayed by years. The problem is that proponents of one standard have the incentive to injure and delay development of the competing standard. When opponents of a standard serve on the standard-setting committee, unanimous agreement is generally impossible, and there is no basis for cooperation.

In summary, the foundation of cooperation is the identification of a basis for cooperation—the identification of shared interests. Most industries have many issues on which the firms agree, including customer education, government actions, and the provision of complementary goods. These factors can be used to establish a basis for cooperation, which may extend well beyond the factors themselves. That is, a solid basis for cooperation may be leveraged to achieve cooperation in other dimensions.

Agreeing to Agree: Baseball Arbitration

Salary disputes between unions and firms are often intractable, leading to long and costly strikes while both sides demonstrate their bargaining power. Management claims that it cannot afford a large wage increase, that the firm will go bankrupt, while the union demonstrates its willingness to take a very long vacation if management does not meet its demands.

Binding arbitration is a technique to block such deadlocks. With binding arbitration, both sides agree in advance to follow the decision of the arbitrator, and each then makes a case to the arbitrator. The case made, however, can be very complex and take a long time, and both sides have a strong incentive to distort the information revealed to the arbitrator in a self-serving way. Thus, the firm will sometimes show carefully selected, misleading records to the arbitrator. The union may show studies from comparable industries that are not really comparable, and may conceal contract terms. Ultimately the arbitrator's job, of finding a fair compromise that insures the health of the firm on which the union relies, is nearly impossible. Moreover, the tendency is for the arbitrator to "split the difference," leading both sides to propose extremely self-serving deals.

Professional baseball has found a nifty trick to minimize the distortion of information provided by the parties. Both parties make a proposal, and the arbitrator is bound to accept one of the proposals. In particular, the arbitrator is prohibited from splitting the difference. This gives each party an incentive to make the most reasonable proposal, just slightly tilted in its own favor. With such a scheme, generally the proposals are quite close together, and it does not matter significantly which one is chosen.

Why should both parties agree to such a scheme in the first place? Because both have a shared incentive to settle and avoid a strike, which hurts both parties. Therefore, each is willing to give up a bit to reach an early, fair settlement.

Punishment

> Diplomacy requires the threat of war.
>
> **—Unknown**

The threat of punishment enforces cooperation. A firm that runs negative advertisements will later suffer negative advertisements about its own products. Saudi Arabia and Kuwait threatened OPEC with an oil glut if the other nations did not cooperate. By and large, they did not cooperate, and in 1986 Saudi Arabia made good on its promise, more than doubling output and sending prices tumbling. The Central Selling Organization (CSO) of the De Beers diamond cartel, which has functioned very successfully for seventy years, punished both Tanzania and the former USSR for selling too many diamonds, and now a majority of the Russian diamonds are marketed by the CSO. De Beers punished by increasing the supply of the particular grades of diamonds produced by these nations, thereby minimizing the damage to overall diamond prices.*

In 1955, the U.S. automobile industry produced 45% more automobiles than in either 1954 or 1956. The reason appears to be the outbreak of a one-year price war between the major companies. (The automobile price war is discussed further below.)

*On 31 May 2000, De Beers announced that it would cease the stabilization operations of the CSO, which supported prices worldwide, in part by buying up excess production. This followed the collapse of price supports for low-quality diamonds, a consequence of the exiting from the cartel of a large Australian mine in 1996.

There are three main issues about punishments devised to enforce cooperation. First, is the punishment adequate to deter bad behavior? American Airlines usually met the prices of bankrupt competitors, but that did insufficient damage to already bankrupt firms. In contrast, De Beers successfully induced Russia and Tanzania to join the cartel and behave appropriately. Second, is the punishment credible? A threat to price at marginal cost, and well below average cost, for ten years or more is not credible. Indeed, threats to engage in ruinous price wars are often not credible simply because they do too much damage to the punisher. Finally, when should one punish?

A punishment is adequate if the behavior to be deterred is unprofitable once the punishment is taken into account. Consider deterring a firm that undercuts on price to grab market share. The punishment might be low prices charged by rivals for months, even years. When is it an adequate punishment? The punishment is adequate when the net present value of the attempt to grab market share is a loss. The punishment primarily serves the role of a deterrent, and must be adequate to convince the industry to cooperate. Thus, a firm that cut prices to grab market share should lose that market share, or most of it, in the subsequent price war, and would make so much less during this time that any increment to market share would be a pyrrhic victory. Preferably, the result of the price war is a return to the status quo, so that the offending firm is not tempted to try again.

As parents know (and children disbelieve), punishments hurt the punisher. The problem with punishing a firm that does not cooperate is that the punishment usually hurts the punishing firms. If the punishment is a price war, all the firms are hurt by the low prevailing prices during the war. If the punishment is blasting the offending firm with negative advertisements, there is a substantial risk to permanent damage to the industry in the minds of consumers. If the punishment is a marketing blitz to regain lost market share, the punishers expend significant resources in marketing.

For example, suppose that AMD threatened American Airlines that if American cut its flights between San Jose and Austin below four a day, AMD employees would stop flying on American. The cost of such a punishment would be enormous, for AMD employees would have to arrange connecting flights to reach San Jose, wasting thousands of employee hours, at least until another airline obtained gates and started flying the routes. The threat is not credible; AMD needs the nonstop flights too much to credibly threaten to take its business elsewhere.

The cost of punishment creates a problem of credibility. Once a firm has misbehaved, the other firms should punish it, to deter future misbehavior. Often, however, the punishers will want to minimize the punishment, agree too quickly that punishment had lasted long enough, and return to cooperation. The problem with inadequate punishment is that it begs future misbehavior. However, adequate punishment may be too costly to the punishers to be credible. Such would be the case with the Doomsday Machine of Dr. Strangelove (discussed above), a device that must be set to detonate automatically, because no sane person would ever agree to detonate it, as it would involve ending humanity.

The problem of when to punish is known as a signal-extraction problem, because the problem of recovering information from a broadcast requires extracting the signal from noise in the environment. The signal is the intentional behavior of other firms. Are they doing what is in the best interests of the other firms? Intel seems to believe that Microsoft does not exploit new features of Intel chips in Microsoft's operating system satisfactorily, therefore reducing consumers' incentives to upgrade their hardware. Microsoft might take the position that this is difficult and that they are developing Windows as fast as is efficient. Intel has to discern whether Microsoft is living up to its side of a cooperative agreement or slacking off, and whether punishment, which might take the form of entry into some aspect of the software business, is appropriate. Thus, Intel is faced with the problem of discerning whether its partner is behaving appropriately. Generally, it is not going to be possible to know with certainty whether a firm has cheated on a cooperative agreement. Instead, each firm will be faced with a likelihood that the others are cooperating, a likelihood it deduces from the information gleaned.

In situations where it is not possible to know with certainty whether a firm has not fulfilled an agreement, the usual approach is to set a critical value for some observable variable and respond when that critical value is exceeded. For price competition, this typically would involve setting a critical sales figure and initiating a price war or a marketing blitz if one's quantity or market share should fall below the critical level. Proctor & Gamble appears to follow such a strategy, insisting on a significant market presence and initiating a marketing blitz when its share falls below a set level.

There is a downside to such a critical value—it invites others to push the firm to its critical value. Thus, a firm that will start a price war when its share falls below 20% is essentially asking for a share of 20.1%. There may be value in ambiguity about the minimum acceptable quantity. The Korean War started because the U.S. secretary of state released a map that showed the area the United States would defend, and that area did not include South Korea, thus apparently ending ambiguity about whether the United States would defend South Korea.

It is not enough for a cartel to devise a suitable punishment, one sufficient to deter defection and credible to impose. The cartel needs a plan—tacit or not—for what to do when a firm fails to impose the punishment. As already discussed, punishment hurts the punisher. Thus, a means for insuring that punishment is actually carried out is required. The cartel needs to punish the firm that failed to punish. Failing to punish might arise either because the punishments themselves are quite costly to impose, or because a defector to the cartel agreement pleads for mercy and promises never to cheat again; that is, the defector attempts to renegotiate the punishment. A plan to punish firms who fail to punish defectors provides a deterrent to such failures of carrying out punishment.

The credibility of punishments is especially implausible when only two firms are involved. In this case, if the firm that is supposed to punish fails to punish, the logic of supporting the cartel requires the original defector to punish the firm for not punishing the defector. It is as if a prisoner is required to punish the guard when the guard shows mercy on the prisoner! With only two firms, the temptation to renegotiate the punishment is difficult to resist. Such possibility of renegotiation reduces the threat of punishment, making cooperation difficult to sustain. With three or more firms, however, such punishments for failure to punish become more plausible. If one firm defects, and the second fails to punish, the third can punish the second for not punishing.

If the punishments are profitable from an individual perspective, the credibility is not at issue—the firms would choose to punish anyway. Thus, a price war as a punishment is credible; cutting price to increase market share generally is profitable individually, even when it hurts the average industry profits.

In sum, enforcing cooperation requires a plan for punishment in the event that firms fail to cooperate. Punishments often are costly to enforce—the enforcement is expensive for the punisher. Such costly punishment creates a credibility problem: Will the punishers actually carry out the threat if someone fails to cooperate? Creating credible punishments requires a means of punishing the punisher who fails to punish. Some punishments, like price wars, are credible because they are preferred to be handled on an individual basis by the firms.

War Games and Credibility

An interesting example of a punishment that strained credibility was the U.S. claim that it would attack the USSR with nuclear weapons if the USSR invaded Western Europe, a threat maintained throughout the Cold War Period. The problem with the punishment is that once the USSR invaded Western Europe, the United States would have much to lose and little to gain from starting a nuclear war. Thus, it is not plausible that the United States should start a nuclear war, in which the United States itself is likely to be destroyed, for the sake of punishing an invader. Game theorists call this problem "subgame perfection," a phrase coined by Nobel laureate Reinhart Selten. The problem of subgame perfection can be thought of as whether threats made at one stage of a game will be carried out when the stage requiring them is reached. If the player is not willing to carry out a threat in the event covered by the threat, the threat is not credible, and the theory of subgame perfection holds that threats that are not credible should not be believed. Thus, if the United States would not choose to start a nuclear war in the event that the USSR invaded Western Europe, the USSR should not believe the threat.

To increase the credibility of the plan to start a nuclear war, the United States stationed 200,000 troops in Germany, thus creating the threat of a reprisal in the event of a Soviet invasion. The troops actually had little direct deterrent effect against the numerical superiority of the USSR. Instead, the troops increased the likelihood that the United States would feel it had to respond, because it was not just Europeans but also 200,000 American soldiers who would have been affected by the invasion.

It has been alleged, but I am unable to verify it, that the war games run by the U.S. military during the 1970s to simulate global conflict often resulted in a successful invasion of Germany by the USSR, an invasion that lasted two days and stopped with Germany, thus minimizing the incentive of the United States to respond. Why, then, did not the Soviet Union actually invade Germany in the 1960s or 1970s? The answer has only become available recently. The Soviet planners were afraid that an invasion of Germany would spark a rebellion throughout Eastern Europe, and that Soviet troops would be inadequate to hold Germany and simultaneously quell the rebellion. This problem of a rebellion in Eastern Europe was underestimated by U.S. military strategists, in spite of the uprisings in 1956 and 1968.

The Joint Executive Committee

As price-fixing is illegal in the United States, studies of cartels usually focus on international cartels in such things as oil, coffee, tin, and copper. These products are commodities, and are thus intrinsically different from manufactured products and services. One study, conducted by Professor Robert Porter,[1] examines instead the Joint Executive Committee (JEC), which controlled eastbound rail shipments from Chicago to the Atlantic Seaboard prior to the first antitrust law in 1890.

Grain was the primary commodity transported, accounting for 73% of transport by the JEC member railroads. The JEC set market shares for each of the railroads; prices for other goods were expected to be in line with the grain prices. Since much of the grain was exported, prices to different Atlantic coastal cities were adjusted to reflect differences in ocean shipping rates, making transportation to different cities competitive with each other. The JEC monitored differences between the share allotment that each of the railroads was expected to have and the actual cost of transportation. If the actual outcome differed from the market shares allotted to each firm, a price war started.

There were ten price wars in the six-year period studied, and over a third of the weeks involved price wars. Thus, price wars were a frequent feature of the cartel,

TABLE 6.1
Circumstances Surrounding the 1955 Automobile Price War

Year	*Disposable Income (Dollars)*	*Interest Rate (%)*	*Durables Expenditures (Billions)*	*Automobile Production (Millions)*	*Auto CPI (Index of Auto Prices)*
1954	$1609	0.9	$14.5	5.51	0.99
1955	$1669	1.7	$16.1	7.94	0.95
1956	$1717	2.6	$17.1	5.80	0.97

and prices were significantly lower during those wars. A very interesting aspect of the study is the effect of the entry of another railroad to transport grain from Chicago to the Atlantic, increasing the number from four to five. The entry did not itself disrupt the cartel, which continued to function smoothly. However, the cartel prices fell 10%, and price wars became more frequent.

Even with a handful of firms and legal cartelization, the JEC was unable to run its cartel without frequent, sustained price wars. Recovery from price wars was clearly a major feature of the cartel design.[2]

The 1955 Automobile Price War

In 1955, 45% more cars were sold in the United States than in either 1954 or 1956. The year 1955 was not unusual economically in overall output, consumer income, or interest rates; indeed, on major macroeconomic characteristics as well as chronology, 1955 was between 1954 and 1956. Spending on other capital goods was approximately the same. However, as the number of automobiles sold jumped, revenue rose significantly. Prices fell. Table 6.1 provides a quality-weighted price index.

Professor Timothy Bresnahan, who conducted the study, concludes that the year 1955 involved a price war, primarily between GM, Ford, and Chrysler.[3]

Recovery

> I thought he was going to hit me, so I hit him back first.

Mistakes will happen. The movie theaters in a particular city collude by agreeing not to compete for movies. They accomplish this noncompete collusion by assigning distributors to theaters, with each theater buying only from the distributors it has been assigned. The scheme, once implemented, runs without discussion or meetings, and is entirely tacit. (The movie theaters think this makes the scheme legal, and at least one jury has agreed.) The scheme was complicated by exceptions that permitted several to bid for movies that would fill several movie theaters.

A price war by several movie houses arose when one bid for the (at that time) new movie *Star Wars,* when that theater was not supposed to bid for it. For the subsequent two years, all of these theaters bid for any movie, regardless of the assigned distributor. Then cooperation returned. The offending movie theater, which caused the bidding war to begin, had apparently made an innocent error and bid for a movie that was not part of its allotment.

There are several lessons in the tale of the cooperating theaters. First, the theaters established exclusive territories to simplify the allocation problem they faced. Rather than being a geographical location, a territory consisted of a distributor and the movies handled by that distributor. Establishing exclusive territories is often practical for a variety of reasons, including ease of monitoring and clarity about rules. Second, the cartel permitted some exceptions, to handle extraordinary circumstances. Such exceptions can be quite valuable, and they may even be necessary. If the value of stealing *Star Wars* is so great that firms would be tempted to do so no matter what punishment would be imposed, it is preferable to open *Star Wars* to more than one, or to all, firms, as a means of avoiding a price war. That is, if the theaters cannot enforce an aspect of the agreement, they should not try. Third, a mistake was made, and not surprisingly it occurred during one of the exceptions. Business-as-usual was well understood; the exceptions less so. Fourth, the theaters punished the offender for a significant amount of time, easily insuring that the theft would not be repeated for a long time. That is, the punishment was more than adequate. Finally, the group found a means to recover from the punishment and return to cooperation. It may not be coincidental that the punishment phase lasted precisely two years.

To err is human, but to really foul things up requires a computer.
—Farmers' Almanac, 1978

A major question for cooperating firms is how to recover from mistakes. The movie theater experience suggests a reasonable rule: punish any detected misbehavior for a fixed period of time. A fixed length of punishment has the flaw that the punishment does not always fit the crime, when the same punishment is used for all misbehaviors. However, establishing a fixed rule has the advantage of making it clear to all parties when they should return to cooperation.

A difficulty with the fixed-time rule is that it may not be credible. A fixed punishment must be large enough to deter major transgressions. For a small transgression, a large punishment may be inappropriate, and thus may not be enforced.* In particular, will Intel sever its very profitable relationship with Microsoft if Microsoft is just a little lazy in improving Windows and in using Intel's increased processing power? Clearly, the sensible answer is no. In such circumstances, the only punishments that are credible are small ones. As a consequence, a fixed punishment rule is not credible in circumstances where smaller punishments can be negotiated after a violation of cooperation. In such circumstances, the punishments must be designed using industry-specific information.

In summary, the theory of cooperation and collusion suggests:

- Cooperate on a variety of matters, not just price.
- Identify the basis for cooperation.
- Share the proceeds of cooperation sufficiently that the relevant parties participate.
- Identify punishments for misbehavior that are an adequate deterrent.
- Identify punishments that will be used credibly.
- Set a trigger to start a punishment.
- Fix a method for recovering from punishment and returning to cooperation.
- A fixed-length punishment is often a good choice—if it is credible.

Who Colludes?

According to a study by Dr. Jon Joyce (who was in the Antitrust Division of the U.S. Department at the time but is now in private practice), the firms convicted of price-fixing are not large firms, and indeed tend to be owner/operator-type firms. Joyce explains this finding as a consequence of incentives—it is difficult to motivate a manager in a large corporation to fix prices. The problem with motivating the manager is that the firm cannot write a contract compensating an employee for illegal behavior. Moreover, few managers are willing to risk jail sentences when it is possible to reach a sharing of the market via tacit understanding.

Included in Joyce's finding are the industries with the largest number of incidents of price-fixing (see table 6.2).[4]

*Nobel laureate Gary Becker asked why not use the maximal punishments for all crimes, e.g., execute jaywalkers. Using a maximal punishment saves on enforcement costs—one only need catch criminals with small probability; a small probability of a large penalty equals a large probability of a small penalty in deterrence. There is a subtle logical flaw in this reasoning. Suppose the penalty for jaywalking is death, and that this penalty is sufficient to deter any rational person from jaywalking. Then, if anyone is caught jaywalking, they must be irrational—and thus qualify for an insanity defense—or be falsely accused. Either way, the penalty should not be imposed in this instance. But the failure to impose the penalty makes it sensible for rational people to violate the law.

Table 6.2
Price-Fixing by Industry

Highway and Street Construction	33%
Electrical Contracting	25%
Furniture Wholesaling	5%
Water and Sewer Construction	5%
Motion Picture Theaters	5%
Refuse Systems	3%

PROBLEMS OF TACIT COOPERATION IN PRICE

People of the same trade seldom meet together, even for merriment or diversion, but the conversation ends in a conspiracy against the public, or in some contrivance to raise prices.

—Adam Smith, *The Wealth of Nations,* 1776

The most difficult kind of cooperation to enforce arises when the interests of the firms involved are mostly in opposition, and the firms have a limited basis for cooperation—particularly in pricing and market shares. Each firm wants a larger share, and a larger share must come from competitors. Thus, it is worth more attention to understand how cooperation in pricing arises, and how it fails. The goal is an understanding of all the problems facing firms attempting to cooperate, rather than a primer on how to collude. Indeed, a careful reading of the problems in price-fixing suggests that it is a bad strategy for most firms.*

There are no fewer than twelve major challenges to sustaining tacit cooperation in price:

- Confessions
- Many producers
- Differentiated products
- Reaction time

*For example, Archer Daniels Midland paid $100 million to settle charges relating to price-fixing of lysine. Three executives were fined $350,000 each and sentenced to two years in jail. ADM now faces heightened federal scrutiny in all its activities, and especially in mergers, because of a "history of collusion." Consult an attorney before taking actions that might break the antitrust laws.

- Environmental randomness
- Motivating managers
- Efficient allocation within the cartel
- Unenforceable contracts
- Risky communication
- Small or failing firms
- Entry and substitutes
- Competition in other dimensions

Confessions

The number one problem of illegal, price-fixing cartels is confession. That is, an executive at one of the companies calls up the U.S. Department of Justice and says (usually through an attorney) that the collusion has been going on for years and that the executive is willing to turn state's evidence, implicating the others, in exchange for immunity. In some cases, executives angry at other cartel members report the conspiracy. Disgruntled ex-spouses have been known to turn in colluders. At the federal level, it appears that a majority of convictions arise in this manner. Cartels that ultimately get caught appear to last about seven years, on average.[5]

Confessions may be motivated by a crisis of conscience—the member genuinely feels sorry about breaking the law. But confessions are often motivated by a crisis of *confidence*. Price-fixers face the serious problem that, as in defection, one very much wants to be first to confess, because immunity from prosecution generally goes to the first to confess. Thus, if the cartel appears shaky or unreliable, the fear that others may confess can send the entire group racing to their attorneys to confess.

Moreover, unlike all of the many other problems facing a cartel, the problem of someone confessing has no economic solution. There is no structuring of the implicit agreement that resolves the problem of confession—because any solution to the problem of confession has to change beliefs. The members have to believe that they are all upstanding, trustworthy individuals who would not confess, but the problem with such beliefs is that price-fixers are committing criminal acts. Would you consider a price-fixer trustworthy? After all, if price-fixers are willing to break the law, would you believe in their honor?

Although there is no full solution, there are several ways to mitigate the problem of confession. The primary one is for fellow price-fixers to be friends. This is the reason collusion seems so closely allied with golf; golf facilitates not only illegal discussions and planning but also trust. Limiting the number of colluders helps, too, for there are fewer candidates to have a personal crisis and confess. A second approach is to insure that everyone shares sufficiently in the cartel's proceeds; a small firm that gets very little should not be included in a cartel, for that firm has little to lose from confessing.* Finally, there is a noneconomic solution—use organized crime to prevent it. Organized crime operates on the principle that it is scarier than the government, and thus confession ceases to be an attractive strategy. Employing an organized crime syndicate to enforce price-fixing is bad business from many perspectives; not only does the syndicate insist on taking a large share of the proceeds, but the price-fixers will be owned now by the syndicate and may be forced to do other illegal activities that could result in even worse penalties.

Many Producers

As a practical matter, few cartels of more than eight firms survive, and the typical number of firms in a price-fixing conspiracy is four or five. A large number of producers creates three separate problems. One is organizational: a cartel with a large number of firms operates like a committee that is too large—it cannot accomplish much of anything. In addition, a large number of producers means that many of them are small companies. A small firm has a relatively large incentive to attempt to cheat on the cooperative agreement—grabbing a large share of the market for itself in the short run, and living with the consequences of the subsequent price war. Third, with many producers, it is more likely that one confesses, dooming all. With confessions, the chain is only as strong as its weakest link.

Differentiated Products

OPEC faces the following problem. If the price of "Saudi light" is $27 per barrel, what should Nigerian heavy sour crude sell for? Light crude contains a higher fraction of relatively valuable gasoline, while heavy oil contains more low-value sludge with which asphalt is made. Saudi light is a relatively sweet crude, which means it contains little sulfur, while the Nigerian oil contains more sulfur, which must be removed at significant expense in distillation to reduce sulfur dioxide emissions. Thus, Nigerian crude is an inferior product, and should sell for less per barrel. But how much less? From the Saudi perspective, $2 less is plenty. At that price, some buyers are indifferent about choosing between the Saudi and Nigerian crude oils, and neither country can sell all it would like to sell at the assigned price.[6] But Nige-

*If permitted to continue operating, a small player who confesses could have a lot to gain by sending all his rivals to jail. However, the granting of immunity also tends to include a prohibition on participating in the industry for many years. This is a mistake on the part of the Department of Justice. If a firm that voluntarily turns in the other firms prior to any DOJ investigation is permitted to stay in the industry, a major incentive is created to turn in co-conspirators.

ria would like to sell more, and thinks a $3 differential is more appropriate. There are some buyers who would not switch from Saudi crude to Nigerian crude unless the price difference was at least $3. How should OPEC price their differentiated products?

OPEC's problem is a good example because the answer to the problem it faces is relatively simple. For any given buyer (refinery), there is a straightforward trade-off. That is, the technology of refining is such that the value of lightness and sweetness can be calculated exactly by using linear programming. Changing an input crude stream (many refineries mix the input streams to optimize the net value of production) changes the most profitable mix of outputs (including gasoline, diesel, heating oil, jet fuel, and asphalt) in a complicated but well-understood way. If all refineries were alike, there would be a price differential that made refineries indifferent about substituting one crude for another, and that differential would determine appropriate relative prices. Unfortunately for OPEC, and fortunately for oil consumers, distinct refineries are different from each other, which complicates the trade-off. Some cannot use sour crude oils, for they lack a desulfurization plant. Some can crack heavy oil to lighter components, while others have much less capacity to do so. There is no single appropriate trade-off for all refineries—a price difference of $2 will make Nigerian crude seem like a bargain to some refiners and yet be a woefully inadequate incentive to substitute Nigerian for Saudi light to others. Consequently, OPEC squabbles about the price differences and rarely reaches full agreement.

Generally, quality differences provide a basis for firms to disagree about their price or market share. While firms with identical products can agree, firms with different products will have a much more difficult time agreeing. The problems are vastly compounded when, unlike OPEC, the firms cannot legally talk with one another—then there is no straightforward mechanism for reaching a cooperative allocation that raises prices.

Reaction Time

Airlines can respond to price cuts by competitors in a matter of days or even hours. In contrast, a cartel of firms delivering milk to schools might not be able to respond for a year—it has to wait for new contracts to be offered by schools. Punishments delivered quickly are much more effective for two reasons: punishments end the profits associated with cheating on a cartel, and speedier punishment reduces the discounting associated with the penalty. The reaction time is composed of two separate factors: the time to detect cheating, and the time to implement the punishment. Either can take a long time; together, they comprise the reaction time of a cartel. Detection depends on the environment in which the firms operate. The time to implement the punishment may be slow because of such components as existing contracts or published price lists.

The reaction time limits the number of firms that can cooperate successfully. Suppose, for example, that a number (n) of similar-sized firms can share monopoly profits of $100 million, and that profits in competition are 5% of that, or $5M. The maximal punishment is to impose the competitive profits forever. If all the firms cooperate, they share $100M, giving each $100M/$n$. A firm that cheats can take at most the entire market for a limited period but then loses that market from the price war and shares $5M afterward. Then it is not profitable to cheat on the cooperative outcome if $d \times \$100M + (1 - d) \times \$5M/n < \$100M/n$.

The right-hand side of the inequality gives the profits per firm under cooperation on a flow basis. When a firm cheats, the profits are composed of two terms—the value prior to the initiation of the price war and the value afterward. These two terms are weighted by the proportion of value accruing prior to the price war, a value labeled d.* The value of d is the cost in present-value terms of a delay of a payment delayed by the reaction time. Thus, if the annual interest rate is 21% and the reaction time is six months, then $d = 0.1$, a value that arises because the cost of six months is 10% when the annual interest rate is 21%. The appropriate interest rate is a risk-adjusted rate. The value d gives the relative value of money received prior to the initiation of a price war. Thus, should a firm cheat on the cartel, it can get at most the entire market ($100M), and the weight d adjusts for the duration. Afterward, it shares the competitive profits, with weight $1 - d$ for the delay.

With a six-month reaction time (very slow) and a 21% interest rate (high), cooperation is sustainable if the number of firms is nine or fewer. We see this by inserting $d = 0.1$ into the inequality and then identifying the values of n that make the inequality true. The high values of the interest rate and the slow reaction time both tend to reduce the number of firms that can sustain cooperation. Moreover, the inequality should be viewed as necessary for sustaining cooperation, but it does not account for many of the other difficulties discussed in this chapter. Fast punishments help insure cooperation, and increase the scope for cooperation.

In particular, the calculus of sustaining cooperation requires optimism. If the firms are pessimistic about their chances of sustaining cooperation, it pays to be the first to defect from the cooperative agreement. Consequently, pessimism about the future of a cooperative agreement tends to cause the agreements to unravel immediately.

*Specifically, d is the present value of a stream of $1 per day from now until the reaction time, divided by the present value of $1 received forever.

Environmental Randomness

The Joint Executive Committee solved the problem of differentiated products by assigning market shares. Then firms that cut price too much, and achieved a higher market share, would be faced with a price war. However, there was substantial randomness in demand: price wars could be set off inadvertently, without any firm misbehaving. For example, if there were an unusually high demand for transportation to Boston, the market share of firms delivering to New York might fall sufficiently to trigger a price war.

Randomness in the marketplace permits a firm that is cheating on a cartel agreement to hide price cuts—it becomes more difficult to extract the signal (did someone cheat or not?) from the noise (random fluctuations in demand).

A particularly thorny difficulty arising from observational problems is the difficulty in observing circumstances of other firms. Paper mills in the southern United States rely extensively on small private sellers of timber, and the paper mills compete at auction for the wood. Generally, paper mills know how much wood other paper mills have, and watch each other carefully. Because most of the costs are fixed, paper mills tend to run at full capacity all the time, and thus the demand for wood is very inelastic. Paper mills typically minimize their competition by using geographic bidding strategies—each bids on the stands of trees closest to its mill and more distant from other mills. (A constraining factor is small loggers who can buy underpriced stands of trees for resale.) A paper mill facing a shortage, however, will go further to acquire trees. Managers in charge of wood acquisition watch each other carefully, but are nevertheless frequently surprised by incursion into "their own" territory. In this business, environmental randomness (fluctuations in the wood available nearby) makes cooperation (to lower the price of wood) difficult, in spite of a mill's efforts to monitor the other firms and identify their circumstances.

Motivating Managers

Large firms generally find it difficult or impossible to motivate managers to engage in illegal conspiracies to fix prices. The penalties for price-fixing include jail time, even if such time is served in a minimum security prison, sometimes known as "Club Fed." Making it difficult to motivate managers to fix prices is, after all, one of the purposes of criminalizing conspiracy to fix prices.

It will usually be difficult and dangerous to induce managers to attempt to cooperate with competitors on price, even in a tacit way. Partly, this is a result of the mind-set of competition—the give and take of cooperating on price is contrary to the "never give an inch" attitude of fierce competition. For upper management to tell managers to find an accommodation with competitors borders on ordering managers to engage in a conspiracy, which is obviously dangerous and ill-advised.

Smart managers who derive a substantial portion of their income from the profits of the organization will have an incentive to increase company profits, which provides some incentive to cooperate. While executives of some large firms have been convicted of price-fixing, price-fixing is apparently much more common in small, owner-operated companies, because these owners obtain most of the benefits of the illegal activity.

Efficient Allocation within a Cartel

Along with difficulties observing the costs and needs of cooperating firms, the problem of efficiently allocating the production is an important problem for the cartel, and one that is nearly impossible to solve tacitly. The problem can be illustrated by milk cartels in Florida and Texas, which have conspired on the delivery of milk to public schools.* Schools buy milk by sealed-bid auction, typically with annual contracts. Cartels have functioned by partitioning the territory, so that each company is assigned a set of schools—a territory. The problem of efficient allocation is to assign the schools in such a way that the low-cost provider performs the delivery. However, as the cartel is increasing prices well above costs, many members of the cartel would like to claim to be the low-cost provider. This problem has no complete resolution without some form of side payments, through which the company that serves a school pays the other cartel members not to bid. Such payments can take the form either of direct transfers or bribes (which is an excellent way to get caught and sent to jail), or of a give-and-take scheme, where winning one school district means a company is disqualified for the next two auctions.[7]

The great electrical conspiracy of the 1950s involved the three leading producers of turbines, which are sold to electrical utilities to generate electric power. Generally, purchase contracts involved bidding by the companies to supply turbines. The three companies, Westinghouse, General Electric, and Allis-Chalmers, used the phases of the moon to determine the winning company. The phase of the moon on the date of the bid determined the winner, with the other firms required to submit noncompetitive bids to create an appearance of competition. The mechanism created a random allocation—the firm chosen was not the best for the job,

*Raising prices of milk sold to schoolchildren creates very bad press and is difficult to defend to a jury. In contrast, movie theaters tend to conspire against distributors, their input suppliers, and thus can offer the defense that conspiring on inputs lowers cost, and that part of those lowered costs are passed on to consumers in the form of lower ticket prices. Juries react well to this argument.

TABLE 6.3
Knockout Auction Earnings

Bidder	*Bid*	*Increment*	*Shared With*	*Total Earned*
1	$1000	$100	1	—
2	$900	$50	1, 2	$25 + $50 + $25
3	$850	$150	1, 2, 3	$25 + $50
4	$700	$100	1, 2, 3, 4	$25

but the one that happened to have the current moon phase assigned to it. This inefficiency is a loss to the cartel—some of the gains from collusion are dissipated by the randomness of the allocation of the demand.

In contrast, some antiques dealers (known as "Rings") run efficient cartels. The dealers nominate a particular dealer to buy an item of interest at the lowest price available. Afterward, the dealers run a type of sealed-bid auction, known as a "knockout" auction, to allocate the item among the members. Suppose there are four firms, and $600 was paid in the original auction. If the bids in the knockout auction were $1000, $900, $850, and $700, the rule says that all four firms share the amount $700–$600, the top three bidders share the amount $850–$700, and the top two bidders share $900–$850. These payments are summarized in table 6.3

The payments are all made by the high bidder, who obtains the object. In this case, the high bidder pays $25 to bidder 4, $75 to bidder 3, $100 to bidder 2, and also pays the $600 for the object, pricing the object to the high bidder in the knockout auction at $800. The auction is intended to provide an incentive to bid high—each bidder shares in proportion to how high his or her bid is relative to others.

The knockout auction helps create an efficient allocation; usually the dealer who values an antique the most will win the bidding by bidding highest. Since it involves explicit side payments, however, the knockout auction makes it much easier for the government to detect an illegal cartel. That is, the cartel faces a trade-off between efficiency and the ease of detection by the government.

Generally, cartels face a trade-off between inefficient production and ease of detection; efficiency of the cartel can be increased only by a means that creates more information that is potentially detectable by the government. Considerations of the ease of detection of collusion suggest limiting participation and using a simple allocation scheme, and accepting some inherent inefficiency of assignment.[8]

Unenforceable Contracts

Cartels must provide their own enforcement. Both domestic cartels and international cartels cannot write contracts that are enforced by courts, for different reasons. Courts will not enforce contracts by domestic firms to illegally fix prices, although the U.S. government occasionally enforces agricultural cartels, and there is no relevant international court to enforce an international cartel agreement. Because cartels cannot rely on outside enforcement, cartels must create their own enforcement internally. Internal enforcement is limited by credibility—many punishments are not credible, as was discussed above.

Risky Communication

Many of the problems of cooperation are mitigated by discussion. For example, the milk cartel faces the problem of which companies should deliver to which schools. This problem is reduced or approximately solved by trading. The firms could start with the allocation that prevailed prior to the cartel, and then improve upon that allocation by (1) not competing and (2) trading deliveries. Such a scheme requires discussion between the parties, which substantially increases the likelihood of detection by government authorities.

Another problem that is reduced by discussion is handling extraordinary circumstances. Suppose that, due to a complex problem of logistics, it is useful for American Airlines to send an extra plane through Denver, a United Airlines stronghold. Without discussion, American's action will be viewed as a threat by United, which might retaliate by price-cutting or sending more flights to Dallas. If, instead, American can say, "I need this flight to Denver, but to compensate you I'm stopping a flight to LA that competes with your flight," a costly price war may be averted. That is, discussion can reduce the signal extraction problem faced in enforcing a cartel agreement.*

Discussion is not a panacea—discussion did not prevent price wars by the railroads under the Joint Executive Committee. Moreover, OPEC discussions sometimes seem endlessly unsuccessful. Nevertheless, discussion clearly mitigates many problems, at a cost of creating a higher risk of prosecution.

Small or Failing Firms

Failing firms are very disruptive to cooperation, because a failing firm has so little to lose. Failing firms have a tendency to take risky bets, hoping to win big, a phe-

*A particularly entertaining example of such communication arose when airlines responded to others' fare cuts with matching fare cuts, using the letters FU in the ticket identifier. The companies agreed to stop such communication in a court settlement. See *Wall Street Journal,* 28 June 1990, p. A8.

nomenon seen clearly in the savings and loan crisis of the late 1980s, where essentially bankrupt savings and loan companies took massive gambles, hoping to stay afloat. FDIC insurance prevented depositors from policing such behavior. Limited liability in the stock market has the identical effect on a failing firm. Shareholders of a failing firm *want* managers to take a big risk, even if that risk is a bad bet on average, because shareholders get nothing if the firm actually fails. (Bond holders, on the other hand, prefer that the firm take actions to stay afloat, and they can be opposed to gambles that have a big risk but a good average return.) Because shareholders tend to control the organization, even if indirectly through the board of directors, failing firms will often undertake risky actions, which may set off a price war. Failing firms often make a large push for market share, eroding prices and inducing strong price competition.

Small firms present a different problem. The problem with a small firm, even if it is not failing, is that it does not have much vested in the industry, and thus gains little from cooperation on price. Consider the entry of MCI and Sprint into long-distance telephony. In the first year following entry, both firms had very small market shares. Those small market shares were a problem for AT&T, because it meant that neither MCI nor Sprint could be induced to cooperate on price. The firms were better off capturing a more sizable fraction of the competitive outcome than a miniscule fraction of the monopoly outcome. As a consequence, cooperation in the near term is impossible; AT&T's best strategy was to encourage the growth of its competitors until they had enough to lose, and were vested in the industry. Then, and only then, does serious cooperation on price become feasible.

Entry and Substitutes

High prices attract entry. A successful cartel faces the threat of entry induced by the cartel's very success. The extreme example of the costs of entry can be seen in the real estate market. For example, the Multiple Listing Service encourages real estate agents to charge a uniformly high commission, 6% to 7%, by conditioning membership on uniform commissions. The absolute size of the commissions has gone up significantly, and the size varies dramatically between the coasts and the central part of the country because of the variation in housing prices. Commissions by real estate agents do not generally reflect costs, and there is little price competition by agents. This state of affairs arises because the Multiple Listing Service successfully discourages price competition.

However, most agents do not earn an abnormally high rate of return, because there is no control on the entry of agents. Thus, a flood of agents dissipates most of the proceeds of the high commissions. The system benefits the most talented agents, who avoid price competition and earn an abnormally high return relative to what they would earn with price competition, while lesser agents, by serving as an agent on one house transaction per year or so, earn a return commensurate with what they could earn in alternative employment selling cars or other durables.

Most of the industries in which price-fixing is common (see "Who Colludes?" above) are relatively easy to enter—the skills are widely available and capital requirements are modest. Thus, because it is difficult to motivate managers to engage in price-fixing, price-fixing is most common in industries in which it has little lasting effect on price. Instead, the advantages of price-fixing are squandered on the addition of less talented, relatively inefficient firms.

Competition in Other Dimensions

Beer producers in Ontario, Canada, were fortunate to have the government create a distribution cartel for them. The government enforced a distribution cartel, and permitted the producers to charge one of two prices—a price for regular beer, and a price for premium beer.* This arrangement would seem to be an ideal situation for cooperation on prices, and prevailing prices were substantially above the U.S. prices. In particular, the price of exported Ontario beer, for example, Molson, sold in the United States, was less than the prices that prevailed in Ontario, in spite of higher transport costs.

However, two other problems substantially reduced the ability of the Ontario brewers to benefit from the government scheme. First, the companies competed in quality, which reduced the margins significantly. In particular, when the government permitted variation in bottle types in the early 1980s, the firms introduced unusual, expensive bottles, without any corresponding increase in price. Many Canadians believe the quality is higher—that they are getting something for the higher prices. Moreover, the union that controls workers in breweries and distribution centers has succeeded in capturing a significant fraction of the profits that flow from the government-sponsored cartel.

Firms may succeed in increasing prices only to fritter the profits away in an attempt to grab additional market share through quality. For many years, the government of Australia regulated airlines with a scheme that required the two Australian airlines to offer the same flights, generally taking off within minutes of each other for each destination. The similarity in product offerings did not result in price competition because the government set the prices as well. (It is difficult to imagine who thought this scheme was a good idea, as neither consumers nor firms benefited from it.) However, unable to compete on price or flight times, the air-

*The government scheme can be traced back to a time when the government kept track of all the alcohol sold to individuals, so that the distribution cartel was also a government convenience.

lines competed in quality, offering very pleasant service, squandering some of the advantage of the elimination of price competition.

Generally, competition in quality undermines cooperation in price only partially, because competition in quality does not result in perfect substitution by customers.

SOLUTIONS TO TACIT COOPERATION PROBLEMS

In view of all the problems of sustaining cooperation in prices, it may seem surprising that firms ever succeed in cooperating. However, firms do succeed, and frequently, too. Many have increased prices significantly over competitive levels and sustained these higher prices for more than ten years. Cartels have been, and can be, successful. While there are many problems facing cartels, there are many solutions as well. Indeed, the perspective of cartel analysts is that the real mystery is why there is not more tacit collusion, when tacit collusion is so easy to sustain. Even with fifty firms, the threat of a long-term reversion to competitive prices is usually enough to make cooperation rational.* Moreover, the threat of rapid reversion to competitive pricing is not the only tool in a cartel's arsenal.

Industry Association

An industry association is an example of what is known as a "facilitating device," which helps a cartel or a tacit collusion function. Industry associations provide a reason for executives to get together, and learn how to know and trust each other. Industry associations perform studies that may suggest mutually beneficial strategies, and dire consequences of a failure to cooperate. An industry association can be a vehicle for cooperative, build-the-market kind of advertising, or it can sponsor research projects that benefit the industry as a whole. Finally, industry associations lobby for beneficial legislation. Much of the work of industry associations is beneficial to customers—improving the market and eliminating costly, ineffective regulation—but an industry association also forges links between competitors, and thus can be a vehicle for softening or eliminating price competition in the guise of "rationalizing the marketplace."

*With fifty similar-sized firms, a single firm can take the entire market until the others respond, earning less than the monopoly profits for that period of time. Alternatively, if it plays along, the firm obtains 2% of the monopoly profits forever. Thus, if that percentage forever is preferred to the entire profits for a short time, then monopoly pricing can be sustained. At a 10% interest rate, it takes sixty-nine days to produce 2% of the present value of the infinite stream of monopoly profits. Thus, if the firms can react within sixty-nine days to an attempt to take the entire market, cooperation is theoretically sustainable.

Published Price Lists

A cartel of four firms, each selling ten thousand differentiated industrial products, successfully raised prices for five years in the following way. First, they used their industry association to create a "substitution list." For each firm, this list gave the nearest substitute offered by the rival, and indicated whether or not it was a perfect substitute (would work in any application) or not. Second, the firms published price lists. There was a price leader, and each firm was supposed to follow the price leader.

Because large buyers could negotiate secret discounts, there was some erosion in the agreement for the largest buyers. The majority of buyers were small buyers, and they were charged the price-list price. Published price lists permitted each firm to see what its rivals were doing, and to do the same, thereby reaching a cooperative outcome.

Initially, secret discounts were given only to the largest buyers. Over time, however, the size of customers that qualified for discounts shrank, until nearly all customers qualified for some discount. Offering discounts to all limited the usefulness of the price list as a facilitating device, and the cartel collapsed. Published price lists are a facilitating device, which is especially effective when most transactions occur at list prices. Because price cuts are readily observed in Internet sales, the Internet itself can act as a published price list.

According to Pankaj Ghemawat,[9] General Electric's introduction of a percentage discount off list or book price for the electric turbine business was quickly imitated by rival Westinghouse, and that coordination of prices arose in just one year.

To cooperate on the pricing of differentiated products using published price lists, it is necessary to construct a substitution matrix, which identifies which products are good substitutes for each other. Such a substitution matrix permits the firms to agree on what products ought to be priced the same. The creation of such a list should not be in the hands of any individual firm, as firms have an incentive to distort the list to favor their own products. Thus, an impartial third party, such as an industry association, is a natural candidate to create a substitution matrix. In some cases, a buyers' cooperative will create the list in a misguided attempt to encourage price competition, but instead facilitates price increases by cooperating sellers.

Exclusive Territories

Dividing the market geographically, a strategy used by milk cartels, has the advantage of making it easy to determine that a firm has violated the agreement, and that negotiating on prices is unnecessary. The milk cartel in Texas tended to identify one firm as the winner in a particular geographic area, and other firms were supposed to bid significantly higher. By reducing the need for an agreement or understanding on price, having exclusive territories helps minimize the need to make the bids depend on costs. Exclusive territories inject inefficiency, however, when the identity of the efficient provider varies over time.

A variant on exclusive territories is exclusivity in product. Thus, colluders may divide the market into types of products; for example, Intel agrees not to make software, and Microsoft agrees not to make hardware. Such agreements rarely have lasting effect, because other competitors are induced to enter, and Intel now faces competition from AMD, Cyrix, and other smaller firms.

Preannouncing Future Price Increases

The future will be better tomorrow.

—J. Danforth Quayle

American Airlines has used the "price increase preannouncement" very successfully. The typical announcement, made to the business press, comes in the form "Jet fuel price increases require an increase in ticket prices. In two weeks, our prices will go up 10%. Of course, we have to meet the competition." Then, if Delta and United follow, American goes through with the price increase; otherwise, American withdraws the increase.* Such preannouncements are a means of suggesting cooperative prices, using the business press as a facilitating device. The prewar tobacco industry tended to follow Reynolds to the penny, and the postwar U.S. auto industry is often accused of price leadership. Price leadership, via announcements, is a useful way of talking to competitors without meeting with competitors or entering into agreements.†

The Capture Theory

Nobel laureate George Stigler (1971), with others, invented a model of the interaction of government and industry known as the capture theory. In its simplest form, this theory suggests that the group that cares most about regulation is the regulated industry, and that over time the industry will capture the regulators. Captured regulators will tend to design regulations for the benefit of industry, and, in particular,

*For example, in April 2000, American announced a surcharge increase for freight, but did not implement it when other carriers did not follow suit. It again announced the surcharge increase July 3, scheduled to take effect August 3, and implemented it when other carriers followed suit.

†As with most business strategies, it is a good idea to discuss a proposed strategy with an attorney; an attempt to engage in price leadership could be construed as a violation of the antitrust laws.

what began as consumer protection regulations turn into regulations that prevent entry, soften competition, and benefit the firms at the expense of the consumers.

Perhaps the best example of the capture theory is the capture of the Interstate Commerce Commission (ICC) by the trucking industry. The ICC was originally created in 1887 to assist the railroad industry in establishing profitable, stable prices. Trucking was regulated in 1935, probably as a way of protecting the railroads from trucking competition. Over time, the trucking industry obtained minimum prices and, perhaps most importantly, the creation of significant entry barriers. The minimum rates and entry barriers were such that the elimination of regulation caused a fall of approximately 25% in full-load trucking rates. Prior to the 1980 deregulation that was implemented partially a few years earlier, the ICC prevented entry into trucking by requiring a potential entrant to show that the existing firms could not handle the demand on the route. Trucking firms were prohibited from offering rebates for late delivery or for other performance guarantees. The deregulation of the trucking industry doubled the number of firms, from 16,784 to 33,823 over seven years. Prices and trucking firm costs for full truckloads fell to a quarter of their regulated values. Trucking firm stock values fell 10% to 20%. Most studies find excessive profits accrued to trucking firms during the regulatory period. What began as the suppression of the trucking industry turned into regulation to benefit the trucking industry.[10]

Incrementalism

Sometimes it takes small steps to reach cooperation.[11] Suppose you do not trust your rivals, and they do not trust you. In such a situation, a tacit agreement to divide the market is unlikely to work. However, if you take a small step toward agreement initially, and that step is followed by commensurate steps from your rivals, over time a successful division of the market might arise. For example, American has gradually pulled out of the southern United States (except Miami), closing hubs in Nashville and Raleigh, providing increased dominance to Delta. Delta has reduced its presence in Dallas–Fort Worth (DFW) and other Texas cities like Austin. Had American suddenly withdrawn from the Deep South, it is unlikely Delta would have viewed American's behavior as an offer to trade. Instead, the small steps acted like a series of offers, and cooperation could be accomplished that would have failed with large steps.

The general problem of signaling that a firm is willing to trade will be discussed in chapter 13. Here, the problem is that a withdrawal signals weakness. The incremental trick is to tie withdrawals to entry. Thus, if American shifts flights from the Deep South to the Midwest, and insures that every flight shift meets Delta (i.e., when a terminated flight had competed with Delta, the new flight also competes with Delta), then the signal is not one of fear of competition with Delta but a refocusing of the geographic strategy. That is, by ending a Raleigh/Atlanta flight competing with Delta, and simultaneously starting an additional Austin/DFW flight that also competes with Delta, the "exclusive territory" model of implicit collusion is suggested to Delta. By stopping with one flight until the rival responds, incrementalism insures that all the firms have a shared understanding. Moreover, the risk is reduced by taking small steps. Finally, the simultaneity of the actions, and their relation to each other, can be signaled by making the announcements in the same press release.

Multimarket Contact

> Good fences make good neighbors.
>
> **—Robert Frost**

Firms that compete in several geographic markets can reach implicit understanding with one another by dividing the markets geographically. The tacit agreement is that each firm has its area of dominance, and the other firms should compete weakly or not at all outside their own area. The firms in the Texas milk cartel used geographic location as a means of dividing the market. Geographic division offers a means of clearly delineating the share of each firm.

Geographic market division is employed by waste-management firms (also known as garbage collectors) in many areas of the United States where garbage is not collected by the municipality. Based on its routes and location, each firm has the advantage of serving a distinct region. The firms typically will not agree to serve a customer who is not on a current route. If one firm initiates a new route, the firm whose territory was invaded retaliates by offering its own new route in the territory of the invader. Ultimately, the competition settles down to one or two companies operating on any given street, with very soft price competition separating them.

A similar phenomenon arises in the purchase of wood by pulp mills in the southern United States, which was discussed above. Pulp mills in the South buy a great deal of wood from private landowners, usually by auction. Because the wood is turned into wood chips, it has a relatively low value, and half the cost can be for transportation. Pulp mills understand which firm will likely win a given auction, and learn not to compete too vigorously outside their own region. Ultimately, the only force leading to significant prices is the need to induce landowners to offer the trees on their land for sale, because the firms learn not to compete. As a consequence, typically prices offered are lowest near a pulp mill (where the wood is most valuable due to lower transport costs), and highest about halfway from the nearest pulp mill. This competition is illustrated in figure 6.1. Two pulp mills com-

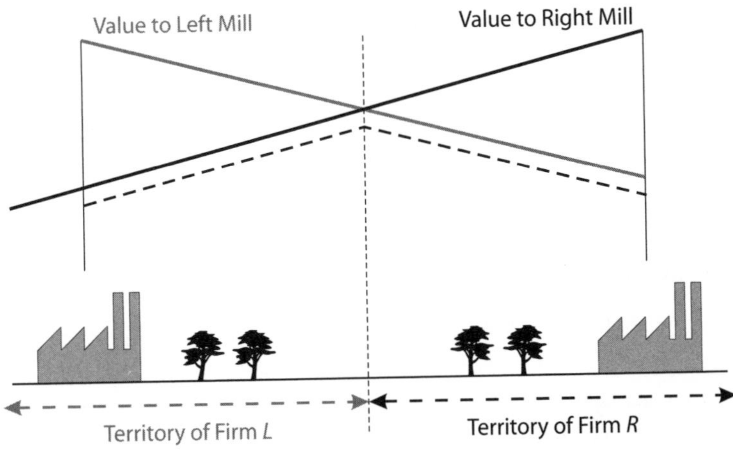

Figure 6.1. Competition between Two Pulp Mills. The value placed on wood by the left mill is denoted in gray, while the value placed by the right mill is denoted in black. Because of transport costs, these values are lower the further the wood is from the mill. Competition produces prices equal to the dashed line—the second highest price. The consequent market territory is denoted below.

pete for the wood for sale in between the two mills. The mills have a value for delivered wood, denoted on the vertical axis directly above the mills (gray line on left, black on right). The value for a particular mill falls as the wood is more distant, owing to transport costs—the value is the delivered value minus the transport cost.

In competition, each mill will pay the value of the competing mill, so that the realized price will be the lower of the two values. (Generally, with more than two mills, it will be the second-highest value.) The price that prevails under competition is denoted with dotted lines, and it is highest in the middle—between the two firms. Even though the value of the closer mill is low at this point, the value of the alternative buyer is higher toward the middle, and thus competition is most intense at the middle.

In such a situation, mills quickly learn which firm is the likely winner. This makes a geographically based market division straightforward; each firm bids in the area it would win anyway, and does not bid aggressively outside its own area. In this way, the price can be lowered to approximately the mill-door price, or "Coca-Cola price," so named because some landowners used to deliver wood themselves on an ancient Coca-Cola truck that had been converted to carry trees.

Geographic competition is the clearest example of multimarket contact easing the difficulties of tacit cooperation, but the principle extends to many other forms of contact. In particular, the apparent agreement of Intel and Microsoft—dividing the computer market into hardware and software—is one of geographic division in a product landscape. Any specialization can serve as a means of softening price competition. For example, Boeing specializes in airframes, while Raytheon specializes in military electronics. While both firms compete on some items such as missiles, the relatively clear distinction between electronics and airframes serves to soften the price competition between the two firms.

Multilevel Contact

Seven firms—Chevron, BP-Amoco-Arco, Exxon Mobil, Tosco, Equilon (Shell and Texaco's joint operation), Valero (which bought assets from Exxon Mobil as part of their merger agreement with the FTC), and Ultramar–Diamond Shamrock—account for 95% of all gasoline retailing in California. The same seven firms also account for over 95% of gasoline refining in California, although the retail shares are usually not the same as the refining shares. Moreover, along with the General American Transportation Exchange (GATX), the same firms account for most of the terminaling facilities—the ports and pipes by which imports are delivered and transported. California gasoline is an example of three levels of vertical contact.

Multilevel contact can be used to facilitate cooperation by reducing the cost of punishment in the event a firm misbehaves. Suppose a company tries to expand its retail sales by price-cutting at the retail level. If the cheating company is a net purchaser of wholesale gasoline, the other firms can reduce their sales of wholesale gasoline, thereby driving up the cost of purchased gasoline by the cheating firm. Such a punishment may have minimal cost to the punisher—the earnings from the increased price at the intermediate level compensate for reduced sales. If the misbehaver is a net supplier of wholesale gasoline, the punishing companies do the opposite, increasing their sales of wholesale gasoline, thereby reducing the profits of the cheating firm. Either way, multilevel contact expands the set of possible punishments dramatically, reducing the cost of punishing most defections. Moreover, multilevel control increases the difficulty of entry. To enter the gasoline business in California, a company must (1) bring gasoline in, (2) find or build a port or negotiate with the sole independent, GATX, and (3) start a retail outlet, either alone or in conjunction with a firm not currently in the gasoline business. While each of these three steps might be feasible individually, the conjunction of them makes entry much more difficult, and perhaps impossible.

Unused Capacity

In the first half of this century, two companies, United Fruit (now Chiquita) and Standard Fruit (now Dole), dominated the importation of bananas into the United

States. These companies excluded rivals by a variety of means, including an attempt to monopolize rail transportation in possible entry sites. But the primary means of insuring cooperation and preventing entry was capacity. Each company had the means of flooding the market within a year. Indeed, each company maintained sufficient land to double its production in one year.

Unused capacity is generally necessary for tacit collusion in price. Such collusion is enforced by an implicit threat to retaliate in the event that a firm fails to follow cooperative pricing. Such retaliation must be sufficiently prompt to be a deterrent, and must be sufficiently inexpensive to be credible. A threat of the form, "If you misbehave, I will build a new unprofitable factory and use its output to bankrupt us both," is hardly credible. Faced with the need to punish, the punisher will likely refuse to carry out the punishment. If, however, the factory is in mothballs, ready to start up at a moment's notice, then the punishment can become credible. Starting up an existing factory is much more reasonable, and may even be profitable, given the misbehavior of a rival.

The ability to divert resources toward punishment may serve as well as unused capacity, and has the advantage of putting the capacity to use. For example, in reaction to the entry of Vanguard Airlines into the DFW–Kansas City route, American Airlines added five low-priced flights on that route. Rather than have unused aircraft sitting in hangars, American could simply divert some aircraft. The key for diversion to work is that the resources are employed in a relatively low value activity, so that diverting them to a low-price market is not too costly.

Capacity should be viewed not just in the form of aircraft and banana lands, but also more broadly. Marketing capacity can serve instead of productive capacity—the key element of punishment is the ability to retaliate against a malefactor at low cost. Indeed, in the situation of brand-name competition, Michael Porter advocates keeping a "fighting brand" on the shelf.[12] A fighting brand is a brand name that gets little marketing but can be quickly promoted as a means of injuring a competitor. The ideal fighting brand is similar to the rival's brand but different from the firm's own major brand, so that promotion of the fighting brand hurts the rival more than the firm itself. Such a construct is unused capacity, with the added benefit that the punishment is inexpensive to apply and therefore more credible.

Grow or Crush Small or Bankrupt Firms

A major problem for tacit collusion is small or, worse still, bankrupt firms. Price wars work poorly against either type of firm. A small firm has little to lose in a price war, having little market share to defend. A bankrupt firm typically is not concerned with a future price war, because its interest is focused mainly on surviving for the next month or two. Consequently, both small and bankrupt firms will rationally take risks that typically set off price wars. Braniff Airlines, for example, flew as a bankrupt carrier for some time, and promoted price competition.

Hastening the demise of nearly bankrupt firms is generally the only successful strategy for dealing with such firms. A price war may be worthwhile if it eliminates the weaker players, permitting the remaining players to cooperate without the hindrance of misbehavior by desperate companies. The logic of such a price war is that the short-term cost is recouped by cooperation later.

With small companies, it may be better to encourage the firms, at least when crushing them is too expensive or impractical. For example, regulators clearly would not let AT&T crush MCI and Sprint in the early days of long-distance competition. Consequently, AT&T's optimal strategy was to encourage these firms to acquire a sufficient market share so that they had something to lose from a price war, and hence would cooperate in setting higher prices. To do so, it is optimal for AT&T to price above the monopoly price for some time, thereby hastening the growth of its fledgling rivals. Once these firms are of sufficient size to have something to lose, AT&T is then in a position to reap high profits via tacit cooperation.

EXECUTIVE SUMMARY—COOPERATION

- Many aspects of business merit cooperation; cooperation is not just about prices.
- Cooperation through tacit collusion requires three elements:
  - A shared interest
  - An ability to detect and punish uncooperative behavior
  - A mechanism for recovering from mistakes
- Cooperation requires that the proceeds of cooperation be shared among the participating parties.
- Punishments need to be:
  - Swift
  - Sufficient to deter misbehavior
  - Credible to impose
- There are many problems to tacitly cooperating in price-fixing, including:
  - Confessions
  - Too many producers
  - Too many products
  - Inability to quickly punish cheating
  - Inability to detect cheating
  - Managers who prefer to avoid jail
  - Unenforceable (illegal) contracts

- Risk associated with communicating
- Small or failing firms with little incentive to participate
- Entry of new firms
- Quality competition
- Inefficient production in order to allocate the proceeds

- Solutions to these problems may involve:
  - Industry associations
  - Published price lists
  - Exclusive territories
  - Announcements of future price increases
  - Government regulation
  - Cooperating in a tit-for-tat manner
  - Cooperation in many markets
  - Cooperation in across the vertical chain
  - Excess capacity

7

Organizational Scope

Organization theory addresses two main questions. First, how should decisions be made? Should a central office make decisions, or should decisions be made locally at far-flung locations? Should a manager tell a worker whether, and how, to fix or replace the worker's broken machine, or should the worker make that determination? Waiting for a manager can be very time consuming and slow the production process down, but granting that authority to the worker may result in more new machines being requested. Should a fast-food franchisee choose the menu and prices, or should the franchiser? Having the McDonald's Corporation choose the menu insures valuable uniformity but eliminates the ability for a restaurant to respond to local tastes and conditions. Centralization of the decision-making process facilitates coordination. However, centralization generally makes it difficult to incorporate local information.

The second main question addressed by organization theory concerns the means of motivating individuals in organizations to achieve high performance. We have met this question already, for one of the problems of centralized organizations is the difficulty in inducing extraordinary performance. The second question of organization theory is the focus of the next chapter (chapter 8), on agency and incentives.

The value of centralization is relatively transparent—decisions can be coordinated to lower costs and improve quality. Coordination permitted General Motors to substantially reduce its costs and successfully compete with the much larger company, Ford, in the 1920s, while maintaining a much larger variety of products than Ford. The merger of Lockheed, which had expertise in stealth-aircraft technology, and Martin-Marietta, a leading producer of missiles, led to the creation of stealth cruise missiles. Wal-Mart reduces its distribution costs by centralizing distribution on a regional basis.

There are two main costs of centralization. One is mistakes—centralization increases the number and cost of mistakes. The retailer Sears, for example, apparently had snowblowers for sale in Puerto Rico. The Chevrolet car named Nova was sold in Puerto Rico with disappointing results, because *no va* in Spanish means "It doesn't go." Chevrolet changed the car's name to Caribe with better results.* Centralization generally forces a "one size fits all" standardized rule on disparate divisions or locales, at the cost of an imperfect fit to every situation. A second problem is that a centralized administration tends to mute individual incentives to produce. In particular, centralization encourages an army of motivationally challenged bureaucrats. It is believed that problems of bureaucracy are the reason that radically new ideas often seem to come from outside of large organizations. Top management often views its own human resources department as an organizational problem that prevents hiring the most talented individuals. The military, with its extraordinary centralization, has produced many striking examples of the mishaps of central authority. In one entertaining incident, an anchor for an aircraft carrier was delivered to the Air Force Academy in Colorado. An aircraft-carrier anchor weighs about fifteen tons, and this one required alteration of the train car just to get it to Colorado. Surprisingly, no one questioned why the Air Force Academy in Colorado needed an anchor, and the culprit was an erroneous parts number. Large organizations create an opportunity to conceal incompetence in the complexity of the organization, and often discourage individual initiative.

Independent bookstores often compete successfully with large chain bookstores in spite of the lower costs and lower prices of the chains. Chains find it difficult or impossible to respond to local market conditions, and, indeed, hire low-paid clerks who are not usually devoted to reading and who may have little idea in what sections of the store Shakespeare and Grisham are to be found. In contrast, owner-operated bookstores pay close attention to what customers are reading, offer service of the "if you liked this, you'll probably like that" variety, and reflect local interests in their selection much more closely than the major chains do. One of the costs of centralization in the bookstore market is the loss of local information, which leaves room for smaller firms.

Clothing retailer Benetton has an interesting mix of centralization and decentralization. All Benetton stores offer the same merchandise, but the automated ordering system keeps track of sales at each retail outlet, and adjusts the quantities

*Although no less an authority than the U.S. Government's Department of Education believes this story to be true, it is remarkably difficult to find a source that doesn't seem like an urban myth, also called a "contemporary legend." Famous urban myths include spider eggs found in Bubble Yum, Exxon dumping gasoline in the desert, and Mrs. Field's (or Neimann Marcus's) $500 cookie recipe. McAfee Associates (no relation to the author) maintains a database of false reports of computer viruses. False reports are considered to be very damaging for the reasons expounded in the fable of the boy who cried wolf.

Box 7.1: Modern Manufacturing

In *Economics, Organization and Management,* Paul Milgrom and John Roberts outline the differences between the classic mass production approach to manufacturing, and the strategy called "modern manufacturing," associated with Toyota and other Japanese firms in the 1970s and 1980s.[1] Milgrom and Roberts emphasize that these approaches are different in a number of self-reinforcing ways, and that either one is a coherent strategy for production. Mass production minimizes average costs, while-modern manufacturing maximizes product value at a reasonable cost.

	Mass Production	*Modern Manufacturing*
Batch Size	Very large	Small
Number of Varieties	Small	Very large
Machines	Specialized, high volume	Flexible
Product Upgrades	Rare	Frequent
Worker Skills	Specialized	Multiple tasks
Inventories	Large	Just-in-time
Compensation	Piece rate, hourly	Based on skills, not job
Decision Centralization	Centralized	More authority at factory floor
Communications	Top down, infrequent	Fast, bidirectional
Subcontracting	Unimportant	Large

Mass production exploits economies of scale, so batch sizes are large. Consequently, extra varieties are relatively costly and there will be few of them. Machines are optimally specialized for the large batches. Upgrades require major retooling and thus are infrequent. Workers can be very specialized under mass production. The loss of one component shuts down an assembly line, so inventories will be large. Workers can be motivated by piece rates, or in the case of fixed assembly line speed, paid hourly. Decisions flow from top management, which coordinates the large production enterprise. Subcontracting is unimportant; indeed, the coordination gains probably outweigh other considerations.

In contrast, modern manufacturing is based on small batch sizes. Small batch sizes permit frequent upgrades, and a large number of relatively specialized product varieties. Machines are made flexible to accommodate the varieties and upgrades. Workers need to be skilled at a variety of tasks. Inventories are small or nonexistent, because product changes make inventories wasteful. With low inventories, workers need to be able to maintain machines themselves, further encouraging wider skills on the factory floor. Since workers fill many roles, compensation is based more on skills than on the job performed. Decisions need to be made quickly, requiring more autonomy and less centralization, and communications need to flow up as well as down, to alert management to changing conditions. Subcontracting becomes more valuable, because new ideas can be incorporated into design more rapidly.

based on past sales. If yellow sweaters sell better in California than in the Northeast, the system automatically routes more yellow sweaters to California and fewer to the Northeast. Such automated responses can reduce the errors that arise in a centralized system.

A basic question of centralization is whether a product should be made inside the firm or outside the firm. This decision is known as the "make-or-buy" choice. Making a product inside the firm brings the ability to tailor the product to the firm's specifications, and keep the profits that might have gone to an independent seller. However, independent sellers have major advantages, including competition, innovation, and strong incentives. Our investigation of organizational design begins with the make-or-buy question.

MAKE OR BUY DECISIONS

Lockheed Martin, one of the three largest defense industry firms, is a "merchant buyer." This means that when one division needs transistors or landing gear, it does not favor the transistors or landing gear produced within Lockheed Martin.

Indeed, each division is encouraged to buy from the supplier offering the best value.

Lockheed's rationale for its merchant-buyer corporate strategy is that each product that Lockheed produces is usually in competition with the products of other companies, where the best product will win the competition. Thus, to choose an inferior internally produced part begs a loss of the overall competition; it is better to use a superior part made by a rival and win the contract than to use an internally produced part and lose the contract. Moreover, to favor internal production, even when possible, is to breed a weak division, one that survives only with the protection of favoritism, and is ultimately not competitive. Thus, Lockheed's merchant-buyer approach favors long-run, strong divisions.*

The merchant buyer approach provides one strategy for the make-or-buy decision, which is a critical component of the decision to centralize or decentralize an organization. First, the merchant-buyer approach decentralizes the decision; each project manager makes the make-or-buy decision. Second, it asks for internally produced parts to be competitive, essentially creating an internal market for parts in which internally produced and externally produced parts compete on an equal footing.

The main reason to buy, rather than make, inputs to the production process is that at some tasks outsiders can do a better job. When a vibrant competitive market exists for a product, it is unlikely that making the product is a good idea. A large competitive market can exploit scale economies, with plants sized to serve many users. Such a market can exploit scope economies, making a large group of related products efficiently. Large scale also permits a larger number of product varieties to exist, and greater specialization in the production process. Moreover, competition can encourage new product development and new cost reduction practices, and ultimately the benefits of lower costs flow to consumers of competitively supplied goods. Thus, when the market for a good is relatively competitive, it is usually best to buy the good. The suppliers will earn low profits, and the prices will approximate cost. For example, computer makers should not be in the business of making paper or boxes or printing their own forms and manuals. These paper items are supplied by intensely competitive markets.

When an input is idiosyncratic or not supplied competitively, it may be profitable to produce the input internally. There are four major reasons for producing goods internally.

*Lockheed is also a merchant supplier—it supplies parts to other competing firms on equal terms. The rationale for being a merchant supplier is that one would rather win a piece of a large contract by supplying a part than lose the entire contract. The problem with the merchant-supplier approach is that there will be circumstances when a company's own technology is sufficiently advanced that it will win the overall contract if it withholds the technology from competitors. Hence, the logic of merchant buyer is very different from the logic of merchant supplier.

- Holdup
- Coordination in production and design, information leakage
- Double marginalization
- Foreclosure

Holdup

The holdup problem is the ability of one party to expropriate the profits of another party, usually by changing the terms of a contract, or because contracts are impossible to write. Thus, the supplier of coal to an electric utility can raise the prices after the utility has sunk half a billion dollars in a coal-burning facility because the next best supplier is far away. The fear of holdup reduces the incentive to invest, and the fear may be eliminated by integrating the supplier and buyer. When a single supplier provides a critical input, there is a justified fear that this supplier will be able to capture most or all of the profits of the downstream organization. Integrating with the supplier can eliminate the threat and fear.

In some instances, it pays to integrate, not because a firm is threatened with holdup but because a firm that it deals with fears holdup. For example, GM wanted Fisher Body, an independent supplier, to build a car body plant contiguous to the GM plant. Fisher declined, perhaps because physical proximity, along with exactly coordinated plans and designs, would make it extremely vulnerable to holdup by GM. Thus, GM integrated with its supplier, not because GM feared holdup but because its partner feared holdup by GM.

Coordination in Production and Design, Information Leakage

If no one makes an input that a firm needs, that firm may be forced to make the product itself. Usually, however, the problem is not that no other firm can make the input, but rather that if another firm invests in the necessary plant and equipment, trains a labor force, develops necessary technology, and creates a design to produce the input, a holdup problem has been created—both companies now have investments specific to the other party.

A closely related problem is that a firm that learns how to produce an input for one firm can sell the technology to competing firms. Moreover, whenever one works with suppliers, some proprietary information will leak out. When information leakage is a major factor, vertical integration or making the product internally mitigates the problem.

An interesting example of information leakage arises with trade secrets. For example, if the Coca-Cola Corporation purchased its Coke inputs from one supplier, that supplier would be able to deduce the ingredients and their proportions. Even with a small number of suppliers, the information about the relative proportions of the ingredients would be held by a small number of people. In such circumstances, vertical integration may be warranted, although using multiple suppliers is usually sufficient.

An interesting example of the flip side of information leakage occurred when the U.S. Department of Defense decided to sponsor a contest to develop a stealth aircraft. The DOD paid for four firms to perform research, with a plan to proceed to develop the best plan or plans; being chosen to develop was the contest prize. For a variety of reasons, including a desire to prevent the Soviet Union from knowing about the development of stealth aircraft, the DOD did not publicize the sponsorship of the research. Lockheed was not one of the four firms picked, because the DOD was unaware of Lockheed's development of stealth technology at its famous Skunkworks facility. Lockheed heard about the research contest and petitioned to be permitted to enter, using Lockheed's own funds.* Lockheed's entry led to the F-117A stealth fighter aircraft (fig. 7.1). Hundreds of these aircraft were produced without informing most of Congress of the plane's existence.

The problem of information leakage has been brought to the public's attention by the "coincidence" of movies with very similar themes coming out within months of each other. Table 7.1 lists some of the similar movies released in the same season. In some cases, such as the asteroid movies, the coincidence was driven by the topic being in the news; in others, lawsuits alleging copyright infringement and theft suggest information leakage was the source of the coincidence.

Information leakage is especially a risk when trade secrets and proprietary formulas or processes are used. At least one cereal manufacturer will not give plant tours, as a means of preventing access to its production methods. Knowledge of a firm's inputs can help rivals deduce information about a firm's production process. Thus, Coca-Cola would like to prevent potential rivals from knowing the complete list of inputs of its proprietary formula. Secret herbs and spices are not too secret to the suppliers, and even well-meaning suppliers will not have the full incentive to protect trade secrets.

Double Marginalization

Beginning around 200 B.C., the Silk Road was the major trading route for silk. Initially, the Silk Road was contained within what is now China, and connected the capital, Chang'Am (now Xi'an), with western provinces. With the rise of the

*The fact that Lockheed got wind of a secret contest is itself an example of information leakage, one that raises doubt about how successful the Pentagon is at keeping secrets. Still, Lockheed managed to keep its development of stealth technology secret from its competitors.

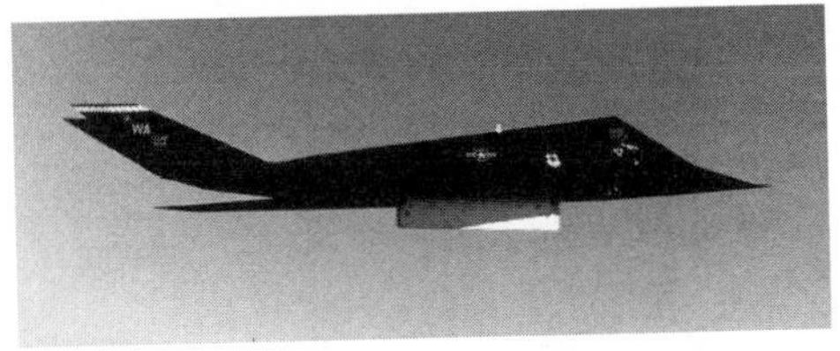

Figure 7.1. The F-117A stealth fighter.

Roman Empire, however, the Silk Road was extended to the Mediterranean Sea and permitted the trade of silk for precious stones, perfumes, medicine, and slaves. The seven-thousand-mile route presented a great number of difficulties for traders, including marauding tribes, vast deserts, disease, and thieves. Not the least of the problems for trade along the Silk Road, however, was double marginalization.

The Parthian empire separated China from the Roman Empire, so Chinese owners of silk did not trade directly with Roman owners of perfumes. As a consequence, trade along the Silk Road generally required the Chinese to trade with Parthians, who traded with Romans. Indeed, the number of middlemen in the process could be much larger. The problem of double marginalization, also known as the "successive monopoly" problem, is that everyone gets a markup, which works like a tax in terms of incentives. With several parties able to take a hefty percentage that they set themselves, the gains from trade between Roman and Chinese

TABLE 7.1
Similar Movies Released at about the Same Time

1991	Robin Hood	Robin Hood—Prince of Thieves
1993	Wyatt Earp	Tombstone
1997	Grosse Pointe Blank	Romy and Michele's High School Reunion
1997	Volcano	Dante's Peak
1998	A Bug's Life	Antz
1998	Armageddon	Deep Impact
1999	Thirteenth Floor	Matrix
2000	Mission to Mars	Red Planet
2000	Sixth Sense	Stir of Echoes

people were weakened, and little trade survived the process. For example, a single intermediary might take 50% of the proceeds, cutting trade to around half what it would be under an unfettered competitive market. With two intermediaries, each able to set the percentage that they took, the first would take half, and the second would take half of what remained, extracting three-quarters of the profit between the two of them. The total volume of trade would fall commensurately. It is easy to see that double marginalization can easily render potentially lucrative trade unprofitable.

Cable television companies sell premium channels like HBO, Showtime, Disney, and the fishing channel to the public, in addition to providing other standard channels. The cable companies are free to charge what the market will bear for the premium content. When a company like HBO contemplates a price decrease for its service, it faces the problem that some of the cable companies will keep part or all of the price decrease. Thus, if HBO charges $5 per subscriber and figures that a $1 price cut would induce a 40% increase in demand, which is profitable, HBO faces the problem of inducing cable companies to pass on the price cut to consumers, when the cable company is more likely to pass on only a fraction of the price cut. As a result, HBO has less incentive to reduce the price than it would if it contracted with customers directly. HBO's price is higher than it would be if HBO were the direct seller to the public. For this reason, Time Warner's ownership of HBO can actually reduce the price of the service to the public. As a major cable provider, Time Warner internalizes the value of increasing the sales, since it makes both the HBO profit and the cable profit. The same logic, however, dictates that Time Warner will have an incentive to favor its subsidiary HBO over rival Showtime, and could even choose not to provide Showtime at any price. Time Warner's ownership of HBO eliminates double marginalization of HBO's price but creates a preference for its own content over content of rivals.

Buying a supplier has a second effect along the lines of elimination of double marginalization—buying a supplier increases the proportion of costs that are fixed. When Amazon buys books from Ingram and other book intermediaries, all of the costs of the books are variable costs, not incurred unless Amazon makes sales. In contrast, when Amazon integrates backward and builds warehouses, computerized inventory systems, and automated mailing robots, all of these costs, as much as 40% of the cost of the book, become fixed costs. The proportion of costs that are fixed rises as the firm integrates vertically. This matters because fixed costs tend to affect pricing in a different way—overall, less than variable costs. Once integrated, Amazon's low marginal costs and high sunk costs will tend to make it more aggressive in pricing and quantity. Such aggression risks a ruinous price war if another firm is in a similar position. Indeed, it may have been Amazon's plan to integrate backward into book supply that prompted Barnes & Noble,

Amazon's chief competitor, to attempt to take over Amazon's largest supplier, Ingram Books.

Foreclosure

Time Warner's merger with America Online received antitrust scrutiny because of the threat that Time Warner would refuse to provide its content to Internet providers other than AOL, or would provide Time Warner content at disadvantageous terms as a way of promoting AOL. Such fears raise the specter of foreclosure, which is the elimination of rivals by a refusal to deal, or of raising rivals' costs, which is the attempt to injure competitors by charging them more for necessary inputs. In the Time Warner/AOL merger, Time Warner is viewed as an input supplier to AOL, providing Time Warner's vast array of content—movies, news, magazines—to the Internet. AOL can use these inputs strategically to harm rivals in the Internet service market. In addition, as a major cable provider, Time Warner is in a position to bundle cable modem service with an AOL Internet connection, thereby promoting AOL in areas where cable modems face few good substitutes.

By far the most interesting reason for a company to buy a supplier and make the product itself is to foreclose a rival from access to the supplier, or to prevent a rival from foreclosing the company's access to supply. Time Warner, which owns HBO, can favor HBO and exclude Showtime from Time Warner cable subscribers. (Typically, Time Warner provides Showtime, owned by rival Viacom, on similar terms as HBO.) In reverse, since HBO is the most popular premium channel, Time Warner can provide HBO to other cable companies at high prices, thereby disadvantaging them.

Computerized reservations systems, like Sabre and Apollo, are used by travel agents (and are now on the Internet) and represent inputs into the airline business, by facilitating the purchase of tickets. Initially, American Airlines's Sabre system favored American flights, in some cases showing American connecting flights in preference to competing nonstop flights. After a legal dispute, American agreed to use an impartial point system to determine which flights would be listed first. A second round of legal disputes revealed that American's point system favored flights that connected through Dallas or Chicago, American Airlines's two largest hubs, and especially disadvantaged Denver, a United Airlines hub. American agreed to a more impartial determination of the points. American's parent company has since sold the Sabre system.

In some cases, it makes sense to purchase a supplier to prevent a rival from foreclosing opportunities. Multimedia companies, like Disney and AOL Time Warner, have used this logic to justify massive vertical integration into delivery of entertainment to the consumer.

Tapered Integration

In some cases, it makes sense to make and to buy simultaneously, a system known as tapered integration. Automakers use tapered integration for two distinct reasons. The ability to internally produce parts provides valuable information about costs of external suppliers and permits the automaker to prevent holdup by suppliers. Thus, GM can quickly move to produce a part that is currently supplied by a poorly performing company. Internal production capacity disciplines the external suppliers, providing a credible threat by the buyer of its willingness and ability to produce. Internal production capacity is especially valuable when there are only a few potential suppliers, each with substantial market power.

Why not produce all the inputs internally, if there is external market power? External purchases discipline internal divisions. An internal division that is needed may become inefficient and lazy in the absence of market discipline. External purchases provide a reference point, so that a poorly performing internal division is quickly and readily identified, allowing management replacement, new investment, and other changes to happen in a timely manner. Tapered integration can often provide the benefits of both internal and external production, creating the benefits of competition, restraining holdup by external suppliers, and exploiting valuable coordination between the internal supply division and the downstream business unit.

What does tapered integration cost? Suppose the scale economy is 2.5%. This means that a doubling of output, a 100% increase, reduces average cost by $0.025 \times 100\% = 2.5\%$, which is a modest but significant economy of scale. Consider having 10% of production done in house. Since 100% is ten times 10%, producing 10% of the output in house costs 25% more per unit. Ninety percent is 10% less than 100%, so 90% costs 0.25% more per unit. Overall, the average cost of producing 10% in house and 90% externally will be

$$10\% \times 25\% + 90\% \times 0.25\% = 2.725\%.$$

That is, with a scale economy of 2.5%, producing 10% in house costs about 2.7% more. Is this a good deal? If the internal production permits negotiating a 3% price decrease on the external production, the internal production will pay for itself in enhanced bargaining power. Such a significant decrease in price is likely when the external production is supplied by a monopoly, or by a few firms with market power. Indeed, the discipline of internal production might account for a 10% decrease in the external price, more than compensating for the increase in average costs.

Informational Issues

A major motivation for GM's purchase of Ross Perot's Electronic Data Systems Corporation was the perceived benefit GM could receive from the electronics expertise of EDS. When Barnes & Noble attempted to purchase Ingram Books, the information that Ingram received by selling to Barnes & Noble's competitors who were well informed about local conditions would become available to Barnes & Noble. Similarly, the Lockheed Martin–Marietta merger permitted the companies to share secrets about both stealth and missile technology.

Prevention of information leakage and acquisition of information are important reasons to produce internally. However, managing a large-scale, far-flung enterprise has significant difficulties of its own. Not only is there Sears's problem of snowblowers being offered for sale in Puerto Rico, but mechanisms need to be in place to provide management with appropriate information. It is not merely a question of how to produce incentives for information to be provided, but how to limit the information so that important information is not lost in a flood of extraneous, irrelevant detail. Managing information flow is a challenging task for modern organizations. The revolution in information technology has not made the problem easier, but it has made it more important. Reductions in the cost of providing information exacerbate the problem of information overload, and make it more difficult to identify significant developments and facts. As part of their answer to the FTC's request for information related to their proposed merger, Exxon and Mobil produced over 25,000 bankers' boxes of documents, representing perhaps as much as 100 million pages of information. The *index* of these documents ran thousands of pages, and an index to the index was needed. Management of such a conglomerate requires not just a means of getting relevant information, but the ability to screen out unnecessary detail. How will 100 million pages of information be processed and used? How will this information be incorporated into decisions?

In off-shore oil auctions, firms sometimes participate in consortiums that bid jointly. It should come as no surprise that consortium members have submitted independent bids on the same tract, thereby bidding against themselves. Such bids are often mistakes, created by two different branches of the organization.

Corporate Cultures

Firms with very different cultures often have great difficulty merging. Distinct cultures are a very important reason why a firm might choose to buy, rather than make, an input. Indeed, fitting the culture to the production process is an important aspect of business strategy that is partially explored, in a very limited way, as an issue in multi-tasking, discussed below.

There have been some very high-profile clashes of corporate culture. The merger of GM and EDS was stormy for its entire duration and ultimately ended in divorce. These organizations have very different cultures. GM was hierarchical and paid employees primarily with salary or hourly compensation, while EDS was less hierarchical and used incentive compensation extensively. Sony and Columbia Pictures experienced similar trouble, allegedly over Sony's difficulty in understanding that entertainment professionals should not be treated like employees. IBM's takeover of telephone equipment maker Rolm created similar problems. Internet auction company eBay's takeover of tony auction house Butterfield's did not extend eBay's influence into art and antiques as desired. In all of these cases, the organizations that had evolved to solve particular production and development problems were very different, and clashed mightily when the merger took place.

THE MULTIDIVISIONAL FIRM

Committee—a group of men who individually can do nothing but as a group decide that nothing can be done.

—Fred Allen

In the decade after World War I, four companies developed a new management technology for managing large conglomerates. Those firms were General Motors, DuPont, Sears Roebuck, and Standard Oil of New Jersey (Exxon). When Sears Roebuck moved from being a mail-order company to operating retail stores, it needed a new approach to management. The central warehouse that served the mail-order business so well did not work well for geographically dispersed retail stores. General Motors attempted to centralize some aspects of its automobile business, so that R&D and parts production were not unnecessarily duplicative and exploited scale economies associated with integrated operations, while still encouraging individual car marques to compete on quality and innovate. GM aimed to provide a vast array of products at reasonable prices, to compete with Ford's low-cost, one-size-fits-all approach. After the court-mandated 1911 breakup of the Standard Oil Trust, Standard Oil of New Jersey decided that a vertically integrated company that controlled production, refining, and distribution was the optimal competitive vehicle. The company embarked upon the creation of the first fully integrated oil field-to-consumer company, which meant managing very disparate operations—oil exploration, drilling, pipelines and transportation, refining, and retail sales—over a wide geographic area. This required a new approach to management and operations control. Finally, DuPont's explosives business, built up during World War I, had very different customers than its paints and consumer chemicals business, necessitating very different management approaches within the same organization. In all four cases, the companies developed what has become known as the multidivisional firm.

Multidivisional firms are organized into divisions based on one or more criteria, usually one of

- Product divisions; e.g., appliances, consumer electronics
- Customer divisions; e.g., military and civilian aircraft
- Technological divisions; e.g., aircraft, electronics
- Geographical divisions; e.g., by state, by nation, by region

Divisions have a substantial amount of autonomy, operating essentially as independent firms. Such divisions with nearly complete autonomy are known as business units. For example, GM's various car divisions, including GMC, Chevrolet, Pontiac, Oldsmobile, Buick, and Cadillac, operate as separate companies for marketing, pricing, and sales, but share some production and R&D. Thus, GM operates divisions based on customer type. Boeing also has aircraft divisions based on customer type—military and civilian. In contrast, Sony divisions tend to be based on products, with consumer electronics, electric parts, and movies in separate divisions. Sony also operates divisions based on the continent in which they are located. Most companies that operate worldwide have divisions based on nations or continents. In order to comply with local laws, and to handle time zones and languages, it helps to have a division that specializes in each nation or in a small group of nations.

Multidivisional firms offer a means of breaking management problems into manageable portions by dividing the firm into smaller divisions, each of which is managed like a separate enterprise, subject to some overall direction from top management.

The most difficult problem associated with the multidivisional firm is a problem of setting transfer prices: How is one business unit, which provides an input to another unit, to be compensated? Consider the business unit, Autolite, that produces alternators for Ford. Suppose Autolite can make alternators for $40 each and has a fixed cost of around $20 per alternator. Ford should use its own alternators when the market provides them for more than $40, but Ford saves money by switching to an outside supplier when the price of that supplier is less than $40. Thus, in order to get Mercury or another division to make the correct decision about the use of Autolite alternators, the correct price is the marginal cost, $40. At that price, however, Autolite loses money, and if compensated at a rate of $40, Autolite cannot afford to make any investments. In order to get Autolite to make sensible investments in fixed costs, the right price for it to receive is the outside market price, say $65. This is a general problem; the transfer price that makes the buying unit make the right decisions is marginal cost, while the transfer price that makes the selling unit make the correct decisions is the average cost of outside competitors, which is larger than marginal cost.

There is no definitive solution to the problem of setting transfer prices. Many companies use average cost, a decision that has three major defects. First, the selling unit makes no profit. This can be fixed by providing a modest markup over cost, in which case the selling unit's profit can go up as its costs rise. Second, average cost does not guide the investment decisions of the selling unit in any sensible way. Third, the incentives of the buying unit are also distorted, because the buying unit is paying sunk average costs on a marginal basis.

Other companies use, where possible, the outside market price (or the avoided costs) as the transfer price. This approach generally provides good incentives to the selling unit. Moreover, the incentives of the buying unit are not too bad, because the buying unit is paying what it would pay even if it did not buy internally. The typical problem here is when the buying unit is forced to do business with the selling unit, in which case the selling unit can provide a shoddy product at the market price of a higher-quality one. This seems to have been the case with Lucas Electric, the electrical parts supplier for British Leyland. Lucas is credited with giving Jaguar its reputation for unreliability. The unreliability of Lucas was the basis of the following joke:

Q: Why is there no ice available for drinks in England?
A: Lucas freezers.

The problem with Lucas was corrected by buying from German supplier Bosch. In response to declining sales, Lucas's quality improved.

Using market prices or avoided costs helps provide good incentives to the selling units without making buying units make serious mistakes. However, buying units are not capturing all the profits they are generating, because some of these profits are captured by the selling unit. Consequently, any transfer pricing scheme will tend to induce some business unit to underinvest and sell too little. *Often, this problem of inadequate incentives is the reason the two business units are in the same firm in the first place*: there was a problem with a market solution that could be mitigated or solved by integration of the operations. Thus, replication of the marketplace inside the firm is rarely a full solution to the management of complex enterprises—other command and control mechanisms are needed.

Divisionalization

Divisionalization refers to the use of multiple corporate divisions as a means of committing to a greater output. There is an enormous overlap between car models sold by distinct divisions of the major U.S. manufacturers, including similar models by Chevrolet and Pontiac, by Ford and Mercury, and by Plymouth and Dodge. The similarity in the offering of these divisions seems too great to justify multiple divisions unless there is another purpose. One candidate explanation is that multiple divisions will naturally choose a larger output than a single division would choose.

The parent company might want to commit to greater output in order to forestall entry, to discourage rival investment, or to encourage rivals to reduce output.[2] The use of multiple divisions accomplishes this goal when the managers of the divisions are compensated based on the profitability of the division. Managers within the same parent company will behave as if the division were an independent firm when their profitability determines compensation, and consequently the proliferation of divisions acts like an increase in the number of firms, generally increasing industry output.

Franchised fast-food operations are often geographically close to each other. The franchise faces a trade-off in the location of franchises. By spreading the franchises far apart, the average profitability of the franchises increases, increasing the overall profitability and hence the amount the franchise can extract from each firm. However, spreading the franchises increases the profitability of entry by competing franchises. Consequently, the franchise has an incentive to pack the franchisees more tightly than is efficient, as a means of deterring entry of competitors.

Divisionalization is a strategy for insuring an output larger than a single firm would select. When divisionalization succeeds in deterring rivals from expanding or induces exit, divisionalization can be profitable; some of the increased output is offset by reductions of competitors' outputs, and thus the increased output has a more limited effect on price than demand would indicate. In contrast, when the divisionalization fails to induce contraction by rivals, it is costly for the entire industry. Divisionalization as a strategy carries the risk that competitors will imitate it, and every firm will be worse off. However, when a firm is first into a market that can sustain multiple firms, divisionalization offers a strategy to reduce the number of entrants, and may be profitable overall.

TRANSACTION COSTS

The transaction costs approach to understanding markets and organizations was invented by Nobel laureate Ronald Coase,[3] and developed by Professor Oliver Williamson.[4] In its roughest form, the transaction costs approach to organizations dictates that the design of organizations, firms, and contracts minimizes the costs associated with production and trade. In particular, organizations will be designed to minimize transaction costs, although the methods of production sometimes affect transaction costs, and thus such costs usually cannot be minimized without consideration of all costs. Transaction costs include costs of writing contracts and of managing teams of workers, but they also include the costs of providing incentives, costs of assessing worker performance, and costs of workers angling for perks. The transaction-costs approach provides an alternative view of the design of organizations, one encompassing the make-or-buy centralization issue and agency approaches.

The transaction-costs approach to analyzing the performance of organizations requires an accounting of all the transaction costs, and consideration of alternative organizational arrangements that might reduce the transaction costs. A major benefit of the transaction-costs approach is the attention paid to costs that are difficult to measure and that are not just obvious, quantifiable costs. In many cases, substantial real costs are ignored by a standard analysis. On the other hand, the emphasis on difficult-to-quantify costs necessarily means that predictions are qualitative, and bottom-line implications are generally no better than guesses.

There is no consensus of how to categorize transaction costs, and all authors seem to have their own list. Some authors are very vague, with a couple of uselessly large categories. Others omit significant categories of costs associated with performing transactions. The following eleven categories represent an attempt to provide a useful list of significant costs that is comprehensive and without redundancies.

- Specialized investments and holdup costs
- Coordination costs
- Motivation and incentive costs
- Information acquisition costs
- Information processing costs
- Contracting costs
- Search costs
- Enforcement costs
- Bargaining costs
- Measurement costs
- Influence and lobbying costs

Some transaction costs create direct monetary costs, others lower the value of output, still others impose delay or loss of goodwill. The type of expense is not categorized.

Specialized Investments and Holdup Costs

Specialized investments—investments useful for a specific party and no others—create a significant risk of holdup. Consequently, specialized investments can create major transaction costs through the fear of holdup. The presence of specialized investments insures that markets are "thin," involving only one other party. The holdup risk created reduces incentives to invest, and creates incentives to protect against holdup. For example, internal production capacity may be maintained expensively to mitigate the bargaining power of a supplier.

Coordination Costs

Coordination costs include the management time spent coordinating the activities of various people and enterprises. For an automobile manufacturer, coordination costs include all those costs required to insure that parts fit together and that the final product works as desired. Moreover, the coordination costs include the efforts required to insure that assembly lines move smoothly, that the output of one workstation is transferred to the next workstation, that adequate inventory exists so that each worker is not idled for lengthy periods, and that all of the efforts required to insure that complex teams perform as desired are being made.

Motivation and Incentive Costs

We will meet, in the next chapter, the costs of providing incentives in the form of a risk premium that needs to be paid to compensate for the increased risk associated with incentive compensation. In addition to the direct costs such as the risk premium, incentive costs include the management and accounting required to operate these compensation schemes. Moreover, incentive compensation requires measuring performance, which can be attributed to a cost of providing incentives, or directly as a measurement cost.

Information Acquisition Costs

A great deal of information is expensive to obtain. Information that is "free," such as state regulations governing the operation of retail stores, nevertheless needs to be obtained from the relevant state agencies, checked for accuracy, and summarized in a useful manner. Other information, such as the estimate of the value of oil in a tract up for bid, the likely number of competitors for a new technology, or the cost of building a nuclear reactor, might require expensive studies.

It is a mistake, often a very large mistake, to view information held by the firms' own employees as free. Extracting information held by employees is generally costly. Project managers for major mining companies have a strong tendency to overstate the attractiveness of the project they are proposing, because their careers will be more likely to prosper the more projects they oversee. Similarly, the managers of bidding for spectrum for the offering of new wireless phones faced a moral hazard problem—if they did not bid, they looked like losers. If they bid and won, no one would know for a decade whether they had paid too much. As a consequence, winning in the auction looked attractive no matter what the price. Inducing honesty in such a situation requires offering a bonus (perhaps in the form of an alternative project to manage) to managers who recommend *against* pursuing projects; that is, it is costly to induce honesty.

Information Processing Costs

While useful information is costly to obtain, processing of information is also a costly endeavor, and is growing ever more costly as information technology makes the provision of raw data cheaper and more prevalent. Indeed, managing the processing of information has become a major challenge.

Contracting Costs

These costs include the costs of writing contracts and employing attorneys.

Search Costs

There are returns to searching—lower input prices, buyers willing to pay higher prices for output. Search costs can be substantial, especially when looking for a product in a foreign country.

Finding suitable employees is such a significant challenge that firms often contract with other firms for the provision of employees. Moreover, as part of the provision of temporary employees, temp agencies generally have a charge if the employees leave to go permanently to the company that hired them as temps. Such charges reflect the very real costs of searching for employees. Included in these search costs would be the costs of checking references and administering tests, and perhaps even attempting trial employment.

Enforcement Costs

Contracts give rise to failure to perform. Enforcement of contracts, and of penalties for nonperformance, often involves the use of expensive attorneys and can easily cost a significant amount. Penalties for contract breach, a significant aspect of enforcement costs, will be considered in chapter 14.

Box 7.2: Transaction Costs Analysis in Action

How does the modern manufacturing approach to organization stack up against the mass production approach in terms of the incurred levels of transaction costs?

	Mass Production	*Modern Manufacturing*
Specialized Investments	High	Low
Coordination	Medium	Very high
Incentive	Low	Medium
Information Extraction	Low	High
Information Processing	Low	Very high
Contracting	Medium	High
Search	Low	High
Enforcement	High	Medium
Bargaining	High	Medium
Measurement	High	Medium or high
Influence	High	Low

The modern manufacturing approach to production, in most areas, has much higher transaction costs per unit produced, because it relies on information technology. Indeed, the modern approach did not become feasible until improvements in information technology made the kinds of coordination, information processing, and measurement costs sufficiently low. Only in areas where the very size of the enterprise makes costs large—bargaining and influence—does mass production have higher costs.

However, modern manufacturing is designed to lower these costs. Employees are paid based on skills rather than the job to lower both incentive, information extraction, and influence costs.

Employees are given more authority to reduce information extraction costs.

Support for some of these entries can be found in Curtis Taylor and Steve Wiggins, "Competition or Compensation: Supplier Incentives under the American and Japanese Subcontracting Systems," *American Economic Review* 87, no. 4 (September 1997): 598–618.

Bargaining Costs

Negotiation takes time and is often quite costly. The costs created by bargaining—either in the market or within the firm—are significant costs that are affected by organizational arrangements.

Measurement Costs

Production, raw materials, workers' hours, failure rates of goods and many other items all need to be measured. Workers who are paid piece rates need their hours monitored. Hourly workers also need their hours monitored—to insure that they work the number of hours for which they are paid, and are paid for the number of hours that they work, as underpayment could incur Department of Labor sanctions. Products designed to meet specific quality standards must be tested for quality. For example, a natural-gas pipeline that carries gas for a variety of producers must verify that each company puts in gas of similar quality. Some companies inserting gas into the pipeline have an incentive to insert low-quality gas, since the gas is blended by the pipeline. Such a cost is mitigated when the pipeline is vertically integrated and carries only its own gas. Measurement costs are both real and large.

Influence and Lobbying Costs

Everyone rises to their level of incompetence.

—The Peter Principle, Dr. Lawrence J. Peter

I don't want any yes-men around me. I want everybody to tell me the truth even if it costs them their jobs.

—Samuel Goldwyn

A major source of transaction costs was first described by Paul Milgrom,[5] and involves the costs of employees angling for better jobs, manipulating or gaming the system, and extracting resources from organizations. Jobs carry perks and nuisances—good or bad locations, nice surroundings, hazardous working conditions, travel—that make them more desirable or less desirable. These job attributes are usually not priced by the company, so that employees care about their job assignment.* The desirability of certain jobs over others leads employees to invest in trying to influence the decisions of the firm in ways that benefit the employee but not the firm. Such attempts to manipulate the firm's decisions will tend to distort the decisions away from profit maximization, and will waste valuable employee and management time.

Influence costs are a consequence of size and centralization of firms. The larger the firm, the more discretion that can be wielded. The more centralized the operations, the more susceptible is management to attempts to influence costs. Moreover, the more centralized the operations, the larger the difference that influence efforts can make to the organization. Influence costs are generally increased by merger and vertical integration.

The faster the change in an environment, the more serious the influence cost problem, because external change means the firm needs to change to keep up. The problem with change is the group that is well positioned risks losing this good position, and the group that is poorly positioned has a chance to change that condition, so both groups tend to fight hard. With a rapidly changing external environment, the optimal firm scale typically shrinks, as a way of minimizing influence costs. Large firms caught in rapidly changing environments often have difficulty adapting; witness the problems of Sears, IBM, and the Soviet Union.

Firms counter influence costs by restricting the authority and discretion of decision makers. As a means of mitigating influence costs, American Airlines assigns flight attendants to routes according to their expressed preferences and seniority, following a nondiscretionary rule.

Increasing the costs of influencing decisions will not necessarily reduce influence costs, although it does reduce the quantity of effort devoted to influencing outcomes. In the war of attrition model studied in chapter 14, an increase in the costs of battle has no effect on the total costs of the war. More generally, increasing the costs of influence activities can either increase or decrease the total waste arising from influence efforts.

One common means of restricting or reducing influence activities is to use a group of outsiders to provide advice on key decisions. The advantage of outsiders, usually management consultants, is that they offer unbiased, fresh opinions and have no vested interests or hidden agenda. Moreover, management consultants

*An interesting exception involves the pricing of premium offices by the Economics Department at Arizona State University, which auctions the offices annually. See William J. Boyes and Stephen K. Happel, "Auctions as an Allocation Mechanism in Academia: The Case of Faculty Offices," *Journal of Economic Perspectives* 3, no. 3 (Summer 1989): 37–40.

often bring a perspective unavailable from within the firm, a perspective that arises out of experience with a variety of firms, including the company's competitors. Besides the significant expense of hiring management consultants, there is usually a certain amount of undesirable information leakage. Management consultants may learn some of the best practices of a firm but will take that information with them when they leave and may divulge these practices to other clients, some of whom may be competitors. Thus, use of management consultants involves both gains and losses.

Transaction Costs Summary

Organizational design should account for transaction costs—setting discretion, authority, and communication in order to mitigate these costs. Because so many of the costs are difficult to quantify, the transaction-costs approach is often qualitative in nature. Alternative organizational arrangements can be assessed to determine the relative levels of each of the costs, but an assessment of the absolute levels is usually impossible.

PRICES OR QUANTITIES

Nobel laureate Ronald Coase's view of the choice to direct production inside the firm, or to use markets, was that the decision was determined by cost minimization, or value maximization.[6] An alternative view, promoted by Professor Martin Weitzman,[7] is that the decision to centralize involves deciding between a choice of a price mechanism or a quantity mechanism. Within a firm, the firm can just order the quantity desired independently of the price system used by markets. In contrast, when using a market to decide, prices determine decisions. In Weitzman's view, such a decision hinges on a review of the mistakes that are made by the two systems, with the choice to internalize production arising when the errors of a command system have smaller impact than the errors of a price system.

If markets are perfect, then there is no question that the market decisions are efficient, so the question concerning the choice of using markets versus internal production must be made to resolve some inefficiency in the market. Weitzman posits that whether prices or quantities are used, they must be set prior to the resolution of market uncertainty. Here, I present a simplified version of Weitzman's theory.

Suppose that there are only two possible supply curves, represented in figure 7.2 by S_H and S_L, and a demand curve represented by D. The best outcome would be to have the price and quantity represented by the intersections of the supply curves and demand, depending on which one was relevant. However, if the decision—either price or quantity—must be made first, which is better?

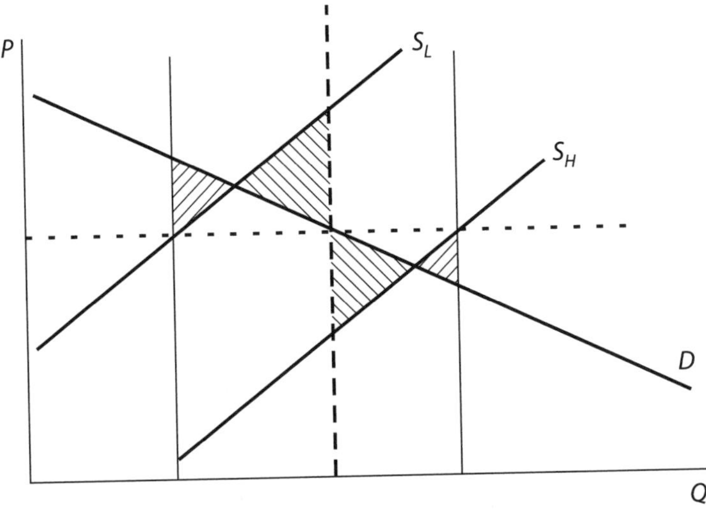

Figure 7.2. A graphical analysis of prices versus quantities.

When prices are used to direct decisions, suppliers in competition produce at the point where the price equals the supply. Consider the dotted horizontal line, which reflects a price in between the two desired outcomes. When supply is low at S_L, there is too little output and the price is too low. This gives a loss equal to the area of the left triangle—shaded with upward sloping lines—which is the value (demand) minus cost (supply) of units that were efficient to produce, but were not produced because the price was too low. The case of high supply, S_H, is exactly analogous. Here, the supply is large, and the price is too high. Too many units are produced—the quantity (illustrated with a solid vertical thin line) is larger than the efficient quantity. The rightmost triangle is the loss arising from the production of units that cost more than they are worth to the company.

Similarly, when quantities are used to determine the outcome, the quantity must be set prior to the resolution of uncertainty. The vertical dashed line is a quantity that balances the loss in the high state from the loss in the low state. When supply is low at S_L, too much is produced, and the second-from-left triangle represents the loss created by producing units whose marginal cost exceeded their value. Similarly, in the high state of supply, too little is produced, and the lower triangle illustrates the value of the production that was lost.

Thus, the question of whether prices are preferred to quantities boils down to the question of whether the leftmost and rightmost triangles, together, are smaller than the combined inside triangles. As drawn, this is certainly true. However, notice that as demand becomes more vertical, pivoting around the center point, the inside triangles shrink, while the outside ones grow; clearly, it could go either way. With a modicum of Euclidean geometry, it is possible to see that the outside triangles are smaller whenever demand is flatter than supply. In this case, prices minimize the loss; otherwise, using quantities is preferable.*

Intuitively, when demand is very elastic—a large-quantity response for minor changes in price—it is better to set the price at approximately the right level and let the quantity be optimally supplied; only a minor mistake is made, because the demand is flat around the price. In contrast, when supply is very elastic and demand is not so elastic, the mistake that is made by setting price is large; essentially demand is dictating the quantity (from its inelasticity).

It might appear that absence of demand variation matters to the theory, but that is not so. Demand variation introduces additional losses to both price setting and quantity setting, but these losses are the same for both systems and do not favor one system over another. Neither demand nor supply variation favor the choice of prices versus quantities; what matters is the relative elasticity.

How does Weitzman's analysis help us understand the design of organizations? When demand is relatively elastic, prices are favored. Hence, either markets internal to the firm or subcontracting is preferred when demand is relatively flat. Conversely, when supply is relatively elastic, prices induce large over-responses in quantity, and quantity-based mechanisms are better. The analysis suggests that internal transfer pricing, or markets, are better with elastic demand.

NET PRESENT VALUE

How should projects for a firm to carry out be selected? Our analysis thus far has focused only on the question of whether projects should be carried out within the firm or be subcontracted to other firms. But which projects should be undertaken at all? The standard, most common approach is that of net present value (NPV). Calculate the present value of the project's costs and revenues, and undertake the project if it has a positive NPV. This section reviews NPV and discusses its utility and flaws in comparison to alternatives.

Receiving money in the future is not as good as receiving money now. At a minimum, with the money now, one can invest it in interest-bearing accounts and have more money in the future. To convert money that comes in the future into money today, one must discount the future sum by the appropriate rate of interest, which is known as finding the present value.

For example, at 10% per year, $100 becomes $110 in one year, and that $110

*Specifically, when the slope of demand plus the slope of supply is positive, prices are preferred; otherwise, quantities are preferred.

becomes \$121 a year after that. Thus, at 10%, \$100 today produces \$121 in two years. At the same interest rate, then, a rock-solid promise (e.g., a U.S. bond) paying \$121 in two years is equivalent to \$100 today. More generally, if r is the interest rate (10% = 0.1), the future value after n years of a sum of money equal to PV today is

$$FV_n = PV(1 + r)^n.$$

One obtains the formula for present value by dividing by the compound interest term:

$$PV = \frac{FV_n}{(1+r)^n}.$$

When the interest rate varies, the logic is the same, but the expression is more complex. For example, if the interest rate is r_1 in the first year, r_2 in the second year, and so on, the future value will be

$$FV_n = PV(1 + r_1)(1 + r_2) \ldots (1 + r_n).$$

When one receives a sequence of payments, the present value of those payments is the sum of the present values of each of the individual payments. Consider, for example, a lottery that pays \$1 million in each of twenty years, with the first payment arriving immediately, the second one year after, and so on. At a fixed interest rate of r, this lottery payment has the present value of

$$PV = \$1M + \frac{\$1M}{1+r} + \frac{\$1M}{(1+r)^2} + \frac{\$1M}{(1+r)^3} + \ldots + \frac{\$1M}{(1+r)^{19}} = \$1M\frac{1+r}{r}\left[1 - \frac{1}{(1+r)^{20}}\right].$$

How much is the lottery worth? Table 7.2 provides the answer for a variety of interest rates, and suggests that many lotteries are misleading when they advertise their payouts. Even at 6%, the payout is worth \$12 million, not the \$20 million a lottery would typically proclaim.

An important feature of the present-value calculation is that it can be run in reverse. Thus, start with \$12,158,116.49 invested at 6%, and one can pay out \$1 million per year for twenty years. That calculation is illustrated in table 7.3. We start the process on January 1 of the year, make a payment on January 2, then collect 6% interest over the course of the year.

Table 7.3 illustrates how one can invest \$12,158,116.49 at 6% and produce the lottery stream of payments—\$1 million per year for twenty years. The first

TABLE 7.2
Present Value of a $20 Million Lottery

Interest Rate	4%	6%	8%	10%	15%	20%
PV of Lottery (000s)	$14,134	$12,158	$10,604	$9,365	$7,198	$5,844

column gives the year. The second column shows the status of the account on the first of the year, prior to the payment. This balance starts at the present value of $12,158,116.49. A payment is made, so the balance drops by $1 million, to $11,158,116.49. A year later, 6% interest on $11,158,116.49 has been collected, so the balance now stands at $11,827.603.48. Then another payment is made, and so on. As the table illustrates, this process continues for twenty years, when the last payment is made and the account is exhausted.

Generally, losses and expenditures enter the present value as negative numbers, and no other change is necessary. The exception to this rule arises when borrowing and saving require different interest rates. For example, an individual who earns 6% on saving but pays 11% on credit cards would need to use a more complex formula that would keep track of whether the individual was a net borrower.

Consider a mining company that finances investment out of retained earnings, which are either invested in mines or in other investments. The company investigates a silver mine site and establishes that, after an immediate investment of $2 million, followed by $1 million each in the years one, two, three, and four, the mine will start to produce silver, and will produce $750,000 per year for each of the subsequent forty years. How much is this project worth? Should the company undertake the project? Using lottery logic, an expenditure of $6 million produces revenue of $30 million, which is logic that explains why the government cannot successfully run a mining operation.

The workhorse of capital budgeting is the net-present-value approach. This approach dictates finding the net present value of the project, and undertaking the project if the net present value is positive. As in any present-value calculation, the net present value will depend on the interest rate used. Table 7.4 sets out the return on the silver mine for several interest rates.

The net present value of the project can be calculated (in $ millions) as

$$NPV = -2 + \frac{-1}{(1+r)} + \frac{-1}{(1+r)^2} + \frac{-1}{(1+r)^3} + \frac{-1}{(1+r)^4} + \frac{0.75}{(1+r)^5} + \ldots + \frac{0.75}{(1+r)^{44}}.$$

Table 7.4 shows that the silver mine earns a handsome profit at 5%, breaks about even at 10%, and loses a substantial amount of money at 15%. This is the

TABLE 7.3
The Lottery Run in Reverse

Year	*Balance on Jan 1*	*Balance on Jan 2*
2001	$12,158,116.49	$11,158,116.49
2002	$11,827,603.48	$10,827,603.48
2003	$11,477,259.69	$11,477,259.69
2004	$11,105,895.27	$10,105,895.27
2005	$10,712,248.99	$9,712,248.99
2006	$10,294,983.93	$9,294,983.93
2007	$9,852,682.96	$8,852,682.96
2008	$9,383,843.94	$8,383,843.94
2009	$8,886,874.58	$7,886,874.58
2010	$8,360,087.05	$7,360,087.05
2011	$7,801,692.27	$6,801,692.27
2012	$7,209,793.81	$6,209,793.81
2013	$6,582,381.44	$5,582,381.44
2014	$5,917,324.33	$4,917,324.33
2015	$5,212,363.79	$4,212,363.79
2016	$4,465,105.61	$3,465,105.61
2017	$3,673,011.95	$2,673,011.95
2018	$2,833,392.67	$1,833,392.67
2019	$1,943,396.23	$943,396.23
2020	$1,000,000.00	$0.00

nature of mining—most of the costs occur up front, and substantial earnings occur decades out. Thus, the economics of mining are unusually sensitive to interest rates. Figure 7.3 illustrates the NPV as a function of the interest rate. The vertical axis is the net present value, in millions. The horizontal axis is the interest rate, expressed in proportion (10% = 0.1). As the interest rate rises, the distant profits

TABLE 7.4
Return on a Silver Mine

	Amount Per Year	Amounts (000s) r = 5%	r = 10%	r = 15%
Year 0	−$2,000	−$2,000	−$2,000	−$2,000
Year 1–4	−$1,000	−$3,546	−$3,170	−$2,855
Year 5–44	+$750	$10,588	$5,009	$2,848
Net Present Value		$5,042	−$160	−$2,007

fall in value, and the overall value of the project falls. As the interest rate rises farther than is illustrated on the diagram, the net present value actually starts to rise. Higher discounting reduces present-value profits, but it reduces the present value of the expenditures for years 1 to 4 by an even larger amount. In the example, the net present value of the project begins to rise at an interest rate of 39%. Of course, it stays negative at this point.

The NPV is often expressed as a return on investment, which is just the NPV divided by the initial investment, which is known as the project profitability. However, as we saw in the mining example, the initial investment often is spread over time. In this case, the profitability should be expressed as the overall NPV divided by the NPV of the stream of investments. For example, at an interest rate of 5%, the silver mine (table 7.4) had a profitability of $5,042/$5,546, or 90.9%, which is a healthy rate of return by most company's standards. (As a practical matter, most mining companies use interest rates in the 12% to 18% range, so the project described, which is based on a real project in Mexico, has a negative NPV and would not be undertaken without a substantial increase in silver prices.)

There are two other common methods for assessing whether projects should be undertaken: the internal rate of return (IRR), and the payback period. The internal rate of return solves the NPV formula for the interest rate that results in an NPV of zero, and dictates undertaking a project when the interest rate is low enough. The internal rate of return approach is fatally flawed, and should not be used. First, the IRR often has multiple solutions for the interest rate, which begs the question of which internal interest rate should be used. That problem is usually solvable, in that using the lowest positive interest rate that gives an NPV of zero does not directly cause problems. Second, the IRR may not exist. Consider a

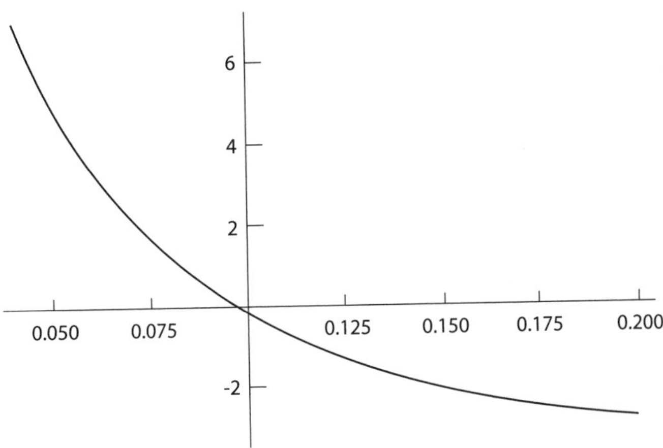

Figure 7.3. Net present value as a function of the interest rate.

project that costs \$100 in year one, produces \$280 in year two, and then costs \$200 to clean up in year three, at which time the project is over. This project has no solution for NPV = 0, as an application of the quadratic formula will demonstrate. The internal rate of return solves the problem:

$$0 = -100 + \frac{280}{1 + IRR} - \frac{200}{(1 + IRR)^2}.$$

In this particular case, the NPV is always negative, for any interest rate. However, there is no direct rule that is helpful when the IRR does not exist—others will have a positive NPV but no IRR.

The third problem with the IRR approach to project selection is that the IRR suggests taking some bad projects. Consider one project that costs \$100 and pays \$120 a year later. This project produces a positive NPV for interest rates less than 20%. If the internal rate of return threshold is 10%, both the NPV and IRR approaches get the same answer, which is to undertake the project. But consider the project that pays \$100 now but will create a cost of \$120 later. The IRR is still 20%—this project is exactly the mirror image of the previous one—but it has a negative NPV. The IRR values these projects—one good, one bad—exactly the same.

The pay-back period is an alternative approach to project selection. The payback period means different things to different people, but probably the most common meaning is the year at which the NPV reaches zero. It is often useful to know the payback period—it determines when the project is producing funds that can be invested in other projects. However, as a decision rule (e.g., choose the project with the lowest payback period), it is woefully inadequate. Consider the decision of which M.B.A. program to attend: Duke or Georgia Tech. In 2000, Duke graduates increased their incomes by $80,000 per year, and tuition was around $60,000. Georgia Tech increased their income by around $60,000 per year, and tuition was $30,000. The payback period for Duke is substantially longer than for Georgia Tech; indeed, almost twice as long. Even at 10%, however, the program is worth substantially more than Georgia Tech's program to the average graduate. When only one project can be undertaken, NPV is a better guide than the payback period or the IRR.

What is an M.B.A. worth? According to *Business Week,*[8] the average Stanford graduate was earning $65,000 when entering, and earned $165,000 upon graduating with an M.B.A. two years later. Suppose this gap persists for the rest of the student's career. The tuition was $29,000 per year for two years. There are a few other expenses—books and so on—so we can round this to $30,000. Note that foregone earning counts as a cost, but room and board, which would be expended whether one went to school or not, are not costs of going to school. Thus, in this simple NPV calculation, the Stanford student loses $95,000 per year (tuition plus lost wages) for two years, and then earns an extra $100,000 per year for the next thirty-five years. The NPVs associated with attending Stanford's M.B.A. program are given in table 7.5. Any interest rate less than 30% makes the Stanford degree worthwhile, which is not to say better than other M.B.A. degrees, but better than none at all. Viewed in an NPV light, business school is a remarkably profitable investment.

There are many practical problems associated with NPV analysis. Often it is difficult to estimate interest rates, project costs, and project proceeds. Project costs may be systematically underestimated, and revenues overestimated, by managers who want their pet project funded.

There are two major conceptual flaws with NPV analysis, but both flaws can be addressed. First, most projects are risky. It can be straightforward to estimate the average return and use the average return in the NPV formula. However, such a procedure—using the average return—will consistently and systematically make errors, because the averages ignore the option value associated with projects. Consider the mining example given above. Mining is risky—perhaps the ore is not present, and perhaps silver prices go down. The ore content is unlikely to change over time, but the prices are likely to change. Thus, delaying the project to learn more about prices tends to be valuable. A cost of implementing the project is that the option to delay is lost, and this cost should be considered in the determination of when to undertake a project. The option value is considered in chapter 10. The second consideration is that risk itself is costly and is priced by the market. Thus,

TABLE 7.5
NPV of a Stanford M.B.A.

	Interest Rate		
	6%	*8%*	*10%*
Stanford M.B.A., NPV (000s)	$1,106	$816	$615

the inherent risk of a project should be taken as a cost. This consideration requires an analysis of the market price of risk. The basic analysis is known as the capital asset pricing theory, which is presented below.

PROJECT SELECTION AND RISK ASSESSMENT

What projects should a firm undertake? From a set of candidate projects, which ones will enhance the firm's value, and which will detract from the firm's value? Will the merger of two firms increase shareholder value by creating offsetting risks? The leading theory has some remarkable implications for the choice of projects. From the leading theory, the surprising answer is that the only consideration on project selection is how the product's returns correlate to the market as a whole.

It often proves useful to think about the selection of a project in terms of purchasing a stock or a commodities contract. When undertaking a project, a firm creates an asset. This could be a new product, a chain of stores, a team of researchers, a computer inventory system, a brand image, or even management expertise. In particular, it need not be a tangible asset. Similarly, when one buys shares in McDonald's, one is buying a piece of McDonald's reputation for clean restrooms and adept ability to select successful children's toys for inclusion in "happy meals," as well as its "brick and mortar" stores. Every project has a cost and produces a random, risky stream of payments, just like a stock certificate. A project has a capital value, and it is the determinants of the capital value that is investigated in this section. In a nutshell, the theory of project selection requires the firm to value a project the way the stock market would value the project were the project an independent firm, and then undertake the project when its value exceeds the cost.

The primary theory of risk assessment is the Capital Asset Pricing Model, or CAPM, pronounced "cap em."[9] There are two main premises of this theory. First, securities are distinguished by two components, the mean return and the variance of the return. Thus, if returns are distributed according to the normal (bell-shaped) distribution, the first premise is automatically satisfied, because those two com-

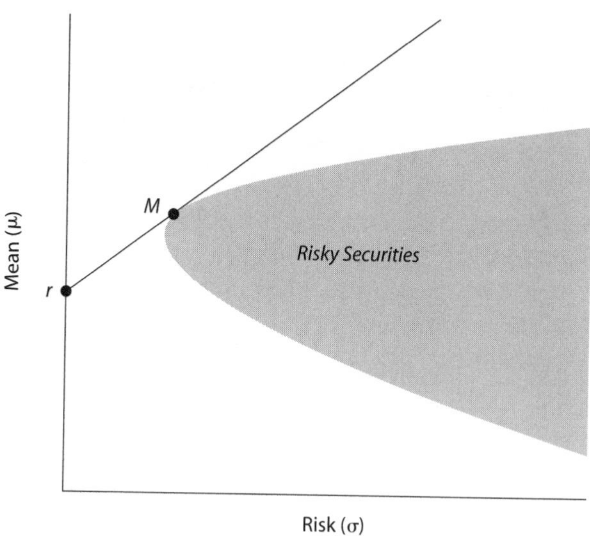

Figure 7.4. Return and risk of various securities.

ponents, and those two alone, characterize a normal distribution. The second premise is that there is an available risk-free investment, with a return *r*. Usually, U.S. government bonds are considered to serve as risk-free investments, because the likelihood of U.S. government default is so low.

These two premises permit the drawing of a picture like figure 7.4. In this figure, the horizontal axis represents the risk, measured as the standard deviation, associated with various securities, so that points on the right represent securities with higher risk than points on the left. The vertical axis represents the mean return. The risk-free rate, *r*, is denoted by a black dot on the vertical axis. The area shaded in grey represents the available pool of risky securities. Each point in this area can be thought of either as an individual investment or as a portfolio of investments. Thus, one can generate a new security by having a portfolio containing two or more securities, by combinations of the securities. For example, if $1000 invested in Dell is one security, and $1000 invested in Microsoft is another, a composite security composed of $500 in Dell and $500 in Microsoft can be created. The average return of such a security is the average of the Dell and Microsoft returns. However, the variance of the return of the composite investment is not the average of the variance of the returns. Instead, the variance depends on the degree of correlation between the underlying assets. Correlation is measured by the correlation coefficient, denoted by ρ (the Greek letter rho). The correlation coefficient ranges from 1, which is perfect positive correlation, to -1, which is perfect negative correlation.

The security denoted by a black dot labeled *M* in figure 7.4 plays a special role in CAPM—this security has the highest slope of any line connecting the risk free return *r* with another security. That is, it maximizes the rate of return per unit of risk. Alternatively, the security *M* minimizes the standard deviation per unit of return in excess of the risk-free rate. Risk is measured by the standard deviation, denoted by σ (the Greek letter sigma). The security *M* should be thought of as a market index averaging many securities; many studies use the Standard and Poor's (S&P) 500 index as a proxy for *M*.

Since the market asset *M* is the "best" risky asset, any risky asset can be priced by viewing it as a combination of the market asset and the risk-free asset. Define the common financial term β (the Greek letter beta) by the ratio of the expected excess return on a given asset *X* to the excess return of the market security *M*:

$$\beta = \frac{EX - r}{EM - r}.$$

Here, *EX* denotes the expected return of *X*, and *EM* denotes the return on *M*. A β of $\frac{1}{2}$ means that the asset returns less than the market rate, while a β of 1 means a return equal to the market rate. The price of the security *X* must be set by the market so that market participants are willing to hold it, but do not have an infinite demand for it. This, in turn, implies that the market risk of X (σ_X) is priced the same as the risk of the market asset (σ_M), that is,

$$EX = r + \beta(EM - r) = r + \rho\frac{\sigma_X}{\sigma_M}(EM - r).$$

The CAPM pricing formula says that the return on a given asset is the risk-free rate, plus a term that is the net return of the market security, $EM - r$, weighted by the relative variance, σ_X/σ_M, times the correlation with the market return. Let us consider each of these terms in turn. First, $EM - r$ is the price of market risk. Any security with risk associated with the market must bring a return that is higher than the risk-free rate. Second, the price of risk is linear in the amount of risk. Thus, the risk pricing is scaled by σ_X/σ_M, which accounts for the amount of risk, relative to the market. When σ_X is low, the risk is low, while if σ_X is high, the risk associated with the security is high. Finally, the only risk that matters is market risk; that is, risk uncorrelated with the market, called idiosyncratic risk, brings no excess return over the risk-free rate. The reason for the zero price for idiosyncratic risk is that risk uncorrelated with the market can be completely diversified by being spread among millions of shareholders, and thus imposes no real risk on shareholders. Risk negatively correlated with the market brings a return *lower* than the risk-free rate, because such risk helps reduce market risk in a portfolio. Negative correlation with the market is a good, and the holder of an asset with a negative ρ pays for the privilege by obtaining a return lower than the risk-free rate.

An implication of the basic pricing formula is that a stock's β, its excess return over the market excess return, equals the correlation coefficient ρ times the ratio of the standard deviations. Thus the well-known β reflects both a stock's correlation with the market risk and its overall variance. Low values of β are desirable in that they carry a smaller risk premium than high values of β.

An equivalent formulation of the basic pricing formula is

$$EX = r + \rho \frac{EM - r}{\sigma_M} \sigma_X .$$

This formula is interpreted as follows. First, the price of risk is the ratio $(EM - r)/\sigma_M$, which is the return required for market risk per unit of market risk. The amount of risk imposed by the security X is σ_X, so the term to the right of ρ is the price of market risk times the amount of risk associated with this asset. This is multiplied by the correlation ρ to adjust for the extent to which the risk of the stock worsens or improves the overall risk of an investor's portfolio. Thus, the risk adjustment to the risk-free rate of return r is the correlation ρ of the return, times the market price for the risk the asset provides.

The price of the asset can be deduced from the returns. As with bond prices, the price of the asset is the inverse of the return. A bond that pays $\$B$ in the future, and has a price of $\$P$, has a return which is $\$B/P - 1$. Similarly, an asset that is expected to pay $\$A$ in the future has a return of $\$A/P - 1$, where the price is $\$P$. Assets with a stream of payouts require a present value calculation, but the principle is similar.

In spite of the widespread application of CAPM analysis in financial markets, the two premises of CAPM are justifiably controversial. First, people usually care about more than the mean and variance of returns. Assets can have the same mean and variance, yet impose significantly different risks. Consider, for example, an asset that pays nothing or \$100, with equal probability. This has a mean of \$50 and a variance of \$2500. Alternatively, consider the asset that pays \$55.02 with a probability of 99% and −\$447.49 for 1% of the time. These assets have the same mean and variance, but are perceived quite differently by most individuals. CAPM requires them to be treated the same.

Second, the risk-free return is also problematic. Historically, U.S. Government bonds were considered a good proxy for a risk-free return. However, bonds have been offered only recently with inflation adjustments, and government inflation adjustments are imperfect because the consumer price index is an imperfect measure of inflation. As the 1970s made clear, government bonds do not provide a risk-free real return. The theory hinges critically on the existence of such a risk-free asset. A subtle aspect of the risk-free rate of return problem is that a beta that exceeds 1, and many of them do, requires the ability to sell the risk-free asset short. It is not clear that this is possible.

Third, many assets are not publicly traded. In particular, about three quarters of Americans count a single-family home as a large asset in their portfolio. The risk associated with this asset varies from person to person, and thus the optimal portfolio will vary idiosyncratically. Consequently, rather than care about the overall market risk, people care about some combination of the market risk and their idiosyncratic risk, which effectively produces a distinct security *M* for each individual, and undermines the CAPM analysis.

Fourth, it is not at all clear what the market portfolio *M* should be. Many researchers used the S&P 500 as a proxy for *M*, but the proliferation of index funds suggests that there is no clear answer. Empirically, implications of CAPM have been challenged for two decades. Nevertheless, CAPM remains the prevailing theory of asset pricing.

This section began with the question, How should firms select projects to undertake? CAPM provides a direct answer. First, the *only* consideration is how the asset generated by the project, which might be a division, or some capital equipment, or a team of workers and some office space, performs relative to the market return and risk. CAPM permits the computation of the rate of return necessary to sell the asset to diversified investors, which permits the calculation of the value of the asset. This value can be compared to the cost of creating the asset; when the value exceeds the cost, CAPM suggests that the project that creates the asset is worthwhile.

CAPM suggests that only market risk is priced—all other risk is idiosyncratic and has a price of zero. This is a stark prescription of the theory, one that does not seem compelling. The concept of the *market* pricing of risk, however, is an exceedingly important one. CAPM emphasizes that risk is priced not by the individual firm but by the market, and that firms should value risk at a market price. Whether that market price is determined by a single "superfund" portfolio, or by multiple securities, is not important for the insight that the market, rather than the firm, prices risk, and that financial officers and corporate planners must respond to the market pricing of risk to maximize shareholder value.

There are many considerations that complicate the practical application of the CAPM theory. First, the cost of a project includes the opportunity cost of a manager's time, which can be high when there are many potential projects, and in any case is determined by the alternative uses of the management expertise. Second, it is often impossible to estimate the correlation of the returns of some project with the market returns. At best, one can hope to say that the returns appear to be negatively correlated, or not strongly correlated, with the market.* Third, it is not clear what the market return is. Many researchers used the S&P 500 as a proxy for the market return, but the growth of the NASDAQ relative to the S&P 500 during the 1990s shows the folly of that approximation. Thus, even if one had an idea of what determines the returns of a project, identifying the relationship of those returns with the market is problematic. Fourth, the variation in returns, relative to the market, is difficult to estimate. Fifth, many firms use a non-market-based internal rate of return, which adjusts for optimistic estimates of project returns by managers, making the application of market rates problematic for internal reasons. Nevertheless, CAPM remains useful and suggests the relevant considerations to project selection even when the pricing formula cannot be applied quantitatively. Some examples of betas are provided in table 7.6.

The value of beta for copper is approximately 0.65, while the value for gold is around zero, or possibly even slightly negative. Thus, the risk inherent in price fluctuations is moderately significant for copper. A copper mine should value its risk at around 65% of the price of market risk, but risk is neutral or even a good thing for a gold mine. Knowledge of a project's relevant betas provides insight into the economic cost of risk, and the return necessary to justify that risk. In particular, it is possible to compute betas for most commodities like copper and oil, and for assets like computers and automobiles, and to assess the risk costs of these items in a project. Such costs are especially important in long-lived projects like oil wells and mining.

EXECUTIVE SUMMARY—ORGANIZATIONAL SCOPE

- An important aspect of organizational design is the make-or-buy decision: when to centralize operations and when to decentralize operations.
- The provision of incentives to employees is the second major aspect of organizational design.
- There are four main reasons for making an input internally:
  - Holdup by suppliers
  - Coordination or information leakage
  - Elimination of double marginalization
  - Foreclosing rivals from inputs
- In many cases, tapered integration, which involves partially supplying one's own needs, is preferable to either full integration or no integration.

*For example, projects that provide assistance to unemployed workers, retail outlets that specialize in low-income families, and private provisions of prisons tend to be countercyclical to the business cycle, and hence should be negatively correlated or weakly correlated with a market portfolio.

TABLE 7.6
Some Estimates of Beta

Company	*Beta*
Sony	0.9
Time Warner	1.0
Exxon-Mobil	0.5
AOL	2.5
Delta	0.9
Microsoft	1.7
Dell	2.0
Apple	0.7
Dollar General	1.2
Sears	0.9
Wal-Mart	1.2
McDonald's	0.9

Source: Charles Schwab

- Advantages to purchasing inputs include competitive supply, an organization designed to optimize the input, and the use of a distinct corporate culture for the input supplier.
- A multidivisional firm splits production according to one or more criteria:
  Product divisions
  Customer divisions
  Technological divisions
  Geographical divisions
- Divisionalization creates the ability to commit to higher production levels than might be optimal from the overall firm's perspective.
- Transaction costs theory suggests designing the organization to minimize transaction costs, which include costs arising from holdup, coordination, incentives, information acquisition and processing, contracting, search, enforcement, bargaining, measurement, and lobbying.

- Another aspect of centralization involves the use of transfer prices with autonomous divisions or centrally set quantity choices.
- Transfer prices are preferred when there is little variation in the value of the transferred good.
- For deciding to undertake a project, use of the net present value (NPV) is preferable to the internal rate of return (IRR).
- The Capital Asset Pricing Model (CAPM), used to evaluate stock prices, is also useful conceptually as a means for evaluating project selection.
- CAPM provides the price of risk correlated with the overall market. Risk that is uncorrelated with the market can be diversified and has a market price of zero, while risk that is negatively correlated with the market is valuable.
- In many instances, the market risk of a project can be estimated. For example, the correlation of metals prices with the market is known. Thus, the NPV for a project to dig a mine should have a correction for market risk.

8

Incentives

The second main question addressed by organization theory concerns the means of motivating individuals in organizations to achieve high performance. To address this issue, traditional "agency theory" focuses on the trade-off between risk and incentives. Consider motivating a real estate agent. Real estate agents earn a combination of salary and commission. In most areas, real estate commissions are around 6% of the sale price. This amount is split between two companies—a listing agency and a selling agency. The listing agent was hired by the seller to place advertisements, post the house in the Multiple Listing Service (MLS), advise on showing the house, and so on. The selling agent brought the buyer to the house. In many areas, the portion of the commission going to the selling and listing companies is split equally, with 3% going to each agency. These may be the same company, of course. The 3% going to the listing company is equally split between the listing agent and the company, so the listing agent receives $1\frac{1}{2}$% of the sale price as a commission, and the company keeps the other $1\frac{1}{2}$% to cover its expenses (offices, secretaries, and the like). Usually, the agency pays a salary in addition to the commission to the agent. The salary is a fixed monthly amount that does not depend on sales.

To increase their incentives, an agency can reduce the salary and increase the commission, and this is precisely what the RE/MAX agency does. Agents at RE/MAX receive little or no salary and keep around 95% of the commission—nearly 3% of the sale price. RE/MAX agents consider that they have stronger incentives and hence work harder. The RE/MAX agency, of course, attracts agents who perform better—better performing agents will make more money at RE/MAX than poor performers.

In contrast to traditional agency theory, modern incentive theory focuses on the side effects of increased incentive pay. The RE/MAX scheme, by creating strong incentives to be either a listing agency or the selling agent, reduces the incentive to help other members of the agency. At a standard agency, the salary component of compensation comes with an expectation that the agent will assist other agents. Because the salary component is a large fraction of compensation, in a traditional agency there is more of a team mentality than at RE/MAX. RE/MAX's strong incentives to sell are in effect negative incentives to cooperate and assist. Because the rewards to agents for selling their own listing are high at RE/MAX, the cost of helping others is also high, and the rewards are low.

Examination of the incentives and compensation of individual employees is a major tool for investigating organizational design. The logic for a large emphasis on the case of individual employees is that the contracts and compensation for an employee of a company serve as a proxy for how a corporation should treat a division. Thus, in many of the examples, employees can be thought of as divisions—the logic is the same. For example, the question of what decisions an employee should make is quite similar to the question of what autonomy a division should possess.

AGENCY

Agency theory, also known as principal-agent theory, concerns the design of contracts to provide incentives to perform, which is the second major issue addressed by the theory of organizations. Consider an encyclopedia salesperson who goes door to door selling encyclopedias. If the salespersons are paid a straight salary, they have no real incentive to go door to door—their earnings are unaffected by their effort. In particular, if it is cold and drizzling rain, they can sit in a coffee shop with their compensation intact. If, in contrast, the salespersons are paid a pure commission—a straight fraction of the revenues generated, for example—they have an incentive to work hard, because when they sit in the coffee shop, they earn nothing. However, a pure commission with no salary imposes a substantial risk on the salespersons. In particular, even with a great deal of effort, they may have little to show for it.

Commissions are an example of incentive compensation—compensation linked to performance. Incentive compensation includes commissions, bonuses, and royalties. Bonuses usually reflect past performance; for example, an employee might get an annual bonus if the year's performance is sufficiently good. It is often the case that bonuses depend not just on an individual's performance, but also on how well the business unit performs, so that the employee has no incentive to sabotage coworkers. Royalties are a flow of payments depending on performance, but are usually paid to a person who has no current involvement. For example, royalties paid to an author reflect how well a book is currently doing in the marketplace, even though the author's primary contribution ended when the book was written.

Still, royalties are similar to commissions in that the better the book sells, the more the author earns, which is presumably influenced by the author's talent and effort in writing the book.

Simple agency theory balances the incentives to perform induced by commissions and incentive compensation with the risk imposed on the employee. The view is that a large corporation, or even a relatively wealthy employer, is better able to withstand the risk created by a business enterprise such as encyclopedia sales than the salesperson. Thus, the optimal incentive arrangement—typically a mix of salary and commission—reflects a balancing of risk sharing and incentives.

In areas of the United States where house prices are very high, real estate agents may sell only a couple of houses per year on average. A pure commission like RE/MAX's compensation scheme imposes risk on real estate agents. On a pure commission, some agents might average $40,000 per year or more, but they also have a 50% chance of having no earnings at all—an extraordinary risk. Thus agencies with a stableful of agents are much better positioned to handle risk, and they share the risk with the agents by paying them part salary, part commission.

When compensated with a mix of salary and commission, an incentive problem is created. Employees drawing a salary can choose to relax, reduce their efforts, and spend a lot of time around the watercooler. Essentially, when the employer insures the employee against unforeseen risks, the employer necessarily reduces the incentives to perform. This problem is known as a problem of "moral hazard," which means that an insured person has a reduced incentive to take care, to take preventative measures, and to reduce or mitigate risks.

> [T]here's a lot of debate on this subject—about what kind of car handles best. Some say a front-engined car; some say a rear-engined car. I say a rented car. Nothing handles better than a rented car. You can go faster, turn corners sharper, and put the transmission into reverse while going forward at a higher rate of speed in a rented car than in any other kind.
>
> **—P. J. O'Rourke**

The same problem of moral hazard is familiar from health care. Under simple insurance, an insured person has an incentive to visit doctors too often, because the bill is paid by the insurance company rather than the individual. Moreover, the doctor has an incentive to perform too many tests on the patient, again because neither the doctor nor the patient is paying the full cost of the tests, but the benefits of the tests (finding out what is wrong, eliminating possibilities, and reducing the chance of a lawsuit by the patient) accrue to the doctor and the patient.

Automobile and homeowner insurance contracts tend to involve a deductible, an amount for which nothing is paid, along with coverage of amounts over the deductible. The deductible provides an incentive to reduce risks, because the agent has some exposure to the cost of an accident. Like a salary component in compensation, accident insurance limits downside risk. Conceptually, the problem of designing insurance schemes is similar to the problem of designing compensation contracts, and in both cases the answers are similar: limit downside risk, using insurance payments or salary, and provide incentives, using a deductible or a commission.

Reducing Risk Facing Employees

When outcomes are risky, incentives usually impose some risk on agents. The reason is that the agents may fail to perform; in this case, their earnings must fall, in order to provide incentives. One goal of the design of incentive compensation is to make the risk as low as possible. The method for reducing risk is to base compensation on outcomes that are within the employee's control, as far as possible. A real estate agent has a much easier time selling in a thick market with lots of transactions than in a thin market, where few buyers are chasing few sellers. Thus, one strategy for reducing the risk that working on commissions creates for the agent is to reduce the salary in boom markets and increase it in thin markets.* In order to be useful, such a change in the salary must be negatively correlated to the market randomness that affects commission compensation. Moreover, it is generally best not to make the salary change too often, for otherwise the salary itself becomes a source of significant uncertainty.

A second procedure for reducing the risk inherent in incentive compensation, while maintaining incentives, is to eliminate the dependence of commissions on the performance of others. For example, it is better to make the pay of the manager of a business unit depend mostly on the performance of that business unit, rather than depend mainly on the performance of the entire corporation, since the corporation's performance includes more than the business unit's performance. As the manager has much more control of the performance of the business unit, the same incentives can be provided at less overall risk when pay is based on the performance of the business unit. For example, an encyclopedia salesperson might not be rewarded based on the performance of the encyclopedia division but on the salesperson's own performance, provided dependence on the performance of oth-

*A natural method for making the salary depend on the thickness of the market is to make the salary depend on how well other employees perform, which will be discussed below under yardstick compensation. Such a procedure works when there is a sufficiently large comparison group, so that their performance accurately proxies for the overall market. In contrast, dependence of the employee's compensation on the performance of a small or varying group actually becomes added risk for the employee.

ers does not help reduce the overall risk. Some care must be taken when targeting incentives to individual performance. Incentives not only strengthen efforts, but incentives direct efforts, and strong but misguided incentives can do more damage than no incentives at all.

The Cost of Incentives

Even when the risks have been minimized, some risk is imposed on the employee. Agency theory shows that there is a cost of providing incentives, and that the cost includes a risk premium—the employee must be provided with compensation for the risk the employee is asked to bear. Alternatively, a reduction in incentives permits an employer to reduce average compensation for two reasons. One is that the fall in intensity of effort, as incentives fall, means that employees need not be compensated for as much effort—their job becomes just a bit more pleasant. Moreover, the risk facing the employee falls, and the risk premium falls right along with it.

The structure of the incentive compensation matters significantly to its cost. The popular salary-plus-commission structure of compensation has the advantage that the employee's downside is protected somewhat by the salary. The net compensation to the employee has the form shown below:

$$\text{Net} = \text{Salary} + \text{Commission} \times [\text{Average Sales} - (\text{Risk Cost} \times \text{Variance})].$$

The net compensation is composed of three elements. First, there is the salary component. Second, there is an average amount earned from commissions, which is the commission rate times the average sales. Finally, there is a risk premium, which is the cost of risk times the variation in earnings. The variation in earnings is the variance of sales times the commission. Thus, we can see that increases in the commission proportionately increase the cost of risk.

Employees have alternatives. Whatever the contract offered, it must offer as much as the competition offers to obtain qualified employees. With an increase in commission, the salary can be lowered, but average total compensation must rise to accommodate the increased risk of the higher commission. Moreover, increasing the commission will tend to change the pool of employees, often favorably.

Efficiency Wages

Bonuses and incentive pay are not the only types of incentives that can be provided. An alternative approach to providing incentives is to pay workers a salary that is more than their market value, with a threat of termination in the event of bad performance. Such contracts are known as efficiency wages. The efficiency wage, with a threat of termination, is the means with which Toyota compensates input suppliers. That is, Toyota pays the input suppliers more than their costs, and significantly more than the value of the Toyota supplier to another firm. Hence, the supplier is willing to work very hard not to lose the position, which permits Toyota to obtain good performance even when the performance is only sporadically observed.

Efficiency wages are an excellent motivational device when performance is difficult to measure. For example, the performance of teachers in the classroom is hard to measure, and student evaluations confound quality with easy grading. In this environment, pay for performance generally has perverse effects, as will be discussed later in this chapter. In contrast, giving the teacher an efficiency wage may work very well. While a quantitative assessment of a teacher's performance is very difficult to make, a qualitative assessment—whether the teacher is performing at an acceptable level—may be much easier to obtain. Paying more than the competition, and then firing workers who appear to perform poorly, creates strong incentives even in environments where performance cannot be measured and is very difficult to observe.

Making Firms More Aggressive

In some cases, the moral hazard problem can be used to the firm's benefit. For example, compensating the sales force based on the amount of, or the revenue from, their sales will make them more aggressive than if they are compensated based on the company's profits. Inducing additional efforts at selling, even if it comes at the cost of some price-cutting by the sales force, can be useful by making rivals contract their output. Facing a firm that has compensated its employees to induce aggressive price-cutting, a rival may reduce output as a means of propping up the price. Such a reaction by rivals renders the original compensation scheme profitable for the firm.

The differing interests of bondholders and stockholders can also be used to commit a company to an aggressive marketing strategy. Stockholders have limited liability—the worst thing that can happen to stockholders is that they lose their investment. Moreover, stockholders get nothing whenever the bondholders cannot be paid back. Thus, stockholders do not care about whether a firm is barely bankrupt or has lost $5 billion—either way the stockholders have lost their investment. This indifference to the various negative outcomes induces a risk-loving attitude on the part of the stockholders. For example, a fifty-fifty risk of gaining $2 billion or losing $5 billion is overall a bad bet. But from the perspective of a stockholder of a failing enterprise, it is a good bet, because it gives a 50% chance that the stock is worth something. With the losing outcome, the firm is just *more* bankrupt. Since the bankrupt firm is not worth anything to the stockholders, the stockholders of a failing firm would win from the bad bet. The bondholders, of course, lose from such risks.

If the management of a company tends to implement the wishes of the board of directors, who represent stockholders, increased leverage (a greater portion of debt financing) can make the firm more aggressive in the markets in which the firm competes.[1] The stockholders would like the company to price aggressively, taking market share from rivals, because there is a good upside to this outcome, and some of the downside occurs when the firm would go bankrupt anyway. Thus, a highly leveraged firm ought to be more aggressive in pricing than its less leveraged competitors. As a practical matter, few firms are sufficiently likely to go bankrupt for this effect to be more than an academic curiosity. At the business unit level, however, a poorly performing unit may be shut down; managers may have a useful incentive to take aggressive actions to become profitable in order to preserve their reputation and position.

Agent Selection

An important aspect of incentive compensation is that it affects the pool of employees who are willing to work for given terms. This can be observed directly from the compensation equation that has already been discussed:

$$\text{Net} = \text{Salary} + \text{Commission} \times [\text{Average Sales} - (\text{Risk Cost} \times \text{Variance})].$$

The higher average sales are or the lower the risk cost is, the higher the net is. Thus, higher commissions with lower salaries attract those able to sell more, as well as those who are less averse to risk and hence have lower risk premiums. Attracting employees with higher average sales is a useful property of incentive compensation. Lazy or inept employees earn little under a primarily commission-based pay structure, and thus tend to avoid jobs with significant commissions in favor of salary-based jobs. Giving high commissions with low salaries not only provides incentives but also weeds out lazy employees.[2]

High commissions also favor employees who are not averse to financial risk. Usually, this includes employees who are already wealthy—financial risk is most easily borne by those with a substantial cushion. Few employees, however, are in this situation. Thus, high commissions tend to attract employees who view the risks as low. This means that high commissions will tend to attract the overconfident as well as the talented.

Increasing the portion of compensation arising from commissions or bonuses

- Increases effort,
- Requires an increased average compensation to compensate for increased risk,
- Attracts more talented agents,
- Attracts risk-loving agents,
- Attracts overconfident agents.

Managing Creative Talent

> You are the pits of the world! Vultures! Trash.
>
> **—John McEnroe**

Managing creative individuals, such as film directors, actors, animators, architects, musicians, computer program architects, or university professors, requires a very different management technique than is appropriate for an assembly line. Sony discovered that its management technology did not mesh with creative talent after Sony's takeover of Columbia Pictures, and it was an expensive discovery, indeed. Sony's heavy-handed management strategies were apparently responsible for a sequence of expensive box-office failures.

Creative workers tend to be easily offended and desire creative control of a project. The market demand for their services in large part determines the extent of their ego and difficulty. With a large demand, creative workers can indulge in childish behavior without threat of severe sanctions. When there are few employers, such fits of pique risk unemployment and such behavior is more restrained. From a strategic perspective, little can be done about this kind of behavior except accommodate it when necessary.

Even when a firm is the sole buyer of a type of creative talent, however, the talented individual should be managed differently than other employees to maximize the value of the output. For example, flexibility is important. Some creative workers will labor through the night if properly encouraged, but the cost of this is workers who do not work 9 A.M. to 5 P.M. but instead set their own hours. It is critical that immediate supervisors know what the workers are doing, both to assess their productivity and to verbally reward them when the job is well done. Words are an inexpensive and critical form of compensation for creative talent. Such words must be informed—the creative worker wishes to feel appreciated—to be useful. Indeed, ill-informed praise is likely to be damaging. In keeping tabs on the workers, however, it is critical that management not appear intrusive or controlling—such management techniques will alienate the talent. Managing talent requires a very different organizational form than is useful in other situations, but the reward to the firm is workers who will work extremely hard for compensation that is a small fraction of their value.

MULTITASKING

Multitasking relates the provision of incentives to agents in organizations to the design of the organization itself, in particular addressing the question of how the provision of incentives interacts with the use of employees versus independent contractors, and with the make-or-buy decision.

Consider a chain of convenience stores that wants to provide fresh bread twice per day in each store. The convenience store chain contracts with a bakery to provide bread, and now faces the problem of arranging delivery. A simplified version of the tasks that must be performed, for the delivery alone, includes:

- Planning the route
- Driving the truck
- Maintaining the truck

In addition, other items besides bread might be put on the truck to economize on average costs. How should the delivery of bread be organized? There are two popular methods. First, independent contractors may be used. Second, employees may be used. Moreover, there are striking differences in the two organizational approaches, and it is rare to find hybrid or intermediate cases.

Some of the differences between bread delivery by independent contractors and employees are summarized in table 8.1. In almost every dimension, the independent contractor has authority where the employee does not. It is possible for employees to own their own trucks, or for independent contractors to have the route set by the company, but such anomalies are rare. Generally, independent contractors have authority over all of the choices associated with the delivery of bread, except that the bread must be delivered. Occasionally the company will specify the timing of delivery, and independent contractors are provided with incentives—if the bread is late, they are paid less (or not at all). In contrast, employee drivers are generally paid by the hour, although sometimes they are salaried, and rarely are they provided with significant financial incentives for performance. The company makes all of the relevant choices—setting the schedule, maintaining the truck, selecting the route; and the company also owns the tools with which the driver performs the job: the truck itself.

Why do we not see independent contractors driving the company's truck? Employees provided with incentives to arrive quickly? Independent contractors compensated for truck maintenance? Workers, whether employees or independent

TABLE 8.1
Organization of Bread Delivery

	Independent Contractor	*Employee*
Route	Sets own route	Company sets route
Truck Ownership	Owns truck	Company owns truck
Compensation	Incentive	Salary or hourly wage
Maintenance	Contractor controls	Set by company
Carry Other Items	Yes	No

contractors, face competing demands for their time. If the worker owns the truck, the worker has very strong incentives to maintain the truck—the truck is a valuable asset, often the individual's most valuable physical asset. Thus, the truck owner will drive cautiously over potholes, perform maintenance regularly, and drive carefully to preserve the value of the truck. In contrast, the worker who does not own the truck has weak incentives to maintain the truck—the worker's wealth is not tied to the health of the truck. As a consequence, company-owned trucks are driven very hard.

Now consider the effects of incentive compensation, say for on-time delivery of the bread. On some days traffic is unusually bad, so that the only way to get to the store on time is to take risks. The truck owner will trade off the increased compensation associated with driving faster with the increased wear and tear on the truck, and will strike a balance between risk to the truck and the return to speed. The driver of the company-owned truck, in contrast, may drive over curbs, drive on the shoulder to skirt traffic jams, and employ other shortcuts that may severely injure the truck but increase speed, in the event traffic is unusually heavy. Incentive compensation—pay for performance—has very different effects on the owner of a truck and on the employee who does not own the truck. The owner faces competing incentives (protecting the value of the asset) that moderate the owner's response to the incentive compensation.

The incentive for the owner to maintain the truck is clear—maintenance is an investment that increases the return on the capital asset. Moreover, when incentive pay for fast delivery is increased, the owner trades off the increased costs of maintenance against the return from increased speed, again achieving a more balanced response. In contrast, the employee who does not pay for maintenance will not have an incentive to account for increased costs of maintenance in setting the driving speed. If the employee is charged for the maintenance, the employee will tend to minimize maintenance where possible. As the benefits of maintenance accrue primarily to the truck owner, it is very difficult to provide incentives for the employee to balance the competing goals of truck maintenance and speed. Indeed, since it is difficult to measure the employee's performance in terms of maintenance and driving care, generally an efficiency wage compensation mechanism will outperform incentive compensation. Efficiency wages work well when important aspects of job performance are difficult to monitor consistently and systematically.

The analysis of the setting of routes and the ability to carry items for other companies is similar. If the employee sets the route, the employee will minimize the hassle, making the driving pleasant, while the owner, facing incentive compensation, will take more challenging routes to insure better on-time performance. Carrying other items involves increased risk of not delivering bread on time. With the independent contractor, failure to perform has a cost, and thus the independent contractor has adequate incentives to trade off returns for carrying bread versus the returns for carrying competing items. In contrast, the employee, if permitted to run a separate business while carrying on the employer's business, has a massive incentive to try to earn money on the side and minimize the effort at carrying bread.

The theory of multitasking considers how best to design authority and choose asset ownership to minimize the cost of performing a set of related activities.[3] Incentive compensation often encourages one activity at the expense of others that are more difficult to monitor and reward. Multitasking concerns the management of multiple tasks, and how to provide appropriate incentives so that all the desired tasks are accomplished. Multitasking incorporates the fact that performance is measured with error, and that ownership of an asset creates incentives to maintain or improve that asset; and conversely, when the asset is owned by others, a moral hazard problem may arise. There are three key issues in multitasking theory:

- Measurement errors
- Substitution across tasks
- Risk

Measurement errors mean that it is difficult to verify whether or not some tasks are performed appropriately. It is difficult to verify if a truck is driven in a way that balances wear and tear with the desire for on-time delivery. Measurement errors imply that the firm cannot directly specify the way the truck is driven; instead, the best the firm can do is to attempt to provide incentives to drive the truck carefully. Ownership of the truck by the driver provides those incentives. In the absence of truck ownership by the driver, incentives to drive the truck carefully, for example, by fining the employee whenever an accident occurs, would impose a great deal of risk on the employee.[4]

Employee substitution across tasks implies that increased incentives on one task will tend to reduce performance on other tasks. A major insight of multitasking theory is that incentives are often complementary. If the company wishes to increase effort in one dimension, and increases the reward for performance in that dimension, the indirect effect is that performance in other dimensions suffers. Consequently, the optimal response to increased incentives for one task is to increase the incentives for other tasks as well, thereby striking a balance between tasks that compete for the employee's time. For the independent trucking contractor, ownership of the truck provides a strong incentive, which made the firm want to impose strong incentives in other dimensions. In contrast, the employee who does not own the truck faces weak incentives to maintain the truck, and this makes weak incentives for other tasks the correct response.

There are two major reasons why independent contracting does not solve all of the firms' problems. First, independent contractors face much more risk than employees, and must be paid a risk premium to absorb this risk. Thus, it will pay to use independent contractors only when the return to the increased incentives and performance exceeds the risk premium. Second, in some cases, employees must be reassigned or coordinated with other workers. The need to rapidly reassign employees is generally more consistent with pay based on skills rather than pay based on performance.

A very important conclusion of the theory of multitasking is that when a very important aspect of the job is difficult or impossible to measure, *all* incentives ought to be weak. An extraordinary example concerns schools. It is difficult to measure whether teachers do a good job with students. Teachers with high expectations often frustrate students in the short run; it is only years later that such "tough love" is appreciated. The best teachers make students work harder. Thus, it will generally be very difficult to base a teacher's compensation on how well they educate and enlighten students—the success rate may not be quantifiable for years after any particular class ends.

When they are unable to measure what really matters, many states have turned to standardized tests, and have penalized teachers whose students perform poorly on the tests. Such schemes have the effect of diverting teaching efforts toward "teaching to the tests," a common outcome of such backward incentives. It is reasonably clear that this is a poor teaching technique, one that arises when teacher compensation is based on students' test scores.

Providing incentives based on what is measurable, rather than on what matters, is a recipe for perverse and undesirable effects. Medicare doctors who are paid by the patient minimize care and maximize throughput.

In addition, multitasking has important implications for the design of jobs. Consider two tasks, one of which is easy to monitor, and the other nearly impossible to monitor. It is possible to provide strong performance incentives for the easy-to-monitor task. If, however, the same employee performs a difficult-to-monitor task, providing strong incentives on the easy-to-monitor task will tend to undermine performance on the more difficult task. Thus, if possible, it is desirable to have some employees performing only easy-to-monitor tasks, and to provide these employees with strong incentives. Difficult-to-monitor tasks should also be grouped together, but with relatively weak incentives, or with incentives provided via efficiency wages and not by measured performance.

The concept of multitasking sheds some faint light on differences in corporate culture. Since the desirable incentive systems, authority lines, and asset ownership vary with the task at hand, firms that specialize in one type of production problem will tend to have many employees with a similar set of incentives and authority. Another firm, solving a different set of production problems, may have very different incentives and authority. When firms with very different employee arrangements merge, the understanding and expectations of one group will clash with the other, and ultimately one set will come to predominate, much to the disgruntlement of the other faction. A very extreme example of such a clash is going on in Hong Kong, which is being absorbed into China. China understands that it is undesirable to kill the competitive nature of Hong Kong and has promised to keep the institutions and autonomy in place, but this promise has already proved very difficult to keep. The parallel to GM's purchase of Electronic Data Systems (EDS) is clear—in both cases, a bureaucracy is having difficulty preserving a spirit of independence.

In summary, increases in incentives in one dimension often have deleterious effects on efforts in other dimensions. Thus, it is often desirable to provide commensurate incentives in all relevant dimensions. Providing incentives based on what is measurable, rather than on what matters, is a recipe for perverse and undesirable effects. When a critical aspect of the job is difficult to quantify accurately, it is best to provide weak direct incentives and efficiency wages, using a threat of firing or reassignment to a lesser position if important but unmeasurable tasks are not carried out. Finally, tasks with similar incentive strengths should be grouped together, where possible.

Common Agency

Common agency refers to a situation in which several firms or organizations are represented by the same agent.[5] For example, grocery stores retail the products of competing brands; travel agents book flights on all airlines; insurance brokers may sell policies of many companies; and real estate agents show potential buyers house listings of multiple real estate brokers. Inside a nonhierarchical organization, employees may report to several managers, also creating a common agency situation. In the language of multitasking, common agency creates a situation where distinct incentives are set by different firms.

Common agency creates competition for the agent's time and effort. Computerized reservations systems are given free to travel agents (with restrictive terms), in a competition for the travel agent's time. Compensation schemes must take into account the desire of an agent to choose the most rewarded activity. Consequently, in a common agency setting, the incentives offered by other firms matter to the outcomes obtained by any one firm. If one insurance company pays an insurance broker more for selling its policies, the broker will put more effort into selling that company's policies, and less into other companies' policies. Consequently, the optimal response of the other companies is to increase their incentives—up to the point where they stop using the agency.

Food manufacturers pay groceries significant sums of money for good shelf placement for their products. Grocers are common agents for a large variety of food manufacturers, all of whom want a large expanse of the best real estate–shelf space at eye level for the average customer. If one manufacturer pays for more such space, less is available for other firms. But how can a manufacturer get the best space? The company who has an employee visit the grocery store in person can negotiate for the best space, while the company that negotiates over the phone cannot readily monitor the location and may be sold a site that looks good on paper but has poor lighting and is down a dead-end aisle. Monitoring directly confers an advantage.

When one firm can monitor the performance of an agent more readily than other firms who use the same agent, the firm that can monitor has a striking advantage, because it can provide stronger incentives than the other firms. Consequently, a firm with a monitoring advantage does well, and thus it may pay to invest in direct monitoring.

Summarizing the effects of common agency:

- The incentives offered by other firms affect the outcomes obtained by any one firm.
- The firm offering the strongest incentives tends to get the most out of the agent.
- Incentives tend to be complements, so that each firm responds to an increase in incentives by one firm with increases of its own.
- Firms that can monitor the agent's performance most easily have a striking advantage, because they can provide strong incentives to perform.
- Consequently, as a means of offering strong incentives, it may pay to invest in increased monitoring.

TOURNAMENTS AND YARDSTICK COMPETITION

Consider the company that unleashes a door-to-door sales force to sell a new product. How should the sales force be compensated? An incentive approach requires an analysis of the returns versus effort, as a way of calibrating the incentive compensation. But with a new product, the returns to effort are unknown; such an incentive system will likely misjudge the circumstances, providing either too strong incentives, with the sales force tripping all over each other in their mad dash to make a sale, or too weak incentives, with the sales force sitting in hotels watching HBO. Similarly, paying efficiency wages requires a meaningful chance to observe employee's effort or laziness, which may not be possible to do when the employees are in distant areas, like the World Bank employees who allegedly never venture from the Hilton Hotel in Third World countries.

In some situations, compensating employees similarly to sports tournaments, with the best performers obtaining a bonus, provides appropriate incentives without detailed knowledge of the environment.[6] The new-product sales force can be compensated with a minimal salary, plus a fixed bonus that is awarded to the top few performers. There are two main virtues of such tournament compensation schemes. First, they insure that the average compensation is reasonable even when the employer has little knowledge of the difficulty of the job. The reason is that the overall compensation is set to be commensurate with alternative employment; when the job is especially difficult, the employees work less hard as a way of equalizing the return to their alternatives. Such a response—doing less when the job is more costly—is generally efficient.

The second advantage to tournament compensation is that it removes common risk from the compensation scheme, and therefore reduces the risk facing the employees. Provided that the employees face strongly correlated risks, the risks affect all the employees and thus cancel out. For example, suppose that a major challenge to the traveling sales force is bad weather. Sometimes it is sunny and the sales force can sell one hundred units each on average, and sometimes the monsoon strikes and ten is a good day's work. Provided that all the sales force is in the same general area, their compensation in a tournament will not depend on whether there is a monsoon—the same amount is paid either way. In contrast, incentive schemes tend to compensate much more highly during nonmonsoon periods, creating income risk associated with weather, which is outside the employee's control. An efficiency wage scheme might require firing all the workers because of a monsoon. In such a circumstance, tournaments work much better than common alternatives.

Tournaments encourage effort by compensating the best performers. Alternatively, yardstick competition encourages effort by paying for performance over the average performance, and marries incentive compensation with adjustment of the compensation based on the performance of others. Where a tournament might give a $10,000 prize to all the employees in the top 10%, a yardstick reward might provide for a payment of $1000 for every sale over the average quantity. Like tournaments, yardstick compensation can mitigate common risk in the environment, and provide incentives in circumstances where a reasonable success rate is unknown.

Ratchet Effect

> Accomplishing the impossible means only that
> the boss will add it to your regular duties.
>
> **—Doug Larson**

The government of Ontario, Canada, experimented with incentive compensation for hospitals, rewarding hospitals that reduced costs significantly. The program was discontinued as a failure after a few years. Few hospitals showed improved performance, and the hospitals that did lapsed back to their old inefficient ways. The reason was the nature of the program. Hospital managers got to keep the proceeds of cost savings, but only for one year; the following year the budget of the hospital was cut to extract the savings for the government. Thus, a permanent decrease in expenditures followed a one-time budget surplus; few hospital managers considered this to be a good deal for the hospital.

A major failing of tournaments is the information generated for the firm. Once the firm has learned the ability of employees, the firm has an incentive to adjust the expectations upward, and compensation downward. In particular, when a firm learns, thanks to a tournament or incentive compensation system, that employees can produce significantly more than the employees had been producing, the firm makes that enhanced level the new baseline, paying a premium only for performance in excess of the new baseline. This phenomenon is known as the ratchet effect, for the firm continually ratchets up expectations.

The ratchet effect discourages a response to incentive compensation of any form, and encourages employees to conceal their ability. Many unions discouraged superior performance by new members and set maximum performance goals, a means of combating the ratchet effect.

There is no easy cure for ratchet effect problems. Establishing a reputation for continuing to reward superior performance is probably the best strategy when it is available, but it is often difficult to resist the temptation to hold up a successful employee by revising expectations. In 2001, the Graduate School of Business of the University of Chicago set a $175 million, five-year fund-raising target. Within eight months, it had raised $100 million; ten months later it raised another $20 million. It will be interesting to observe whether the school succeeds in avoiding the ratchet effect temptation to increase the target.

EXECUTIVE SUMMARY—INCENTIVES

- The provision of incentives to employees is a major aspect of organizational design.
- Incentives are provided to employees by tying compensation to performance.
- Incentives necessarily impose some income risk on employees, and the risk premium is the cost of the provision of incentives.
- It is valuable to minimize the risk by tying, as closely as possible, the employee's compensation to the employee's behavior.
- Paying *efficiency wages* involves paying more than market rates, which provides incentives by the threat of termination from a high-paying job.
- High incentive payments (high commissions and low salaries) tend to attract two groups—the very able and the risk-loving.
- A crucial aspect of the provision of incentives is the effect of incentives for one behavior on other behaviors.
- When one aspect of a job is very important and difficult to measure, incentives to perform other aspects of the job need to be weak, so that the important aspect is not lost.
- Providing incentives based on what is measurable, rather than what is important, is a recipe for perverse effects.
- Jobs may be designed to minimize the problems of providing incentives.
- *Common agency* is the situation where several firms utilize the same agent.
- In a common agency situation, firms compete for the agent's efforts.
- Firms that can monitor the agent most easily have a significant advantage, so it often pays to increase monitoring.
- A tournament is a useful compensation system when the cost of effort or success is difficult to assess.
- The *ratchet effect* is the tendency to reward success with increased standards.
- The ratchet effect reduces the incentive to succeed.

9

Antitrust

At a very general level, the antitrust laws prohibit firms from coordinating their actions, through merger or agreement, in a way that would lessen competition. There are three significant reasons for managers to be quite familiar with the antitrust laws. First, the antitrust laws restrict the set of legal actions that a firm can take, prohibiting profitable strategies on occasion. Second, private antitrust suits are often used as a means of harassing a competitor. Even if a firm does not engage in such uncooperative behavior, it might be the target of a private antitrust suit. Third, managers personally can face significant fines and prison sentences of three years or more for violating the antitrust laws, so it is important for managers to have a familiarity with the laws.

MAJOR LAWS

The antitrust laws are enforced by two agencies: the Antitrust Division of the U.S. Department of Justice and the Federal Trade Commission. The Department of Justice ordinarily enforces antitrust laws by using the Sherman Act, although it may proceed with a Clayton Act violation as well. The Federal Trade Commission is charged with enforcing the Clayton Act, but it has no authority to bring criminal charges that may arise under the Sherman Act. As a practical matter, cases are divided between the two agencies based on relative expertise and current capacity. When the Department of Justice charged Microsoft with antitrust violations, the FTC handled a greater number of merger analyses to pick up DOJ overflow.

An interesting feature of the antitrust laws is that firms might be prohibited from bidding together, and yet be permitted to form a consortium or merge. Thus, in the 1995 Personal Communication Services (PCS) auctions, four major firms, including Airtouch and Bell Atlantic, formed a consortium to bid in the auction.

This consortium was legal, yet the firms individually could not legally cooperate during the auction. Thus, in some cases joint ventures can serve to legally implement what might otherwise be price-fixing.

Sherman Act (1890)

The Sherman Act of 1890 represents the beginning of serious antitrust legislation in the United States, and remains a major foundation of antitrust legislation. The two main clauses of the Sherman Act are Sections 1 and 2:

> *Section 1. Trusts, etc., in restraint of trade illegal; penalty*
> Every contract, combination in the form of trust or otherwise, or conspiracy, in restraint of trade or commerce among the several States, or with foreign nations, is declared to be illegal. Every person who shall make any contract or engage in any combination or conspiracy hereby declared to be illegal shall be deemed guilty of a felony, and, on conviction thereof, shall be punished by fine not exceeding $10,000,000 if a corporation, or, if any other person, $350,000, or by imprisonment not exceeding three years, or by both said punishments, in the discretion of the court.
> *Section 2. Monopolizing trade a felony; penalty*
> Every person who shall monopolize, or attempt to monopolize, or combine or conspire with any other person or persons, to monopolize any part of the trade or commerce among the several States, or with foreign nations, shall be deemed guilty of a felony, and, on conviction thereof, shall be punished by fine not exceeding $10,000,000 if a corporation, or, if any other person, $350,000, or by imprisonment not exceeding three years, or by both said punishments, in the discretion of the court.[1]

It is not at all clear from the act precisely what was intended by the Sherman Act; some scholars maintain that it was no more than a requirement for the courts to create antitrust laws via legal precedent. Early court rulings by Justice Rufus Peckham led to what became known as the Peckham Rule. Peckham noted that competition tends to lower prices, increasing the volume of trade. Thus, combinations, contracts, or conspiracies intended to restrict output or raise prices are illegal, while combinations intended to increase output are legal.

There was significant opposition to the Sherman Act at the time of its early enforcement. Many, including President Teddy Roosevelt, felt that the act was quite vague, and preferred legislation that enumerated a list of proscribed activities. It is a fair criticism even today to say that it is very difficult to tell in advance whether an action complies with antitrust legislation. President Howard Taft, however, felt that enforcement of the Sherman Act was quite reasonable. Generally, the courts ruled that mergers and trusts intended to increase prices were illegal, and all others were legal.

The famous *Standard Oil* case of 1911, leading to the breakup of the Standard Oil Company into thirty-three separate companies, was the first case to use a "rule of reason" analysis explicitly. This analysis judges a restraint of trade to be legal if it has a procompetitive basis, rather than an anticompetitive basis. The rule of reason requires a weighing of the effects and motivation, in contrast to a per se illegality. An action is *per se* illegal if it is illegal no matter what the motivation or effects. Supreme Court Chief Justice Edward White's opinion was that the Sherman Act was extremely broad and, on the face of it, eliminated perfectly reasonable contracts. Indeed, according to Chief Justice White, one reading of the Sherman Act might be that all contracts are illegal, insofar as contracts, by setting the terms of trade, restrain trade. The legislature could not have intended to prevent all contracts, and thus must have intended to prevent unreasonable contracts. In applying the act, then, judicial discretion is necessary. In addition to introducing the rule of reason explicitly, Chief Justice White's opinion also stated that the Sherman Act did not prohibit a firm from being a monopoly, but meant that some exclusionary practices could not be used in the attempt to obtain a monopoly.

Starting with the breakup of Alcoa in 1945, and most recently in the Microsoft case, the courts employ a two-part test for the Sherman Act. First, does the firm have monopoly power in a product market? Absent monopoly power, a firm has no ability to reduce competition or influence prices. Second, did the firm use illegal tactics in acquiring or maintaining the market power? In particular, did the firm engage in "the willful acquisition or maintenance of that power as distinguished from growth or development as a consequence of a superior product, business acumen or historic accident"?[2] That is, monopoly itself is not illegal, but some means of acquiring and preserving it are illegal.

Clayton Act (1914)

Enacted in 1914, and amended in 1936 by the Robinson-Patman Act, the Clayton Act adds detail to the Sherman Act, supplementing and extending Sherman Act enforcement. The Clayton Act does not carry criminal penalties, but it does allow for monetary penalties three times the amount of damage created by the illegal behavior.

Section 2 of the Clayton Act prohibits price discrimination that would lessen competition. This law is not applicable in selling to final consumers, but usually it is applicable when selling to firms that compete with each other. The logic of the act is that a lower price of an input to one firm will create a competitive disadvantage for other firms. In the classic case, volume discounts given by Morton Salt

Box 9.1: You Say Tomato

Celebrated restauranteur Wolfgang Puck, who started the trendy Los Angeles restaurant Spago, began selling frozen pizzas in the late 1980s. At least, *he* thought he was selling pizzas. The Federal government disagreed.

At issue: must a pizza have tomato sauce? According to the Department of Agriculture, yes. According to Puck, he knew more about pizza than federal bureaucrats knew.

The resolution: Puck agreed to call his sans-tomato pizza *California-Style Pizza,* which you can find on his line of frozen pizzas today.

Source: Kathleen A. Hughes. "Do the Feds Also Make It Taste Like a Soggy Piece of Cardboard?" *Wall Street Journal,* 7 November 1987.

were ruled illegal in 1948 because volume discounts disadvantaged small grocery stores relative to larger stores that qualified for the volume discounts. The discounts were not cost-based.* Section 2 of the Clayton Act provides for two main defenses. First, a cost-based defense is permitted; if the cost of serving one firm is higher than that for another, it is permissible to pass on the higher cost. This defense has been used rarely in practice. The second defense is that of "meeting competition." A firm is permitted to offer a discount to match the price offered by a competitor, without lowering prices to all. For example, a steel mill in Pittsburgh could lower the price of its steel to a customer in Chicago to match the price provided by a plant in nearby Gary, Indiana, without lowering the price to its Pittsburgh customers.

Section 2 prohibits a variety of subterfuges for concealing price discrimination, including brokerage commissions and indirect payments. Section 2 also prohibits buyers from attempting to extract illegal discounts from sellers.

*A second use for the prohibition of price discrimination arises out of the local price-war theory—a large firm moves into a market and uses its large resources to drive many of the small, local firms out of business, so as to control the market. There are various problems with this theory. Why does the large firm have better access to capital than successful local enterprises? If the large firm isn't more efficient, why can it eliminate local firms permanently? The Standard Oil Company was alleged to have engaged in such predatory practices, financing a price war with profits earned elsewhere, and picking off rivals one by one. The Utah Pie Company successfully used the theory in a 1967 suit against nationwide rivals.

Section 3 of the Clayton Act prohibits a variety of exclusionary practices that lessen or eliminate competition. This section rules out a variety of transactions between the seller of a good and buyers who are themselves firms. The section has been interpreted to prohibit

- Tying (must buy one good to get another)
- Requirements tying (buyer agrees to buy all its needs from the seller)
- Exclusive dealing (buyer agrees to deal only with seller)
- Exclusive territories (buyer agrees to operate only in specified region)
- Resale price maintenance (buyer agrees to a minimum resale price)
- Predatory pricing (pricing below cost to eliminate a competitor)

In order to be illegal, these activities must reduce competition or work to exclude or eliminate a competitor.

Section 4 of the Clayton Act permits private enforcement of the antitrust laws. In particular, those harmed by violations of the antitrust laws are entitled to treble damages (three times the actual damages) and the cost of bringing the suit, including attorneys' fees. Consumers, and firms in the same line of commerce, who were injured by the violation of the antitrust laws have standing to sue; those with collateral damage will not generally have standing. For instance, a firm driven out of business by predatory pricing will have standing to sue; however, the shareholders and employees of that firm will not, nor will the suppliers of other inputs to the bankrupt firm. That is, there may be parties injured by the illegal behavior who are too indirectly injured to have standing to sue.

The damage to consumers of illegal acts is clear—prices are increased by the monopolization, attempted monopolization, or lessened competition created by violations of the antitrust laws. (Predatory pricing is a notable exception.) However, the injury to firms is more complex. If the firm is driven out of business directly as a result of anticompetitive behavior and as part of the violation of the antitrust laws, its lost profits are an antitrust injury. Assessing antitrust injury is quite complicated when a firm is a user of a good whose price was illegally increased. Such a firm may have substituted other inputs, limiting the damage created. The Supreme Court has ruled that even if a downstream firm passed on the price increase, it is still entitled to collect the amount of the overcharge created by the antitrust violation.

Predatory pricing (pricing with the intent to drive competitors out of business) has generated a great deal of controversy. There have been many successful predatory pricing cases, although many analysts argue that it is an irrational strategy on the part of firms. The most convincing evidence comes from an in-depth study of American Tobacco, which found that American Tobacco had engaged in successful predation and was able to buy out its rivals at distressed prices.[3] Consistent with the theory, American Tobacco benefited from a reputation for starting price wars and paid less than other majors for acquisitions.

It is generally accepted that pricing below marginal cost is evidence of predatory intent, for such pricing is difficult to rationalize. There must be some method of recouping losses incurred on current sales, and setting higher future prices is a logical hypothesis. Proving that prices are below marginal cost is difficult, especially when costs fluctuate substantially, when there are peak-load-capacity issues, or when there are joint costs that must be allocated across various goods. Conceptually, the issue of pricing below marginal cost is straightforward, but verifying whether prices were below appropriate marginal cost is often difficult or impossible. As a consequence, prices below average variable cost (known as the Areeda-Turner test after the inventors) has become a standard accepted by many courts. The logic is the same—it is generally better to stop production than price below average variable cost. The problem, of course, is that it is difficult to identify average variable costs. Providing labor with guaranteed severance pay implies labor is not fully a variable cost—the severance must be deducted from wages.

Section 7 of the Clayton Act specifically addresses mergers, and prohibits direct or indirect share acquisition that would lessen competition or create a monopoly. Thus, the Clayton Act covers much of the territory covered by the Sherman Act, and in particular permits a second challenge to a merger, with the more transparent standard of a lessening of competition, rather than the problematic "attempt to monopolize" language of the Sherman Act.

FTC Act (1914)

The Federal Trade Commission Act created the FTC and gave it a mandate to prevent unfair methods of competition and deceptive practices. The FTC commissioners have the ability to decide quickly that a practice is unfair and move to stop it. The FTC commissioners have a quasi-judicial standing in such proceedings and can issue restraining orders and stop deceptive practices. The FTC has prevented Volvo from showing ads with monster trucks crushing other cars but not the Volvo, because the advertisements were faked. In particular, the roof supports of other cars were cut, while the Volvo was reinforced. The oil-treatment company STP (which stands for scientifically treated petroleum) was not only forced to stop advertising that STP promotes longer engine life but was also forced to run advertisements apologizing for deceptive advertisements. Recently, the FTC blocked bankrupt toy seller Toysmart from selling its customer list, because that would have violated Toysmart's privacy promises.[4] McDonald's "shakes" cannot be called milkshakes because they have too little milk to qualify as milkshakes.

The FTC Act does not generally create more powerful antitrust enforcement than the Clayton Act. However, it was recently interpreted to prohibit *suggesting* collusion to competitors, even when turned down. Under either the Sherman or Clayton Act, the suggestion that firms might fix prices, if turned down, has not lessened competition and probably did not attempt to monopolize, and therefore is not illegal. The FTC Act, however, may make such a suggestion illegal.

Exemptions and Special Treatment

A variety of industries are handled separately from the standard antitrust laws. Banks are scrutinized by the Federal Reserve, which may prevent mergers, although banks also receive FTC or DOJ scrutiny as well. Some of the industries with special treatment, either by explicit legislation or existing precedent, are

- Labor unions
- Baseball[5]
- Agriculture
- Research joint ventures
- Oil companies[6]
- Newspapers
- Industries protected by states (e.g., state-sponsored agricultural cooperatives)
- Business lobbying organizations*

Government agencies other than the DOJ and FTC may still have powerful effects on the form of competition, even when they have no antitrust authority. The Federal Communications Commission oversees the telecommunications industry, and thus acts as an adviser to the DOJ and FTC. In response to the increasing complexity of the telecommunications industry, the FCC has expanded its capacity to perform economic analysis at least threefold in recent years.† The Federal Energy Regulatory Commission (FERC) insures that Soviet economic policy continues even after the Communist regime has disappeared.‡ Finally, the Department of Defense has a major impact on the defense industry. The DOD orchestrated the consolidation of the defense industry, although without any apparent consideration of what the end result should be. As a large buyer of jet fuel, the DOD was

*In particular, trade associations that lobby the government for regulations that would restrain trade and lessen competition are generally legal.

†The FCC was one of the last agencies to switch to tone-based telephones from the old rotary-dial system. One FCC staffer remarked in 1990, "We regulate twenty-first-century technology with nineteenth-century technology."

‡For example, it is a FERC regulation that insures that the Trans-Alaska Pipeline is always at 95% of capacity, no matter how much oil goes through it. The capacity is defined as 105% of utilization. This bit of government psychosis insures that the prices for capacity obtained via bidding are always high.

consulted on the likely effects of several large oil company mergers in the past several years.

Collusive Bidding in Hostile Takeovers

An unusual exemption from the antitrust laws arises when firms are attempting to take over another firm. When two firms are bidding, one may pay the other to stop bidding; this has happened half a dozen times over the past twenty years. Typically, this lowers the price that the winning bidder pays.[7]

Why is this not illegal price-fixing? In a standard auction, paying one bidder to exit would be conspiracy and price-fixing. However, the courts have consistently ruled that the 1934 Securities and Exchange Commission Act, which regulates the trading of company stock, preempts the antitrust legislation that preceded it. Congress passed control of securities to the SEC and left no role for additional antitrust enforcement, according to several decisions.

Predation, Foreclosure, and Tying

The Sherman and Clayton Acts prohibit a variety of activities that would lessen competition or create a monopoly. One important aspect of these laws is that the acquisition of a monopoly itself is not illegal. In the 1945 *Alcoa* case, the court specifically stated that the acquisition of a monopoly does not prove monopolization. When a monopoly is acquired by "superior skill, foresight and industry," having a monopoly is legal. However, some means of acquiring a monopoly are illegal, as the justices ruled in the *Alcoa* case. The court singled out:

- Signing of exclusive agreements with electric utilities forbidding the sale of power to competing aluminum producers
- Price-fixing with foreign companies to prevent imports
- Increasing the price of raw materials provided to competitors to squeeze their profits
- Expanding capacity to eliminate competition.

An important precedent was set in the *United Shoe* case in 1953. The United Shoe Machinery company engaged in two practices that were ruled to contribute to monopolization. First, United Shoe rented, or leased, its machinery and refused to sell the machinery. Second, United Shoe insisted on manufacturer repair and prohibited third-party repair. The court reasoned that the insistence on manufacturer repair of machines, enforced by a refusal to sell the machinery, discouraged the entry of third-party service companies, known now as independent service organizations, or ISOs. The lack of third-party service increased the scale required to enter the shoe-machinery business—not only would an entrant have to manufacture shoe-making machinery, but it would have to provide service as well. Since *United Shoe,* there have been many lawsuits by ISOs against manufacturers who provide service for their own equipment, with mixed results. Usually, manufacturers have no duty to help ISOs, but heavy-handed exclusionary tactics may be illegal.

The courts often take a dim view of a *refusal to deal.* Generally, such a refusal may require a procompetitive reason in order to be legal. A refusal to deal is especially problematic when it involves an *essential facility,* without which it is impossible to operate. The original essential-facility case involved a monopoly on railroad bridges into St. Louis. Without access to one of the bridges, it was not possible to get a train to St. Louis. Generally, an essential facility is something necessary to own to compete, and it can include buying cooperatives and selling channels. Microsoft Windows is likely an essential facility for microcomputer manufacturers. The major logic of refusal-to-deal cases is that a firm is denied access to an essential resource or input, which renders the firm uncompetitive, hence injuring competition and violating the law. In the original essential-facility case, the Supreme Court held that access to the bridge had to be made available to all firms.[8]

Predatory pricing involves pricing in such a way as to bankrupt or induce exit of a competitor. A two-part test is used to determine if a firm has engaged in predatory pricing. First, were the prices below cost? Marginal cost is the right concept, for competitive firms will not price below marginal cost. However, often marginal cost is not observable, and average variable cost is used; average variable cost has the virtue of being more readily observed and also representing the shut-down point of a competitive firm in classical economic analysis.* The second part of the predation test is to determine whether the firm could reasonably recoup the losses if it succeeded in driving a firm or firms out of business. This part of the predation test rules out many unreasonable predation claims, because it would be difficult or impossible to injure competition by pricing below cost. As soon as prices were raised (to recoup the investment), entry would occur. In one instance, a claim that a firm would recoup its losses twenty years later was dismissed as unreasonable.

It is quite common for firms to want to place restrictions on input suppliers and downstream retailers. For example, a firm might want its retail outlets to offer service, provide exchanges and issue refunds, and promote the product. Firms want input suppliers to provide an input of good quality in a timely manner, with guaranteed delivery. As a consequence, firms enter into contracts with upstream and

*Unfortunately, average variable cost is more difficult to observe than many analysts realize. For example, a team of workers may be lost if laid off, so that the team is more like a fixed cost than a variable cost. The concept of variable cost is especially murky when multiple products, with interdependent cost functions, are offered.

downstream firms; some of these contracts, known as "vertical restraints," have been found illegal. The contracts are called vertical restraints because they restrain other firms in a vertical (upstream suppliers or downstream retailers) relationship.

At best, the logic of decisions based on vertical restraints is murky and confused. One principle is that when a firm sells a product to a retailer or final consumer, the firm cannot force behavior on the purchaser. Thus, the buyer of a GM car cannot be required to use GM parts. The courts see through the ploy of voiding the warranty in the event that substitute parts are used; the warranty can be voided only if the substitute parts actually caused a problem covered by the warranty, and then only the relevant portion is voided, not the entire warranty. Beer retailers cannot be prevented from selling Coors beer east of the Mississippi. Resale price maintenance, which imposes a minimum price on retailers, is illegal. Indeed, resale price maintenance is illegal per se. A finding that a firm engaged in resale price maintenance is sufficient to show that the firm broke the antitrust laws.*

Firms often create exclusive territories for retailers. Car dealerships have exclusive territories, for example. Generally, exclusive territories are illegal if the purpose is to limit price competition, but are legal if the purpose is to promote competition. A major motivation to have exclusive territories is to prevent the manufacturer or upstream firm from exploiting successful retailers. For example, a franchise might encourage franchisees to open up, but only to open company-owned stores near the successful franchises. (Taco Bell has been accused of this behavior.) Such opportunistic exploitation, of course, undercuts the incentive to open the initial franchises. As a consequence, exclusive territories can be procompetitive—assuring franchisees of protection against exploitation by the franchiser.

In contrast to exclusive territories, which are often (though not always) legal, exclusive dealing is often illegal. A typical case of exclusive dealing prevents a retailer that carries one manufacturer's product from carrying any other manufacturer's product. The Alcoa contracts with electric utilities, which prohibited the utilities from providing electricity to competing aluminum producers, represents an example of illegal exclusive dealing. Exclusive dealing is illegal if it affects a substantial share of commerce in a "relevant" market; that is, if a market in the antitrust sense (which need not coincide with common parlance) is significantly affected.

Exclusive dealing ties the purchase of one product to the nonuse of another. Tying, in contrast, requires purchasing one product to be permitted to purchase

*This finding is especially annoying to economic analysts, because the usual reason that firms engage in resale price maintenance is to encourage retailers to engage in competition on grounds other than price, such as service and education. Presumably, sellers have an interest in preventing retailers from competing on price only when the provision of such services is efficient; otherwise, sellers would like retailers to cut their margins and compete on price.

another. For example, IBM required the use of IBM cards, and United Shoe required the use of United Shoe repair. Both of these tying contracts were judged illegal. Market power in one product that is used to limit competition in another product through a tying arrangement is illegal. In particular, tying product sales to manufacturer-provided service is illegal. Similarly, Microsoft's requirement that AOL promote Internet Explorer, in order to have its service registration bundled with the Windows operating system, represented an illegal tying arrangement. Tying represents the extension of monopoly power in one market into another market.*

The antitrust laws were intended to promote competition and to protect competition from practices by monopolies. An unintended consequence of the antitrust laws was the creation of a new means for corporations to harass each other. In chapter 14, we will meet several examples of corporations damaging each other by the use, and misuse, of the antitrust laws.

MERGERS

When two firms above a minimal size begin the process of merging, the Hart-Scott-Rodino Act of 1976 requires that the firms inform the government prior to the merger, and provide certain information concerning the relationships between the products and services of the two companies. Both the FTC and the DOJ's Antitrust Division have jurisdiction, but these two agencies will choose which of them will handle the merger rather than have both exercise authority. The agency has up to twenty days to request more information, known as a second request. Once a second request is issued, the firms are prohibited from merging until they are in "substantial compliance" with the second request. Complying with a second request can be remarkably arduous; the Exxon-Mobil merger generated over 100 million pages of documents.

Occasionally, firms will attempt to hide competitive issues associated with merger by inundating the agency with documents, providing a copy of every scrap of paper and the least informative index that complies with the law. (This was not the Exxon-Mobil strategy; document production was large because the companies were large.) The document-blitz strategy is typically ineffective, because it strongly signals that there is a major problem with the merger, and the government can call on other sources, such as competitors and consumers, to identify the competitive problems hidden in the mass of documents.

Horizontal mergers, in which the merging parties have products in common,

*IBM was almost certainly not trying to monopolize the card market; rather, cards represented a useful way of metering demand, letting IBM price discriminate in the machine market more successfully.

generate the largest concern by the government. Until relatively recently, the primary theory was that increased concentration in a market made collusion and cartels more likely. Now, however, there is an increasing focus on unilateral effects of merger—that merger will lead to increased prices in spite of significant, but imperfect, competition to the merged entity.

Agency concerns over vertical mergers are growing. For example, the FTC was concerned over Barnes & Noble's planned purchase of Ingram Books, and over vertical aspects of the merger of BP/Amoco with Arco, particularly concerning the supply of oil to the California market, where Arco has a large retail presence. The merger of AOL with Time Warner presented a number of vertical concerns, many of which required remedy.

When either the FTC or the DOJ considers that a serious competitive problem is raised by a merger, it can request an injunction stopping the merger until a trial can be held. Typically, the agency works with the firms to identify the competitive issues and to find remedies that would eliminate the competitive problem. When the government and the firms cannot find common ground, the government will request a court order preventing the merger, and a trial date will be set. Many mergers are approved without remedy, and many are approved after a remedy for existing antitrust problems is found. Exxon and Mobil, for example, sold Mobil's interest in a pipeline, thousands of retail gasoline stations, and a California refinery. BP/Amoco agreed to sell Arco's Alaskan oil interests, but only after the government sought a preliminary injunction.

There are three broad classes of remedies. The weakest and least effective is a promise. Microsoft issued promises to the DOJ over Windows 95 and Internet Explorer, promises the government alleges were later violated. Promises to provide inputs to competitors on an equal basis and to provide access to facilities are also used. Because the government has difficulty monitoring whether promises are kept, both the FTC and the DOJ tend to take a dim view of promises, although they have been used. The next level of remedy is a fire wall, through which two companies merge but their divisions are kept separate. In one case, the remedy required that compensation to the manager of a division be based exclusively on that division's performance. In another case, a firm promised to keep information about customers generated by one division secret from its other divisions. Fire walls work best in defense procurement firms. Major defense contractors routinely guard national security secrets and are more familiar with fire walls than other firms; and they probably are more credible when they promise to respect fire walls.

The most common remedy is a divestiture of one or more divisions. Few large mergers arise without some divestitures. For example, both General Electric and RCA had small-appliance divisions. One was sold to Black & Decker, leading to the well-known Black & Decker brand of kitchen appliances.

DOJ Guidelines for Horizontal Mergers

The U.S. Department of Justice and the Federal Trade Commission issue very similar guidelines to assist firms in understanding the government position concerning mergers. In principle, the guidelines set out which mergers will be challenged by the government and which will be approved without challenge. In practice, however, there is sufficient dispute concerning the application of the guidelines to make the guidelines a rough approximation at best.

The guidelines present a three-step approach to assessing the competitive effects of horizontal merger. The first step identifies the product market, and uses the following logic: Start with two related products sold by the two merging firms. Would a hypothetical monopolist controlling both of those products choose to raise price by a significant amount, and for a significant amount of time? If so, then the products represent a market. If not, which is usually the case, then another product must be added to make a market. Take the closest third product, perhaps produced by a third firm, perhaps by one of the merging firms. Would a hypothetical monopolist choose to raise price if it controlled the prices of all three? If so, the three together represent a market; otherwise, it would be necessary to keep adding products to the group until a hypothetical monopolist would raise prices. Generally, the "significant amount" by which prices must rise is 5%–10%, and the significant duration is one to four years. This is usually called a SSNIP (pronounced "snip")—a small but significant nontransitory increase in price.

The logic of the guidelines test for a product market is that if a monopolist would not choose to increase prices over a group of products in a meaningful way, then the products cannot comprise a market for antitrust purposes. Even a monopoly will not exercise market power. The logic of the test rests on an old notion that the primary threat to competition is collusion. The DOJ guidelines identify the smallest collusive group that will successfully increase prices.

The second step of the guidelines is a test to determine the geographic market. The geographic market test follows exactly the same logic as the product market test—to identify an area in which both of the merging firms operate. Next, the smallest area in which it would pay to increase prices a significant and nontransitory amount must be found. This area represents a geographic market.

The logic of the geographic market definition is that an area must be sufficiently large for a monopoly or cartel to exercise market power; otherwise, consumers would substitute areas outside that market. A street corner will not be a retail gasoline market, even if there are four stations on the corner, because consumers will typically drive a few blocks, even a mile or so, to save ten cents per gallon on a tank of gasoline. On the other hand, a sizable county might well comprise a retail gasoline market. If prices were raised throughout a county, a hypothetical monopolist would lose business on the edge of the county, because of substitution by drivers to stations outside the county. Nearer the center, however, it would not pay to drive outside the county to save 10%. If the increased revenue in the center outweighs the losses near the edge, the county constitutes a market for retail gasoline under the guidelines approach.

Once the product and geographic markets have been identified, the final step of the guidelines requires assessing the competitiveness of the market. The standard approach involves evaluating the market shares of the firms, to judge how concentrated the industry resources are.[9] Traditionally, the concentration of the industry was assessed by using "concentration ratio four," or CR4, which is the sum of the market shares of the four largest firms. However, starting in the early 1980s, CR4 was replaced with the Hirschmann-Herfindahl Index (HHI). The HHI is the sum of the squared market shares of the firms. For example, if the market shares were 40%, 30%, 20%, and 10%, the HHI is computed by squaring each of these numbers, and then summing them, to obtain

$$\text{HHI} = 40^2 + 30^2 + 20^2 + 10^2 = 1600 + 900 + 400 + 100 = 3000.$$

Many analysts think of an industry with a given HHI as behaving similarly to an industry with the same HHI but with equal-sized firms. Thus, an HHI of 1000 corresponds roughly to ten equal-sized firms, and an HHI of 2000 to five equal-sized firms. If there are n equal-sized firms, the HHI will be

$$\text{HHI} = n\left(\frac{100}{n}\right)^2 = \frac{10{,}000}{n}.$$

This equation can be solved for n, the number of equal-sized firms corresponding to a given HHI. That number is 10,000/HHI. Thus, it is not uncommon to hear government analysts talk about a market with two and a half firms, which is a proxy for an HHI of 4000. Similarly, the HHI of 3000 found above is viewed to be similar to three and a third equal-sized firms.

The merger guidelines consider an industry to be unconcentrated if the HHI is less than 1000, moderately concentrated if the HHI is between 1000 and 1800, and concentrated if the HHI exceeds 1800. Thus, ten or more equal-sized firms mean there is little concentration, while five and a half to ten equal-sized firms create a moderately concentrated market. High concentration arises with five or fewer equal-sized firms.

The merger guidelines require assessing the effect on concentration by considering how much the HHI changes, and whether the market is concentrated after the merger. The change in the HHI is found by computing both the premerger HHI and the postmerger HHI, the latter assuming that the merged firm has a market share equal to the sum of the merging parties' shares.[10] Consider the example given above, with four firms, and market shares of 40, 30, 20, and 10, and an HHI of 3000. If the two smallest firms merge, the hypothetical new market shares will become 40, 30, and 30, with an HHI of 3400 and a change of 400.

The merger guidelines dictate a likely challenge if the postmerger HHI is moderately concentrated and the change exceeds 100, or if the postmerger HHI is concentrated and the change exceeds 50. A change of 100 arises if a firm with 10% of market shares merges with a firm with 5%. Thus, if there were nine firms with 10%, and two firms with 5%, a merger of a firm with 10% and a firm with 5% just squeaks through the guidelines—the HHI rises from an unconcentrated 950 to a moderately concentrated 1050, but the change is just 100. It is relatively rare for the guidelines to be strictly enforced, for many very competitive industries are concentrated by the guidelines standards; the calculations should be viewed as a basis for discussion rather than a strict rule.

There are a variety of alterations to the basic calculations, which relax or tighten the guidelines. Two major relaxations involve a safe harbor that arises when one firm is not too great—has less than 35% of the market—and the other has less than 1%. A more significant exception is the "failing firm defense," which permits a firm going bankrupt to merge with another, when the alternative is for the failing firm's assets to leave the industry. The logic is to preserve capital in the marketplace; if the capital will leave unless there is the merger, it is better for society if the merger takes place. The failing-firm defense has been used successfully in many local newspaper mergers, and in the Greyhound bus company's takeover of its major competitor, Trailways. This instance of the failing-firm defense was viewed with extreme skepticism by many analysts, but was later given significant corroboration when Greyhound itself went into receivership.

In the view of the government agency, efficiencies of a merger may offset some of the risk of increased prices. From the government's perspective, increases in efficiency are a good thing, and thus are certainly relevant to the decision of the government to pursue a case. However, efficiencies are not exemptions found in law, since typically they must be huge to offset an increase in market power.* Efficiencies were used as defenses in several defense industry mergers, and evidence showing that 75% of efficiency increases accrued to the Department of Defense was persuasive. Moreover, the experience with the early defense mergers showed that

*Even a merger to monopolize a market might lower prices if costs fall sufficiently, so that the monopoly price with the low cost is below what the marginal cost would be without the merger. Since competition has been reduced even as consumers are made better off, efficiency defenses are generally ignored by the courts.

the merging parties underestimated efficiencies, which was compelling evidence in subsequent cases.

Entry appears twice in the analysis. The product market can include the products of firms that are not currently in the marketplace but are likely entrants. In particular, imports that are unprofitable to import currently, but would be imported in the event of a SSNIP (a small but significant nontransitory increase in price), would count in the product market definition. Imports can be very significant to a minimization of the market shares of the merging parties. However, the impact of imports tends to be relatively cut-and-dried. If the import costs plus transportation costs are just above currently prevailing prices, imports count; otherwise, imports are too expensive. The threat of "imports" from other geographic regions can be used to make geographic regions seem large.*

The importance of entry may appear a second time in the analysis—in market shares. If rapid entry is the likely consequence of any significant increase in price, the capacity of firms not in the marketplace may be counted toward assessing the market shares. Such was the outcome in the analysis of the space-station market in the merger of RCA and GE. These two firms were the only two with current plans to bid for many components of the space station. However, the ability of other firms, especially defense contractors like General Dynamics, Lockheed, Boeing, and Northrop, to provide the same components was not seriously questioned. Consequently, market-share analysis for many space-station components, including zero-gravity toilets, included a number of potential competitors. (Since none of the parts had yet been produced, even GE and RCA were only potential competitors.) Because of the large number of potential competitors, GE and RCA were permitted to merge without a divestiture of space-station production units. In the actual bidding, however, major components of the space station that expected to receive bids from both GE and RCA actually received bids from only the merged firm GE/RCA and not from any of the other potential competitors.

Generally, for entry to mitigate the government's concern over the anticompetitive effects of a merger, entry must be expected very rapidly, usually in one to four years, depending on the industry. In many industries that have environmental-impact issues, like pulp and paper or power generation industries, entry in this time frame is not feasible. Consequently, in many practical situations, entry will not ameliorate the government's concern over possible price increases.

There are three major situations that increase the government's concern over a merger dramatically. First, if firms are already price discriminating, the merger guidelines suggest defining very narrow geographic and product markets. The rea-

*In one entertaining incident, a judge was shown a film of the quickest drive between two banks. Because the drive involved thirty miles of hairpin turns and precipitous cliffs, the judge concluded that the firms were not in the same geographic market.

son is that the ability to charge different groups significantly different prices means that the different groups fall in different markets. Price discrimination was a key to the analysis of the geographical-market size of retail gasoline. Major gasoline sellers tend to charge significantly different prices in areas with inelastic demand, in spite of proximity to stations with lower prices. Apparent market areas, judged by one company's pricing techniques, could be as small as a square mile.

Second, if there appears to be a significant likelihood that the merging parties can, postmerger, unilaterally increase price, concerns about the merger increase. Unilateral effects have been a growing concern of both the Department of Justice and the Federal Trade Commission because of heightened attention paid by academic economists to unilateral effects. In particular, the FTC's opposition to the merger of the office supply superstores Staples and Office Depot was based on a unilateral-effects theory. Because these companies were each other's closest and most significant competitor in many markets, the FTC viewed that the merger would facilitate price increases. The FTC provided documents from Staples and some economic data to the court showing that in a market with two competing superstores, the prices were lower than when only one superstore was present. According to economic experts familiar with the case,[11] the economic analyses by various experts canceled each other out, and documents determined the court's finding in favor of the FTC. This is not an uncommon outcome. Often complex economic analysis is unpersuasive, and documents produced by the parties determine the outcome. When these documents are inflammatory, especially when the documents of one firm identify the other merging firm as the "main" or "primary" competitor, the court will often oppose a merger of the two firms. This is a major reason for the court's agreement with the FTC in the *Staples* case. Similarly, documents that reveal attempts—even unsuccessful attempts—to engage in predatory pricing, to share a market, to soften price competition, and generally to engage in acts that indicate an attempt to increase prices above competitive levels, are likely to be taken as significant indications of probable competitive problems arising from the merger.

When the industry, such as the cardboard manufacturing or tobacco industry, has a history of collusive behavior, the government will be much more leery of a merger than if the industry seems to have been historically competitive. The logic is that the industry has been collusive because of some, usually unidentified, structural reason, which will likely remain after the merger. Thus, past collusion is viewed as a good predictor of future collusion.

Typically, the United States is much more aggressive in challenging mergers than the governments of other nations. However, the European Commission, headquartered in Brussels, is increasingly involved in mergers, and may require divestitures not required by the U.S. agencies. Recently, the European Commission prevented General Electric's takeover of Honeywell, which appeared to have survived scrutiny by U.S. antitrust authorities.

The Premium Fountain Pen Market

An interesting example of product market analysis arose in the merger of Gillette and Parker Pen. Gillette owned both the Papermate and Waterman brands of writing instruments. Parker is a well-known pen maker. The Department of Justice and its economics expert, George Rozanski, alleged that premium fountain pens constituted a relevant antitrust market. In particular, the government alleged that this market excluded ordinary fountain pens and instead was composed of pens of higher quality, the kind with solid-gold or gold-plated nibs, superior filling systems, and brass fittings. Such pens generally cost over $50. In addition, the government's expert appears to have excluded pens costing more than $400, although it is unclear whether he was viewing these as a separate market from premium pens, or just did not have data on pens over $400.

In contrast, the merging parties, and their economic expert, Professor Carl Shapiro, argued for a much more inclusive market. The merging parties focused especially on fountain pens with prices near $40, because Sheaffer sells many pens in this range, as do Pellikan, Lamy, Elysee, and others. Because most of the sales in the $50 to $400 range are in fact closer to $50, the case for exclusion of $40 pens is difficult to sustain. In addition, Professor Shapiro argued that the fountain pens were not a relevant market because a substantial number of customers would shift to rollerball pens if the price of fountain pens increased significantly. Professor Shapiro introduced evidence from consumer purchases to support his claims, while Dr. Rozanski relied on industry documents and affidavits.

United States District Court Judge Royce Lambert (District of Columbia) agreed with the merging parties and denied the government's request for a preliminary injunction. Interestingly, Judge Lambert agreed with the government that fountain pens costing less than $50 should be excluded from the specified market. However, the court also agreed with the merging parties that other writing implements besides fountain pens belonged in the market. As a consequence, the government claims concerning the too-narrow fountain pen market failed.[12]

Vertical Mergers and Antitrust Enforcement

Vertical mergers—those between a firm and an input supplier, or between a manufacturer and a retailer—traditionally have received much less scrutiny than horizontal mergers, which involve firms in the same industry. However, in recent years, vertical aspects of merger cases are becoming much more carefully scrutinized.

A case in point is Barnes & Noble's attempted takeover of Ingram Books. Ingram is an intermediary in the book business, buying books from publishers and warehousing them for resale to owner-operated bookstores and to chains, including Barnes & Noble. There were two significant areas of concern in this merger. First, Barnes & Noble was in a war with Amazon over the Internet market for books.* Thus, the purchase of Ingram—Amazon's largest supplier by far—could be interpreted as an attempt to foreclose Amazon by denying Amazon access to the raw material of Internet book sales, books.† In addition, Ingram obtained a great deal of information from its position as the main source of supply for independent booksellers. The advantage of supplying independents is that the independent booksellers collect a great deal of information about the likes and dislikes of their customers, because one of the main products of an independent bookstore is personalized service. As a consequence, the demand of the independents reflects a greater knowledge of the customers than is available through alternative sources. Only Ingram is in a position to aggregate that knowledge of the market and order books accordingly. The independent sellers feared that if Ingram was purchased by Barnes & Noble, it would favor Barnes & Noble over the independents, further damaging them in their competition with major chains.‡ Ultimately, the merger of Barnes & Noble and Ingram was not consummated.

Another example of a merger that received significant antitrust scrutiny was Microsoft's purchase of Intuit, a merger that was also abandoned. This case involved both a horizontal aspect—Intuit's very successful financial software program Quicken and Microsoft's relatively unsuccessful program Money—but the vertical aspect was almost certainly more important than the horizontal aspect. Indeed, Microsoft was having difficulty getting Money off the ground, so the competitive overlap was relatively minor. At the time of the proposed merger in 1994, Money was the weakest of the four competitors, with Meca's Managing Your Money and Computer Associates' Simply Money being the other two competitors.

*The companies had several lawsuits against each other, including Barnes & Noble's suit to stop Amazon's use of the slogan "Earth's largest bookstore," and Amazon's suit to stop Barnes & Noble's express checkout.

†There are other book intermediaries, yet virtually all market participants agree that Ingram is the best broad-based intermediary. The largest intermediary other than Ingram handles a large number of school texts. In addition, an intermediary is not absolutely necessary, because a company can deal directly with publishers. However, this requires warehousing—publishers sell large lots and are slow to ship old books. Indeed, Amazon opted to backward integrate into book warehousing.

‡This fear seems apparently reasonable but is somewhat tortured. If Barnes & Noble were to favor itself through Ingram's sale policy, Barnes & Noble would risk sending the independents to competing suppliers, who would improve, attracting more independents, and ultimately would kill off the informational value of Ingram. The risk of such a major bad outcome should restrain Barnes & Noble from all but the most minor shifting of profitable books to itself.

Quicken had about three-quarters of the market, and the other three competitors were roughly similar in size. The main fear was that Microsoft could use its operating system to foreclose competition in the financial software market, and perhaps in the tax-preparation software market, where TaxCut, Intuit's very successful program, was dominant. The fear that Microsoft could use the operating system as a means of foreclosing competition was enhanced by Microsoft's success in the word processing, spread sheet, and presentation software markets.

Vertical mergers create a possibility of foreclosing competition by denying access either to inputs or to retail distribution. At a less dramatic level, a vertical merger might lead to "raising rival's costs," which amounts to an increased price rather than a refusal to deal. A key element of antitrust analysis is that antitrust guidelines protect competition, not competitors. Thus, just because a competitor is harmed by a price increase, one cannot conclude that competition has been harmed; there may be alternative competitors, or customers may have other means of protecting themselves against price increases.

An interesting vertical merger case concerned the plan of Silicon Graphics, maker of powerful computer workstations, to purchase Alias Research and Wavefront Technologies, two of the three leading firms that produce graphics software. The products in this software market are used to produce special effects in movies, for instance morphing and the dinosaurs in the film *Jurassic Park*. These products run exclusively on the workstations of Silicon Graphics. Thus, the FTC feared that the merged entity could favor its software at the expense of the rival firm, SoftImage, now a subsidiary of Microsoft, thereby using control of the input—the workstation—to foreclose a rival.[13] In addition, the FTC was concerned that the merger would enhance the ability of Silicon Graphics to price-discriminate, using software.[14]

The commission accepted a three-part remedy in exchange for permitting the merger. First, Silicon agreed to insure that Alias's software would be compatible with a competing workstation, in an attempt to encourage entry into the computer graphics workstation market. Second, Silicon Graphics agreed to keep its operating system open, so that other software producers could produce competing software that would run on Silicon Graphics workstations. Finally, Silicon agreed to create a fire wall to prevent the flow of information about customers between the software and hardware divisions. This remedy addressed a concern that information about competitors could be passed inappropriately. For example, suppose a third-party software company needed help in making its program run on a Silicon Graphics workstation. It would show new features to the workstation team. If the workstation team were to pass the information about the new features on to the graphics division, the graphics division could benefit inappropriately, free-riding on the investments of the third party.

Conglomerate Mergers

In antitrust usage, conglomerate mergers refer to mergers with no obvious vertical or horizontal dimension. It is usually considered that conglomerate mergers present few antitrust concerns, although this is not necessarily the case. For example, a merger of two firms selling identical products in different geographic regions has no horizontal overlap. However, if the merged firm competes with another firm that operates in both geographic regions, it may become possible to divide the market along the lines of the multimarket contact analysis conducted earlier. Generally, however, the FTC and DOJ have focused only on horizontal and vertical aspects of mergers.

EXECUTIVE SUMMARY—ANTITRUST

- The two major antitrust laws are the Sherman Act and the Clayton Act.
- These laws prohibit mergers and conspiracies that lessen competition.
- Many specific practices are prohibited, including
  - Tying the purchase of one good to the purchase of another,
  - Requiring a buyer to deal with one seller,
  - Splitting the market with a competitor,
  - Imposing a minimum price on retailers (resale price maintenance), and
  - Predatory pricing.
- Both the FTC and DOJ have jurisdiction over mergers (mergers of firms in the same output markets).
- The FTC and DOJ divide the cases based on their relative skills, and historically have focused mainly on *horizontal* mergers (mergers of firms in the same industry).
- Concern over *vertical* mergers (mergers of supplier and buyer) is growing.
- The threats to competition from vertical mergers include foreclosure (denial of access to an important input) and raising rivals' costs.
- The agencies have issued guidelines that are stricter than common practice for assessing the anticompetitive conduct of mergers.
- Evidence of price discrimination increases government concern over the likely anticompetitive effects of merger.
- The likelihood of entry mitigates merger concerns. Efficiencies created by merger are considered, but the government is often skeptical that the merger is necessary to achieve efficiencies.
- Conglomerate mergers, those with neither a horizontal or a vertical component, are generally viewed as benign.

There are three kinds of lies: lies, damned lies, and statistics.

—Benjamin Disraeli[1]

Elementary Statistics

Statistics are a critical element to understanding business strategy, because almost every endeavor has some random component. Better sports teams sometimes lose. Machines break down. Market surveys indicate demand that does not materialize when the product is introduced. An oil field is unexpectedly profitable, or dry. A large safe falls out of a window.

Many approaches to strategy ignore randomness. The standard Net Present Value (NPV) approach to valuation of a project ignores the option value of postponing a project. This is often a mistake, because in many cases the option value is quite valuable, and consideration of the option value may significantly change the optimal time to undertake the project. Option values are not an issue only when there is no random component to the outcomes, or no possibility of relevant information being learned. For example, in off-shore oil tracts, it is generally useful to know if nearby tracts have oil; the presence of oil nearby is very relevant information. Thus, even if the NPV is positive, it may be preferable to wait until a neighbor drills, and base the decision to drill on the neighbor's success.

Probability and statistics represent central tools in the analysis of insurance, physics, biology and genetics, agriculture, economics, finance and equity valuation, and medicine. The systematic study of probability began in the late seventeenth century, with the work of Jacob Bernoulli and Gottfried Wilhelm Leibniz, who were motivated by two kinds of problems—games of chance and fair-interest-rate determination.* Probability and statistics are technical fields. While the presentation is simplified, it still is the most technical aspect of strategy.

*Relative to almost all other scientific pursuits, probability developed very late, probably because the idea that things are intrinsically random is difficult to understand; people want to find a cause for events, and random chance is somehow unsatisfying. In contrast, calculus was developed by Archimedes around 220 B.C., lost, and then rediscovered by Isaac Newton and Leibniz.

OPINION POLLS

We've lived by the crystal ball and learned to eat so much broken glass tonight that we're in critical condition.

—CBS anchor Dan Rather

In the 1948 presidential election, the *Chicago Daily Tribune* was sufficiently confident of Thomas Dewey's victory that it printed the paper with the banner headline "Dewey Defeats Truman." Truman won, and showed the headline with satisfaction in St. Louis (see fig. 10.1). In the 1992 election, opinion polls forecast that third-party candidate Ross Perot would obtain less than 10% of the popular vote, when he won 19%. Why?

The problem in 1948 was that the poll was taken by telephone. Taking the poll by telephone created a bias—poor people typically did not own telephones, and thus were excluded. The poll, therefore, did not sample all of the people, but a selected subset, and that subset excluded many of the relatively poor in the voting population. Those excluded people were much more likely to vote for Truman. In one sense, the polls were accurate—a majority of telephone owners voted for Dewey; but the poll had not sampled the group of interest—all voters—but instead had sampled an unrepresentative group of voters. The problem with the 1948 opinion poll is not conceptually different than the problem with a sitting president polling his staff about who should be elected, or asking the people in a Wendy's hamburger restaurant which fast-food restaurant they prefer.

The problem in the 1992 election was more complex. Polls now attempt to adjust for the likelihood that someone votes as well as who they say they will vote for. The 1992 polling error arose as a combination of two factors. Perot voters were more likely to vote than had been expected. The likelihood of voting is forecast using information about individuals—where they live, income, etc.—and is based on historical voting patterns. When the likelihood of voting changes dramatically—with Perot voters more likely to vote—there is no means of forecasting that change with historical data. Moreover, some people were embarrassed about supporting Perot and did not admit they were voting for him.* Interestingly, the Iowa Electronic Market (IEM), a futures market that trades primarily in election futures, closed the day before the election with Perot getting 19% of the vote, which was much more accurate than the opinion polls.†

*More people voted for Perot than exit surveys indicated; that is, some people who voted for Perot apparently denied it moments later. Perhaps this is not surprising in light of Perot's subsequent behavior.

†The IEM has a major advantage and a major disadvantage when compared to opinion polls. The major advantage is that participants are using real money, often as much as $1000, to participate. This provides a disincentive to misrepresentation, when compared to opinion polls. However, the IEM was set

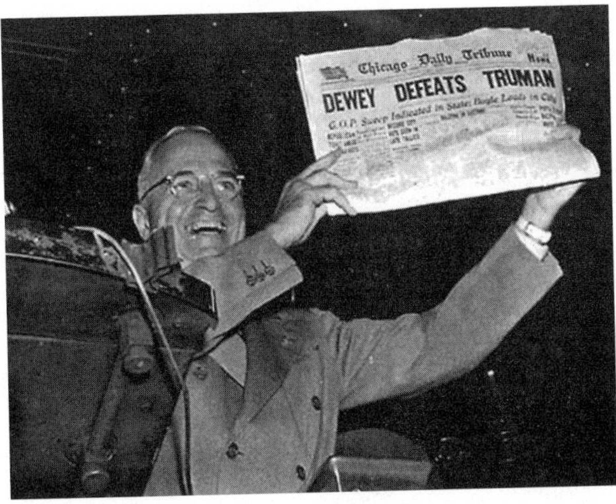

Figure 10.1. In this famous 1948 photo taken in St. Louis, Truman holds up the *Chicago Daily Tribune,* whose headline proclaims, "Dewey Defeats Truman," when in fact Truman won. *Source:* National Archives.

In spite of the problems in 1948 and 1992, opinion polls represent the simplest example of statistical analysis and are the natural starting point for understanding statistics. The analysis of opinion polls begins with a study of coin flips, in particular flips of a coin that might not be a fair coin but instead a coin that has heads arise with a probability not equal to 50%. Each person voting is viewed as a coin toss: voting Democratic with one probability, and otherwise voting Republican. (Third-party votes will be ignored for the moment.) Note that the proportion that votes Democratic gives the probability that a voter polled at random will vote Democratic. Suppose that 40% vote Democratic and 60% vote Republican. If two voters are sampled, there will be two Democratic votes, denoted DD, with probability $0.4 \times 0.4 = 0.16$, or 16%. Two Republican votes (RR) occur with probability 0.36 (0.6×0.6), and there will be one of each party with probability 0.48.[2] Now take a third voter, who is an R 60% of the time and a D 40% of the time. The odds of all Ds fall to $0.4 \times 0.4 \times 0.4 = 6.4\%$; of all Rs to $0.6 \times 0.6 \times 0.6 = 21.6\%$. There are two Ds and one R with probability 28.8% and two Rs and one D with probability 43.2%.[3] Outcomes that are close to the true probabilities are becoming more frequent as the number of voters rises, because some of the randomness is canceling out.

up by academics to study markets, and thus is more heavily represented by academics. The sample is composed only of computer users, creating a bias akin to sampling only telephone users.

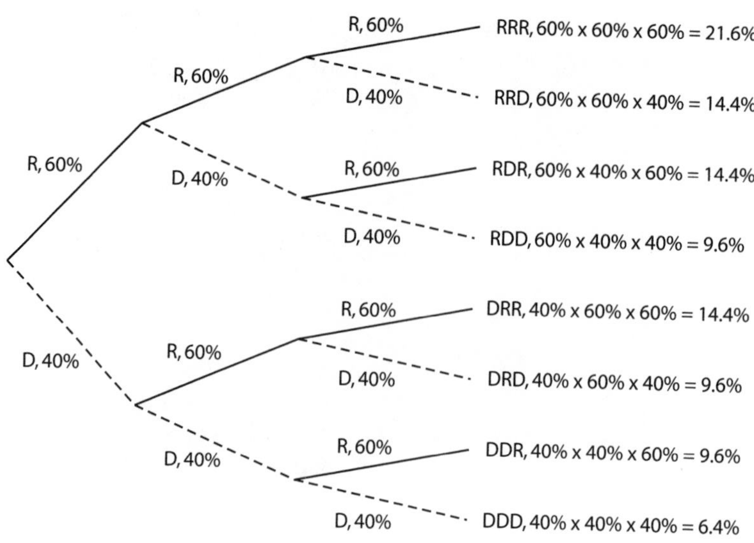

Figure 10.2. Calculation of the Probabilities with a Sample of Three. The solid lines denote an R and the dashed lines denote a D. There are eight possible outcomes, three of which have two Rs and one D, and three of which have two Ds and one R.

Figure 10.2 sets out the various ways of sampling three voters, and shows the outcomes that can arise. Note that to get the likelihood of any outcome, like RDR, one multiplies the probabilities of first meeting an R, then a D, then an R. Three of the outcomes have two Rs and one D—RRD, RDR, and DRR. Each of these corresponds to a two-thirds sample of Rs, and the probabilities must be added to get the overall probability of two Rs. Similarly, there are three ways to get two Ds.

With samples like 10 or 20, it is still possible to be pretty far away from the true proportion. However, as the samples get large, the odds of getting mostly Ds shrink. Indeed, the odds of being very far away from the true proportions of 60% Rs and 40% Ds become quite small. Figure 10.3 presents the likelihood of various proportions of Rs for a series of samples. The curve denoted with a circle corresponds to polling 25 voters drawn at random. In this case, the odds of being near the true proportions of 0.6 are fairly low—the probability of sampling between 0.5 and 0.7 is about 70%. That is, 30% of the time, a sample of 25 voters will be wrong by at least 10%. For this reason, a sample of 25 is relatively unreliable. This calculation is represented in figure 10.3 by the probabilities between 0.5 and 0.7. The figure is a histogram with cells of 4% length. On the horizontal axis is the proportion of Rs. On the vertical axis is the probability of observing the proportion of Rs. Thus, to find the probability of the proportion of Rs being between 0.5 and

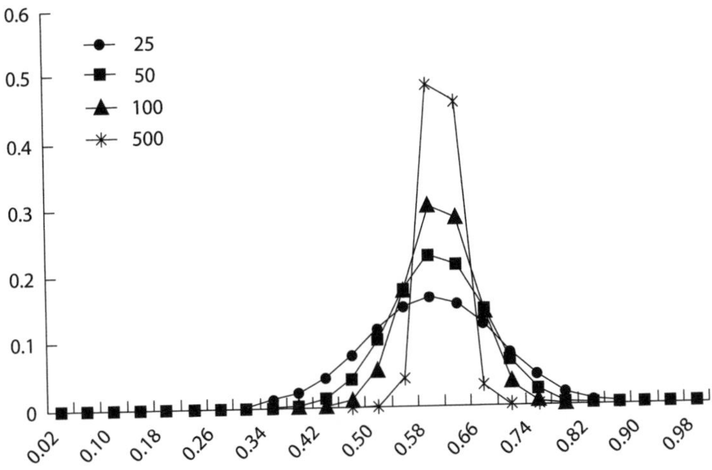

Figure 10.3. The likelihood of an average falling in a ±2% cell.

0.7, one would add the height associated with each point above the horizontal axis in that interval.

One could compute figure 10.3 following the procedure outlined for samples of sizes 2 and 3—compute the odds of every exact proportion. Thus, for a sample of 25, the odds of having all Ds, and hence 0% Rs, is 0.4^{25}—0.4 multiplied by itself twenty-five times. This number is 0.0000000001129. The likelihood of 4% Rs is the likelihood of getting exactly one in the sample of 25. This turns out to be 0.00000000422, forty times as large.[4] There are some mathematical conveniences to these calculations, but ultimately this is how they are computed—by using computers to do a great deal of multiplication.

Samples of size 50 are represented by the curve marked with squares. Note that this curve has more probability concentrated near 0.6, the true proportion of Republicans. Indeed, the likelihood that a sample of 50 voters has been 50% and 70% Republicans is 89%. Thus, a sample of 50 will be wrong by at least 10% only 11% of the time.

Note that we must specify two distinct percentages to describe the accuracy of a sample. How often will a sample be accurate? Consider throwing darts at a bull's-eye on a dartboard. How often will the throws be within an inch of the target? Within two inches? Within five inches? On the board? Clearly, any thrower will be within two inches at least as often as within an inch. Accuracy in samples is analogous. A sample of 50 will be within 10% of the true proportion of Republicans 89% of the time, and more than 10% off the remaining 11%. It turns out that a sample of 50 will be within 5% only 52% of the time.

Increasing the number of voters polled will always tend to increase the accuracy, because errors will tend to cancel out. If, by chance, most of a sample of 25 are Democrats, the odds are good that the streak of Democrats will not continue in the second 25.* Thus, the larger sample will tend toward the true proportion. We see this in figure 10.3. As the sample size, listed to the left, grows, most of the probability is concentrated around 0.6. By the time the sample size reaches 1,000, the probability of being within 10% is 99.999999991296%. Indeed, the probability of being within 3% is 95.1%. One sees this statement made often in newspapers—a poll that sampled around 1,000 people has an accuracy of ±3%, nineteen times out of twenty. That is, the sample outcome will be in error by no more than 3%, 95% of the time. Put another way, 5% of the time the error will be greater than 3%.

How accurate is a sample? There turns out to be a simple formula, known as the "square root" formula, that is approximate but very close. Let n represent the sample size. Then, for random samples exceeding 20, at least 95% of the time the sample will be within

$$\pm\frac{1}{\sqrt{n}}.$$

Thus, a sample of 1,000 is within $1/\sqrt{1000}$, which is 0.031, or 3%. For a sample of 25, the accuracy is one-fifth, or 20%. This accuracy is met at least 95% of the time. To get within 1%, one would have to solve the equation $1/\sqrt{n} = 0.01$, yielding a sample size of $n = 10{,}000$! That is, to get the error from 3% to 1% requires about a tenfold increase in the sample size.†

Suppose Pepsi surveys 36 people and finds that 70% of them prefer Pepsi to Coke. What is the probability that a majority of similar people prefer Pepsi? The accuracy associated with a sample of $n = 36$ is one-sixth, or 16.6%. Thus, using the square root formula, Pepsi can conclude that there is at least a 95% chance that a majority prefer Pepsi. Indeed, there is a 95% chance that 53% or more prefer Pepsi. (However, it will probably turn out that the survey was taken in Pepsi headquarters, so that we are 95% confident that a majority of Pepsi executives prefer Pepsi.)

*However, if there are unusually many Ds in the initial sample, it does not follow that it is likely to have unusually many Rs in a second sample. The odds have not changed for the second sample. Adding a usual second sample to an unusual first sample will tend to move the overall average more toward the true proportion.

†It is very important that the sample be a random sample. In particular, sampling people whose opinions are correlated to each other—perhaps because they are all members of a club, or family members—will not produce independent draws and is akin to polling the same person more than once.

Consider a new drug to combat a disease. With the old drug 41% got better. In a sample of those getting the new drug, 51% got better. Are we 95% confident that the new drug is better? That depends on the sample size. If the study of the new drug involved more than 100 people, the accuracy is no worse than 10%, and we can be 95% confident that the new drug does better than 41%. But if the study was of 25 people, the 95% confidence level is $\pm\frac{1}{5}$, or $\pm 20\%$.

Why 95%? This number is called the level of confidence, and the $\pm 3\%$ gives the accuracy or "confidence interval." In the previous example, we can be 95% confident that the percentage who prefer Pepsi falls in the interval $70\% - 16.6\%$ to $70\% + 16.6\%$, or 53.3% to 86.6%. We could, instead, have asked only to be 90% confident, in which case our interval shrinks—the accuracy with 90% confidence turns out to be $\pm 13.6\%$. How to compute these kinds of intervals is considered below. However, 95% is the accepted confidence level used in most studies. The level of confidence should depend on the purpose for which the statistics are being used. For example, in the medical study, one wants to know which drug is likely to be the most effective, in which case a 50% level of confidence may be appropriate. In contrast, before concluding that someone is a murderer and should be executed, one might want to be extraordinarily confident, much more than 95%. Nevertheless, the 95% confidence level is so prevalent that an effect that is demonstrated with 95% confidence is commonly referred to as "significant." For example, when medical researchers find a drug to have a significant effect, this typically means they are 95% confident of some effect. Similarly, when the Department of Labor says training programs significantly increase wages, they mean that a study found a 95% chance of some wage increases. This can be important, since it is possible to be 95% confident that a training program increases wages, but by some tiny amount. Statistically significant does not mean large.

One curious fact is that it does not matter how many voters there are, provided we are sampling in an unbiased manner. The reason is that, provided our sample is randomly selected and not, for example, a telephone survey or other biased sample, the odds of being more than 3% away from the true probability depends only on how many voters we sample, not on how many voters there are. Sampling a population of voters is like flipping coins—the odds depend on the coin and on the number of flips, but not on the number of times the coin was not flipped—the number of voters not sampled.

The more voters there are, however, the more difficult it will be to obtain a truly random sample. For example, to find the proportion of voters expecting to vote Republican, it is necessary to sample voters randomly across the fifty states. It is not always necessary to sample voters in each state, but it is necessary not to rule out any state, to select randomly from the pool of voters. The problem is not the total number of voters, but the number of groups of voters. One must take care to sample across the same voters in the same groups.

Consider the procedure of sampling a thousand voters from New York State. One does not learn the proportion of Republicans in the United States, but only the proportion of Republicans in New York State, which is not the same thing at all. So instead, one might pick a state at random, and sample a thousand voters from that state. On average, this will not produce a biased sample, but the error can be quite large and *not* $\pm 3\%$. Why? Again, we have learned only about one state, not about the United States overall, although we have learned about a randomly chosen state. In order to get an accurate assessment, we need to choose randomly over the entire nation. It may be that some states are not represented in any particular sample. The most important thing is that the sample is not biased by the

Box 10.1: The Whiz Kids

Shortly after the United States entered World War II, Text Thornton, a low-level government official, persuaded the Assistant Secretary of War for Air to let him take over the Harvard Business School, as a wartime emergency, in order to train a group to manage the Army Air Corps. The individuals were trained in modern statistical and optimization methods. The graduates of the program, nicknamed the Whiz Kids, were instrumental in the design of operations research techniques to solve logistics problems. For example, the design of convoys to elude German submarines involved several trade-offs. A convoy is only as fast as its slowest ship, so that it is desirable to group fast ships with fast ships and slow ships with slow ships. Large convoys can be protected by a relatively small number of destroyers, but small convoys are harder for German U-boats to spot. The contribution of the Whiz Kids was not only to recognize the trade-offs, but to quantify the trade-offs statistically and to develop formulas to help solve them.

Thornton went on to found the major defense-contractor and nuclear-plant manufacturer Litton Industries. Several of the Whiz Kids went to Ford Motor Company after the war ended, and Whiz Kid Robert McNamara became president of Ford Motor Company and later U.S. Secretary of Defense.

exclusion of certain groups, as the telephone survey was. The second most important thing is that the sampled individuals are not correlated. Sampling individuals from the same state creates a correlation in the sample, which is akin to sampling the same person more than once.

Pollsters and marketers generally do not sample in an unbiased way. Instead, they attempt to produce a "synthetic" sample—picking people who represent various income groups, races, religions, and so on, with the same frequencies as those found in the United States or in another target group. The advantage of using synthetic samples is that one can correlate the outcome with various socioeconomic factors. Suppose, for example, in the overall sample of 1,000, 60% planned to vote Republican. Of the 510 women in this sample, however, only 48% planned to vote Republican. What can we conclude about the plan of women to vote? The answer can be given with the square root formula: with a probability of 95%, women will be within $1/\sqrt{510}$, which is 4.4%. Note that the accuracy is less for subgroups, because fewer of the subgroup were sampled. Thus, to obtain the same accuracy of 3%, we would need to sample 1,000 women.

So why, if it only takes a sample of 1,000 to obtain 3% accuracy most of the time, is it so difficult to forecast the outcome of an election on election night? Moreover, with a sample of 10,000, the accuracy has increased to 1%—enough to call most political races. The forecasting problem was dramatically brought to the nation's attention in the year 2000 presidential election, when all three networks declared Al Gore the winner in Florida at 8 P.M. EST; then retracted an hour later and put Florida back in the "too close to call" column; then declared George W. Bush the winner around 2 A.M. EST. Simply put, the problem is that the precincts that report early are generally different in nature from the precincts that report late. Typically, smaller precincts report early, and smaller precincts are more likely to be in suburban or rural areas. Consequently, the early returns usually favor the Republican candidates, but early Republican leads tend to narrow as election night progresses. In the 2000 election, all the networks correctly forecast that California would go for Gore, in spite of Bush's 51% lead to Gore's 44%, with 22% of the precincts reporting. The problem for the networks in trying to forecast a close race is to obtain a large enough sample so that they can predict the number of votes in slow precincts, even though the votes in slow precincts are statistically different than those in early precincts.

It doesn't matter, in the analysis of opinion polls, whether there are only two outcomes. Suppose there are three parties: R, D, and I. We sample a thousand people and find 54% R, 42% D, and the remainder I. What is our accuracy on R? It is still ± 3%. The logic for this result is that one can create two outcomes: R versus not-R. The two party analysis applies to this case, and thus we can still conclude that the Rs will get 54% ± 3%.

THE PRECISION OF STATISTICS

People commonly use statistics like a drunk uses a lamppost: for support rather than for illumination.

—Attributed to Mark Twain by some sources

Opinion polls are relatively easy to understand, because they work like coin flips. But the same logic applies to other random outcomes, like income or stock prices. It is useful to begin with some descriptive statistics for random variables that have a numerical outcome. The first is the average, which has the technical name "mean." This familiar concept is found by adding the outcomes weighted by the likelihood of the probability of that outcome. Thus, if there are three outcomes, 1, 2, and 3, with probabilities 40%, 40%, and 20%, the mean is $1 \times 0.4 + 2 \times 0.4 + 3 \times 0.2$, which is 1.8. The mean is a measure of the typical outcome of something random.

The median is another measure of the typical outcome. The median is the number that no more than half are above and no more than half are below. In the three-outcome random variables described above, the median is 2, since 40% are below and 20% are above.[5]

The mean and the median both have advantages. The median gives the middle outcome, with half above and half below. The median income is a better measure of the income of the typical American than the mean income. Mean income weights the outliers—for example, Bill Gates Jr.—quite heavily. Thus, in countries with few rich people, mean income can be high while median income, and the income of most people, is low. In the United States, the mean household income in 1996 was $47,101, while the median income was $35,172. The mean value is often more useful in a business context, where the emphasis is on the average outcome. For example, total sales are the number of transactions times the average, or mean, sale amount.

In addition to measures of typical outcomes, it is useful to have a measure of the typical variation. If the mean is the average outcome, what is an average amount of variation? That is generally assessed by the "standard deviation." A deviation is the distance from the mean. In the three-outcome example above, the mean was 1.8. How much does the random outcome vary from the mean? This random variable and calculations of the mean and standard deviation are summarized in table 10.1.

The left column gives the outcomes of the random variables—1, 2, and 3. The second column gives the probabilities of the three outcomes. These must sum to 1.0, or 100%. The third column provides the product of the first two columns, which effectively weights the outcome by the probability of that outcome. The sum of that column is the average, or mean, which in this case is 1.8. The fourth col-

TABLE 10.1
Computations with a Random Variable

Outcome	*Probability*	*Outcome Weighted*	*Deviation*	*Deviation Squared*	*Deviation^2 Weighted*
1	0.4	0.4	−0.8	0.64	0.256
2	0.4	0.8	0.2	0.04	0.016
3	0.2	0.6	1.2	1.44	0.288
Sum	1.0	Mean = 1.8	0.0	2.12	$\sigma^2 = 0.56$

umn gives the first column minus the mean, which is the deviation from the mean. Thus, 1 is 0.8 less than the mean, and 3 is 1.2 greater than the mean.

The variance, often denoted by the notation σ^2 (which is the Greek lower-case letter sigma, squared), is the average of the square of the deviations. The fifth column computes the squared deviations, and the sixth column weights the squared deviations by the probabilities from the second column. The sum of the sixth column is the average of the squared deviations, and in this case is 0.56.

The standard deviation is the square root of the variance. In words, the standard deviation is the square root of the average of the squared deviations. In concept, it works like this: The deviations measure how much different from the mean the various outcomes are. On average, the deviations must be zero, for that is the whole idea of the mean. What, then, is the average deviation? One might compute the average of the absolute values, which arise by discarding the negative signs. It turns out, however, that this concept is difficult to use in applications. In contrast, the average of the squared deviations will have several useful applications. Thus, the standard deviation first squares the deviation, to make the deviations positive, then averages these squared deviations, then takes the square root to return to deviation units, rather than squared deviation units.

In the three-outcome example, the standard deviation, denoted σ, was $\sqrt{0.56} = 0.748$. This value is intended to represent a typical variation from the average outcome. One way to think about the standard deviation is that it is a measure of the precision of a statistic. The standard deviation is the most common measure of variation of a random variable. The standard deviation for U.S. family income is about \$30,000, which indicates a fairly large variation in income—two-thirds of the mean income.*

*For variables that can't be negative, it is sometimes useful to consider the standard deviation divided by the mean, which is known as the "coefficient of variation."

A formula that is occasionally useful is called Chebyshev's Inequality, discovered by Russian mathematician Pafnuty Chebyshev. Consider any numerical variable. This variable could be income, number of compact disks owned by families, or the change in the population of Las Vegas each year. Let σ be the standard deviation of this variable and b any number greater than one. Then the proportion of the population that is at least $b\sigma$ away from the mean is not greater than $1/b^2$. For example, with an average income of \$47,000 and a standard deviation of \$30,000, how many people have incomes exceeding \$100,000? The figure of \$100,000 is 1.77 standard deviations away from the mean; that is, \$53,000 is 1.77 times \$30,000, which makes b equal to 1.77. Thus, there cannot be more than $1/b^2$ of the population with incomes greater than \$100,000, or 32%. Chebyshev's Inequality is useful when one is entirely ignorant about distributions, other than the mean and the variance. Chebyshev's Inequality is an upper bound on the probability, so 32% is too large. The actual number is 10.5%.[6]

Chebyshev's Inequality is useful when little is known about the distribution in question. In many situations, much is known about the distribution, which can be usefully exploited. The most important distribution is called the normal distribution.

THE NORMAL DISTRIBUTION OR BELL CURVE

The normal distribution, also called the bell curve due to its bell shape, can be found on the German fifty mark note, in honor of its discoverer, the Swiss mathematician Leonhard Euler. An illustration of the normal distribution, with a mean of 0 and variance of 1, is provided in figure 10.4. This figure gives the relative likelihood of various points by the area beneath the bell-shaped curve. For example, the probability that the random outcome falls between -1 and $+1$ is the area beneath the curve between these two points, which is shaded. This area turns out to be 0.682, or 68.2% probability.

The normal distribution is symmetric around the mean. Using the normal with zero mean and variance equal to one provided in the figure, the probability of an outcome exceeding one can be deduced as follows. First, we just learned that 68.2% of the outcomes fall between -1 and 1. The remainder is 31.8%. which is evenly divided between outcomes greater than 1, and outcomes less than -1, because of symmetry. Thus, an outcome greater than one occurs 15.9%—half of 31.8%—of the time.

Many things that vary appear to follow the normal distribution. Height, shoe size, and IQ are approximately normal. The distance acorns fall from the tree is approximately normal. Income, however, is decidedly not normal, nor is the amount of oil found in off-shore oil tracts.

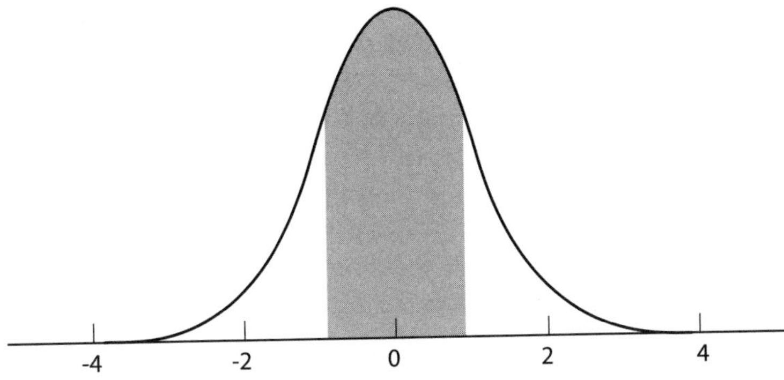

Figure 10.4. The Normal Distribution. The likelihood of an outcome between any two points is given by the area under the curve between those two points. An example is shaded.

It turns out that *averages* are approximately normally distributed. Take people's incomes, which are not normally distributed. Individually, incomes will not appear normally distributed. Averages of a random selection of 100 people, however, will be approximately normal. Call the mean income μ (the Greek letter mu), which is traditionally used to denote the mean, and the variance by σ^2. Then the variance of the average of n people's income has mean μ and variance σ^2/n. Averaging a group, the mean is the same, but the variance of the group average is $1/n$ of the variance of the individual. It makes sense that the variation of the group average is considerably less than the variation of the individual because while some in the group are high, others are low, canceling out. Thus, if individual income has a variance of \$900 million, the variance of the average of a group of 100 would be \$9 million.

The fact that averages behave like a normal distribution permits us to compute the odds of the average of a group falling close to the mean with considerable precision. Table 10.2 provides the probability that a normally distributed variable exceeds the mean by a given number of standard deviations. These values are sometimes referred to as Z statistics or Z scores, and are written as $(X - \mu)/\sigma$. In words, the Z value represents the number of standard deviations that an outcome is from the mean, or the size of a deviation from the mean measured in standard deviations.

From the table, the probability of exceeding the mean by two standard deviations is 2.3%. The normal distribution is symmetric, which means the probability of being two standard deviations below the mean is also 2.3%. Thus, 4.6% are more than two standard deviations from the mean, and 95.4% are within two standard deviations from the mean.

IQ tests are constructed to have a mean of 100 and a standard deviation of 15.

TABLE 10.2
Normal Distribution Z statistics

Z	*0*	*1*	*2*	*3*	*4*	*5*
Probability $(X - \mu)/\sigma > z$	50%	15.9%	2.3%	0.13%	0.003%	0.0000003%

Therefore, 15.9% of the population have IQs over 115, because 115 is one standard deviation over the mean of 100. Similarly, 2.3% have IQs over 130, because 130 represents two standard deviations over the mean. A bit more than one-tenth of 1% have IQs over 145. There should be about 80 Americans with IQs exceeding 175, which is five standard deviations, a number that is computed by multiplying the probability of an IQ exceeding 175, five standard deviations over the mean, by the number of Americans. Finally, an IQ of 200, which is six and two-thirds standard deviations over the mean, would appear once in every 76,429,353,031 people. Normal probabilities are symmetric, so the probability of having an IQ less than 85 is 15.9%; less than 70, 2.3%; and so on. Thus, the fraction of the population that have a room-temperature IQ (70) is a bit more than 2%. It is not clear why these people are so common driving on streets and highways.

Normal distributions are useful to assess risk of a group of projects or investments. Consider, for example, the capital needed to minimize the risk of bankruptcy for a well-diversified insurance company. The insurance company writes n tornado policies on houses that are far enough apart that the likelihood of the same tornado hitting multiple insured houses is small. The policies pay $100,000 when a tornado strikes an insured home, and otherwise pay nothing; and tornadoes strike with probability 0.0001, a one-in-ten-thousand chance. Thus, the average cost of the policy to the company is $10, and the variance is 999,900.[7] The company sets aside $11.50 per customer. What is the likelihood of bankruptcy? The key to solving this problem is to note that the mean cost remains $10, no matter how many policies are written, but the standard deviation is $\sqrt{\sigma^2/n} = \sqrt{999{,}990/n} = 999.95/\sqrt{n}$. The company goes bankrupt when the average claim exceeds $11.50, which occurs when the deviation exceeds $1.50. The deviation divided by the standard deviation is a Z statistic, and it is

$$Z = \frac{1.50}{999.95/\sqrt{n}} = \frac{\sqrt{n}}{666.63}$$

Thus, to choose the probability of bankruptcy is to choose the desired value of Z. In particular, to obtain a probability of 0.003%, which means going bankrupt every 30,000 years on average, one chooses $Z = 4$, and then solves for the number of policies. In this case, the solution is a bit over seven million policies.[8]

Note that an economy of scale is revealed by the risk pooling that arises with averages. In order to insure a low probability of bankruptcy, a large firm with many policies can hold back a smaller amount per policy than a small firm. Costs—money held back to deal with unlucky outcomes—fall on the order of $1/\sqrt{n}$, where n is the number of policies.

This insurance scheme fails when the outcomes on the policies are correlated. The insurance company that writes a million hurricane insurance policies in south Florida has not successfully diversified its risk.

The source of the formula for political polls, considered earlier, can now be clarified. With large samples, a poll is just an average of the variable that is 1 when the person says R, and 0 when the person says D. This variable has a standard deviation that is less than $\frac{1}{2}$. Thus, the standard deviation of an opinion poll of n people is no greater than $1/(2\sqrt{n})$.[9] To obtain 95% confidence, we would need 2.5% on either side of the confidence interval, which yields $Z = 2$ from the table. (The exact value is $Z = 1.96$). This gives a 95% confidence of an error of $\pm 1/\sqrt{n}$. Using $Z = 1$, instead, would give a confidence interval of $\pm 1/(2\sqrt{n})$ and a confidence level of 68.2% (15.9% on the outside in each direction).

CONDITIONAL PROBABILITIES AND CORRELATION

Does drinking coffee promote cancer or not? It seems as if the results of a new medical study, linking coffee to some dire consequence, is announced every month. These studies tend to be quietly withdrawn a few months later. Is red wine better than white wine, or tequila, for your arteries? Is red wine better than no alcohol? Does salt cause high blood pressure? Early studies convinced most Americans to reduce their salt intake. Later studies found either no effect of salt on blood pressure, or an effect only for a relatively small portion of the population who have severe problems with high blood pressure. The pendulum is swinging again—the most recent studies favor an effect of salt on high blood pressure.

Why are medical researchers having such difficulty figuring out what appear to be simple questions? The basic reason is that researchers can rarely perform controlled experiments on humans. Consider the question of whether salt increases hypertension. If doctors could take a group of people, divide them into two subgroups, feed a lot of salt to one subgroup and less salt or none to the other, and then observe whether the blood pressure of the salt eaters rose relative to the non–salt eaters, the question could be answered in short order. However, usually it is not possible to assign patients randomly into treatment groups and observe the effects. Instead, researchers attempt to tease out these effects from observed behav-

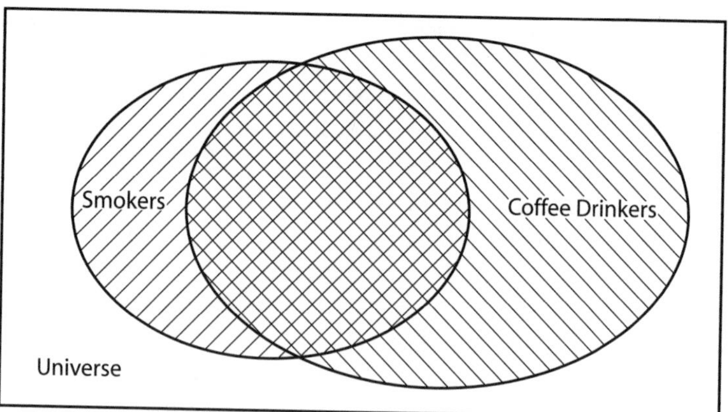

Figure 10.5. A Venn diagram, with smokers, coffee drinkers, and others.

ior, but this can be very difficult. For example, it was once reported that coffee drinkers are more likely to get lung cancer than people who do not drink coffee, but this is probably not because of the coffee but because those who drink a lot of coffee are more likely to smoke cigarettes also. Knowing this, researchers attempt to adjust for cigarette smoking, by comparing nonsmoking coffee drinkers to nonsmoking noncoffee drinkers.

A useful conceptual tool for probabilities is the Venn diagram. A typical Venn diagram is presented in figure 10.5. Here, the rectangle represents the entire population. Those who smoke are in the left-side oval. Those who drink coffee are represented in the right oval. Finally, the overlap of the ovals, which is crosshatched, shows those who both smoke and drink coffee. In this figure, we can see that a greater number of coffee drinkers smoke than noncoffee drinkers. The areas in a Venn diagram are intended to represent overall probabilities. As illustrated, too, a majority of smokers drink coffee—the area of the coffee-drinking smoking group exceeds the area of the smoking but noncoffee-drinking group.

The Venn diagram is helpful in conceptualizing the use of new information to update, or revise, probabilities of possible outcomes. Once we know that someone is a coffee drinker, we know the person is much more likely to smoke than if the person abstains from coffee. Indeed, the probability of drinking coffee for smokers is just the probability of both drinking coffee and smoking (the cross-hatched area in the diagram) divided by overall the probability of smoking. This calculation is an example of "Bayes' updating," which computes the probability of one event, A, conditional on another event, B, as the probability of both events happening (A and B) divided by the probability of B.

For example, of the 103,874,000 households in the United States, 20,433,000

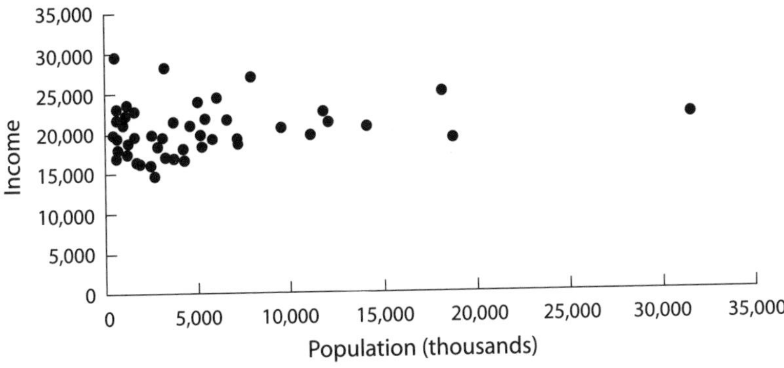

Figure 10.6. Population and income by state.

are in rural areas. Twelve percent of households have an African American head of household, and 1,651,000 of African American–headed households are in rural areas. Thus, the probability of an African American–headed household being in a rural area is the probability of a household being both African American–headed and rural (1,651,000/103,874,000 = 1.6%) divided by the probability of a household being African American–headed, which is 12% of total households. Thus, 13% (1.6%/12%) of African American households are rural, while 20% of households overall are rural. What is the probability that a rural household is headed by an African American? To obtain this, we simply divide the number of African American–headed rural households by the number of all rural households to obtain the figure 10%.

In many cases, it is useful to summarize the relationship of two variables with a single number, the correlation coefficient. Do people in more populous states earn more money? The correlation coefficient is designed to answer this kind of question. Figure 10.6 shows the data on population and income by state.

It is not obvious if there is any relationship between the population of state, given on the horizontal axis, and the average income. But, in fact, there is a correlation, and it is positive—a 19% correlation. The correlation coefficient is a statistic constructed to measure how closely two variables relate to each other. The correlation coefficient ranges from −1 to 1, with −1 a perfect negative correlation (a straight line sloping downward), and +1 a perfect positive correlation (a straight line sloping upward). For state income and population, the correlation coefficient is 0.19, or 19% of perfect correlation.

For any two variables, the correlation coefficient is the average of the product of the Z statistics of those variables. Thus, to compute the correlation coefficient, one first computes the Z statistics (variable minus mean, all divided by standard devia-

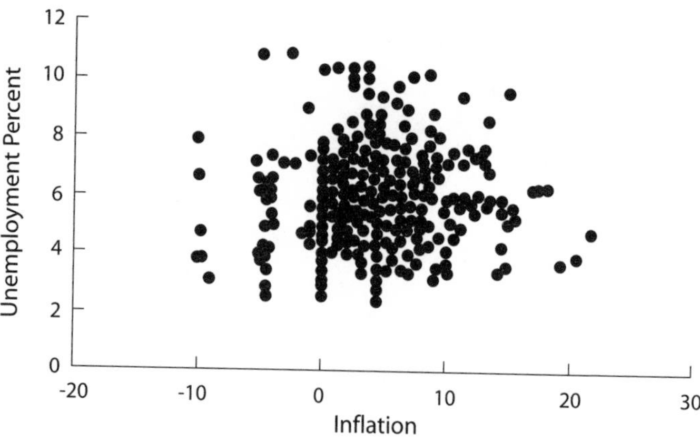

Figure 10.7. Phillips relationship.

tion σ) for each of the variables, multiplies the two *Z* statistics, and then averages this product. The effect of this procedure is to first standardize the variables, by subtracting the mean and dividing by the standard deviation, so that the two variables are comparable in scale. All *Z* scores have a mean of zero and a standard deviation of one, and thus computing *Z* scores creates comparable scales. In particular, standardization eliminates effects of measurement scale—adding a constant or multiplying by a constant will not affect the correlation. This standardization is important in eliminating effects that have nothing to do with correlation, such as the units by which the variables are measured. It does not matter to correlation whether income is measured in dollars or Swiss francs, for example, for the correlation coefficient.

The correlation coefficient measures to what extent large values of one variable are associated with large values of another. If one variable affects another, the correlation coefficient measures the predictive content of the first variable. For example, consider the classic economic question of the whether unemployment and inflation are related. The relationship is known as the Phillips curve, after its discoverer, economist Edmund Phillips.

A plot of the data on monthly unemployment and inflation from January 1948 to July 2000 is provided in figure 10.7. The data come from the Bureau of Labor Statistics. The correlation coefficient is 0.1. This value represents a weak correlation. Interestingly, it is a positive correlation; that is, a higher unemployment rate is associated with a *higher* inflation rate, in contrast to the theory, which specifies a higher unemployment will be associated with lower inflation.*

*The modern theory, formulated by Nobel laureate Robert Lucas, indicates that there is no long-term systematic relationship between inflation and unemployment. Unanticipated inflation may reduce un-

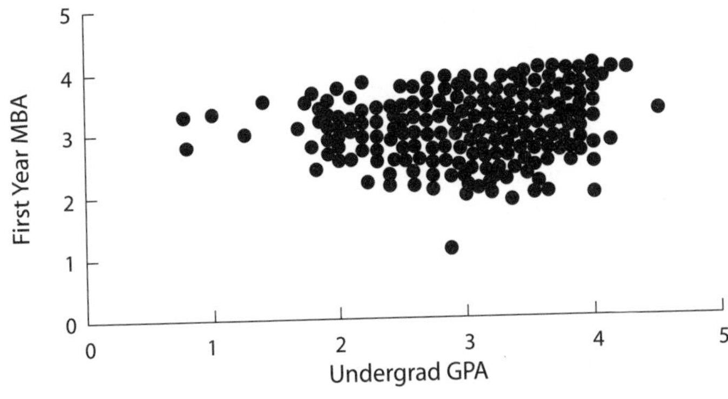

Figure 10.8. Undergraduate grade point average as a predictor of M.B.A. scores.

How well does undergraduate performance predict success among M.B.A. students? Figure 10.8 provides an indication, by plotting the grade point average (GPA) of first year M.B.A. students against their undergraduate success. The correlation is 24%—meaning that 24% of the variation in GPAs for first-year M.B.A.'s is accounted for by differences in their undergraduate performance.[10]

There are two major things to keep in mind when interpreting correlation coefficients. First, correlation is not causation, a point illustrated in the next section. That two variables are correlated does not prove one causes the other. There may be a third cause that makes both move together.

Second, correlation helps one find monotonic relationships—when one variable is high, the other tends to be high. Thus, the correlation coefficient may help assess the effect of income on spending on computers or automobiles, for example. If the relationship is U-shaped, so that it is partly decreasing and partly increasing, the change in direction will tend to cancel out, and a low correlation is the result. In sum, correlation does not prove causation, and the absence of correlation does not prove the absence of a relationship between two variables.

It is useful to bear in mind that small samples affect correlation coefficients in the same way described with variance—with a small sample, one may discover spurious correlation, which would tend to disappear with a larger sample.

Figure 10.9 illustrates various degrees of correlation. When variables are weakly correlated, as when Rho $= \frac{1}{3}$, there is a substantial amount of variation. As the cor-

---

employment, essentially by fooling people into thinking that they are richer than they are, but expectations adjust and people won't be permanently fooled. Anticipated inflation will have no effect. The original Phillips theory associated unemployment with the price level. It turns out that the correlation of prices and unemployment is stronger and positive—29%!

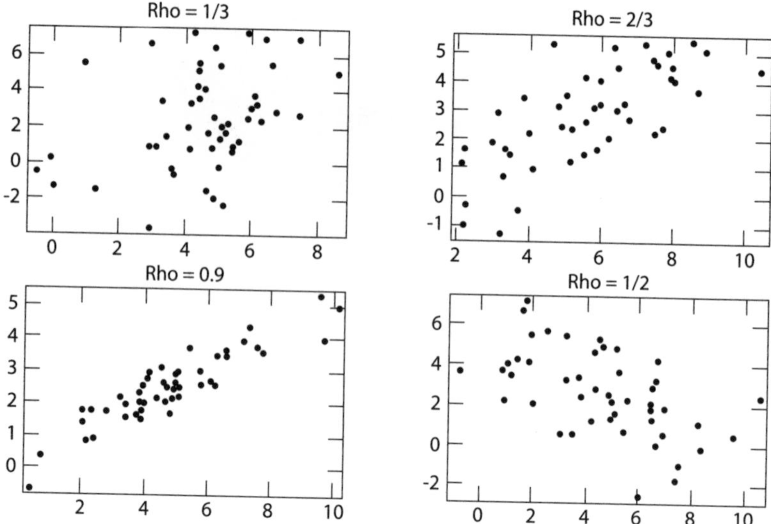

Figure 10.9. Examples of Correlation. The correlation coefficient, Rho, ranges from perfect correlation with value 1 through no correlation and value 0 to perfect negative correlation with value −1.

relation coefficient increases toward $\frac{2}{3}$, the data start to line up, falling roughly between two parallel lines. A 90% correlation generally means the data fall on a thick line—very close to a straight line. Finally, figure 10.9 also illustrates a negative correlation, in which case the data tend to slope downward.

The Predator Theory of Tornadoes

It is often observed that tornadoes usually damage mobile homes. This observation has given rise to the predator theory of tornadoes—mobile home sales increase the food supply of tornadoes, which brings tornadoes. Do the data support this whimsical theory? Table 10.3 presents data for the five years from 1995 to 1999, by month, for both tornadoes and mobile-home sales.

Other than a possible seasonal effect, it is not obvious that mobile-home shipments and tornadoes have a relationship. A quick spreadsheet calculation shows that the correlation coefficient is 0.37—mobile-home sales explain 37% of the incidence of tornadoes. Put another way, every standard deviation increase in mobile-home sales—about 3,317 mobile homes—tends to increase tornadoes by 0.37 standard deviations, which turns out to be 94 tornadoes. This works out to be one tornado for every 35 extra mobile-home sales.

Does the data confirm the correlation coefficient? Figure 10.10 shows a plot of

BLE 10.3
a on Tornadoes and Mobile Home Shipments

	Tornadoes					*Mobile-Home Shipments*				
nth	*1999*	*1998*	*1997*	*1996*	*1995*	*1999*	*1998*	*1997*	*1996*	*1995*
	212	47	50	35	36	26,784	26,362	25,969	26,963	25,270
	22	72	23	14	7	28,770	27,549	29,044	27,039	24,216
ar	56	72	102	71	49	34,205	31,813	32,717	30,309	29,409
r	176	182	114	177	130	33,148	33,266	31,482	32,473	26,228
ay	311	312	225	235	390	30,550	31,397	31,180	33,710	30,108
n	289	376	193	128	216	32,887	33,567	28,953	31,376	30,838
l	100	80	188	202	161	26,799	31,085	31,316	29,135	24,634
ug	79	61	84	72	54	30,890	32,556	31,211	34,220	33,038
ep	56	104	32	101	19	28,875	32,710	34,138	31,439	29,609
ct	18	86	100	68	74	28,239	35,185	26,524	35,865	32,663
Jov	9	26	25	55	79	25,675	30,110	24,559	27,935	29,554
Dec	15	6	12	15	18	21,849	26,284	26,284	22,947	24,034

Z statistics for both tornadoes and mobile-home sales. Clearly, a correlation is present—it is rare to observe lots of tornadoes when there are relatively few mobile-home sales. That is, the lower right quadrant of the figure is empty. (There are those who claim to see a tornado shape in the data plotted in fig. 10.10.)

Of course, the reason for the correlation is that mobile-home sales are more common in the summer, and less common in the winter, as are tornadoes. Indeed, the seasonality is readily observed from table 10.3.

Just because variables are correlated, neither may cause the other. Modern meteorological theory suggests that mobile-home sales do not cause tornadoes, although tornadoes, by destroying some existing mobile homes, may cause a limited number of mobile-home sales. Some have hypothesized that many medical correlations are a consequence of the "Type A" personality, people who drive themselves harder than most. Such personality variables play the role of season in the tornadoes and mobile-home-sales case, causing excess consumption of coffee and alco-

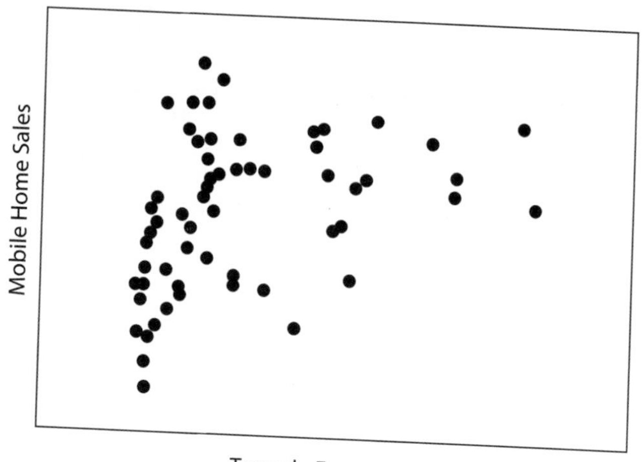

Figure 10.10. *Z* statistic plot.

hol, stress, and heart attacks. Under the "Type A" theory, the reason people who consume only one drink per day outlive others is that such people, being moderate in one thing, are much more likely to eat moderately, exercise regularly, have low stress, and generally enjoy a healthier lifestyle. Even if moderate alcohol consumption were damaging to health, its effects are smaller than the effects of moderation.

SAMPLE SELECTION BIAS

Telephone-based political polls represent an instance of sample selection bias; there is a bias in the sample taken by telephone relative to the population of interest, which includes all voters. Similarly, the characteristics of early adopters of a new product or service are generally quite different from later adopters. For example, the first Internet service providers, such as Compuserve, were designed for very technically oriented customers. These services had a great deal of difficulty adjusting to the provision of service for a larger, less technically oriented population, and ultimately were absorbed by companies, such as AOL and Earthlink/Mindspring, that focused on a less technical customer base.

How much is a house worth? How much have houses gone up, or down, in price? Housing values are consistently and systematically mismeasured—because what is observed is *housing transactions,* and transactions represent a biased sample of housing values. Transaction prices would measure housing values accurately only if the value of houses that do not sell equals the value of houses that do sell. But a rapidly rising market tends to be a thick market, with many transactions. In contrast, when the prices begin to fall, many houses that might otherwise sell are removed from the market, and the market becomes quite thin. House trades represent an example of sample selection bias—the observed sample, houses that trade, represents a biased set of all houses. An extreme example of this phenomenon was the often-repeated claim that, in the 1980s, the value of Tokyo real estate (which rarely trades) was higher than the value of all real estate in the continental United States. This might have been true if all of Tokyo real estate was valued at the value of the few units that traded, but only relatively valuable real estate typically traded in Tokyo.

Sample selection bias is familiar in the context of used cars. Is the quality of the average used car for sale representative of the average used car? Clearly not, as people with lemons will tend to try to sell them, while people with cars that perform well will be less likely to resell. Thus, used car prices will understate the value of the cars, because the cars offered for sale will include a higher fraction of lemons.

There are sophisticated techniques, developed by Nobel laureate James Heckman,[11] to correct for sample selection bias. It is important to be aware of this common problem in statistical analysis, because it is a feature of most data.

An extraordinary example of sample selection bias was uncovered by Mark Satterthwaite et al.[12] This study examines the implementation of a system that revealed fatality rates for patients of cardiac surgeons in Pennsylvania and New York State. Following the policy of revealing the fatality rates for surgery, the fatality rates fell, making the policy appear to be a major success. In fact, however, the *overall* fatality rates were not falling. Instead, many physicians declined to perform surgery on the patients most likely to die during surgery, so that the cases most likely to benefit from surgery went without surgery. These patients were much more likely to die without the surgery, but they presented a bad risk for surgeons whose personal statistics would be hurt. In addition, more surgery was performed on patients not likely to die, either with or without the surgery. Thus, the effect of revealing the surgeons' fatality rates was to shift the patients who received surgery from the most needy group to a middle group that excluded many of the most needy and included some less needy. The appearance of improved performance was actually a severe case of sample selection changes. The patients most likely to benefit from surgery, but also the most likely to die, were excluded from the sample. The authors estimate that the policy of publishing the fatality rates of cardiac surgeons killed as many as 125 more people per year.

THE HOT HAND

Everyone is familiar with the feeling of doing everything right, of being charmed, "in the groove." In basketball, this feeling of success is known as the "hot hand."

A majority of basketball fans believe that players will get hot, and score more often. Similarly, most of us are familiar with the ham-fisted feeling that nothing is going right, that further action compounds the problem and hence it is best to quit temporarily and return when one is performing up to speed. Many gamblers believe that runs of luck are either with them or against them. Generally, the hot hand is a misperception.[13] Random chance will give rise to runs of successes and runs of failures—the mere presence of a run is not a sign that the odds have changed. Moreover, people systematically underestimate the likelihood of a run of successes or a run of failures.

Even in flipping coins, there is a significant chance of a run. Denote a coin flip with the face up as an H (head), and the other side as a T (tail). Many people would identify the sequence THTTHHHHHT as having a run of Hs toward the end, but such runs, statistically speaking, are surprisingly common. Consider, for example, the odds of a run of five heads (or five tails) in flipping a coin ten times. The probability of such a run is 7/32—nearly one-fourth of the time![14]

To illustrate the problem of identifying streaks, consider figure 10.11, which presents two diagrams of dots. Which is a random array of dots? Most people identify the left figure as having holes in the center area, and some clusters of dots that appear not to be random. In contrast, the right-hand figure seems random—the dots are spread around randomly. This, of course, is incorrect, or why else would it be discussed? The left figure was generated with each point randomly assigned over the entire rectangle; such holes and clusters are *common* in a random assignment. The figure on the right, in contrast, has a structure. Divide the box into fifty cells, ten on the horizontal and five on the vertical. The boxes are illustrated in figure 10.12. Each of these cells has exactly one point. This kind of "filling" of the figure is highly unlikely to arise in a random assignment over the entire rectangle. Indeed, the probability that all fifty boxes are filled by the fifty points is 0.00000000000000000034%.

The hot-hand phenomenon appears in many other contexts. Early reports indicate that the phenomenal batting of Sammy Sosa and Mark McGwire in 1998 was the result of good hitting, but not a consequence of a "hot bat." The so-called canals of Mars seem to be a consequence of a linguistic mix-up—astronomer Giovanni Schiaparelli called the geologic features of Mars "canali," meaning channels in Italian, which was translated into English as canals, suggesting a nongeologic origin. Schiaparelli warned that the names were fanciful. Combined with fanciful observation and the general difficulty of recognizing whether patterns existed or not, some were convinced that a civilization built canals on Mars—seeing a pattern where none existed. The canals of Mars were the "hot hand of astronomers."

An additional aspect of hot-hand phenomena is that better players are more likely to be judged to be having streaks. That is, highly successful athletes are more

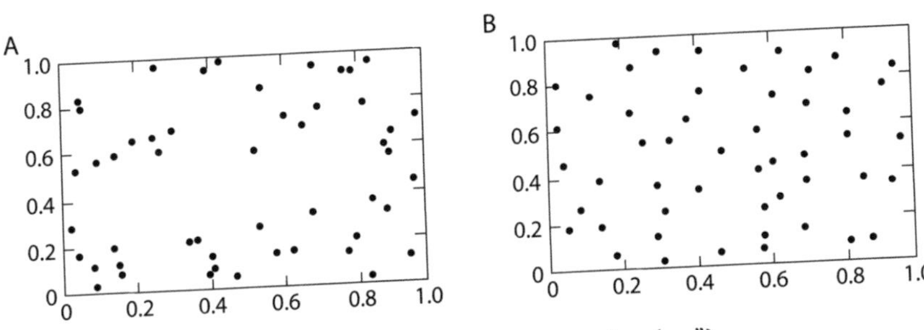

Figure 10.11. Which picture is more "random"?

likely to be thought to be having streaks of success, perhaps because such streaks are more likely with more talented players.[15]

Do mutual funds display a "hot hand"? Should you shift your money to the fund that was more successful last year? There is considerable research on this topic, but the researchers did not generally distinguish between funds that are persistently better and funds that are temporarily better than average. Recently, professors Judith Chevalier and Glenn Ellison[16] have demonstrated that there are significant differences in the performance of mutual-fund managers. Managers who are younger, who graduated from top universities, and who have M.B.A.'s, consistently outperform their complement. Some of the enhanced performances of young M.B.A.'s from top universities can be attributed to differences in choices—M.B.A.'s manage funds with higher systematic risks, so a higher return may be just a compensation for the increased risk, and younger managers manage funds that have smaller management expenses. Ultimately, however, it appears that some managers are just better than others. A streak may not be a hot hand, but a sign of a superior manager.

The hot-hand phenomenon—meaning the incorrect belief in transitory patterns—is very common. Psychologically, it is natural to want to impose a pattern on randomness and to underestimate the likelihood of streaks, and thus draw false conclusions from streaks. This phenomenon is especially prevalent among amateur stock-market investors and a few self-proclaimed professionals, who often consider that they can predict the peaks and troughs of a stock from observation of the past performance, a strategy known as "chartism." In contrast, the prevailing theory of the stock market holds that all relevant, public information is incorporated into the current price, and thus the past behavior is uninformative about the future direction of the stock.[17] The prevailing theory is that stocks follow a "random walk," which is a sequence of random values, where each value is the previous value, plus an average increase, plus a shock or error term, which can be thought of as the effect of new information on the share price, and which is uncorrelated with past

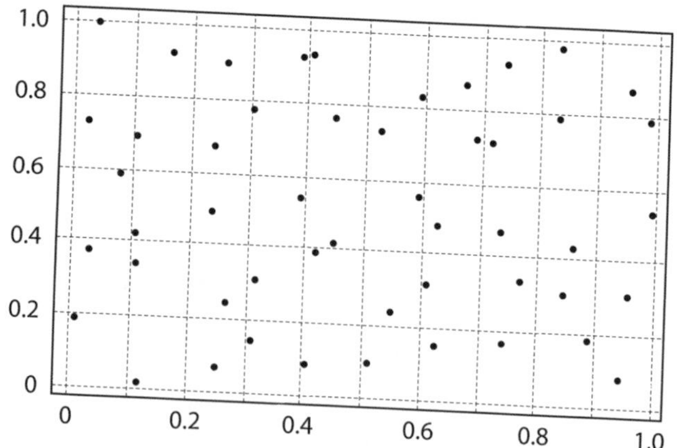

Figure 10.12. The Nonrandom Figure. Each smaller rectangle contains exactly one point, which is a very unlikely configuration. Most people expect random points will be evenly dispersed, when the opposite is true.

shocks. There is more than adequate research to debunk the proposition that charting works, but nevertheless, charting remains popular, as does thinking one is just luckier and "knows when to stop," and therefore can beat the house in Las Vegas.

Chartism finds adherents because of a misunderstanding of randomness that is similar to the misunderstanding embedded in the hot-hand phenomenon. Most people expect fewer strings of high values than actually arise in a random walk. In fact, however, it is very unlikely that a random walk will stay near its expected value—random walks wander around (hence the name). The misunderstanding may be due to the fact that averages tend to get close to their mean as sample sizes grow. However, a random walk is not an average—it is the *sum* of a series of random variables, but it is not divided by the number of variables as an average would be. Consequently, the variance of a random walk actually grows as the observation period gets longer. Indeed, the variance of a random walk, 1,000 days in the future is a thousand times greater than the daily variance. Figure 10.13 plots the results of a random walk with 100,000 steps. Each step adds a normally distributed random variable, which is zero on average, and has a variance equal to one, to the previous value. Note the apparent patterns—significant declines and substantial periods of increase. Random chance produces apparent patterns, which are not real patterns. Indeed, in the process of adding 100,000 random variables, each with mean zero and variance equal to one, together, the sum is very likely to exceed 100 at some point in the process. For the same reason, the process is very likely to wander below −100, because that requires a relatively small string—less than 1%—of negative outcomes. Similarly, getting 200 ahead, out of 50,000, say, is not very much as a percentage, but it produces the kind of startling rises and falls seen in

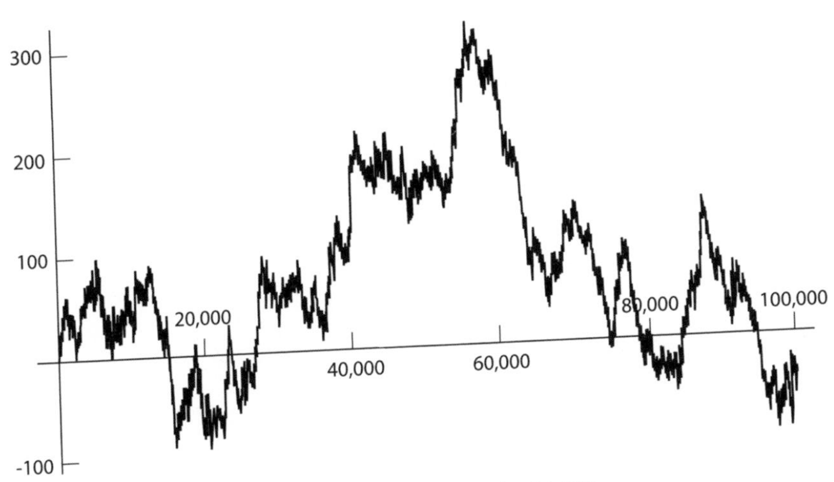

Figure 10.13. A random walk with 100,000 steps.

figure 10.13. As the series runs for a long time, there are likely to be streaks, as are visible in figure 10.13. Indeed, random walks can produce apparent patterns that may look more like the expression of some underlying phenomenon than would be seen in real stock-market price patterns!

OPTION VALUES

A call option is the right to buy something at a set price, sometimes called the strike price. For example, the right to buy 1,000 shares of Microsoft stock at a price of \$100 per share is a call option. One is not required to buy the shares, and if the price is below \$100 on the option's expiration date, the call option is worthless. In contrast, if the share price on the expiration is \$112, the call option is worth \$12,000—\$12 per share, because the option gives the right to buy shares for \$100 that could be sold for \$112.

Note that a share of stock is equivalent to owning an option that never expires and has a strike price of zero. Ignoring tax considerations, such an option should be valued at the stock price, because one can freely convert the option to the stock at any time.

European call options can be exercised only on the day they expire, while American call options can be exercised on any day prior to their expiration. As it is easier to understand the pricing of European options, we start with those. For example, suppose that the possible prices of Microsoft stock are \$99, \$100, \$101, \$102, and \$103, with probabilities given in table 10.4. The option value is computed by finding the expected profit of owning the option. In the example, the option pays

TABLE 10.4
A Random Payoff

Outcome	*Probability*	*Profit/ Share*	*Weighted Profit*
\$99	10%	\$0	\$0.00
\$100	20%	\$0	\$0.00
\$101	40%	\$1	\$0.40
\$102	20%	\$2	\$0.40
\$103	10%	\$3	\$0.30
Sum	100%		\$1.10

whenever the price exceeds \$100, and it pays the share price minus the strike price. This is a random variable, and the mean of this variable is the option value.

An increase in the strike price, to \$101, does not reduce the option value by \$1. This is because the increase only matters when the option produces a positive return. In particular, an increase of the strike price to \$101 produces an option value of \$0.40. With a strike price of \$100, the option was "in the money" (has a positive payoff) 70% of the time, so that the increase costs the holder the \$1 with a probability of 70%. Hence, the option value falls by \$0.70, which is \$1 times a probability of 70%. Note the relationship between the two options, one with a strike price of \$100 and one with a strike price of \$101, which arises because of the probability distribution determining the share price.

In concept, option pricing works like the example. One computes the probability distribution of earnings from the option, and then averages the earnings to find an average value. Consider a European call option with a strike price s. The share price is normally distributed with mean equal to μ, and a variance of σ^2. The share price, at the time of the expiration of the option, is denoted by X. To value the option, it will be useful to express the strike price as a Z statistic, $Z = (s - \mu)/\sigma$. The expected value of the option, then, is just the expected value of the random variable that is the larger of 0 and $X - s$, the share price minus the strike price. This can be expressed as

$$\text{Max}\{0, X - s\} = -s + \text{Max}\{s, X\} = \sigma\left[-\frac{s-\mu}{\sigma} + \text{Max}\left\{\frac{s-\mu}{\sigma}, \frac{X-\mu}{\sigma}\right\}\right]$$

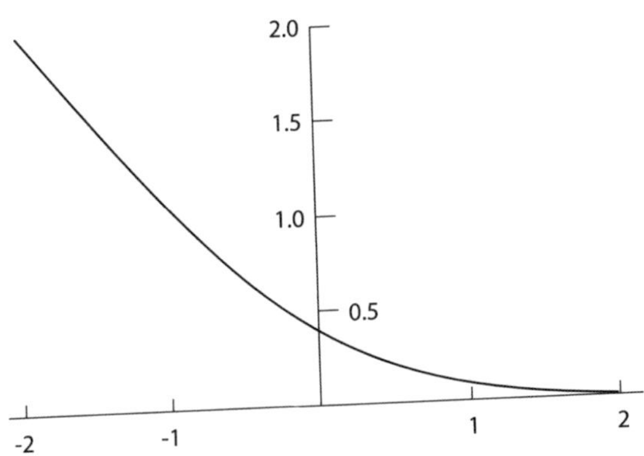

Figure 10.14. The option value as a function of the strike price in standard deviations.

Note that this expression for the option value is expressed entirely in terms of the share price standard deviation σ, and the *Z* statistic for *s*. The option value can then be computed using a table. A graph of the term in square brackets is provided in figure 10.14. This figure gives the value of the option in standard deviations of the share price on the vertical axis. The strike price of the option is measures in terms of its *Z* statistic. Thus, for example, suppose Microsoft is trading at $100 and has a monthly standard deviation of five. Microsoft's value a month hence is normally distributed, with a mean of $101 and a standard deviation of five. An option that has a strike price of $101, then, gets a *Z* statistic of 0. Consequently, the option value is about 0.4 standard deviations, or two. In contrast, if the strike price is $106, the option has a *Z* statistic of 1 ($106–$101 divided by the standard deviation of five), which gives an option value of 0.083 σ, or $.42. A strike price of $91, which is two standard deviations below the expected value of $101, has an option value of just over two standard deviations, or just slightly more than the $10 difference between the average return and the strike price. These values—the option value and the difference between the expected price and the strike price—are close because when the strike price is two standard deviations below the expected price, the option is almost always exercised.

The possibility of initiating a project creates an option. A paper manufacturer that considers building a pulp mill has several options, including time and location. If the market can support just one more mill, building the plant exercises the option, and hence the option value is lost. It may be the right decision to build the plant, but the loss of option value should be subtracted from the NPV; it is a real cost. In some cases, building a plant creates an option value. Building a plant to meet technical specifications of other nations, for example, creates an option to export that would not be available without the new plant. Building an oil refinery in Phoenix, Arizona, that is capable of creating gasoline to meet the California Air Resources Board (CARB) standards permits the option of selling the gasoline in California or elsewhere. How would one go about valuing the option? In principle, one would estimate the likelihood that shipping the gasoline to the California market would be profitable, and would determine how much profit would be earned. This permits valuing the option to sell in the California market, which can then be compared to the cost. Option values are encountered frequently in business decisions. Building a spur line to a railroad permits transporting inputs and outputs by rail as well as trucks. Locating in a major metropolitan area permits access to specialized labor resources and other resources that are not available in smaller areas. For example, there are only a few cities with stores that provide 24-hour computer-parts sales. Typically, one will not need to buy a hard drive at 2 A.M., but the option may have positive value.

The field of option pricing is exceedingly technical and sophisticated, and is outside the scope of this book. The examples provide some of the flavor of option pricing—at its core, option pricing is about estimating the likelihood options are exercised and their value when they are exercised. It is important, however, to consider some principles that can be deduced from our relatively simple option examples.

- Options are valuable.
- Options are more valuable the more variation there is.
- Options can be priced by computing expected values of exercised options.
- Exercising an option causes the option value to be lost.
- Initiating a project closes some options and creates others.
- Option values matter most when useful information will arrive in the future.

In 1995, there were three major digital formats for the new-generation cellular phones, known as PCS (Personal Communication Services) phones. There was the European standard, called GSM (Global System for Mobile Communication Services), and two other standards, TDMA (Time Division Multiple Access) and CDMA (Code Division Multiple Access). Roughly speaking, GSM was less sophisticated and easier to implement than TDMA, and TDMA was less sophisticated and closer to being ready to implement than CDMA. By waiting to offer service, a firm retained the option of choosing the better technology for the job, and seeing the bugs and wrinkles removed from the standards first. In particular, CDMA was years away from being ready for data transmission, while GSM-based modems already were available in 1995. While estimating the likelihood of technologies working successfully is notoriously hard, nevertheless it was clear that waiting a few years would resolve most of the questions about the technology for the new generation of phones. However, waiting created two costs. First, other firms arrived at the market first, building networks that might be harder to replicate. Second, early entry might sway the market toward the firm's desired standard, while staying out would let others choose the technology. In the end, all of the major U.S. telecommunications firms except MCI entered, and, perhaps not surprisingly, all three standards were employed, although GSM had a limited following. Faced with the difficulties of estimating the option value of waiting, all three options were chosen, although of course by different firms.

Scenario Analysis

Scenario analysis is a means of accounting for the unknown in analysis of a market and of the firm's position within that market. The approach involves specifying a limited number of scenarios, each of which represents a group of possible outcomes. For example, a firm contemplating a price cut considers the likely moves by its rivals—doing nothing, matching the price cut, cutting prices by a greater amount. The outcomes under these scenarios can be calculated. Probabilities can be associated with scenarios by considering the likely payoffs to the rivals under the scenarios and determining the rivals' likely best responses. Similarly, a firm offering a new form of cellular service might run three scenarios—demand as expected, greater than expected, and less than expected. When the choices of a competitor are uncertain, perhaps because the competitor's technology and resources are not known with precision, more scenarios can be generated. For example, if there will be zero, one, two, or three competitors, there are twelve possible scenarios—three demand states times four competition states. Because of the tendency for the number of scenarios to proliferate, it is usually necessary to lump many of the scenarios together to keep the number manageable.

With probabilities attached to the scenarios, the expected profitability of a price cut can be assessed. Unfortunately, the probabilities are rarely more than a gut instinct. Moreover, there seems to be a consistent tendency to underestimate the likelihood that the scenario is different from the expected scenario, perhaps because of the psychological resistance to randomness that is explored above.

An important aspect of scenario analysis is the evaluation of options. Often, investment decisions are based on a scenario analysis, and at some point the correct scenario will be clarified. It may pay to wait until the decision of another firm to enter is resolved, or until the extent of demand is resolved, prior to making an investment decision. Scenarios should be formulated to facilitate the evaluation of options, because correct evaluation of options can minimize or even eliminate downside risk. For example, if another firm is building a factory to enter an emerging market, it may pay to wait and see if this firm experiences a high level of demand, rather than to start building right away. Because the other firm has a head start, the cost of delay does not involve a loss of a first-mover advantage—that is already lost. Delay eliminates the low-demand scenarios; elimination of the low-demand scenarios may be worth more than the value of slightly earlier entry, especially when it is possible to avoid the mistakes of the first entrant.

The most common approach to scenario analysis is to lump possible outcomes together to keep the number of scenarios manageable. However, there is an alternative approach that is preferable in some circumstances and belongs in the scenario toolkit. Consider two companies competing to buy a copper mine in a sealed-bid auction. Both companies are aware that there is substantial uncertainty not just in whether there is ore present, but how much ore, in what purity, and how much rock must be sifted through to reach the ore. Each company drills some core samples and uses dynamite-based imaging techniques to assess the nature of the rock below the surface, and it obtains estimates of the relevant variables. From experience, however, each company knows that there is substantial error associated with the estimates. Indeed, the companies are quite good at forecasting the likely outcomes of each of the variables, and each uses a spreadsheet for the analysis. How should the companies bid? That depends not only on the evaluation of how much ore is present, but also on the evaluation of the other company's estimate.

The standard scenario analytic approach would assign to the other firm a few possible estimates of the value of the mine and compute a good bid, given the expected value of the mine and the likely competing bids. This approach fails miserably; the expected value held by the competitors is strongly correlated with the actual value of the mine, because the competitors' estimates, and hence bids, are usually large precisely when the samples indicated the mine looks promising. The standard approach can be supplemented by increasing the number of scenarios—a "scenario configuration" becomes a listing of the scenario held by each company. Thus, if the company normally calculated five scenarios for the value of the mine—high, medium plus, medium minus, low plus, low minus—there would be twenty-five scenario configurations for two companies, because in a bidding context a scenario configuration must account not only for the scenario held by the firm, but the scenario held by its competitor as well. The standard scenario approach becomes unmanageable even with two firms and five scenarios; with six bidders and eight scenarios, there are more than a quarter of a million scenario configurations.

The alternative approach is to give up on keeping the number of scenarios or scenario configurations manageable, and instead use a spreadsheet to perform the analysis. As spreadsheets are already used to perform scenario analysis, the only real loss from proliferation of the number of scenarios is the understanding of the individual components of the analysis—it becomes a rote calculation rather than a

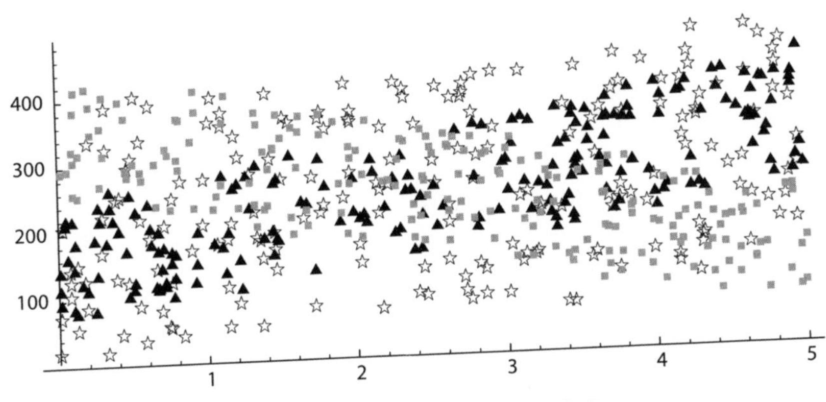

Figure 10.15. Complex scenario analysis.

group of comprehensible stories. This is a significant loss, which can be mitigated by producing graphs that treat the spreadsheet like a black box.

The major disadvantage of the scenario proliferation approach to scenario analysis is the loss of a clear understanding of the drivers of the environment in which the firm operates. This disadvantage can be mitigated by the production of correlation graphs showing how high-level variables interact. Suppose, for example, that demand for laptop computers has been modeled in a way that depends on fifteen fundamentals—income, interest rate, various business activity measures, prices of other goods, growth rates, and so on—each of which has two to five reasonable levels, for a total of 15 million scenarios.* How can one understand the effect of an increase in the federal funds rate, for example? The answer is to produce graphs or scatterplots that relate demand to interest rates. Such plots can be used to show how important variables affect demand. Moreover, by using color diagrams, a third variable can be represented by the color of the plot. Figure 10.15 provides an example, illustrating how demand is affected by interest rates and the price of another good in a complex system. Each triangle, star, and box in figure 10.15 represents the outcome of a scenario analysis, one for each scenario. These scenarios may be calculated and graphed using a spreadsheet program like Excel. The horizontal axis represents one input like the federal funds rate, and the shapes (triangles, stars, and gray boxes) represent demand in three distinct groups of scenarios. Each point represents a full scenario. It is possible to detect, from this picture alone, that demand is falling as the federal funds rate increases for the gray

*It is almost invariably a mistake in this approach to assume the variables are independently distributed. In particular, macroeconomic variables like income, interest rates, growth rates, and so on have a known covariance structure. Accounting for such covariances is a major challenge for scenario analysis generally, but a larger challenge the more scenarios there are.

box scenarios and demand is rising for the triangle scenarios. It is more difficult to ascertain what happens with demand in the star scenarios, although there is a slight apparent upward slope. Such pictures as this one can be used to provide insight about the nature of large groups of scenarios that arise when many different variables are uncertain. With the use of color rather than shapes, it is quite feasible to consider three or more classes of scenarios.

To summarize, the conventional method of scenario analysis involves a limited number of cases that have good stories attached to them. The advantage of the conventional approach is that these stories are readily interpretable and make sense. The disadvantage of the conventional approach is that there are, in reality, many more possibilities than the limited number of stories. Proliferating scenarios into the thousands and above increases the realism of the scenario approach, but at the cost of an inability to understand how high-level variables interact overall. This disadvantage can be mitigated by using statistical analysis and graphs to summarize the interaction of important variables.

EXECUTIVE SUMMARY—ELEMENTARY STATISTICS

- Probability and statistics play a significant role in the formulation of strategy, because the world has many random aspects.
- A sample is *biased* if it samples an unintended group or subgroup of the intended group.
- As samples get larger, the likelihood that the sample reflects the true population grows.
- The precision of an estimate requires two statistics—an error or *confidence interval* (e.g., ±3%) and the likelihood of falling within that error or *confidence level* (e.g., 95% chance of ±3%) because there is always some chance that the estimate falls outside any given error.
- With opinion polls, there is a 95% chance that the poll is within $\pm 1/\sqrt{n}$, where n is the sample size.
- The *variance* is a measure of the average amount of variation in a random quantity.
- The normal distribution, or bell curve, is characterized by a mean, or average value, and a variance.
- Sample averages approximately follow normal distributions. This permits calculation of confidence levels for averages in a manner akin to the analysis of opinion polls.
- The *correlation coefficient* measures the co-movement or statistical relationship between two random quantities.

- The correlation coefficient ranges from -1 to 1, with -1 a perfect negative relationship and 1 a perfect positive relationship.
- Correlation is not causation. Some quantities are correlated even though they have no influence on each other, usually because of a "third cause" that influences both.
- Sample selection bias can be created by choices—people who choose an action are usually different in salient respects from those who did not choose the action. In some cases, it is possible to correct for sample selection bias.
- Most people see patterns in random outcomes, a phenomenon often called the "hot hand" in basketball.
- This tendency to see patterns in random data arises from the expectation that "random" means uniform, when random sequences often involve apparent streaks.
- Chartism in the stock market is an example of the hot-hand phenomenon.
- A call option provides the right to purchase something at a prespecified price.
- Options are valuable and can be priced by using sophisticated mathematics.
- Options are more valuable the higher the variance of the outcome and the more information that will be available in the future.
- Exercising an option eliminates the option value. Thus, it may pay to wait to preserve an option value.
- Some investments create an option value by delaying a decision point, and these investments are more valuable than an NPV analysis would suggest.
- Scenario analysis is a common tool to deal with uncertainty.
- A new development in scenario analysis is the analysis of thousands of scenarios using statistical methods. Some intuition and understanding are lost relative to standard scenario analysis, but greater complexity can be handled.

I bought some batteries, but they weren't included.
—**Steven Wright**

Pricing

In many corporations, the selection of prices used to be something of an afterthought. Some companies still use a fixed markup over average cost. Others follow the prices of their competition. Pricing was often a subsidiary consideration in a marketing department or division, a branch of the organization devoted to analyzing and changing customer perceptions of the product. The neglect of pricing strategy was a curious phenomenon, for pricing is fundamental to business strategy and the way firms make money. Perhaps more important, misunderstanding the pricing behavior of rivals can give rise to ruinous and unnecessary price wars.

In the past twenty years, pricing has grown from an afterthought in most organizations to a major strategic concern. Some companies have created pricing divisions. American Airlines estimates its yield management program generates $500 million per year in additional revenue. One estimate holds that American changes prices half a million times *per day*. Actually, with more than fifty distinct fares on every flight segment, and prices depending on where passengers connect, it is not really that surprising that American changes its prices so often. In response to subtle shifts in the number of seats purchased relative to normal bookings for a single flight (e.g., Austin to San Jose at 9:22 A.M.), American changes future demand forecasts and re-optimizes its prices not just on that flight, or even that route, but on other routes as well. American Airlines excels at the phenomenon known as *price discrimination,* which means charging different customers different prices for the same good.

The Internet offers new opportunities and new challenges for pricing. Customer histories will be available to some firms, offering the opportunity to base price offers on the history of the customer's purchases. In particular, it becomes possible to offer higher prices to those who have shown, by their previous purchases, a willingness to pay a price higher than the market price. (It is a better idea to offer discounts to price-sensitive customers rather than add surcharges to those whose history suggests a tolerance for higher prices.)

This chapter is concerned with pricing strategies, the largest component of which is price discrimination, sometimes known as *value-based pricing,* which involves charging what the market or individual submarkets, will bear. There are two major flavors of price discrimination strategy—direct and indirect.[1] Direct price discrimination involves charging customers different prices based on observable characteristics of the customer. A senior-citizen discount at a movie is an example of direct price discrimination, as is the Hertz rental car "gold" agreement offered free to high-level frequent flyers. Discounts offered to corporate buyers are also direct price discriminations. All of these differences in prices depend on observed differences in the customer type—their age, flying pattern, or employment. Indirect price discrimination involves making offers that are available to all, and letting customers choose which offer is best for them. The classic example of indirect price discrimination is the quantity discount, such as "buy one and get the second at half price." Newspaper coupons are also examples of indirect price discrimination, for the coupons are available to all and customers choose whether to use them or not. Pricing of bundles of products tends to involve self-selection—using distinct objects in the same way as a quantity discount. In some cases, however, bundling permits a surcharge over the pricing of individual components for the larger purchase.

Long-distance companies offer a blizzard of telephone plans, with different monthly charges and per-call charges. Potential customers then choose among these plans, to find the one that best suits their calling profile. Identifying the best plan for a given usage pattern is sufficiently complex that there are computer programs to assist the consumer. In designing its offerings, a long-distance telephone company must address a variety of issues:

- What types of potential customers are present? If all customers were the same, there would be no point in offering multiple plans. Multiple plans enhance profit for the company because they permit the company to offer selective price cuts to price-sensitive customers.
- How will customers choose plans? What is the demand for the plans? How is the demand for one plan affected by a change in the terms of another plan? What alternatives do customers have?
- Can customers "mix and match" the plans? Can customers join together to take advantage of quantity discounts, or make many small purchases to take advantage of promotional discounts?
- How will rivals react? American Airlines offered the first frequent-flier program, and United responded with plans of its own in two weeks. Many

> other Internet service providers followed AOL's $20 per month, no-hourly-charge plan the same week.

This chapter is devoted to addressing such questions in a systematic way.

ILLUSTRATIVE EXAMPLES

There is almost no limit to the creative use of price discrimination. However, the potential for price discrimination remains largely untapped—there are many more applications. This section presents some clever and significant examples of price discrimination.

International Pricing by the Pharmaceutical Companies

Many residents of Texas find that prescription pharmaceuticals are consistently less expensive in Mexico, and consequently there is a substantial flow of prescription drugs into the United States from south of the border. What is less commonly known is that U.S. drug prices are high relative to Canada's, and prices in both countries are high relative to most European countries'. Extreme examples include Clozapine, an antipsychotic, and Fluoxetine, an antidepressant. U.S. prices were six times the price in Spain, and well above prices prevailing in continental Europe. An international comparison of these drugs is provided in table 11.1.

Methyl Methacrylate

Methyl methacrylate (MM) is a plastic with a variety of industrial uses, as well as a quite valuable use in the manufacture of dentures. According to George Stocking and M. Watkins (1947), the two manufacturers of MM, DuPont and Rohm & Haas, followed a uniform pricing policy and acted as a cartel.[2] Their pricing certainly corroborates this claim: they sold the powdered version of MM for industrial uses at $.85 per pound, and the liquid MM for $22.00 per pound to licensed dental laboratories. The liquid was a prepared mixture consisting of both monomer and polymer versions of MM, while the powdered version was a polymer.

The price difference was too great, and attracted bootleggers who extract the dental formulation from the powder and sell the result to dentists.

Rohm & Haas considered adulterating the powdered version so that it would be unsuitable for use in dentures. The goal was to induce the Food and Drug Administration to prohibit the use of the powdered version in dental uses. A licensee of Rohm & Haas suggested:

TABLE 11.1
International Pharmaceutical Price Differences

Country	*Clozapine* *100 mg (90)*	*Fluoxetine* *20 mg (30)*
Austria	$59.92	$36.36
Belgium	$75.62	$37.52
Canada	$271.08	$37.59
Denmark	$66.04	$32.06
Finland	$64.39	$29.64
Germany	$89.55	$51.56
Italy	$131.51	$33.09
Luxembourg	$78.03	$36.69
Netherlands	$75.82	$35.47
Portugal	$112.56	$29.27
Spain	$51.94	$25.93
Sweden	$73.72	$38.50
U.K.	$294.93	$33.54
U.S.	$317.03	$72.16

Source: Larry Sasich, and E. Fuller Torrey, *International Comparison of Prices for Antidepressant and Antipsychotic Drugs* (Washington, DC: Public Citizen, 15 July, 1998).

A millionth of one percent of arsenic or lead might cause them [the FDA] to confiscate every bootleg unit in the country. There ought to be a trace of something that would cause them to rear up.

Rohm & Haas apparently did not put this policy into effect, although an internal document described it as "a very fine method of controlling the bootleg situation." Rohm & Haas resorted to the less effective strategy of planting a rumor that they had adulterated the powder: less effective, but less likely to kill customers.[3]

Hand-Me-Down by Armani

The fashion company Armani has three distinct brands or lines of clothes: Armani Via Borgo Nuovo, Armani, and Emporio Armani (called Mani in the United States). The three lines differ in price and in offered designs, but not in the type of clothes offered. Moreover, there is a distinct time pattern to their offerings.

New designs are introduced by Armani Via Borgo Nuovo at a very high price. After a few months, the design is replaced, and the now older design is passed on to Armani, and from there to Emporio Armani, which typically sells Armani designs that are several years old. Employing multiple brands helps prevent Armani from cutting prices of brand new designs to obtain more sales, a temptation that was the undoing of the Italian designer Fiorucci.

Starting around 1980, Fiorucci attempted to expand its relatively specialized business that focused on the young upper middle class. To do so, Fiorucci expanded to sales channels to include department stores and lowered the prices to be competitive with other department store offerings. Fiorucci's customer base stopped buying, because the exclusivity of the designs was gone. The loss of the fashionable image reduced the attraction of the clothes for the mass market, and ultimately Fiorucci went out of business.[4] It will be interesting to see if the new mass-market Armani stores, called Armani Exchange, succeed where Fiorucci failed.

IBM LaserPrinter E

In May 1990, IBM introduced the LaserPrinter E, an inexpensive alternative to its very popular and successful LaserPrinter. The LaserPrinter E was virtually identical to the original LaserPrinter, except that the E model printed text at five pages per minute (ppm), while the LaserPrinter could reach ten ppm.

The slower performance of the LaserPrinter E was accomplished by adding five chips to the E model. According to Mitt Jones (*PC Magazine,* May 29, 1990):

> The controllers in our evaluation unit differed only by virtue of four socketed firmware chips and one surface mounted chip. PC Labs' testing of numerous evaluation units indicated that the LaserPrinter E in effect inserts wait states to slow print speed . . . IBM has gone to some expense to slow the LaserPrinter in firmware so that it can market it at a lower price.

The LaserPrinter E sold for about 60% of the price of the original LaserPrinter. This was in line with the newly introduced Hewlett-Packard IIP printer, which was the first laser printer popular with households.[5] In constructing the IBM Laser-

Printer E, IBM has reduced the incentive of high-end customers to buy the low-end device by slowing down the low-end device.

Sony MiniDisc

The Sony MiniDisc is like a compact disc in performance, but it is the size of a $3\frac{1}{2}$-inch floppy disc. Like the floppy, the minidisc has a protective case. Like a CD, a minidisc is read with a laser. Like a CD-R, the minidisc is recordable.

Sony makes two sizes of minidisc, a 60-minute and a 74-minute version. The difference in the 60-minute version is a code written on the disc itself, which tells the player/recorder not to use a portion of the disc. These instructions are embedded in a "nonrewritable" area so that aftermarket resellers cannot overwrite the instructions.

At the time of this writing, 74-minute minidiscs sell for around $4.50, while the 60-minute versions sell for $3.00. The discount for the 60-minute version is much greater (in percentage) than when the products were first introduced. As with the IBM LaserPrinter E, Sony has gone to considerable trouble to create a less valuable version of the minidisc, so that it can charge less for it.[6]

An Electric Utility's Individualized Pricing

In the late 1980s, the turbine generator was developed, which made it much more practical for large users of electricity to generate their own electricity at costs comparable to the costs of large electric utilities. As a consequence, traditional pricing of electricity for industrial customers threatened to lead to bypass of the electric utility altogether—customers would prefer to produce their own power rather than pay the electric utility's standard rates.

Niagara Mohawk Power Corporation developed a very sophisticated response to the new threat. For its largest customers, it calculated precisely what it would cost for the customers to use modern technology to generate electricity themselves. This calculation is feasible given (1) the available technology (which is publicly observable) and (2) the customer's history of electricity purchases. (Some care has to be taken to deal with the value of reduced marginal costs to the customer, along with potential peak-load problems, differences in reliability, the value of self-sufficiency, and other factors.) Then the utility makes an offer the customer will not refuse—power at slightly less than self-generation would cost. The offered schedules come in the "block declining" form, with marginal costs stepping down as the demand rises, just to keep the utility competitively priced with self-generation.

Somewhat smaller customers would not find it profitable to enter into self-generation. These customers were offered an *option* of lower-usage charges (both peak and off-peak) reflecting actual marginal cost, with a fixed monthly access charge. The access charges were carefully chosen to extract revenue from the buyer, and ranged from $32,900 to $107,000 per month. Since the new plan was optional, both the utility and the customer were better off than before the offer was made; the customer paid more but also bought more power, with less financial risk. Niagara Mohawk used both direct and indirect price discrimination. The offers made to a customer depended on the customer's usage history, but the offer was an option with the right to continue under the old pricing scheme.[7]

IBM's Punchcard Metering

In the early part of this century (about the 1930s), IBM charged $1 per thousand for punchcards that cost much less to manufacture, and it required users of IBM machines to use these IBM cards. IBM had the strategy of renting the tabulating machines at a very low price and then making up the difference in cards. This was advantageous because it let IBM charge intensive users of data processing more, since the intensive users used more cards, and intensive users valued computation more highly. In this way, IBM used indirect price discrimination (the customer decided the amount of usage) to charge higher-value customers a higher total price, essentially metering machine usage by punchcard usage.

In 1936, the Supreme Court struck down this practice as illegal tying (see chapter 9), but the value of the practice, when legal, is clear. A high marginal cost combined with a low fixed charge permits sales to a wider variety of buyers without significant threat of arbitrage, since the only mechanism for arbitrage is for buyers to use non-IBM cards. While some buyers may be willing to risk cards that fold, spindle, and mutilate, many, even most, will not.

IBM is also credited with the invention of FUD—fear, uncertainty, and doubt—which is a means of suggesting that the quality of the IBM product is higher than the competition, and justifies the higher price. This concept was perhaps best expressed in a series of advertisements implying, "No one was ever fired for buying IBM."

Buying Paint from an Airline

Alan H. Hess considered the ramifications of the airline pricing model applied to hardware, in a way that suggests additional applications of price discrimination in our future.

Buying Paint from a Hardware Store:[8]

Customer: Hi, how much is your interior flat latex paint in Bone White?

Clerk: We have a medium quality, which is $16 a gallon, and premium, which is $22 a gallon. How many gallons would you like?

Customer: I'll take five gallons of the medium quality, please.

Clerk: That will be $80 plus tax.

Buying Paint from an Airline:

Customer: Hi, how much is your paint?

Clerk: Well, sir, that all depends.

Customer: Depends on what?

Clerk: Actually a lot of things.

Customer: How about giving me an average price?

Clerk: Wow, that's too hard a question. The lowest price is $9 a gallon, and we have 150 different prices up to $200 a gallon.

Customer: What's the difference in the paint?

Clerk: Oh, there isn't any difference; it's all the same paint.

Customer: Well, then, I'd like some of that $9 paint.

Clerk: Well, first I need to ask you a few questions. When do you intend to use it?

Customer: I want to paint tomorrow, on my day off.

Clerk: Sir, the paint for tomorrow is the $200 paint.

Customer: What? When would I have to paint in order to get the $9 version?

Clerk: That would be in three weeks, but you will also have to agree to start painting before Friday of that week and continue painting until at least Sunday.

Customer: You've got to be kidding!

Clerk: Sir, we don't kid around here. Of course, I'll have to check to see if we have any of that paint available before I can sell it to you.

Customer: What do you mean check to see if you can sell it to me? You have shelves full of that stuff; I can see it right there.

Clerk: Just because you can see it doesn't mean that we have it. It may be the same paint, but we sell only a certain number of gallons on any given week. Oh, and by the way, the price just went to $12.

Customer: You mean the price went up while we were talking?

Clerk: Yes, sir. You see, we change prices and rules thousands of times a day, and since you haven't actually walked out of the store with your paint yet, we just decided to change. Unless you want the same thing to happen again,

I would suggest that you get on with your purchase. How many gallons do you want?

Customer: I don't know exactly. Maybe five gallons. Maybe I should buy six gallons just to make sure I have enough.

Clerk: Oh, no, sir, you can't do that. If you buy the paint and then don't use it, you will be liable for penalties and possible confiscation of the paint you already have.

Customer: What?

Clerk: That's right. We can sell you enough paint to do your kitchen, bathroom, hall, and north bedroom, but if you stop painting before you do the bedroom, you will be in violation of our tariffs.

Customer: But what does it matter to you whether I use all the paint? I already paid for it!

Clerk: Sir, there's no point in getting upset; that's just the way it is. We make plans upon the idea that you will use all the paint, and when you don't, it just causes us all kinds of problems.

Customer: This is crazy? I suppose something terrible will happen if I don't keep painting until after Saturday night!

Clerk: Yes, sir, it will.

Customer: Well, that does it! I'm going somewhere else to buy my paint.

Clerk: That won't do you any good, sir. We all have the same rules.

DIRECT PRICE DISCRIMINATION

Direct price discrimination is conceptually the simplest pricing tool available to business. It involves charging customers more, or less, depending on the identity, or type, of the customer. There are a number of means of identifying customer types:

- Location
- Other possessions or purchases
- Status
- Age
- Employment
- Gender

The goal of direct price discrimination is to charge each customer, or customer group, the price that maximizes the firm's profit for that particular customer. Thus, with direct price discrimination, the firm attempts to identify customer characteristics that are correlated with the value customers place on the firm's products, and condition the prices on these characteristics. For example, students are typically more sensitive to prices (have lower willingness to pay) than nonstudents. As a consequence, for many items it is advantageous to charge students less than the regular price. Frequently, restaurants near university campuses offer student discounts, as do some movie theaters. The desirability of offering student discounts is not a consequence of the number of students, but rather the responsiveness, or elasticity, or student demand to a price cut. This responsiveness of quantity to price is generally quantified with the concept of elasticity, which measures the percentage of increase in quantity demanded that arises from a 1% decrease in the price. For example, with an elasticity of two, 10% increase in price should decrease the quantity demanded by approximately 20%.[9] The *monopoly pricing rule* states that the profit-maximizing price-cost margin is one over the elasticity of demand. In symbols:

$$\frac{p - mc}{p} = \frac{1}{\epsilon},$$

where p is the price charged, mc is the marginal or incremental cost,[10] and ϵ is the elasticity of demand.[11] The relevant demand is the demand facing the firm, rather than the industry demand. For example, when the elasticity is two, the price should be double the marginal costs, or a 100% markup. We immediately observe that the profit-maximizing price is higher when demand is less elastic. Moreover, provided that costs are positive, the left-hand side is less than one. Thus, a profit-maximizing firm sells on the elastic portion of demand (where elasticity exceeds 1). When marginal costs are zero, as is approximately satisfied in the software industry (marginal costs are mostly demands on the help desk), the profit-maximizing prices make the elasticity of demand equal to one. That is, with no marginal cost, the profit-maximizing price is the point on the demand curve so that the elasticity is one.

Generally, a firm would like to set a price for each customer so that the monopoly pricing rule would hold for that customer's demand. (Such pricing is sometimes known as value-based pricing, which is a more pleasant term than price discrimination.) The desired price discrimination is illustrated in figure 11.1 for the case of students and nonstudents. Students have a relatively elastic demand: a large quantity change for a given price change, when compared to nonstudents. As a result, the optimal price for students is lower than the optimal price for nonstudents. The price for nonstudents is P_N, while the for students price is P_S.

There are two major impediments to implementing such a plan. The first is informational: It is not straightforward to observe customer willingness to pay, and the customers with inelastic demand have a significant incentive to conceal their

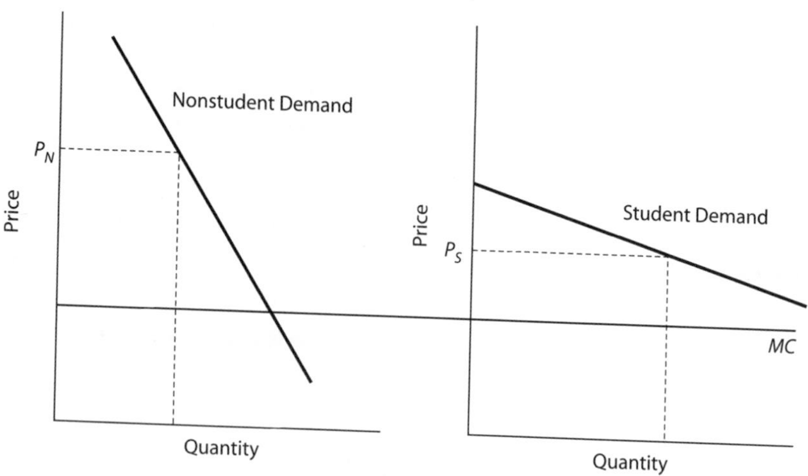

Figure 11.1. The profit-maximizing price for nonstudents, P_N, exceeds the profit-maximizing price for students, P_S.

willingness to pay in order to avoid higher prices. Second, the attempt to charge different prices creates an incentive for customers to arbitrage the price difference, with customers who obtained the low price selling to customers who were charged the higher price, much as some Texans who buy prescription drugs in Mexico do.

A natural barrier to arbitrage is geography, especially national borders. Methods of preventing arbitrage come in five forms:

1. Transportation costs
2. Legal impediments to resale
3. Personalized products or services
4. Thin markets and matching problems
5. Informational problems

The landscaper who charges more in a wealthy neighborhood than in a middle-class neighborhood has engaged in direct price discrimination. The landscaper conditions price on the location of the customer. Because the product is sold on a delivered-and-installed basis, transporting the landscaper's work from a middle-class neighborhood to a rich neighborhood is prohibitively expensive. Such arbitrage would amount to digging plants up, moving them, and replanting them, thereby eliminating most of the value of the landscaper's services.

Objects that are expensive to move are natural candidates for geographic price discrimination. Heavy, low-value items such as gravel and stone are impractical to reship unless price differentials are very large. Oil companies sell gasoline to stations on a delivered basis, so that they can charge more in areas that are less competitive, where the demand facing the retail station is less elastic. To save five cents per gallon, stations are unlikely to be willing to pump gasoline out of underground storage tanks once the fuel is installed there, given the costs and potentially enormous environmental risks. On a larger scale, Saudi Arabia sells oil on a delivered basis, also to charge less in areas with more elastic demand. (The areas with elastic demand tend to be poorer areas, which provides a convenient political rationale for charging the lower prices—supporting the Third World.) Saudi Arabia prevents arbitrage by the simple expedient of threatening to cut off a buyer who attempts to arbitrage the price differentials.

Governments also prevent arbitrage. As noted earlier, pharmaceutical companies routinely sell drugs in Mexico at prices substantially less than in the United States.[12] However, attempts to arbitrage such differences are often stopped at the border, especially if a reseller attempts to bring in a large quantity of pharmaceutical drugs. The U.S. government makes large-scale importation of pharmaceuticals impractical, although recently Congress has been considering changes in the law to encourage such importation.

Many drugs designed for human medicine are also useful in veterinary medicine. The drugs for veterinary use often sell for substantially reduced prices when compared to those for human use. Attempts to arbitrage this difference are hindered by government regulations. In contrast, the government advocates the use of generic equivalent drugs. Nevertheless, the perception that generic drugs are not equivalent to the associated brand-name drugs is pervasive and justifies significant differences in price, even when the generic drug is manufactured by the same company. The difference is price of the generic drug reflects a prevention of arbitrage by informational means.

As noted above, Niagara Mohawk (NiMo) offers buyer-specific prices for electricity to its buyers of large amounts; this is calculated to deter the buyers from installing their own generation capacity. For larger users, generation capacity is inexpensive on a per-megawatt basis, so prices must be low to these users. NiMo's practice is akin to the hypothetical landscaper who charges according to the client's location and other observable characteristics.

Personalized prices have not been practical on a very large scale in the past. Unless the item for sale was relatively valuable, the transaction and administrative costs associated with personalized or individualized prices were too great. However, Internet sales offer an entirely new method of creating personalized prices, by putting the computational power of modern computers to the task. It is quite reasonable for a company to base the price offer on any item on the history of sales with that particular customer. Customers could reasonably pretend to be brand-new customers (by obtaining new Internet addresses and deleting cookies from their machine), but it would be very difficult for customers to alter their history of purchases. In particular, customers who pay more than the median price on an item may get classified as poor searchers and obtain less attractive price offers. For example, Compaq's iPAQ handheld computer comes in two flavors—the 3630 and the 3650. The units are apparently identical. The 3630 is sold in retail stores and the 3650 on the Internet. Offering two models makes it more difficult for consumers to realize that Internet units are less expensive, since comparisons are more difficult.

The airline industry is extraordinarily accomplished at price discrimination. It uses direct price discrimination through the use of frequent-flyer programs, and indirect price discrimination by conditioning the price on a variety of restrictions and requirements, such as Saturday night stay-overs. The price gaps are so large that customers regularly throw away flight segments to reduce their total prices; airlines attempt to prohibit such arbitrage by canceling flights when any segment is not used. Airlines also prohibit the transfer of tickets, citing government regulations intended to prevent terrorism. These regulations do not prohibit the transfer of tickets, but instead require a valid ID from the passenger. Prior to the imposition of the nontransferability, there was a tiny market in the exchange of airline tickets. This market did not function very well (preventing significant arbitrage), because it was difficult for someone with a ticket to sell to find the buyer who valued that particular ticket. The inefficiency of the exchange market is a problem of matching, or thin markets. At any given location, there are few buyers and sellers for any one flight, even if there are thousands of buyers and sellers for the thousands of flights. Airlines succeeded in closing this market in the nick of time, because the Internet would have created a booming market in ticket transfers, as tickets are cheap to mail and relatively valuable—the perfect commodity for an Internet exchange.

From a theoretical perspective, the threat of arbitrage typically bounds the price difference that prevails between two classes of customers. Offer a sufficiently lower price to one group, and the other group will attempt to purchase not from the original seller, but from favored buyers. As a consequence, a price difference that is too great will lead to significant leakage of the low price to the group with inelastic demand. To compensate, it is optimal to charge the group with elastic demand a price *higher* than the monopoly price that would prevail if that group were served individually, and to charge the group with inelastic demand a price lower than their monopoly price. That is, the effect of a threat of arbitrage is to raise the price of the favored group and lower the price of the unfavored (high-value) group. For example, if there is a significant threat of nonstudents obtaining fake student identification, it is optimal to raise the student price and lower the nonstudent price, relative to the levels that prevail in figure 11.1.

To reduce the flow of pharmaceuticals from Mexico to the United States, it is better to both increase the Mexican price and reduce the U.S. price, rather than reduce only the U.S. price. If the U.S. market is sufficiently important relative to the Mexican market, and arbitrage is sufficiently prevalent, it can be profitable to leave the U.S. price unchanged and to raise the Mexican price to the U.S. price as a means of preventing arbitrage. In particular, if the U.S. government mandates a "most favored customer" law that requires the pharmaceutical companies to give U.S. consumers the best world price, the price to U.S. consumers may not fall, but instead the price charged to the rest of the world may rise.

INDIRECT PRICE DISCRIMINATION

Indirect price discrimination uses consumer choice, or "self-selection," as a price discrimination tool. The general mechanism is to offer a set, or menu, of prices and quantities, and let consumers choose those that suit them best. The classic example is the quantity discount. By offering a quantity discount, one can selectively offer lower prices to the larger customers, without having to lower prices to smaller customers. The major advantages of indirect price discrimination are (1) it is unnecessary to observe the individual characteristics of the consumer, and (2) arbitrage is prevented by the design of the pricing scheme. Thus, in the case of indirect price discrimination, customers implement the price discrimination plan for the firm.

Coupons

Coupons are a common method of indirect price discrimination. Coupons work as a price discrimination tool because they are costly to use. Coupons require looking through the paper or coupon flyer, collecting the coupons for products one can use, bringing the coupons to the store, and remembering to hand them to the cashier. As a consequence, people with a low value of time typically find coupons a worthwhile investment of their time. These same people are typically more price-sensitive than those with a high value of time, and thus a coupon provides a discount to people who, on average, are more price-sensitive.

In-store coupons, either placed on the package or in a flashing display near the item, typically amount to a temporary price cut, because the cost of using the coupon is minimal. Thus, in-store coupons are better thought of as an introductory price (discussed in the next chapter) than price discrimination. In contrast, coupons delivered in a large package of coupons will be utilized by people with a low value of time, because finding appropriate coupons requires a significant investment of time relative to the value of the coupon.

Quantity Discounts

Quantity discounts are pervasive. Quantity discounts include special status and offers to frequent fliers, buy-five get-one-free offers at gas stations, restaurants, and other retailers, frequent-buyer programs, and Sam's Club and other discount retailers that offer very large bundles of paper towels, light bulbs, tooth paste, and other consumables at lower prices per unit than at the grocery store. Lexus offers an automatic $500 discount on the second Lexus purchased. Telephone companies offer a dazzling array of plans that include some plans that are strictly dominated by other offers. These dominated plans should never be chosen because there are lower cost alternatives offered by the same firms, but the dominated plans are chosen anyway by confused consumers.*

Few quantity discounts are actually based on cost. While costs occasionally justify modest discounts for buying in quantity (such as larger bottles of detergent, milk, and the like), the cost differences tend to be minimal. On occasion, one observes quantity surcharges. For example, laundry detergent in the larger container may have a higher price per ounce.

The theory of quantity discounts is simple in one sense, and very complex in another.[13] In many circumstances, linear, or "two-part pricing," schemes, which include a fixed charge and a marginal, per unit charge, are sufficient to implement any desirable indirect price discrimination scheme. In such schemes, the consumer is permitted to pay a lower marginal charge in exchange for a higher fixed charge. The higher the fixed charge, the lower the prevailing marginal charge.[14]

The theory of optimal menus is intensely complex and is beyond the scope of a strategy book. A straightforward and intuitive proposition arising from the theory is that a firm should always offer one scheme that charges the customer marginal cost plus a fixed charge. Consider a firm that does not offer such a plan, and consider the group that buys the largest quantity under the current set of plans. Add to the existing menu a plan in which this group can buy up to the same quantity at the same costs that prevailed previously, with a decrease in marginal charge (falling to marginal cost) as the number of units rose. Those with the greatest demand would opt for the new plan, because it is worth a slight increase in total cost

*KT&T Communications registered the names "I Don't Know" and "I Don't Care" as Texas long-distance companies, so that consumers responding with those phrases, when asked what long-distance company they would like, would have unknowingly chosen KT&T. KT&T offered rates significantly higher than larger competitors such as AT&T or MCI.

to get a reduction in the marginal cost, in order to consume more units. Since this group pays more, the firm is better off as well. By offering a plan that looks like the current lowest marginal cost plan up to a quantity, then goes lower but above marginal cost, the firm and the largest customers can both gain. The firm is *guaranteed* not to lose, because if a consumer does choose the plan, the firm gets at least as much as it received before the plan was offered, and more when the consumer buys more.

It is possible to optimize price discrimination menus, as Niagara Mohawk has done. However, in most industries, demand is much too dynamic to be fully optimized. Generally, a modest number of offers is adequate to get most of the revenue that can be extracted using indirect price discrimination. It is preferable to identify some target customers and design schemes for them, paying close attention to the incentives to arbitrage across the schemes. The key element of the design is the prevention of arbitrage, which is accomplished by reducing the quality of the inexpensive plans, making them unattractive to large consumers. This can be accomplished by adding unpleasant restrictions (for example, Saturday night stay-overs, extensive forms to fill out, long periods on the telephone on hold, waiting in line at retail outlets) as well as high marginal costs. Finally, control of the risk created by a plan can be an important aspect of the design of indirect price discrimination.

For consumable products like electricity, gasoline, telephone, and food items, the quantity that a customer desires will vary from month to month. This risk must be considered in the design of an indirect price discrimination scheme, for most such schemes expose the customer to price risk. Indeed, in principle, risk can be used as a means of price discrimination. For example, cellular phone plans provide a fixed number of minutes at a given fixed cost, and then a marginal charge for minutes over the plan limit. A consumer whose usage fluctuates from 200 to 1,000 calls will be willing to pay more for a reduced marginal charge than a customer whose usage is steady at 600, even if both have the same average usage.

Unfortunately, less wealthy customers are usually much more averse to risk than richer customers. In this case, risk cannot be used directly in a manner like coupons, which exploit the poorer customer's relative willingness to waste time. An attempt to offer a low price to the price-sensitive by bundling the low price with high risk will deter the price-sensitive and attract the wealthy, and thus backfire. This strategy will rarely be successful with retail customers, with one very important exception: lotteries.

With retail consumers, poorer customers may enjoy lottery outcomes more than richer customers. (Poorer individuals spend a large fraction of their income on lottery tickets.) Thus, bundling a lottery outcome that is actuarially a poor bet for the customer (like most lottery tickets) with a price cut can be a successful strategy for indirect price discrimination. For example, a product may be sold for $10 or for $11 with a 1% chance of winning $90.* Those customers who do not put a premium on gambling will choose to pay $10.00, while those who put a premium on the gambling aspect will choose the more expensive bundle. If the lottery outcome is worth $1.80 to the gambling lover,† the bundle represents a discount of approximately $.80 to those who love gambling. Lotteries can assist price discrimination in this manner.

Internet auctions of standardized products permit price discrimination on the value of time (the auctions often take days to complete) as well as on a preference for randomized outcomes.‡ Since the decision to purchase a standardized good by Internet auction entails both waiting and risk, the auctions appeal to those who place a low value of time and take pleasure in gambling on outcomes. Thus, Internet auctions appeal to those who are poorer and hence are likely to have more elastic demand, and therefore offer a twofold price discrimination strategy.

Product Branding

Informational problems and issues give rise to especially notable price discrimination. Product branding offers an avenue of price discrimination by providing a perception of higher quality for the brand-name product than for its identical generic. For instance, competition by generic drugs does not prevent profitable high pricing of brand-name drugs, and some economic analyses suggest that brand-name drugs essentially do not compete with generics but rather with other brand names.[15]

The price discrimination function of product branding is enhanced by actual quality differences.[16] In some cases, the expedient method of producing two distinct qualities of product is to produce a high-quality product and damage a fraction of the output, to produce a damaged or *crimped* version. It has been alleged that an overnight delivery service deliberately holds back second-day air packages for delivery on the second day to insure that next-day air is significantly better. This policy insures that many of the next-day-air customers do not perceive second-day air to be a "usually next-day air" product. Intel produced the early version of the 80486SX processor by disabling the math coprocessor in its regular 80486

*Very small chances of very large payouts work better; the numbers are for illustration only.

†As state lottery payouts are in the 50% range, with a $1.00 ticket paying $.50 on average, a 1% chance of winning $90.00 should be worth approximately $1.80. As noted above, a one-in-a-million chance of winning $900,000 will work better as an inducement.

‡Internet auctions of unique goods represent a matching of buyers and sellers that offers significant efficiencies relative to other transactions means, and thus are not generally a price discrimination tool.

chip. IBM's LaserPrinter E and the Sony MiniDisc, which are classic examples of crimped products, were discussed above.

A very subtle version of product crimping allegedly is employed by American Airlines. On flights with a high proportion of full-fare passengers, American improves the quality of the meal service, thereby rewarding full-fare passengers and injuring, on average, discount flyers.[17]

Product Bundling

One of the most important and under-exploited means of price discriminating is bundling products. Pure bundling, called tying by some authors, combines two or more products into one product. Thus, a car comes with a radio, engine, tires, and other amenities. Microsoft Office is a product that includes a word processor, spreadsheet, slide design, and projection program. A computer comes with a hard disk, a floppy drive, and a CD-ROM or DVD drive and is often bundled with a keyboard, monitor, and printer. Pure bundling is a blunt instrument, which is effective when consumers always want two products together. It would be a major nuisance for consumers to buy a car without tires, and very inefficient to expect consumers to buy a car body, engine, radio, and so on and then contract with another company to install the engine and radio. Left and right shoes come bundled together for the same reason.* Generally, price discrimination does not play a role in pure bundling, because only one price is used.

In contrast, mixed bundling, which involves selling the bundle at a discount,[18] is an extremely effective means of indirectly price discriminating. To offer a price cut on a given product to any given group, one should find another product that only this group buys and sell the bundle for less than the sum of the separate prices. Package-vacation costs are often based on this logic. Typical vacation packages involve stays in relatively low quality hotels. Airlines give a price break on such packages because the package does not threaten the loss of higher fares charged to their best customers, who would not stay in such hotels even with the price cut.

A remarkable feature of product bundling is that it is a successful strategy even with products that are unrelated. Consider two products that apparently have no connection to each other, such as a business suit and a drill.† Suppose the suit sells for $300 and the drill for $75. By offering a discount on the pair to, say, $350, the company is simultaneously offering a discount on the suit (for drill purchasers) and

*A company in South Carolina proudly advertised: "Shoe: Buy One, Get One Free."

†This example is chosen because a Detroit clothier advertised, "Buy a suit, get a drill," which seems a very odd mixture of products. Another example arose from the savings and loan institutions, which frequently gave a free toaster to those opening accounts.

the drill (for suit purchasers). If the initial prices are set at the profit-maximizing level, the $25 discount on suits for drill purchasers will have a negligible effect on profits, because profits are approximately constant around the maximum level. Thus, the cost in lost revenue of the discount is paid for by an increase in suit purchases by drill purchasers, for a net zero effect on profits. However, there is also an increase in drill sales, which represents pure profit for the firm! That is, the cost of the price cut is balanced by the increased sales on either good; the fact that there are increased sales on both goods means that the bundle should sell for less than the sum of the independent prices.[19]

In practice, of course, bundling drills and suits will not be very successful—few firms sell both, and the ability to discriminate, while present, is tiny. However, the same logic suggests that firms can often profitably offer a discount on bundles of items it already sells. The key to successful bundling is not the demand conditions but the threat of arbitrage. When a discount is offered for buying two products, someone desiring one product can buy both and sell the other. If the firm cannot discourage such behavior, the bundling strategy will prove ineffective.

A peculiar example of product bundling was related by AT&T chairman Michael Armstrong, who said that one of the most popular promotions for enticing new customers was a combination of long-distance phone service and coupons for oil changes at Jiffy Lube.[20]

PEAK-LOAD PRICING

Most movie theaters offer "matinee" pricing, which is often half the regular price. Florida restaurants offer "early bird specials," which appeal to senior citizens. Happy hours, involving discounted drink prices before 6 P.M., have been discontinued in most locales by bars and taverns only after intense lobbying by anti-drunk-driving groups. Large industrial users of electricity are given price breaks during low demand periods. Hotels in Florida are substantially cheaper in the broiling humid summer than in the mild, pleasant winter, while the reverse pricing pattern arises in most ski areas. Such price differences do not reflect price discrimination, but instead are usually cost-based.

When restaurants, movie theaters, or airplanes are full, the cost of serving additional customers involves expanding capacity—renting more restaurant space, expanding a theater, using larger or more planes. The cost during a peak reflects the cost of capacity expansion. In contrast, off peak, the incremental costs are low, because incremental costs should not reflect a need to expand capacity—capacity is more than adequate. Thus, incremental electricity costs at the peak reflect the cost of capacity expansion as well as generation (fuel and labor), while off-peak prices reflect only generation costs. Peak electricity costs can easily be five times the off-peak costs. The cost of a Florida hotel room in July is the cost of offering the existing room, which involves personnel, cleaning the room, towels, bedding, and depreciation of the facility, but does not involve constructing a room. In February, the only way to produce additional rooms is to build them, and thus the incremental costs involve capacity expansion costs.

Similarly, for an airplane that is half full, incremental costs involve an extra meal, a very, very slight amount of fuel resulting from additional weight, and some addition to the cost of cleaning the plane. The incremental cost is usually less than $5. When the plane is full, however, the incremental cost is the cost of using a larger aircraft, which either reflects the rental rate of the aircraft or the cost of canceling or rearranging another flight in order to use the aircraft on that route. Such costs can easily amount to tens of thousands of dollars.

As a practical matter, airlines rarely add an additional flight—the logistics are too complicated. The incremental cost of booking an airline seat tends to be either the expected cost of buying off a customer from an overbooked flight or the cost of perhaps turning away a business traveler at the last minute. If a business traveler would pay $2000 for the flight, and the flight is full 20% of the time, the incremental cost of booking a seat is 20% of $2000, or $400. Similarly, if a $350 travel voucher, which costs the airline $200 to fill, is required on the overbooked flight, the cost to the airline of booking an additional seat is 20% of $200, or $40, plus the usually negligible cost of travel on a later flight. Note that the probability of overbooking can be forecast and depends on how many seats are already booked, so that the cost can range from nearly zero (a mostly empty flight hours before takeoff) to the full cost of the voucher (an overbooked flight moments before takeoff). The cost of vouchers rises as the excess bookings rise, and are higher when alternative flights are full.

Peak-load pricing allocates the costs of capacity to the relevant demand. For example, with electricity generation, all of the costs of capacity are allocated to the peak hours. Peak-load pricing is sensible because the peak hours determine the necessary capacity, and off-peak consumption can increase without any corresponding increase in capacity. Efficiency dictates that the peak-time demanders pay the cost of incremental capacity.

Peak-load pricing is important in such industries as airlines, hotels, and electricity generation in which a significant fraction of costs are fixed capacity costs, because incremental costs vary so strongly with demand. Using average cost as an indicator of incremental cost is ill-advised, since average cost will be much larger than incremental cost in off-peak times, and much lower during peak periods. Average cost pricing (using average cost plus a markup) may result in losses during peak periods and the failure to recover the cost of capacity. Instead, it is necessary to estimate peak and nonpeak costs, and price accordingly. Yield management accounts directly for peak and nonpeak costs by considering the foregone value of a sale, which depends on the likelihood of a future buyer being turned away. In the yield-management theory, the opportunity cost of a sale is the inability to make a future sale. Yield management is essentially a price discrimination strategy for peak-load-capacity problems.

Aluminum Smelters and Electric Utilities

A major component of the cost of creating aluminum is electricity, which accounts for around 30% of the total cost. As a consequence, aluminum smelters are very sensitive to the price of electricity and tend to locate their plants where electricity is inexpensive, primarily in the Pacific Northwest. In addition, however, aluminum smelters can be quickly shut off, and at minimal cost—primarily idling the labor force. As a consequence, aluminum smelters are an ideal "interruptable" power user, and offer a major advantage to electric utilities—customers who can be quickly turned off during peak demand. Not surprisingly, aluminum smelters get very attractive rates, because aluminum smelters increase overall capacity usage substantially without increasing the peak capacity usage.

Natural-Gas Pipeline Peaks

By and large, U.S. natural-gas pipelines carry natural gas from Texas and Louisiana to the Northeast and the Midwest for electricity generation throughout the year and to heat homes in winter. As a consequence, the peak occurs in the winter. Pipelines have strong economies of scale; quadrupling the capacity requires a pipeline with twice the diameter, a similar number of pumping stations, and overall about twice the cost. Pipelines have been subject to price regulation by the Federal Energy Regulatory Commission for two generations; such price regulation not only prevents high prices, but it also prevents low prices, ensuring that the firms earn an adequate rate of return to justify the capital expenses. As a consequence of both of these factors, natural-gas pipelines have been constructed to handle demand on all but the coldest weeks—most interstate natural-gas pipelines reach full capacity only two to ten days per year.

Since most of the costs of a pipeline are fixed costs, incremental costs are nearly zero most days, but are astronomical on the few days when capacity is reached. As a practical matter, no one would pay the incremental costs on the peak days. It would be cheaper to stay in a hotel than to heat your house with natural gas priced at the incremental cost, which bears all of the cost of the pipeline amortized over a few days per year.

As a consequence, some of the pipelines are not viable under incremental cost pricing—their capacity is too large to lead to prices that recover costs. The pipelines lobby intensively to preserve regulated average cost pricing, while buyers of natural gas lobby for the pipelines to be forced to auction all their capacity, which would force the price below average cost. Tens of millions of dollars is expended in this fight. Companies subject to peak-load pricing need to choose capacity strategically—excess capacity can easily render the industry unprofitable.

YIELD MANAGEMENT

There are two major groups of air travelers: business travelers and tourists or leisure travelers. Business travelers are often insensitive to price, especially when the cost of the airfare is reimbursed by the business, while tourists have elastic demand. Yield management is composed of two main features. First, seats are reserved for full-fare passengers, by limiting the number of discount seats available. Second, discount seats are full of restrictions—stay-over requirements, advanced booking, change fees, and nonrefundability—making them less attractive to the business traveler.

Airlines routinely discriminate on the basis of flexibility and Saturday night stay-overs, for business travelers put a premium on flexibility and generally will pay more to be home with their family over the weekend, while tourists often can commit to a travel plan weeks or months in advance and will usually prefer to be away for more than a week, including a weekend. Thus, a "full fare" fully refundable ticket might cost $1200 while a nonrefundable ticket with a Saturday night stay-over costs $300. This is a static method of price discrimination. Airlines, however, have developed a more sophisticated version of price discrimination that reflects dynamic considerations, and such plans are known as yield management, revenue management, or dynamic price discrimination. Yield management involves reserving space for high-value customers who appear late in the process.

An important aspect of yield management is the premium business travelers place on flexibility. Business travelers often wish to leave "as soon as the meeting ends" to return home. Business travelers are willing to pay $500 or even $1000 extra to take the next available flight. To serve that demand, the airlines need to keep some last-minute, expensive seats available. However, business travelers account for less than half of all travelers, so reserving all the seats would leave the planes quite empty; clearly it is preferable for the airline to sell some, but not all, of the seats in advance at lower prices.

Sophisticated yield management systems exploit variation in demand over time, and involve updating. There are systematic changes in business and tourist demand over the calendar year. Business travel is reduced during the Christmas holidays, but most of the few business travelers during this time will pay remarkably high prices to get home by December 25. Thus, it makes sense to keep fewer seats available during the December holidays but price the full-fare seats higher. This kind of price discrimination, which exploits seasonal effects, is akin to actuarial life insurance—it exploits past history to price optimally. Moreover, as the flight becomes imminent, it may become optimal to sell some additional discount seats if few business travelers have booked seats. That is, one might reserve twenty seats for business travelers, but if only two of those seats are taken a week before the flight, six might be released for lower fares.

Yield management exploits other information beyond calendar-year effects. In particular, unexpectedly high demand for one flight may signal lower demand for another flight. An increased popularity of flights to Dallas's downtown Love Field airport may indicate that fewer business travelers will use flights to Dallas–Fort Worth, making it desirable to release some full fare seats to DFW. Exploiting such correlations is complex in detail but simple to understand. The current tourist and full-fare prices for a flight from San Francisco to New York optimally depend not just on how full that particular flight is, or even how full other flights on the route (San Francisco to New York) are, but also they depend on flights from San Jose to New York and from San Francisco to Newark. Moreover, if flights out of New York to Europe are very full, this may indicate that fewer travelers will fly from San Francisco to New York as a way of getting to Europe, suggesting a need to reduce prices for San Francisco to New York, while more travelers to Europe will take the alternative route through Chicago, suggesting higher prices for routes through that city.

One aspect of yield management is that it prices the option value of a ticket in a dynamic way. Booking a ticket early now forecloses the option of booking it later at a higher fare, so the value of the future flexibility is lost to the airline when the ticket is booked. Flexibility has a value, the *option value,* which is lost when the ticket is booked. Option pricing is familiar from finance theory and was discussed previously. However, yield management is more sophisticated than option pricing, because it adds the element of price discrimination to option pricing. The goal of yield management is to compute not the expected value of the option but the maximum willingness to pay.

Yield management works well with perishable products like hotel rooms and air travel (space not utilized is lost). Most airlines, major hotel chains, telephone companies, and rental-car companies use yield management systems. Many natural-gas companies and resort chains also use yield management systems. Others using yield management include Disney, Eurotunnel, Pepsi's Taco Bell subsidiary, Stanford University, and UPS.

The mathematics of yield management can be illustrated by considering a simpler problem, eliminating direct price discrimination, and focusing only on the central problem of how many seats to reserve for business travelers.[21] First, simplify the problem to consider only two classes of seats: full-fare seats for business travelers, with an associated payment of P_F, and discount seats, with a payment $P_D < P_F$. The problem of how many seats to reserve for business travelers can be viewed as equivalent to the problem of when to stop selling discount seats. Suppose q seats have been sold, and $Q - q$ seats remain, out of the total Q. The airline is contemplating requiring all additional potential passengers to pay full fare. Let n be the probability that the *next* request for a seat comes from a passenger who will not pay full fare. Let s be the probability that the plane sells out, so that a seat sold at a discount today displaces a full-fare passenger. Then refusing to sell another discount seat will produce revenue of P_F if either the next person to call will pay full fare (probability $1 - n$) or the next will not pay full fare and the plane sells out at full fare, which has probability $n \times (1 - s)$. Thus, it is better to sell an additional discount seat if:

$$P_D > P_F \times (1 - n + n(1 - s)) = P_F \times (1 - ns).$$

The probability ns is the probability that the plane does not sell out and that the next person to call will not pay the full fare. This person is lost—and one extra seat goes empty—if no discount seat is available. In this case, charging the discount fare adds P_D to the revenue. Otherwise, selling at the discount fare means not earning the differential between the full fare and the discount fare. Thus, if

$$ns > \frac{P_F - P_D}{P_F},$$

it is more profitable to sell the discounted fare, as the discount fare exceeds the expected profits of withholding the seat. This condition is equivalent to the previous condition.

The implementation of this formula is a statistical problem: how to estimate the two probabilities n and s, which will generally depend strongly on the time remaining before the flight, the number of seats remaining, and the time of year. In addition, a more sophisticated analysis accounts for the statistical dependence of n and s on the extent of booking on related flights, season, time to departure, and other variables. Fine-tuning the discount and full fares is an even more complicated problem. At its heart, however, yield management is a formula like the one provided above.

One important aspect of yield management is that low capacity utilization is not an indication of poor pricing. Indeed, average capacity utilization is not indicative of anything; instead, the relevant statistic is the probability that the plane is full. Suppose business travelers are willing to pay four times what tourists

Table 11.2
Weeks to Release by Venue

Venue	*Week after Theatrical Release*
Theatrical Release	0
Airlines and Hotel Pay-per-View	16
Home Video	27
Home Pay-per-View	34
Premium Cable (HBO)	61
Network TV	Substantial variation

will pay for a given seat. If the plane is full half the time, and half full the remainder, average capacity utilization is 75%, which may sound low. However, since business travelers are willing to pay so much more than tourists, such a capacity utilization is probably too high—too many business travelers are being turned away. From a pricing perspective, the correct measure of capacity utilization is the proportion of full flights, rather than the proportion of occupied seats.

How much does yield management matter? It has been estimated that American Airlines obtains an additional $500 million per year based on yield management.

Theatrical Yield Management

A very different form of yield management arises with movies. Movies have a definite release venue pattern (table 11.2).

Delay in each of these releases improves the value of the former, but, to be effective, such delay must be expected by consumers. Indeed, the National Association of Theater Owners (NATO) lobbies distributors to delay the video release, to increase the value of the first-run theatrical release and reduce the number of people who wait for video. Studios attempt to commit to a delayed release in video, for example, by announcing the video release date at the time of the theatrical release. However, there is little reason, other than the value of commitment, to delay the video release of a movie that did poorly at the box office. Over time, the distributors have reduced the delay prior to video release, thereby increasing the number of customers who wait for the video rather than see the movie at a theater. In

TABLE 11.3
Delay prior to Video Release by Year

Year	*Average Window*
1993	6 months, 21 days
1994	6 months, 12 days
1995	5 months, 28 days
1996	5 months, 18 days

the early 1980s, most movies were not released in video until a year or more after theatrical release. Table 11.3 shows that, by 1996, the average fell below six months.

Movie studios have a major incentive to cooperate on the timing of video releases, because customer perceptions of the delay are not influenced as much by any one studio's timing as by the average timing of the industry. Cooperation on the timing of video release appears to be waning. Collectively, delaying video release helps the industry, but each distributor has an incentive to release its movies early.[22]

Robert Crandall on Airline Pricing

Robert Crandall, the aggressive and charismatic CEO of American Airlines, led American Airlines and the U.S. airline industry through deregulation and introduced frequent flier miles, yield management, and the SABRE system. Here is what he wrote in the airline magazine *American Way,* in May 1998, about airline pricing (reprinted by permission). It is worth reading, both for his discussion of yield management and the challenges of charging distinct customers dramatically different prices for the product, and for his eloquent reminder that even when a free market has some problems, regulation is usually worse.

> In recent months, there has been lots of discussion about airline ticket prices in Washington and in the news media. Since airline pricing often seems mystifying, I'd like to devote this month's column to some of its hows and whys.
>
> Prior to airline deregulation in 1978, the US government set domestic air fares. To do so, it measured average industry costs by length of flight; all airlines were required to charge the same price for flights of the same length. Today, as in nearly all other businesses, the forces of supply and demand de-

termine ticket prices. However, the distinctive economics of the airline industry have created a very complex fare structure.

First, airlines have extremely high fixed costs, and much less ability to change the amount of product offered than do most businesses. Airplanes, terminal facilities, maintenance hangars, and many of our other productive assets cannot be added or deleted in response to short-term fluctuations in demand. Second, because our industry is very competitive, because the number of flights we offer is a very important determinant of customer preference, and because airlines must seek to satisfy daily, weekly, and seasonal peaks in demand, our industry always provides more capacity than can be sold at list prices.

In much of the world, the problem of excess capacity is less pressing, since the airline system is sized primarily for business travelers, many leisure travelers use charter service, and competition is less open. In the United States, however, which has a huge, fully deregulated airline industry and in which charter services have not flourished, airlines offer enough scheduled flights to accommodate all travelers and seek to fill the many seats that exceed business travelers' needs by offering discount fares to attract leisure passengers. To segment demand, airlines impose conditions on discounted tickets to make them somewhat less flexible than higher-priced tickets.

Airlines pricing decisions are also shaped by the reality that most travelers regard one airline as a ready substitute for any other. Since computerized reservations systems—and now the Internet—give customers perfect information about every airline's prices and available seats, every airline must match all competitors' prices or forgo more revenue from lost business than would be lost by matching prices lower than it would prefer to offer.

These unique economic variables have created an equally unique pricing system. To understand that system, it is important to set aside the notion that every seat has the same value as every other. In fact, each seat and its associated fare represents a product that offers different price and convenience characteristics. Because competition is intense, most customers—business and leisure—manage to secure some level of discount; in fact, nearly 93 percent of American's passengers fly on some form of discount. Generally, the size of the discount is directly proportional to the restrictions imposed, with the most expensive fares offering the most flexibility.

Full fares are unrestricted, and allow the 7 percent of our customers with full-fare tickets complete flexibility with respect to when they travel. Full-fare, unrestricted tickets are worth more than discounted tickets because those who use them are, in effect, paying us to keep some seats unsold until the very last minute—forgoing the opportunity to sell those seats at an earlier date for a lower price. If last-minute travelers willing to pay an unrestricted fare do not appear, the airlines lose; when such travelers do turn up, the airlines—and the travelers—both win.

A typical flight carries very few passengers paying the full unrestricted fare, some paying modestly discounted fares, and some paying heavily discounted fares. If every seat were sold at the deepest discount price, airlines would not be profitable, and would have no choice but to reduce the number of flights offered, in an effort to cut costs and to increase the percentage of seats occupied. Under those circumstances, there simply wouldn't be seats available to people who want—and are willing to pay for—more flexibility than the lowest-priced product provides. That phenomenon is well-illustrated in other countries, where customers who try to book at the last minute are often turned away.

We also hear people say that those who pay full fair subsidize those who pay discount fares. It's really the other way around. We know from experience that reducing fares for business travelers will not increase business demand by enough to offset the revenue lost by cutting prices; thus, selling seats not needed by business travelers at discount prices to leisure travelers causes those passengers to "subsidize" full-fare travelers in two ways: by providing revenue that would otherwise have to be made up by charging still higher unrestricted fares, and by making it possible for airlines to offer far more service than business-travel demand alone would warrant.

Twenty years ago, the airline industry shifted dramatically. What had been a heavily regulated quasi-utility became, overnight, a highly competitive market-driven business. One result has been lower fares—adjusted for inflation, airline tickets are 37 percent cheaper today than they were before deregulation. And since 1982, consumer prices have risen 66 percent while air fares have risen a mere 11 percent. Many more people can now afford to fly, and travelers are offered far more flights than when our business was regulated. By nearly every measure, airline deregulation has been a great success!

Despite that success, there's a movement afoot to re-regulate the airline business. Various interventionist voices are calling for things like limits on the number of flights that established carriers like American may offer in certain markets, and for restrictions on our ability to compete with new carriers. While those spearheading this movement agree that deregulation has been a success, they suggest that "just a few rules" can solve what they believe are imperfections in the way a free market regulates competition.

Today, our customers collectively tell us where we should fly, how much we should charge, and what services we should offer. Because our business is very competitive, we listen carefully. We hope the folks thinking about re-regulation will listen, too—and that they'll remember that free markets have produced lots more successes than regulated ones.

COMPETITION AND PRICE DISCRIMINATION

Generally speaking, competition appears to make price discrimination both more extensive and more pervasive, as shown by the prevalence of price discrimination in the telephone and airline industries. One attraction of price discrimination is in offering a discount to one's rival's best customers, without offering a corresponding discount to one's own best customers. Examples include honoring rivals' coupons and offering discounts to users of competing software. The possibility of offering selective price cuts to attract new customers, while still charging high prices to existing customers, is extraordinarily attractive, although usually a mistake.[23]

Microsoft Word is cheaper to buy to users of the competing program WordPerfect. The program itself insures that pricing is conditional—the program will not run if it does not detect an existing qualifying program, such as WordPerfect.[24] Preventing arbitrage is more complex, however, because consumers can buy (or illegally borrow) a qualifying program, install it on their computer, install Word, and then delete the qualifying program. Such a procedure is a significant nuisance, but the gain is large, too—typically the discount for users of qualifying programs is 35% or more. In this way, Microsoft offers discounts to the users of rival programs.

It will often be the case that the best customers of one's rival are one's price-sensitive customers. Generally, these best customers prefer the rival, and thus need significantly lower prices to be induced to switch. While direct or indirect price discrimination often offers a means of targeting the rival's best customers with price cuts, such a strategy risks a price war, with the rival responding.

Chunnel Competition

The Chunnel, short for channel tunnel, is the 31-mile tunnel under the English Channel that connects England and France. It was built at a cost of $15 billion, and opened on 6 May 1994 with passenger rail service commencing in November 1994. It is actually three tunnels—one in each direction plus a service tunnel.

The economics of the Chunnel was severely impaired by the failure to account for the response of the competition. The primary competitors of the Chunnel are hovercraft and ferries, but both of these are slower than the train through the Chunnel. Hovercraft fares fell by as much as 30% after the Chunnel opened, and the unexpected response of the competition required a restructuring of the finances of the Chunnel after huge losses the first year of operation.

The Chunnel has a colorful history. Napolean proposed a tunnel connecting England and France in 1802, and his proposal would have involved building frequent chimneys to the surface for ventilation. Construction of Napoleon's tunnel was never begun and in 1881 it was canceled because of fears it could become an invasion route.[25]

How to Soften Price Competition

An important aspect of competitive pricing is to soften price competition. One's pricing options are limited by the behavior of the competition, which may insist on a price war in response to aggressive pricing. When possible, it is preferable to adopt a pricing strategy that does not encourage head-to-head price competition. Some factors that can help:

- Reward the sales force according to revenue, or net profits, not quantity sold.
- Encourage nonprice deal sweetners rather than price cuts.
- Reduce quality to justify price cuts.
- Create complex, difficult to compare, pricing.
- Create loyalty of existing customers rather than attract competitors' customers.

The purpose of these strategies is to minimize price competition. It does little good to avoid price competition only to squander the advantages in a quality-based battle for market share.

Enhancing the loyalty of your customers is valuable in two distinct ways. First, it protects your customer base from inducements by rivals. Second, and more subtly, the loyalty of your customers encourages rivals to price higher. The reason is that rivals now face a more difficult time increasing market share, and therefore low prices are discouraged in favor of higher prices and a smaller market share. Similarly, an attempt by a rival to lock in its own customers is a good thing for your firm. Thus, American's AAdvantage program was advantageous not just for American but also for its rivals. Similarly, the response of the other airlines, which offered their own frequent flyer programs, was advantageous to American. An airline's frequent flyer programs create costs of switching, thereby increasing the loyalty of its own customers, which softens price competition.

OPPORTUNISM AND EXCLUSIVE DEALING

In business to business (B2B) contracts, after-the-fact opportunism by sellers can be a major concern. Often it takes the form of an "upstream" seller creating new downstream (retail) competitors to the existing downstream firms. For example, Taco Bell franchisees complain that Pepsico, the franchiser, opens new stores wherever franchisees are successful, thereby extracting the profits when a location is unusually successful, while escaping the costs of unsuccessful locations. Both gasoline and automobile dealer franchisees succeeded in obtaining federal protection against unfair termination and nonrenewal. Franchisers are frequently alleged to encroach with company-owned stores on franchisee "territory." Fears of such opportunistic behavior by franchisers have led many states to enact protection against franchiser competition. Texas has a law so narrowly defined (stating the proportion of company-owned stores, the volume of business, etc.) that it applies only to Taco Bell. Thirty-seven states restrict the encroachment of automobile manufacturers into the "relevant market area" of dealers.

Example 1: General Motors

A typical incident of such opportunistic behavior, and the complex issues involved, arose when General Motors planned to license 2,000 independent repair shops as Delco-Tech Service Centers. These service centers would stock GM parts, and employees would be trained to make minor repairs of GM cars. The plan met with vociferous opposition from dealers and was ultimately dropped. From GM's perspective, the plan would have enhanced the value of GM cars by making service more convenient for GM car buyers. Not having car lots, independent service shops can be located closer to suburbs in busy shopping areas. Moreover, licensing independent service shops would permit GM to mark up GM parts and capture some of the profits being earned by independent service shops like Jiffy Lube. These added profits would make selling GM cars more profitable to GM, encouraging GM to slightly cut the price of new cars to encourage the use of additional service. Moreover, the improved service situation would make GM cars more attractive to buyers, increasing the volume sold for any given set of invoice prices and dealer markup. Any decrease in GM's price for new cars would benefit dealers.

From the auto dealers' perspective, however, the price cut would be minimal at best. Meanwhile, the dealers would lose much of the "minor repair" business to the more convenient independents. The dealers felt that they had made large investments in repair facilities, equipment, personnel, and local goodwill in the expectation that they would have little competition from other GM-authorized repair shops. Thus, the dealers argued that GM was expropriating part of their investments with its plan.

The arguments of both sides have merit. Additional service outlets can make the market more efficient, enhancing the value of the product; however, such additional service outlets do undercut the investments made by existing dealers. GM failed to solve the problem with the dealers. Mazda, facing a closely related problem, found a solution.

Example 2: Mazda

In 1990, Mazda had a terrible reputation in the United States for service. Threatening to eliminate a dealer's franchise did little to encourage better service—the franchises were not sufficiently profitable for the threat to make much difference. Mazda's solution was to price the Miata very low to dealers (the $13,800-list-price automobile sold for around $19,000), and tie the quantity of Miatas given to the performance rating of dealers on service. Dealers who had good ratings were allocated more cars (which earned dealers approximately $6500 each), while dealers with bad service and inadequate efforts to fix the service problems lost their now lucrative licenses. Mazda's plan worked well.

Example 3: A Franchise that Understandably Desires to Remain Nameless

A particular franchiser had sold as many franchises as the market would bear; there was little room for additional outlets. The franchise fees involved a $100,000 fixed fee (payable over five years) and 4% of revenue. The franchiser continued to collect income from franchisee revenues, but no avenues for income growth were apparent. The franchiser came up with an interesting scheme to extract further revenue from the existing franchisees. The franchiser had employed a system of certifying the input suppliers to insure quality control. This served the franchisees well—quality was insured by the certification process, and reasonable prices were made possible by the competition of several suppliers. Abruptly, the franchiser decertified all but one input supplier, in which the franchiser owned a controlling interest. That franchiser raised prices by 25% over the course of the next year, which increased the costs of the franchisees by tens of thousands of dollars per year. In this way, the franchiser attempted to expropriate the investments made by its franchisees, who would not have paid $100,000 for a franchise with such high input prices.[26] This is an example of opportunism taken by a franchiser against the franchisees.

Example 4: Coal and Electric Utilities

Coal is heavy, relative to its value; transportation costs can easily account for 50% of the price of coal. Electric power plants, which use coal, are built next to coal mines to avoid the transportation costs, but once these are built, the coal mine has an incentive to increase its prices. The alternatives for the power plant are much more expensive. Similarly, the electric power plant has an incentive to threaten to buy elsewhere, because the alternatives for the coal mine are also much less lucrative. Such bargaining or "holdup" problems are usually solved either by vertical integration (to have one owner of both power plant and coal mine) or by very long term contracts (thirty years or more).[27]

There are six major approaches to solving to the problem of opportunistic pricing by a seller. None of the approaches is perfect, but most help in some circumstances and belong in a firm's toolkit.

Create Competition by Licensing

Licensing a competitor is an extreme solution to the problem of opportunistic pricing. A competitor will police any attempt to increase prices by offering a better deal. Of course, a competitor, once created, erodes future profits. By licensing VHS technology, JVC (Victor Corporation of Japan) committed itself to asking lower prices for the technology, which is generally thought to be the reason that VHS won the standards war with Sony's unlicensed Beta technology. Consumers rationally would bet on VHS, because they correctly would expect that competition would insure that VHS ultimately offered the best value.

Intel's licensing of the 8086 chip technology to Advanced Micro Devices may have accounted for the dominance of that technology, by convincing consumers that the Intel processor would be supplied at a reasonable price not just now but also in the future. This matters crucially when businesses are expected to sink huge investments in the technology. AMD continues to be a major competitor to Intel, which illustrates the cost of licensing.

Creating competition by licensing is a last resort, to be used when the alternative is nonadoption of the technology, because the competitors are likely to constrain profits to very low levels.

Vertically Integrate with the Buyers

Vertical integration (merging the buyers and seller) works well in a limited set of circumstances, like the coal mine/power plant pair. Such a merger mitigates the problem of opportunistic pricing, since the prices become transfer prices within the firm. However, the vertical integration solution works only when the opportunistic behavior reflects a substantial portion of the buyer's business, as in the coal mine case. One would hardly want to merge Kodak with all the retailers of Kodak film, for example. Moreover, such vertical integration can have a major downside in the form of management difficulties, reduced incentives, and other transaction costs.

Long-Term Contracts

Long-term contracts work well in environments where the relevant terms can be easily specified (in the coal mine, it is price and quantity), and the business environment does not change too rapidly. Long-term contracts with recording artists often lead to the production of many bad compact discs to fulfill a contract. It is impossible to specify quality of new music in a contract, so the contracts tend to be in the form, "for the next six compact discs." Such contracts fail to prevent the record label's opportunism, nor do they provide good incentives for recording artists.

Exclusive Contracts

Exclusive contracts are an effective means of mitigating seller opportunism, although at a significant cost when it is efficient to have many downstream firms. Exclusivity prevents a seller from recontracting with a competitor or bringing in additional competitors, and reduces the seller's bargaining power in the event the seller tries to renegotiate. As in marriage, by binding themselves together, both parties increase their incentives to invest in the relationship. In the case of GM dealers, discussed above, by having exclusive contracts the dealers did not need fear new competition, and therefore had incentives to invest in costly equipment and expert personnel.

For a company to give exclusive contracts is problematic when it is more valuable to have multiple firms. For a company to have many retail outlets is a valuable convenience for consumers. How to have multiple retail outlets can be solved by giving each other an exclusive territory, although territory disputes are common. More important, downstream competition in services may be valuable as well, by encouraging retail competition and the higher level of service and efficiency that competition brings. Thus, exclusive contracts work best when the efficient organizational form involves a single firm, and work poorly when the most effective means of distributing goods or services involves many competing firms.

Most-Favored-Customer Clauses

Nondiscrimination guarantees, sometimes called most-favored-customer clauses, require that any offer made to one buyer must be made to all. In the case where firms use simple pricing schemes, nondiscrimination clauses can be very helpful. Consider a franchiser who charges a high fee to engage a franchisee. Franchisees expect that the high fee will insure that few franchises will be sold, and thus that they will face little competition from other franchisees. Once the franchiser has sold as many franchises as the market will bear, however, the franchiser has an incentive to cut the price and sell more franchises.* As with GM's plan to create more repairs shops, the franchisees will be harmed by the additional competitors.

*The incentive to cut the price and sell more once high-value buyers have purchased is known as the Coase conjecture, after Nobel laureate Ronald Coase, who first suggested the problem. Intuitively, a

Nondiscrimination clauses can mitigate the incentive to bring in new competitors, if the price cuts required to bring in more franchisees are made available to all retroactively. In this way, franchisers would cut the charge only if it is efficient for them to have more competitors, because the franchise cannot expropriate the investments of the first franchisees, as the price cut applies to all. Nondiscrimination makes a firm resist price cuts, because the price cuts must be spread widely.

Nondiscrimination clauses work in environments that have simple prices but fail in more complex environments. As we saw earlier in this chapter, menus of contracts, or even quantity discounts, can induce a buyer to select a distinct offer, and permit a seller to engage in discrimination even while making the same set of offers available to all. Moreover, nondiscrimination clauses do not help with territorial encroachment, the increasing of input prices, and other means of expropriating buyer investments.

Uniform, Simple Contracts

Nondiscrimination clauses fail because sellers can engineer discrimination by using menus of contracts or quantity discounts. Menus of contracts typically involve fixed fees—a firm buys a lower marginal charge with a higher fixed fee. Nondiscrimination clauses can mitigate the incentive to engage in opportunistic behavior when the contracts are simple. Simple contracts, the same for all buyers, reduce the scope for discrimination and expropriation of investments. For this reason, franchise contracts are typically a one-time fixed fee plus a percentage of revenue, and a significant fraction of them have no fixed fee.

Simple contracts have the additional advantage of making it clear to all when a firm does engage in opportunistic behavior, which provides an alternative deterrent—the threat of legal action. Legal action is more likely to be successful the less concealed the expropriation is.

---

seller of a durable good competes with future incarnations of itself—consumers can wait for prices to fall. The Coase conjecture has been the subject of intense study by economists. Faruk Gul, Hugo Sonnenschein, and Robert Wilson (*Journal of Economic Theory*, 1986) provide a definitive theoretical analysis. Nondiscrimination clauses have similar effects as renting or leasing—any price cut is made available to all—which is a solution to the Coase conjecture. The value of renting as a solution to the incentive to lower prices was recognized early by IBM. Indeed, the substance of a 1956 settlement with the Department of Justice involved an agreement for IBM to sell tabulating machines, rather than to exclusively lease them as they had done previously. Microsoft's .Net plans appear to recognize that current versions of Microsoft software compete with past versions, a problem that can be solved for Microsoft by renting the software.

PRICING OF COMPLEMENTS

Complementary goods are those for which consumption of one increases the value of the other. Many taverns exploit the complementarity of beer and peanuts by providing free peanuts. Sufficiently strong complementary goods are often sold together—a stereo may be sold with a complete stereo system, and dining-room tables are sometimes bundled with chairs. Often manufacturers offer extended service plans for their products well beyond what would be imposed by the courts in product liability lawsuits.

The theory of bundling helps answer the question about how firms should price complements. In particular, since the purchase of one good tends to increase the value of the other, a bundle discount is unnecessary. That is, customers who buy the dining room table do not need an additional inducement to buy the chairs—they are likely to want chairs anyway. A customer who is buying a computer will not usually need an additional financial incentive to purchase a monitor. Consequently, while there may be a marketing advantage to pricing a computer and monitor together, there is little price discrimination advantage to offering a discount for the bundle. (This is not to undervalue the marketing advantage of discounting, but rather to highlight the advantage of not discounting the bundle, and instead increasing the price of the individual components to achieve the same marketing discount.)

When a firm sells two strongly complementary goods, there is an advantage in offering just the bundle for sale. This assists the firm in capturing the enhanced value for the each good that is created by the sale of the other good. An extreme example is a monitor and a computer, for each is virtually worthless without the other.

In cases of strong competition in one of the goods, there is often no profitable bundling strategy. For example, televisions and VCRs are strongly complementary. A VCR enhances the value of a television, and a VCR is worthless without a television. However, an attempt to sell both items for more than the prices set by the competition fails without some additional product differentiation. Consumers will opt for individual items sold by other manufacturers.

Suppose computer systems of a particular quality sell for \$1000, even though they are worth \$5000 to consumers, and the Palm Pilot (a hand-held computing device that requires a computer for programming) is worth \$500 to customers. The Palm Computing Corporation cannot extract more than \$500 for the Palm Pilot, even with a bundling strategy. The problem that Palm faces is that willingness to pay for computers is set not by their intrinsic value to consumers but by the competition's offering. Thus, a bundle of a desktop computer with a Palm Pilot produces a net value of $1500. At a price higher than this, the customer is better off buying the computer alone for $1000 (producing $5000 in value for a net $4000 gain), rather than the bundle. Bundling a good with a competitively priced complementary good rarely increases value.*

When necessary complementary goods are not competitively supplied, there is an advantage to bundling them. Much of IBM's success in the mainframe computing market can be attributed to its offering of a complete business solution, including hardware, software, and training. By buying this IBM bundle, customers knew the system would work, and if it did not, the responsibility was clearly IBM's. Consequently, confidence in the IBM bundle was high relative to buying hardware from one vendor, software from another, service from a third, and training from a fourth, where any one supplier could duck responsibility for product failure by blaming another.

Offering complete solutions is difficult when several firms are involved. For example, to edit video on a computer, two major products are needed. First, one needs a hardware product (a capture card) for communication between the computer and the video device (camcorder, VCR, television signal). By itself, however, a capture card cannot work. Some kind of video-capture software is also required to control the capture, store the file created, and permit editing. Capture software is created by different firms than the manufacturers of capture cards, perhaps because the required skills to produce the two products are so different. However, capture cards are invariably bundled with capture software. Indeed, capture cards are designed to work with particular software products, and specialized software is created to assist in the interface between the two products.[28] The firms producing these separate items have found a way to coordinate their strongly complementary products. Significantly, Adobe Premiere (arguably the best consumer-market video-editing software) alone sells for about the same price as the Premiere bundled with an inexpensive capture card from another manufacturer. Apparently Adobe has figured out that it makes sense to give away a capture card in order to sell more copies of Premiere. In this case, the two firms have reached a vertically integrated solution without integrating.

*An interesting class of exceptions arises through price discrimination. For example, a medicine might be worth $10 when given to horses, but $20 when given to pigs, because of the availability of a substitute for the equine medicine that would not work for pigs. By selling the medicine alone for $20, or by bundling the medicine and $15's worth of equine vitamins (that have no value for pigs) for $25, arbitrage purchases of equine medicine by hog farmers could be deterred. In order for this strategy to work, it is important that the bundling cannot be easily undone, for otherwise a resale market for the vitamins may arise. In particular, mixing the vitamins and the medicine together would work, while placing the vitamins and medicine separately in the same box generally would fail, as someone could buy the box and use the medicine for pigs and the vitamins for horses.

Another significant example of cross-firm coordination includes Microsoft and Intel. However, these companies generally had difficulty with coordination and have not, apparently, coordinated prices, although they agreed to specialize in software and hardware, respectively, for a considerable time.

PRICE DISPERSION AND THE THEORY OF SALES

Grocery stores announce sale items weekly, and there is a great deal of variation from week to week in the prices of standard, branded items like Coca-Cola, Bounty paper towels, Spaghettios, and other advertised items. Grocery stores play a pricing game with each other week after week, and yet the prices do not stabilize—the variation continues. Indeed, the very unpredictability is what is predictable—the prices on standard items will change, although when and by how much is uncertain.

Prices on standardized, brand name items vary from store to store, often in unpredictable ways. Kodak ASA200 Gold 35 mm film ranges from $3.00 to $4.50 at convenience stores, for no apparent reason. Table 11.4 presents prices for a digital camera offered by various companies on a particular day. Such variation is not atypical but is rather the norm.

There is a very simple reason for such variation: there is no equilibrium that has constant prices. The foundation for understanding price dispersion is to understand that a firm's single price on an item serves two very different consumer types. One type is a comparison shopper, or a well-informed shopper, or generally a buyer who will be informed of price offerings from several competitors and may visit several stores. The second type of consumer is poorly informed, does not seek out multiple price offers, and generally engages in little shopping. In a world mostly full of informed shoppers, firms will price very competitively, with prices at or near marginal cost. Firms that have some customers of the second type, however, will not be willing to price competitively, because it is better to exploit the ill-informed with high prices than to sell a large number of units with no markup over cost.

When a firm is facing a mixture of the two types of customers, its prices cannot be predictable to its rivals. Suppose firm A is expected to be the low-priced firm, and firm B the firm with the second-lowest price. Firm A has an incentive to increase its price to just below firm B's price, which keeps its price leadership role, still wins it the informed shopper, and earns it more money. But then firm B would like to undercut A when it learns that A has increased its price; a small price cut will grab the informed shoppers for B. Predictable, head-to-head competition for the well-informed shoppers is unprofitable because the firms compete only in prices, and if the firms know they face competition, prices of both may be driven

Table 11.4
Fuji Finepix 4700 Prices, 10 June, 2000 (Quoted on Price Grabber)

Retailer	*Price*
The Web Shop	\$629.99
buy.com	\$655.95
firstsource.com	\$656.99
TurboPrice.com	\$664.58
eCOST.com	\$666.99
BuyMoreProduct.com	\$679.27
The Digital Kingdom	\$699.00
BestStopDigital	\$719.00
Computers4sure	\$719.99
Onvia.com	\$719.99
Shop4Digital	\$729.00
MP Superstore	\$739.99
PC Mall	\$779.00
Computability	\$779.00
Buydig.com	\$789.00
Beach Camera	\$799.00
Outpost.com	\$799.95
The Big Store	\$807.95
myPC21.com	\$901.00

to marginal cost. Consequently, it cannot be predicted whether a firm will or will not face competition for the shoppers. Thus, firms must probabilistically prepare to face competition. There is some probability that the other firms will set prices lower to reach the informed shoppers, and some probability that they will not. That is, firms should run sales so that the sale prices cannot be forecast by rivals.

Firms pricing randomly are said to follow "distributional strategies": prices are chosen from a statistical distribution in a random way, rather than in a predictable way. What is predictable is the range of prices used by each firm, rather than the exact price that will be announced on any particular day.

It is not so outlandish that prices might be unpredictable. From the perspective of the manager setting the prices and choosing sale items, the choice may seem very sensible. A grocer might choose a sale on tuna because "it seemed like a long time since we had a sale on tuna," or on paper towels because "our paper towel inventory is bulging." If these reasons are invisible to competitors, then from the competitor's perspective the prices are random. However, when such "introspective" randomization is used, it can often be improved upon, since it may not be sufficiently unpredictable, or may encourage the rival to follow an undesirable strategy.

Randomized attempts to sell to comparison shoppers provide the basis for a theory of sales. According to the theory, sales represent the balancing of the profitability of captive consumers and the additional sales represented by selling to informed shoppers. Consider, for example, two stores and a population of 3,000 customers. Each store sells paper towels. Customers may pay up to $2 for the paper towels, which cost the store $1, but a thousand of the informed customers will investigate prices at both stores and thus obtain the lowest price. Each store also has 1,000 captive, uniformed customers who will be willing to pay up to $2 for the roll. How should it be priced?

It turns out that each store should use the distributional strategy that involves choosing a price on the interval from $1.50 to $2.00. Moreover, the probability of the price choice is not uniform, but has the shape:

$$F(p) = \frac{2p-3}{p-1}.$$

Here, $F(p)$ gives the likelihood of choosing a price less than p. For instance, the likelihood of a price less than $1.75 is $F(1.75) = .50/.75 = \frac{2}{3}$. Why is this the behavior to expect of the firms? This randomized or distributional strategy is stable; given that one firm follows it, the other firm has no incentive not to follow the strategy. Moreover, F is the only distributional strategy that does not leave one firm with an incentive to adjust its strategy. Suppose one firm follows the strategy given by F. The profits of the other firm, if it chooses a price p, are p − $1, times the number of customers it gets. The store gets its 1,000 captive customers, plus another 1,000 if it follows the distributional strategy prices above p, which happens with probability $1 - F(p)$. Thus, the stores obtains

$$\text{Profit} = (p-1)[1{,}000 + 1{,}000 \times (1 - F(p))] = 1{,}000 \times (p-1) \times [1 + 1 - \frac{2p-3}{p-1}] = 1{,}000$$

The profits are the same, no matter what prices are charged. This particular distributional strategy is the *only* strategy that cannot be exploited by the other firm. It is the strategy that produces the highest profits, given an absence of cooperation by the rival. Distributional strategies in pricing are analogous to the strategy in the child's game "paper, scissors, stone," in which two children choose one of these three items simultaneously. If each chooses the same item, the game is a tie. If they choose different items, paper beats stone, stone beats scissors, and scissors beat paper. The only stable play of this game is an even split among the three items—any other play can be exploited by competitors. For example, if one plays paper half the time and scissors the other half, and never plays stone, an opponent can play scissors and win half the time, tying the other half. Unpredictable sales have an effect similar to random play in the child's game—the distributional strategy of sales presents rivals from exploiting one's pattern of pricing.

While the particulars of the determination of the distributional strategy are unimportant, there are several useful insights to be obtained: Distributional strategies

- Arise from competition over a part of the market.
- May not represent the beginning of a price war.
- Cause prices to fluctuate unpredictably.
- Have distributions that are stable over time.

EXECUTIVE SUMMARY—PRICING

- Pricing strategy has growing importance.
- The key issue in pricing strategy is price discrimination—charging distinct customers according to their willingness to pay.
- There are two major price discrimination strategies, direct and indirect.
- Direct price discrimination involves conditioning prices on customer characteristics such as location, status, and other purchases.
- The price should be lower to the group that has more elastic demand (is more price-sensitive).
- The key issue in direct price discrimination is arbitrage. How can the firm stop resale?
- There are five impediments to arbitrage—transportation costs, laws, personalization of the product or service, matching problems, and informational problems.
- When arbitrage prevents full price discrimination, it is preferable to increase the price charged to the price-sensitive group as well as lower the price to the less sensitive group.

- Indirect price discrimination involves the assistance of the customer through "self-selection."
- Examples of indirect price discrimination include coupons, quantity discounts, and multiple rate plans.
- It pays to add plans that share the gains from increasing the quantity purchased by large customers toward the efficient level.
- Risk can be used as a means of indirect price discrimination in some instances.
- Internet auctions permit price discrimination both on the value of time and on preferences for risk.
- Bundling of products is an important and underused means of indirect price discrimination.
- Yield management combines dynamic price discrimination with peak-load pricing issues to create a sophisticated array of prices.
- Yield management, at its core, involves setting aside some product for late-appearing high-value customers.
- Price discrimination carries a threat of heightened price competition. This threat can be mitigated by five means:
  Reward sales force on revenue.
  Encourage the use of nonprice sweeteners.
  Reduce quality to justify price cuts.
  Create complex pricing.
  Encourage loyalty of existing customers rather than try to attract new customers.
- Exclusive dealing provisions offer a solution to some opportunistic behavior, or "hold-up," where one party will not invest because of the threat of expropriation of the proceeds.
- Opportunism can also be mitigated by
  Licensing
  Vertical integration
  Long-term contracts
  Exclusive contracts
  Most-favored customer contracts
  Uniform, simple contracts
- Peak-load pricing involves the recognition that capacity costs should be attributed to the highest demand points.
- Peak-load pricing is most important in industries with a high proportion of fixed costs, such as airlines, hotels, and electricity generation.
- Complementary goods are those that increase each other's value, such as computers and software, automobiles and gasoline, or beer and peanuts.

- It is frequently advantageous to bundle complementary goods.
- When competing sellers have some customers with high switching costs, and others who shop for the lowest price, random sales are common. This is especially important in grocery stores and Internet electronics sales.
- It is important to distinguish randomized strategies from price wars.

12

Auctions

Auctions are one of the oldest market institutions, and were used by the Babylonians. Some of the products that have been sold by auction include the right to televise the Olympic Games, radio spectrum, air travel, condominiums, bull semen, used cars, banks, celebrities' signatures, and cut flowers.* Because governments tend to use sealed-bid tenders for much of their purchasing, an astounding array of goods and services have been procured by auction, including zero-gravity toilets, flood control, building inspection, clerical work, tax collection, voter registration, and stealth-aircraft design.

Most people think of bidding in the context of antiques auctions, or perhaps government procurement of highways and sales of Treasury bills. More recently, Internet auctions have been a huge success, attracting a great deal of attention. However, bidding is a much more prevalent phenomenon than these explicit auctions would suggest. When a painting contractor competes for a job, the contractor is bidding. When a disk-drive manufacturer quotes a price to a PC assembler, the manufacturer is bidding. When an architect prepares a design proposal for a museum, the architect is bidding. When an overbooked airline offers flight coupons to buy back the overbooked seat, the airline is bidding. Bidding is pervasive in a decentralized economy, and indeed is the foundation of market pricing. For this reason, it is valuable to take a closer look at auctions and bidding.

BIDDING

There are two major bidding situations: bidding to buy (e.g., an antiques auction) and bidding to sell (a procurement auction). We will focus on bidding to buy, although all of the insights translate readily to the procurement environment.

*The word "auction" derives from the Latin word *auctio,* meaning "to increase." This refers to oral auctions, where the price is raised by increments until only one bidder is willing to pay the price. The de-

The easiest bidding situations to understand are known as "private-value" environments. A private-value environment involves bidders who know their value for the good for sale.[1] Few items have this property of bidders knowing their own value perfectly, although many are well approximated by the private-value environment. With bidding to sell, a firm bidding to supply computers may know precisely what the computers cost the company. An individual who bids to buy a seat on an airplane may know what it will cost to make alternative arrangements. Most items, however, have some collective uncertainty associated with their value. Consider the sale of a currently popular kid's toy in short supply, such as Playstation or Beanie Babies. Speculators who buy the toy for resale care about the value placed on the toy by others, because that value will influence the future resale price. Thus, speculators do not know their own value for the item—their value is derived from the demands of others. Parents who buy the toy for their own child may have a very good idea of their value of the toy, which is derived from the pleasure of making their child happy versus the pain of having an unhappy child. Private value applies when you will not learn anything about your own value of the good for sale from the bidding or from others' willingness to pay. The speculator in children's toys does not have a private value, while an individual parent does.

The English Auction

The English auction is the most popular kind of auction and is used to sell antiques, prize bulls, and other items. In an English auction, the price starts low and is increased successively. At each increment of the price, some bidder "holds" the item; that bidder wins the item at that price if no other bidder will pay more.

How should a bidder who knows his value bid in an English auction? At any given price, a bidder who does not hold the item faces the question: "Should I bid if no one else does?" If the bidder decides "No," the bidder cedes the item to the current holder or to another bidder. If the bidder decides, "Yes," the bidder then bids and becomes the holder of the item. Losing the item makes sense if the price is higher than the bidder's value. In contrast, losing the item does not make sense if the price is below the bidder's value. Consequently, a bidder who knows his or her value should stand ready to bid until the price equals or exceeds that bidder's value. A private-value bidder in an English auction has a simple optimal strategy—continue to bid until prices exceed the bidder's value.

An important aspect of the simplicity of the optimal strategy is that the strategy does not depend on the behavior of other bidders. Jump bids or other aggres-

---

fense procurement use of the term "auction" means, essentially, to renege on a price agreement; we will not adopt this unusual usage here.

sive bidding techniques should not scare a private-value bidder away from bidding, unless the jump is to a level exceeding the bidder's value.

The effect of optimal bidding in an English auction is that the price is approximately the second-highest value. That is, bidders with the second-highest value will drop out when the price reaches their value.[2] The English auction tends to capture the second-highest valuation for the seller.*

The Sealed-Bid Auction

In a sealed-bid auction, each bidder submits a bid, typically in a sealed envelope. These bids are opened at the same time, and the high bidder wins the item, paying the bid. Unlike the English auction, a bidder's optimal strategy in the sealed-bid auction depends on the behavior of other bidders. Generally, a bidder will base bids on the following formula: Expected Profit = (value − bid) × Probability that bid is highest.

The probability of winning tends to increase in the bid, while the net profits fall as the bid increases, creating a trade-off. The starting point for any bidding procedure is to estimate the probability of winning as a function of the bid. Various procedures using historical data have been employed to estimate this function. For example, bidders in off-shore oil auctions estimate the amount of oil present, and then estimate the value of this oil. Looking at past auctions, the bidders can estimate the winning bid as a proportion of the estimated value. (Because of uncertainty about the amount of oil, off-shore oil auctions are not based on private values, and thus the procedure outlined has serious problems, discussed in the next section, in the off-shore oil application.) Similarly, a bidder for logging rights on U.S. federal land in the Pacific Northwest might look at the winning bid as a function of the government's estimate of the amount of timber on the land. The historical data might look something like the left diagram of figure 12.1. Here, the winning bids range from \$3.50 to \$11.00, and the values ranged from \$6.60 to

*In 1961, Nobel laureate William Vickrey observed that one can implement an English auction by using a special sealed-bid design. The trick is to run a sealed-bid auction in which the price is not the highest bid, but the second-highest bid. In such an auction, the bidders each submit their estimate of the actual value as their bid, and the final price will be the second-highest bid, and hence the second-highest value. This auction has become known as the Vickrey auction in honor of its inventor. Until recently, the Vickrey auction was used only in economics laboratories and in a disastrous series of spectrum auctions in New Zealand. (The Vickrey auction was used in a circumstance for which it is particularly ill-suited—the situation in which one bidder had a value ten or more times the second-highest value. The auction revealed that the spectrum was sold for less than 10% of the highest value. However, the Vickrey auction has found widespread application in Internet auctions, for eBay's bidding robots are Vickrey bidders; the human bidder submits a value, and the bidding robot does the bidding. Forty years later, eBay has attempted to patent Vickrey's insight.

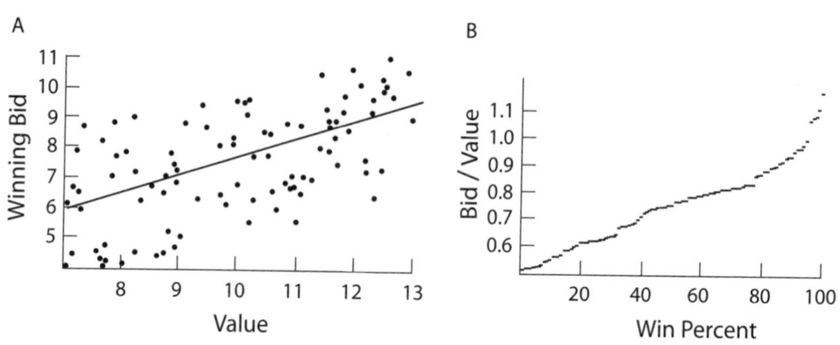

Figure 12.1. (a) Bids as a function of value; and (b) the likelihood of winning for a given bid.

$13.00. Statistically, bids are increasing in values, though the effect is somewhat weak; a regression analysis reveals that bids average 50% of the value plus $2.50. The average winning bid as a function of value is illustrated by the straight line in the left diagram of figure 12.1. Note that there is a substantial amount of uncertainty—bids are often substantially above or below the *average* winning bid.

The left diagram of figure 12.1 presents the raw data but makes it difficult to see what the likelihood of winning is for any particular bid. In contrast, estimating the likelihood of winning when a bidder bids a fraction of the value provides a clearer picture. The right side of figure 12.1 presents the proportion of times that a winning bid was a given fraction below value. Thus, a bid at 50% or less of value never won the bidding. In about 50% of cases, the winning bid was 75% of value or less. This is read off the diagram by finding 50% on the horizontal axis, which gives a bid/value of 0.75, or 75%. The interpretation is that in half of all cases, a bid of 75% of value or less prevailed. Similarly, a bid equal to value would have prevailed in a bit less than 95% of cases. In 5% of the cases, the winning bidder bid more than the value. (This sounds irrational but may have arisen because the winning bidder had a value greater than the bidder doing the estimation.)

The right-hand diagram of figure 12.1 is computed by calculating the bid/value ratio and then ordering these values from smallest to largest. The value of "Win Percent" is then just the proportion below a given bid/value ratio. The Win Percent can be used to calculate the expected profits associated with various bid/value ratios.[3] This calculation is provided in figure 12.2.

Figure 12.2 graphs the profits associated with various bids for a $10 million expected value. Profits are highest at 83% of value, but this level of expected profits is very similar to the much lower bid of 68% of value. Bids from 65% to 87% of value give about the same level of expected profits. This is not atypical of auction bidding; often, a fairly wide range of bids have similar expected profits.

Generally, is it much more difficult to bid in a sealed-bid auction than to bid

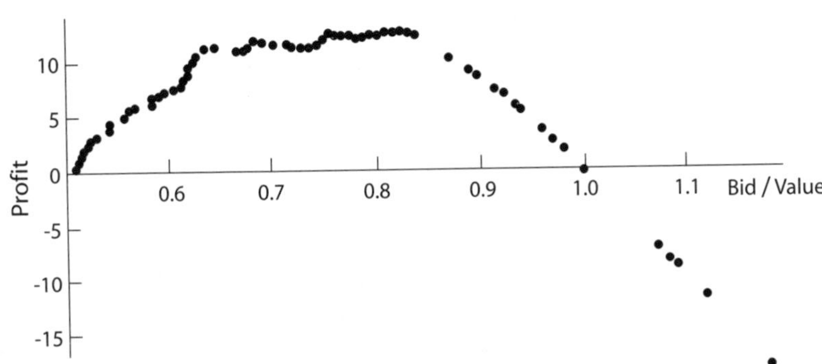

Figure 12.2. Profit, as a function of the bid.

in an oral auction. Moreover, the problems are not confined to the thorny problem of estimating the likelihood of winning. Indeed, estimating the probability of wining is the tip of the iceberg—much more difficult problems face the bidder in a sealed-bid auction. The format of the sealed-bid auction prevents the release of information about others' bids, information that can be used to reduce the risk facing the bidder when the bidder is uncertain about the item's value.

The Winner's Curse

I paid too much for it, but it's worth it.
—Sam Goldwyn

Painters, roofers, and other contractors are familiar with the difficulties of bidding for jobs. Costs often are higher than expected; indeed, costs are *consistently* higher than expected. What appeared to be an easy job may have an unexpectedly difficult feature, and this happens more often in bid jobs than in commissioned jobs. The reason for the consistent misestimation of costs is the bidding process itself, and a phenomenon known as the winner's curse.

The U.S. Department of the Interior has sold thousands of drilling rights for properties off shore of the Texas and Louisiana coasts. Profits in these auctions proved quite low at first, and at least one bidder consistently found less oil than the bidder expected, in spite of substantial expertise in estimating the volume of oil in just such circumstances. Most bidders managed to adjust to the unexpected bidding conditions, but some accounts show Texaco consistently lost money through its winning bids for off-shore oil.

As every Texan knows, oil is inherently speculative—no one knows how much oil is under the surface until drilling has been completed. No one is really sure how much oil a property has until the oil extraction process is complete and the well shut

Table 12.1
Five Estimates of the Value of Oil (in millions of dollars)

1.7	3.0	2.9	3.9	1.5

down. Moreover, different experts make distinct estimates of the amount of oil a geological formation may hold. While the science of estimating oil reserves has improved significantly over the past one hundred years, geologists still arrive at distinct conclusions. As a consequence, bidders often have very different estimates of the amount of oil available in a property. This is a *common values* situation: no one knows how much oil is present, but everyone has estimates. The estimates might be very good, even unbiased (correct on average), but still different from each other.

Half of the off-shore oil leases that are purchased are never drilled. The purchase price is expended whether the lease is drilled or not, so the bids on these tracts represent free money for the government, which regains the tract after five years. Disproportionately many of the tracts that are never drilled received a single bid. The failure of others to bid on the tracts was bad news—it indicated that other firms did not think the tracts were very valuable.

The nature of an auction is that the bidder with the largest estimate of value tends to win. Thus, *the bidder who most overestimates the value of the item for sale will tend to win the bidding.* Even if bidders have unbiased estimates of value, the auction selects bidders in a very biased way, selecting bidders who happen to have overestimated the value by the largest margin.

Consider the problem of bidding on a tract that may contain oil. The prospective bidder assembles a team of five first-rate geologists to study the surveys and to examine the data on nearby tracts and geologically similar tracts in other regions. At the end of the day, the five geologists come up with five estimates of the value of oil on the tract. These estimates are presented in table 12.1.

The five estimates average 2.6 and have a sample standard deviation (a measure of the variation around the mean) of 0.99. If these geologists are typical, other geologists also will have similar variation in their estimates. Estimates will tend to follow the bell-shaped normal distribution already discussed. This distribution has the property that an estimate is equally likely to be above the average as below. Moreover, there is a 16% chance of exceeding one standard deviation, a 2.3% chance of exceeding two standard deviations, and one-tenth of 1% chance of exceeding three standard deviations. The standard deviation, then, is very informative about "usual" variation.

The more bidders in an auction, the more likely that the winning bidder has greatly overestimated the value. A bidder who is more optimistic than one bidder

[TAB]LE 12.2
[Adj]ustment Needed, in Standard Deviations, for Given Number of Bidders

[Nu]mber	2	3	4	5	10	15	20	50	100	500	1000
[Co]rrection	0.564	0.846	1.03	1.16	1.54	1.74	1.87	2.25	2.51	3.04	3.24

will usually have an estimate closer to value than a bidder who is more optimistic than ten bidders. Indeed, we can quantify the effect of the number of bidders when the estimates arrive from a normal distribution. With two bidders, the larger estimate is, on average, 0.56 standard deviations above the mean. The smaller estimate is 0.56 standard deviations below the mean, and they average the mean. But that does not matter because it is the bidder with the larger estimate who typically wins the bidding. Thus, bidders should reduce their estimate of value by 0.56 standard deviations to account for the winner's curse. By doing so, they have corrected their estimate for the bias created by the auction.

Table 12.2 presents the winner's curse corrections for various numbers of bidders. These values represent the average overestimate of the highest of a number of estimators. With five companies estimating value, the highest is 1.16 standard deviations over the mean on average. Thus, to get an accurate estimate of value given that a bidder knows he or she is highest, the bidder needs to reduce the estimate by 1.16 standard deviations. Similarly, the highest of 100 is, on average, 2.5 standard deviations over the true value.

An interesting feature of the corrections is how slow the correction grows in the number of bidders. With four bidders, bidders should reduce their estimates by an entire standard deviation to account for the bias created by the auction. With 100 bidders, the correction is 2.5, rising to 3 standard deviations when there are 500 bidders. A standard deviation may be quite large in practice, running around 15%–20% of average value in off-shore oil auctions. Thus, with 20 bidders, the winning bidder's estimate of value is around 30% above the true value, on average.[4]

The winner's curse risk is much more severe in sealed-bid auctions than in regular English auctions. The reason is that a severe winner's curse in an English auction requires *two* or more bidders to overestimate the value significantly, while in a sealed-bid auction it takes only one bidder to significantly overestimate the value. Moreover, in an English auction, bidders can sometimes see that other bidders have dropped out of the bidding. Thus, it is safer to bid aggressively in an English auction, because the risk is mitigated by the actions of other bidders. In contrast, a sealed-bid auction presents an opportunity to outbid all other bidders, including the second highest, by a large margin. The overall winner's curse correction is the same in either auction; in both cases the correction is the average overestimate of the highest estimate of value. The risk to a bidder of bidding with an uncorrected estimate of value, given that other bidders are savvy and correct for the winner's curse, is lower in an English auction because other bidders drop out. Moreover, in an English auction, it is possible to dynamically update one's estimate of value, given the bidding behavior of other bidders.

There are a variety of factors that may change the magnitude of the winner's curse correction. A well-informed bidder may have a small winner's curse correction because of a small standard deviation. That bidder's competitors, unless equally well informed, face larger winner's curse corrections. When one is bidding against a well-informed bidder, winning means that one must outbid someone who knows the value approximately. In an English auction, this can be fatal—if the informed bidder is not willing to pay a given price, the other bidder probably should not be either. When a bidder outbids a well-informed bidder in a sealed-bid auction, the well-informed bidder may have reduced his or her bid to make a larger profit, so that price is less than value. Still, bidders facing a well-informed bidder should bid cautiously. Consequently, it pays to *appear* well informed, because it makes other bidders rationally choose to bid cautiously.[5] It also pays to be well informed, so that one is less likely to fall prey to the winner's curse.

It is quite common for bidders to find that auction prices exceed their estimate of value. In many cases, these estimates are the result of intensive expert analysis. Bidders are understandably frustrated at losing even when they bid their value. There are two very different reasons for bids to exceed value. In some cases, bids exceed values because naive or inexperienced bidders fall prey to the winner's curse. This appears to have happened frequently in the first decade of the off-shore oil auctions. Firms that understood the economics of competitive bidding lost to firms like Texaco that did not. It is better to lose such auctions, but it is very frustrating for the bidders who are shut out of the competition.

Alternatively, however, some firms value items more because they have very different expectations about the future value of the items. In the 1994 Federal Communications Commission spectrum auctions, which sold the rights to use part of the radio frequency for wireless communication known as PCS (Personal Communication Services), some bidders planned to offer traditional, cellular-type communications. Others considered an array of futuristic devices, including palm-computing devices and child-tracking devices. The Internet was in its infancy at the time, and palm-computing devices amounted to the dysfunctional Apple Newton, so the forecast that there was a major market in wireless palm computing was a brave forecast, indeed. MCI took the position that it would be cheaper to buy spectrum rights, because MCI believed bidders were overpaying for the spectrum, while AT&T and Sprint bet differently. It remains to be seen who was right, although MCI's forecast appears unlikely.

TABLE 12.3
NPV of a Hypothetical Silver Mine

ROR%	10	12	14	16	18	20
NPV, $M	3.77	2.35	1.35	0.61	0.06	−0.36

While grand expectations for future technological advances can account for major differences in estimated value across firms, small differences in interest-rate expectations can do the same. Silver mines generally require four years of investment with no return before silver starts to be produced. A mine may have a forty-year time horizon. Suppose after an initial investment of $2 million in year one, $1 million per year will be produced in years five to forty. How much is this project worth? Table 12.3 provides the answer, in the form of net present values (NPV), for several internal rates of return (ROR).

Since internal rates of return in mining average around 15%, with a significant dispersion across companies and over time, we see that major differences in NPVs can arise from modest differences in the way discounting is performed. In evaluating the likely bid of a competing company an estimate of the silver content in a mine may be less important than the rate of return used by that competitor, or the company's expectation of future silver prices. In assessing the competition, bidders often focus on objective quantities such as the likely silver content in a mine, or the number of telephone subscribers, and ignore the other factors that go into assessing NPV. Not only are these other factors often quite significant, but it may be possible to accurately assess them. For example, a firm that will not undertake projects with a long development lag may have been using a high internal rate of return. Sometimes internal rates of return are made public, and if not, sometimes they can be deduced by past choices. As the example in table 12.3 illustrates, variation in rates of return may dominate variation in all other factors, making estimated rates of return the most significant information about competitors in some situations. This means it is important to learn competitor's rates of return and to keep one's own secret.

Updating

Bids carry information. When people sell stock, they are making a bet against that stock, and the reverse when they buy stock. Such bets reveal something about the beliefs of the buyer or seller. In auctions, the willingness of a bidder to place a given bid is informative not just about that bidder but also about the value of the object for sale.

Updating beliefs based on the bidding behavior of other firms is the flip side of the winner's curse. The winner's curse amounts to the absence of a high bid being bad news about value—no one else is willing to pay what the winner will pay. For the same reason, the presence of another bid is good news about value. Insofar as bidders base their bids on real information about value, bids provide relevant information about value.

How should one use this information? Consider again table 12.1, with the results of five geological studies of a given off-shore oil tract. A bidder possessing this information preliminarily came to a value estimate of $2.6 million, and is competing in an English auction. After the bidder performs some statistical analysis to account for the winner's curse, the $2.6 million estimate is corrected to be $2.3 million. Now suppose Exxon places a bid of $2.3 million. We can conclude that Exxon expects the tract is worth at least $2.3 million. Should we be willing to bid $2.4 million? Perhaps. First, if Exxon is a savvy bidder (and it is), Exxon has also made a winner's curse correction. Therefore, Exxon's estimate had to be at least $2.6 million to induce it to submit a $2.3 million bid. Seeing that two companies' estimates (ours and Exxon's) were $2.6 million or more, we can reduce our winner's curse correction, resulting in an increase in our winner's curse corrected value to $2.4 million.[6] The important lesson is that bids carry information content—a high bid by another party should make bidders more comfortable responding with high bids. In particular, the failure of others to bid on a tract is a bad signal about the likely reserves, and many of the tracts receiving only a single bid are never developed. Tracts that receive many bids, in contrast, are more likely to be valuable.

A common problem in bidding is overconfidence in estimates. Bidders believe their estimates are better than the estimates of their competition. Such confidence is rarely justified. Usually it is more accurate to presume the competition is equally clever. However, acting confident is quite valuable, for it signals to other bidders that the winner's curse will be large for them, and thus that they should reduce their estimates. That is, one would like to project the image of supreme confidence, while privately being skeptical.

SELLING STRATEGY AND AUCTION DESIGN

How should you design an auction to sell a unique item? Several books and hundreds of academic papers have been written on this intriguing topic.[7]

- Should you use a sealed-bid auction, or an oral ascending auction?
- Should you reveal information about the item for sale?
- Are royalties or other revenue-sharing devices desirable?
- Should you impose a reserve price or a minimum acceptable bid?

- When selling multiple items, should you sell them sequentially or simultaneously?
- What can be done about collusion by bidders?
- Should the seller conceal the number of bidders from the bidders?
- Supposing there is a natural winner, should the playing field be leveled by handicapping the most effective bidder?

In this section, I consider only the case of a seller who will deal repeatedly with a group of buyers. With a one-time transaction, a seller can attempt to fool buyers, and such attempts may be successful. For example, naive buyers will often fall prey to the winner's curse, and it can be desirable to exploit this tendency. However, such a policy relies on fooling buyers and will not likely provide long-run returns; thus, it offers no sustainable advantage to the firm. In contrast, the insights of auction design will persist over the long term. To provide a concrete example, a one-time seller with no legal liability, who knows that the product for sale is defective, cannot benefit from announcing the defective state of the product. However, a repeat seller more than makes up the loss of admitting the defective nature of the product by being believed when the product is in fact good.

The logic of the winner's curse is very helpful in auction design. In particular, it is desirable to minimize winner's curse effects in most auctions. The reduction of the winner's curse induces experienced bidders to be more aggressive in bidding, because the threat of loss is smaller. In particular, a reduction in the winner's curse reduces the chance of paying too much, encouraging the bidders to bid more aggressively. On average, this policy *increases* the amount paid.[8] To understand why reducing the winner's curse increases the average price, consider the sale of an off-shore oil tract in the Gulf of Mexico. Firms are uncertain about the amount of oil in the tract, which gives rise to the winner's curse. As a consequence, the firms bid cautiously, which in the end results in profits for the winning firm, on average—because all firms reduce their bids. If the actual amount of oil is revealed, the bidders will bid the value of the tract, reducing the winner's profits, and therefore increasing the average price paid. (The average price is the average value minus bidder profits.)

Another way to view the advantage of mitigating the winner's curse is to understand the role of information. Bidders earn profits in auctions in two ways: value/cost advantages (e.g., lower costs of drilling) and informational advantages. A reduction in the winner's curse has no effect on value/cost advantages, but it reduces the informational advantage of bidders by sharing information with all of the bidders.* Such a reduction in bidder profits directly increases the average price paid.

*Informational advantages are not only real, but can be quantitatively more valuable than other advantages. For example, a drainage tract in an off-shore auction is next to or near an existing tract. If he wishes to bid, the owner of the existing tract has a major informational advantage over other bidders.

The release of relevant information mitigates the winner's curse. Consequently, it is desirable to use an oral auction (releasing information about losing bidders' willingnesses to pay) and to release any relevant information that the seller has. Oral auctions mitigate the winner's curse because it takes two bidders, not one, overestimating value to overpay in an oral auction. In contrast, in a sealed-bid auction, a single bidder can dramatically overestimate value and pay too much.* Similarly, the policy of releasing accurate relevant information reduces the winner's curse. Although one loses when the information is negative, the gains when the information is positive more than compensate. Thus, the policy of the U.S. Department of the Interior to release its information about off-shore oil tracts is a good policy. Similarly, both Christie's and Sotheby's auction houses collect and release information about the authenticity of items for sale, and go to extraordinary lengths to insure that the information is accurate.

Royalties also mitigate the winner's curse. A royalty is a payment made by the buyer based on the realized value of the item. For example, the right to broadcast the summer Olympics held in Seoul, Korea, was auctioned with a royalty payment—the amount paid would depend on the size of the television audience. Royalties tie the total payment by the winning bidder to the actual outcome; when the item proves less valuable than anticipated, the payment is also less. Therefore, royalties reduce the risk to the buyer of overpaying, and hence reduce the winner's curse. When feasible, royalties will be advantageous to sellers.†

Information about Competition

Providing information about value is not the same as providing information about the state of competition. Ontario Hydro, the enormous Canadian electric utility, routinely conceals the number of bidders in purchasing auctions from the bidders themselves.[9] Ontario Hydro has found that the loss from concealing the number

---

Kenneth Hendricks and Robert Porter show that in auctions of drainage tracts, the owner of the neighboring tract makes significant profits, while other bidders approximately break even. That is, *all* the profits arise out of informational advantages. See, for example, Kenneth Hendricks, Robert Porter, and Charles Wilson, "Auctions for and Gas Leases with an Informal Bidder and a Random Reserve Price," *Econometrica* 62, no. 6 (November 1944): 1415–44.

*In the outer continental shelf oil auctions run by the U.S. Department of the Interior prior to 1970, the average winning bid was 50% higher than the second-highest bid. This "money left on the table" encourages conservative bidding.

†Royalties are not always feasible. There may be difficulties in monitoring the value of the item sold. For this reason, royalties for movies and books are often based on the gross, rather than net, earnings, and even then, disputes arise. Royalties also shift risk from the buyer to the seller, which can be undesirable. Finally, royalties increase the scope for legal disputes.

when there are many bidders is more than compensated for by the gain when there are only one or two bidders. In fact, Ontario Hydro has discovered an important principle: revealing the extent of competition is generally undesirable for an auctioneer. For example, if one firm always bids on an item, and another firm sometimes bids and sometimes does not, the price will be very high when the first firm is bidding by itself, and reasonably low when two firms are bidding. By concealing the presence of competition from the first firm, the firm will bid between the two levels, that is, less than when it knew it faced no competition, but more than when it knew it faced competition. This leveling of the firm's bid is advantageous. Ontario Hydro gets a lower purchase price when there is only one firm, and it is protected against too high a price when there are actually two firms by the existence of the second firm. Concealing the extent of competition can have dramatic advantages when the number of bidders fluctuates, but is often small. Concealing the nature and extent of the competition, however, can exacerbate the winner's curse in some circumstances, and thus is not a panacea.

Reserve Prices

Reserve prices (minimum bids) are generally advantageous to sellers. Sellers should always impose a reserve at least as great as their value of retaining the object for sale—it is not advantageous to sell for a price less than the seller's value. In particular, the seller's value includes the option of waiting and reselling in the future. This option is often the best recourse for an item that fails to meet the reserve, but it is somewhat tricky to implement. Typically, the items that do not sell are inferior to those that sell; this is the reason that the items did not sell. Thus, the information that an item failed to sell is "bad news" about the item's value. Consequently, the expected future price of an item that did not sell is less than the price expected in the first auction. For example, the Resolution Trust Corporation (RTC) was responsible for disposing of the assets of failed financial institutions, and wound up selling a great deal of real estate. Some of the real estate was sold with a reserve, but some was sold with no effective reserve. In either case, the RTC observed the appraised value of property prior to the auction. Suppose the RTC imposes a reserve equal to 80% of appraised value. Some items fail to sell because they are worth less than that, while others were not investigated by any of the potential bidders and simply attracted no bids. The items worth less than 80% might be worth, on average, 70% of appraised value, while the items that were not investigated might be worth 90% of the appraised value. Suppose one-half failed to sell because no bidder investigated the item. Then the expected value of an item that failed to sell is one-half of 90% plus one-half of 70%, or 80%. Thus, the appropriate reserve is approximately 80% of appraised value—this is the average value of items that fail to sell. When a seller is faced with the sale of a great number of related items by auction, some experimenting with the reserve can lead to a fine-tuned calculation of the optimal reserve price. The key insight is that the reserve should always be at least the seller's value.

Multiple Items

When multiple related items are for sale, the problems facing the seller can be very complex. For example, when the items are sold sequentially, bidders face the problem that, in bidding on the early items, they do not know the prices that will be obtained on later items; while bidding on later items, the bidders cannot revise their bids in light of new information on the earlier ones. The problem of sequential design was dramatically illustrated in the 1981 auction of transponders run by RCA. Seven nearly identical transponders (satellite communications) were sold. The results are presented in table 12.4. When the first transponder was sold, The Learning Channel (TLC) presumably thought it got a good price. When the next six sold for less, however, it became clear that TLC had obtained a bad price, and indeed had fallen prey to what is known as the declining price anomaly, in which identical items, sold sequentially, tend to fall in price.[10] TLC, arguing that its price was unfair, sued; the courts ruled that the Federal Communications Commission had jurisdiction. The FCC tried first to get all the firms to pay the average bid, a suggestion odious to those that had bought at less than the average. Ultimately, RCA was the loser and was paid less than the total of the winning bids.

Sequential auctions make it difficult for bidders to bid sensibly, because information the bidders need—the winning bids of later items—is not available during the early bidding. Moreover, bidders often experience regret; if prices do rise, the bidders wish they had bought earlier when prices were lower.

Simultaneous sealed-bid auctions of related items, used by the Department of the Interior to sell outer-continental-shelf oil leases, are *not* an improvement on sequential auctions. In such an auction, each bidder submits bids on as many items as the bidder chooses, and the high bidder on each item wins that item. Where sequential auctions limit the bidder's ability to optimize across auctions, the sealed-bid simultaneous design *eliminates* the ability to optimize across items. Bidders also face the problem of perhaps winning too much. A bidder desiring to win ten tracts might bid on twenty, but faces the problem of winning more than the bidder can explore. This problem of winning too much reduces bids, and hence seller revenues, and is detrimental to both seller and buyers by creating a coordination failure.

The problem of bidding in simultaneous sealed-bid auctions is worse when the items sold are complementary. For example, problems of sales of electric genera-

TABLE 12.4
RCA Transponder Auction, 9 November 1981

Order	*Winning Bidder*	*Price Obtained*
1	TLC	$14,400,000
2	Billy H. Batts	$14,100,000
3	Warner Amex	$13,700,000
4	RCTV	$13,500,000
5	HBO	$12,500,000
6	Inner City	$10,700,000
7	UTV	$11,200,000
Total		$90,100,000

tion capacity that have arisen because of new competition into electric generation have created a situation where a bidder might want to win plants A and B, or none at all. In a sequential auction, bidders on A do not know whether they can win B as well, but at least know they have a chance of winning B. Moreover, while there is a risk of winning only A, there is no risk of winning only B. In contrast, in a simultaneous design, bidders have a chance of winning A only or B only and no way to insure that they will win the right package. Sensible bidding is nearly impossible in such an auction. The inability to win an appropriate package tends to make bidders cautious, reducing revenues to the seller.

A better design is the "simultaneous ascending auction," or FCC auction.[11] This auction works somewhat like the silent auction employed by charities, although without the abrupt, specifically timed ending common to such auctions. The FCC auction involves rounds of bidding on multiple items, thereby providing the advantages of oral auctions in a simultaneous format. This kind of auction has only recently come into existence, because it requires a computer to operate effectively. Market design is a branch of economics in its infancy, but it is beginning to deliver on the promise of designing more efficient markets.

Collusion

Antiques are often sold by auction, and the bidders in antiques auctions often collude to suppress prices paid. Nearly a third of all price-fixing cases involve collusion in sealed-bid tenders for the construction of roads and highways. Collusion is a serious problem in auctions, and there is no panacea. However, when collusion is suspected, there are a variety of ways to reduce or mitigate it. (The discussion of cooperation in chapter 6 is also relevant.)

- Inform the Department of Justice, and contact your attorney. Price-fixing is illegal, under both federal and state laws.
- Employ a serious reserve price. A high minimum bid will partially compensate for the suppression of prices by the cartel.
- Use a sealed-bid auction. An oral ascending auction permits the cartel to punish cheaters immediately. In contrast, a cheater can win at least one sealed-bid auction before detection.
- Hold sealed-bid auctions infrequently. The less frequent the auctions, the greater the delay prior to any punishment by the cartel, and the greater the incentive for a bidder to cheat on the cartel agreement.
- Bundle the items for sale into large groups. This encourages bidders to defect from any cartel agreement, because the gains from defection rise the larger a single item is.
- Contact potential entrants. By suppressing price competition, cartels make entry attractive. An entrant will tend to undo the effects of the cartel.*
- Keep the identity of bidders secret whenever possible. (Governments generally cannot do this.) Cartels need to identify and punish cheaters. Concealing the identity of bidders encourages cheating generally, and concealing the identity of winning bidders may eliminate a cartel's effective ability to operate.

Natural Winner

In many auctions, there is a natural winner. For example, drainage tracts in offshore auctions are usually won by the holder of nearby tracts. A gypsum deposit near an existing gypsum plant will likely be sold to the owner of the gypsum plant. Incumbent telephone companies are more likely to win spectrum for cellular phones. When one bidder has major logistical or informational advantages, the likely outcome of an auction is that the advantaged bidder wins at a low price—the competition is ineffective at increasing the price. Indeed, when it is costly to make a bid, disadvantaged bidders generally will not enter, and thus the advantaged bidder may win without competition. In such situations, it can be advantageous to handicap the advantaged bidder and level the playing field. Handicap-

*In some cases, it may pay to subsidize entry in order to defeat a cartel. Beware, however, of ineffective bidders entering only for entry subsidies.

ping the advantaged bidder trades off efficiency against revenue generation. By increasing the chance slightly that a disadvantaged bidder will win, the advantaged bidder can be induced to pay a great deal more.

A common means of handicapping is a bidder credit. This allows a disadvantaged bidder to make a given bid at reduced cost, usually by a percentage forgiven. For example, a 30% bidder credit permits a $100 bid at a cost of $70. If the advantaged bidder tends to have 50% higher value, a bidder credit of 30% for disadvantaged bidders will encourage these bidders to enter, and make their disadvantaged bids much more competitive with the bids of advantaged bidders. The bidder credit forces the advantaged bidder to pay an amount much closer to value. Use of bidder credits faces two problems. First, the seller must be able to identify the bidders with advantages. Second, the seller must be able to estimate the magnitude of these advantages. The bidder credit that maximizes revenue generally leaves disadvantaged bidders only slightly disadvantaged; that is, the bidder credit levels the playing field mostly but not entirely.

Buyers can sometimes eliminate the effectiveness of bidder credits by resale. For example, in the Federal Communications Commission auctions of paging spectrum in 1995, bidder credits were offered to minority- and women-owned businesses. A female executive of a major telephone company resigned and started a company to bid on these licenses, with the understanding that she could lease the license back to her former employer at a profit, and even have her own job jack if the new business was unsuccessful. Nevertheless, bidder credits may be a useful means of encouraging entry into an auction in which a natural winner exists.

The alternative strategy for dealing with the natural winner is to impose a high reserve price, which will serve as competition. Setting such a reserve faces two problems. First, it is often difficult to estimate an appropriate reserve, because the natural winner has private information. Second, it may be difficult to stick with the reserve if the natural winner declines to buy—there is a natural tendency to then auction again with a lower reserve. Such a tendency can be exploited by the natural winner to obtain reduced prices. Often, it is better to create artificial competition by handicapping than to use a reserve.

Unintended Consequences

Auction design requires care; auctions are a system, and "minor" rule changes may have major consequences. There have been some spectacular failures in auction design. One of the most entertaining occurred Down Under. The Australian government sold two licenses for satellite television services by sealed-bid auction and required no deposit on the bids. The winning bids were $A212 million (Australian dollars) and $A177 million. The government announced the bids and the winners and asked for the money in exchange for the licenses. Both winners defaulted, so the government announced that the second-highest bidders would get the licenses at their bids, which were $A5 million less. The second-highest bids were submitted by the same two firms. These two firms defaulted again, and the licenses were awarded to the third-highest bidders, again at $A5 million less, with the bids again submitted by the same firms. This process of assign and default continued until the twentieth-highest bids were the winning bids, still made by the same two firms. One other firm had defaulted, and the same two firms won the bids at prices of $A117 million and $A77 million, respectively.[12]

Perhaps these two firms were the firms that valued the licenses most highly. However, we will never know, as the auction failed to perform as expected. Other firms shaded their bids, attempting to obtain a profit if they won, and hence would have been willing to pay more than their bids. Details matter—the auction form is not a cure-all for problems of selling unless designed appropriately.

When to Auction?

> It's a very sobering feeling to be up in space and realize that one's safety factor was determined by the lowest bidder on a government contract.
>
> **—Astronaut Alan Shepard**

> Hey Harry, you know we're sitting on four million pounds of fuel, one nuclear weapon and a thing that has two hundred thousand moving parts built by the lowest bidder. Makes you feel good doesn't it?
>
> **—"Rockhound," from the film *Armaggeddon***

When should you sell an item by auction, and when should you bargain? It is common for management not to auction when it is selling the firm itself, but instead to attempt to bargain exclusively with a single suitor. Such a bargaining process is often in management's interest, maximizing the size of golden parachutes for firm executives, but rarely being in the shareholder's interest. In most enterprises, it is more difficult to obtain a good price by bargaining then by auction. Competition is a stronger force than negotiation.

Generally, the best that a very tough negotiator can do is to mimic the threat that, failing a good agreement, the negotiator will walk. Such threats are much more plausible when there is a satisfactory alternative. Indeed, in some circumstances, the best negotiating skills in the world will not equal the power of a single extra bidder in a competitive process.[13] Threatening to take business to a rival is much more compelling, and credible, when a serious rival exists.

One major problem arises with the use of auctions. Auctions work better when the specifications of the product are relatively straightforward to describe. If the desired product is difficult to describe, it is difficult to buy the product by auction, since one cannot verify that the correct product is delivered. Moreover, the intense price competition created by auctions tends to be won by the lowest-cost, lowest-quality producer.[14] This problem of low quality is exacerbated when the product has not yet been developed. In this case, a continuing negotiation is required, where the price and specification of the product are jointly determined by technological developments during the procurement process. In such a situation, the price established by auctions fails to affect the final amount paid—renegotiation determines the price. This problem of renegotiating the product and payments in light of technological developments has arisen in U.S. Department of Defense contracting. Firms exploit this feature of defense contracting by bidding very low ("low-balling") and then renegotiating later, after the contract has been won. (Interestingly, renegotiation is known as "auctioning" by Air Force procurement officers.) Low-balling has been sufficiently rampant that the Federal Acquisition Regulations prohibit firms from bidding below cost. This regulation does nothing to help the military procure the best product at the best price, and is an unhelpful response to a real problem.

Lawyer Auction in an Auction Suit

Judge Lewis A. Kaplan of the Federal District Court in Manhattan issued a progressive and interesting decision in April 2000.[15] He invited attorneys from twenty-five law firms representing plaintiffs in a growing class action suit to bid in order to be selected as the attorneys to try the case. Each firm was to submit sealed bids listing the maximum amount that would go entirely to the plaintiffs before any payment to the attorneys, and to bid separately on the attorney's fee. For example, suppose a lawyer bid to have $1 million go to the plaintiffs and $400,000 to the attorney. The plaintiffs would get all of any award below $1 million. For an award between $1 million and $1.4 million, the plaintiffs would get $1 million and the attorney the remainder. The attorney would also get 25% of any amount exceeding the sum of the bid for the plaintiff and the bid for the attorney, with the balance going to the plaintiff. Thus, if the recovery was $2 million, the attorney would get the $400,000 plus 25% of $600,000 (the recovery amount exceeding $1.4 million), or $550,000.

What is especially interesting about Judge Kaplan's decision to auction the procurement of auction services is that the case concerned bid-rigging collusion by the celebrated auction houses Christie's and Sotheby's. The judge also promised to keep the actual bids secret.

The auction design by Judge Kaplan provides several interesting incentive effects. First, it provides an incentive for the attorneys to reduce their fees. Second, it discourages an "easy" settlement, because unless the settlement is sufficiently large, the attorneys will recover nothing. Third, the selection mechanism is unclear: Is a large bid by an attorney who promises more to the plaintiffs, but also wants a larger attorney's fee, preferable to one with smaller amounts? For example, is a bid of $1 million to the plaintiffs and $500,000 to the attorney better or worse than $2 million to the plaintiffs and $2 million to the attorney? There is no logical means of comparing these without some expectation of the likely settlement, which, if known, could probably be reached by negotiation, saving a costly trial. Generally, the difficulties in comparing complex bids make it preferable to design auctions that permit bidding on a single variable, with the others specified in advance. For example, attorneys could bid on the share they would keep, with the attorney who bid the smallest amount for the attorney's share being chosen. Alternatively, the attorneys could bid on the amount that the plaintiff would get without sharing, with 35% of any amount over that recovery being shared with the attorney.

Another difficulty with auctions in this environment is that the best attorneys tend to be the most expensive, which makes the bidding on shares problematic. The award of 60% obtained by good attorneys will often dominate the award of 75% obtained by mediocre attorneys. Fixing the attorney's share and letting the attorneys bid on the amount that will not be shared avoids the problem of comparisons.

EXECUTIVE SUMMARY—AUCTIONS

- The English auction, in which prices rise until only one bidder is left, and the sealed-bid auction, in which the highest bidder is chosen, are the two most popular auction formats.
- A strategy for bidding in repeated auction situations is to compute the empirical distribution of bids and optimize against this distribution.
- A difficulty in knowing how much to bid, or the propensity for the firm most overestimating the value to win the bidding, is the "winner's curse."
- Estimated values need to be corrected to avoid the winner's curse. This correction must be larger the more bidders there are or the greater the variance of information is.
- The design of auctions and selling mechanisms should fit the circumstances. It is useful to:

  Reveal information about value to mitigate the winner's curse.

  Conceal information about the extent of competition.

Impose a reserve price or minimum bid.
Sell multiple items in a simultaneous ascending auction.
Handicap bidders with a known advantage.

- Collusion is common in some auctions. Means of minimizing collusion include using sealed-bid auctions, bundling infrequent sales, maintaining higher reserves, encouraging potential entrants, keeping bidder identities secret, and contacting the Department of Justice.

13

Signaling

A CEO advised me to never hire someone who (1) wears a bow tie, (2) smokes a pipe, or (3) has a beard. In all three cases, the offending action was not a direct problem, but rather the CEO thought that the choice signaled other aspects of the candidate's personality. In particular, "people with bow ties are fussy, ineffectual people," "pipe smokers are reflective, *can't-do* sort of people," and "people with beards tend to be academic, rather than action oriented." While these generalizations clearly are not true about many people, bow ties, pipes, and beards are much more common among ivory-tower academics than among successful business executives. Bow ties, pipes, and beards signal characteristics of people, and are often *chosen* to signal some aspect of the individual.

Signaling is pervasive in business; virtually every choice reveals something about the chooser. This chapter is devoted to a few examples of signaling, along with a modicum of theory to help decode signals.[1]

SIGNALING IN ACTION

I was going to have cosmetic surgery until I noticed that the doctor's office was full of portraits by Picasso.

—Rita Rudner

Law Firms' Marbled Buildings

Clients told me that because I was on the main drag in the business district, they thought I was much more serious about my practice.

—Attorney Jack Chrisomalis[2]

Successful law firms spend a lot on appearances. They install marble floors and tables, have immaculate carpets and large libraries with beautiful shelves, and generally devote a great deal of money to the appearance of their offices. This money is not spent so that the working conditions are nice—that is a minor feature, and indeed many very successful law firms have a rabbit warren of standard offices that clients never see. Moreover, corporate clients themselves typically employ spartan accommodations, relative to their attorneys. The purpose of the richly appointed law office is to imply, "We are a successful firm. A less successful firm could not afford, or would not choose to afford, these fine offices."

An inherent feature of signaling is that the law firm does not have a choice about the signal sent by its offices. The choice of plain offices signals a less successful firm. The attorney whose office is located upstairs above the feed store in London, Ontario, looks like a failure before he arrives in court. Thus, a firm does not get a choice to not signal—its office choice must signal quality to prospective clients, no matter what the quality of the attorneys.

Insurance companies and banks often own very expensive office towers, with their name prominently displayed on the building. The purpose of these grandiose buildings is to signal that the company will be around for a long time. A large building implicitly says, "We are a large, successful company and can pay our obligations in the future." The company need not occupy the entire building; indeed, it is best if the company owns the building but occupies only a small fraction of it, so that the rented building space is a visible asset of the company. As both banks and insurance companies rely on customers trusting that the company can pay them in the future, both have a need to signal their reliability.

Service Plans and Warranties

American consumers lost faith in automaker Audi in the late 1970s because of a series of actual and reported problems with Audi cars. In response, Audi introduced the "Audi card," a "bumper-to-bumper" warranty that insures the customer against virtually all problems. The Audi card certainly increased Audi sales. While the Audi card has the direct effect of insuring the car buyer against mechanical defects, such a strong warranty also makes the statement that the car is quite reliable or else Audi could not afford to issue this warranty in the first place. The Audi card helped improve Audi's reputation in the United States, although its reputation foundered again on later reports that the four-wheel-drive Audis flipped on dry pavement.

Sears's Craftsman-brand tools enjoy a very strong reputation for quality. This reputation arises almost entirely from the warranty, which is unlimited. Indeed, Sears used to run a television advertisement featuring a middle-aged man returning a wrench to Sears for the guaranteed replacement; the wrench had been purchased by the man's father many decades before. The warranty is so strong that, in consumers' minds, Sears could not afford to offer it unless the tools very rarely broke.

Many replacement car batteries have a lifetime warranty, in which lifetime is usually defined as "for as long as you own your car." Lifetime batteries are not significantly different in construction from three-year batteries, and indeed the lifetime warranty is based on a simple actuarial proposition. The battery buyer rarely needs replacement if the battery lasts the usual four years, because the car has been sold by the time the battery fails. Nevertheless, lifetime batteries are generally perceived to be of higher quality and are sold that way.

Warranties signal quality, because warranties are more expensive to offer when the product is of poor quality. Suppose, for example, that a high-quality battery fails 5% of the time and costs $50.00 to manufacture, while the low quality battery fails 20% of the time and costs $45.00 to make. With the warranty, the average cost of replacement is $2.50 (5% of $50) for the high-quality battery, and $9.00 (20% of $45) for the low-quality battery. Thus, the high-quality battery, bundled with a full replacement warranty, costs $52.50, while the low-quality battery with a full warranty costs $54.00. At a price of $53.99, the seller of the high-quality battery can drive the seller of the low-quality battery out of business. The higher price signals to consumers that the battery must be of high quality because the seller of a low-quality battery cannot compete at that price. The major point is that higher quality reduces the cost of offering a warranty, providing a pricing mechanism for signaling high quality—the pricing of the warranty.

The signaling value of warranties is used with most car sales. Most car companies offer long warranty periods with extensive coverage, and many subsidize the extended warranty coverage. In addition to directly protecting consumers, these extensive warranties signal that cars are well made. This signaling of reliability is important because the financial cost (which is covered by the warranty) of unreliability is a small part of the total cost of unreliability. In addition to paying for repairs, consumers are without transportation while the car is dysfunctional, may have to rent a car while the car is being repaired, and possibly get stranded in an undesirable location. Indeed, Mercedes and Lexus have gone to the extreme of claiming they will come and get you wherever your car breaks down—adding roadside assistance to the warranty. Signaling reliability via warranties is most important when most of the cost of unreliability is uninsurable, as with automobiles.

Korean automaker Hyundai experienced significant success with its warranty. After some success in selling to the U.S. market in the late 1980s, Hyundai's sales slipped. It developed a reputation for low quality, and by 1997 its sales had slipped to the 1985 level. Starting in 1999, Hyundai introduced a ten-year warranty on engines and transmissions, the highest in the industry. At the same time, Hyundai added many former options as standard equipment and reduced its discounting of its cars. This worked very well, and sales in 1999 increased 82%, and sales in 2000 were up a further 49%. According to Hyundai buyer Ezra Rogers Jr., the warranty made the difference. "I saw it on TV and figured they must think pretty highly of their products to do that."[3]

The $25,000 Rolex Watch

> Clothes make the man. Naked people have little or no influence on society.
>
> **—Mark Twain**

People spend a great deal of time and money on their appearance. Appearance sends a strong signal of personal characteristics, because in many cases appearance provides the first impression that others receive. A great many things are signaled by appearance; this chapter began with the view that bow ties, beards, and pipes signal an ivory tower, academic lifestyle.

Usually, however, people attempt to signal wealth. Tanned skin signals a life of relaxation in the sun. This is a remarkable turnabout, as a century ago tanned skin signaled outdoor labor, while untanned skin signaled wealth. Similarly, thinness is viewed as attractive in Western culture, but is not in other cultures where large body weight signals wealth. Even in America, thinness used to be a signal of tuberculosis or other maladies. Mercedes automobiles, Mont Blanc pens, and Armani suits are also signals of wealth. Having a BMW signals a more active, fast driver than one with a Mercedes, and BMW's marketing—more power to the powerful—reinforces that image. Mont Blanc implicitly proclaims "Attorney at Law."

In the early 1950s, the steel wristwatch made by Rolex was the watch of choice for army officers. Its near indestructibility was useful to military officers who were placed in adverse conditions. Through this means, the Rolex acquired a reputation as a rugged watch worn by professionals, which attracted other recreational outdoor buyers like rock climbers and yachtsmen. After this point, the intrinsic quality of a Rolex ceased to matter significantly; the watch turned into a signal of a rugged life, and increasingly was worn by those who spent most of their time at a desk. Rolex changed the product with the changing clientele, adding solid gold and diamonds and eventually creating a watch that could be afforded only by the very wealthy. Rolex no longer signals the rugged military officer, although you will still find a few officers wearing steel Rolexes. Instead, the new Rolex is now the quintessential signal of extreme wealth.

Body Language

How should you interpret the dress, style, and actions of corporate leaders? In the 2001 NASDAQ crash, analysts struggle to estimate the prospects of former high-flying executives. *Business Week* suggests some interpretations of high-tech leaders.[4]

Cisco Systems CEO John Chambers's unruly forelock suggests, "Who has time to comb? I'm acquiring companies at such a furious rate that even my hair is whipped about." Amazon CEO Jeff Bezos, in trademark relaxed clothes and sloppy grin, is dressed to amble. In contrast, precision grooming signifies unflappable control. Hewlett-Packard CEO Carly Fiorina's perfectly applied lipstick is evidence of her precise approach to administration. Similarly, Oracle CEO Larry Ellison's impeccably trimmed beard signals his overall competence. Some signaling is unintentional, however. In meetings with analysts, the remarkable number of times Xerox executives needed bathroom breaks suggested corporate, not bladder, problems to the analysts.

Apple CEO Steve Jobs, affecting John Lennon's post-Beatles inscrutability, with fingertips pressed together, sardonic smile, and minimalist eyeglasses, is a master of the if-you-knew-what-I-knew approach to inflating stock prices. The Zen approach—technology that will change the world is coming, so invest now—sent Apple's stock price skyrocketing and the technology was . . . pastel color. Yes, pastel. Not a PC killer, but a soothing cup-of-tea approach to computing. This hyperbole by Apple should have prepared us for the Deka Research mystery invention, known as Ginger, or IT. Variously rumored to be an inexhaustible energy source or a Star-trek-quality flying machine like the Solo Trek™ XFV™ (pictured in fig. 13.1 on the right), which was so revolutionary that the reconstruction of American cities to fit the invention would immediately follow, Ginger caught the attention and imagination of some of the nations' leading futurists and technologists. But Ginger, or IT, turned out to be a . . . scooter. (See patent pictures in fig. 13.1 left and center.) It's a scooter. Yes, a scooter. Looks like fun. It's a scooter. Let's start building new cities now.

Education

The original theory of signaling arose in the context of education, and the application remains significant. What is the value of a Harvard diploma? An M.B.A. from the University of Chicago?

Diplomas from prestigious universities clearly convey more than the content of the courses taken. According to the signaling theory, universities serve a twofold screening role. First, admission to the university is itself a screen—admission demonstrates credentials, either academic or friends in high places. Such a screen, however, does not require graduation. Indeed, the efficient means of providing the admission screen is a certification process. One could run an admissions-only university and save the costs of buildings, faculty, and staff other than admissions of-

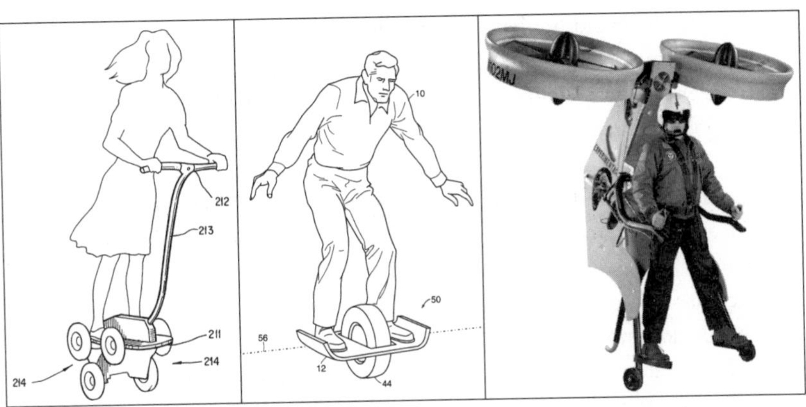

Figure 13.1. Two examples from the Ginger patent application (left and center) and the Solotrek™ XFV™ at right. *Source:* SoloTrek photo courtesy of Millennium Jet, Inc., Sunnyvale, Calif. © 2001. All rights reserved. www.solotrek.com.

ficers. Admission to a prestigious university is a weak signal; generally, employers are looking for *graduation* from, rather than admission to, that university. The diploma, rather than the admissions process, is the valuable commodity.

The second form of screening provided by universities is through grades and graduation. The basis of the theory is the desire of employers to know a difficult-to-observe characteristic of potential employees. How talented are they? How flexible are their minds? Will they do what it takes to succeed? Talented students are willing to work very hard to show employers how talented they are, and therefore they obtain better jobs.

According to signaling theory, students will segregate by major, with the most talented students working very hard to obtain As in difficult subjects, intermediate students earning Bs or lower in difficult subjects or As in easier subjects, and the weaker students earning low grades in relatively straightforward subjects. Thus, students will choose both discipline and a studying strategy and, by doing so, reveal how easy learning is for the student. Students will signal their ability by the courses they take and the grades they produce. Weaker students might be able to produce high grades in difficult subjects, but only at a personal cost that is too high to be worthwhile. In such a way, the university produces publicly observable information about difficult-to-observe characteristics of its students. The students reveal their talent by their performance.

The signaling theory of education is straightforward. Better students find it easier to obtain good grades, and thus good grades, in the appropriate field, signal better job applicants. The interesting and peculiar aspect of educational signaling is that the students did not have to actually learn anything useful in order to succeed in signaling. The key to signaling is to choose an activity, or field of study, that is easier for the desirable type than for the less desirable type of student. For the selection of management trainees, there is no reason the activity cannot be mastering ancient Greek or modern astronomy, provided that the most desirable future managers will find these subjects easier than others.* Making the study useful, in fact, can be positively harmful, if the most desirable type finds the subject so tedious that they do not perform well.†

Of course, it is desirable to make the subject of study useful, provided that the direct value does not undercut the value of signaling too much. Moreover, when one wants to select focused managers, the coursework should facilitate this selection, which is probably the reason for the bias against abstract thinking that dominates some business schools. The general message of signaling for education is that what matters is not what is taught, but who excels at what is taught. Perhaps it is not an accident that the originator of the theory, Nobel laureate Michael Spence, went on to become the Dean of Stanford University's Graduate School of Business.

He's an Unqualified Success

When a plane lands, the flight attendant typically says, "I'd like to be the first to welcome you to . . ." Notice that the flight attendant has not welcomed you, just expressed a desire to do so. Robert Thornton, professor of economics at Lehigh University in Bethlehem, Pennsylvania, has compiled a list—the "Lexicon of Inconspicuously Ambiguous Recommendations" (LIAR)—of useful phrases for letters of recommendation for marginally qualified or unqualified candidates. Thornton's listing in the American Economic Association gives his specialty as Public Employee Bargaining. Some examples from LIAR:

For a lazy candidate: In my opinion, you will be very fortunate to get this person to work for you.

To describe a person who is totally inept: I most enthusiastically recommend this candidate with no qualifications whatsoever.

To describe an ex-employee who had problems getting along with fellow workers: I am pleased to say that this candidate is a former colleague of mine.

*Of all majors, classics and astronomy attract students with the highest combined SAT scores.

†Too much education is usually viewed as a negative signal—some people are never ready for real life. In Siberia, marriage was generally accompanied by a "negative dowry," in that the husband's family provided the dowry. The dowry depended on many things but in particular on the educational attainment of the bride; the highest dowries were associated with a master's degree, and lower dowries with a Ph.D. However, this difference might be attributed to the older age of Ph.D.s.

To describe a candidate who is so unproductive that the job would be better left unfilled: I can assure you that no person would be better for the job.

To describe a job applicant who is not worth further consideration: I would urge you to waste no time in making this candidate an offer of employment.

To describe a person with lackluster credentials: All in all, I cannot say enough good things about this candidate or recommend him too highly.

Count the Pages

> If you haven't got anything nice to say about anybody,
> come sit next to me.
> **—Alice Roosevelt Longworth**

In the economics profession, it is rare to encounter a truly negative letter of recommendation. This politeness may be a result of a general fear of lawsuits, or a remnant of a more civil history. In either case, economists must read between the lines to decode the actual opinion of the writer. Terms like "workmanlike" and "pedestrian" clearly indicate the subject of the letter is uninspired at best. Even "works very hard" can be a condemnation, at least when there is no corresponding success. Then, working hard is a polite way to say that even hard work does not compensate for the candidate's deficiencies.

Such politeness masks intentional manipulation by some letter writers, who describe their own students as being better than they are. Such attempts to manipulate the letter-writing process have led to a pure signaling, and quite jaded, interpretation of letters: count the pages. This theory holds that what is written is irrelevant—the writer can *say* anything. However, it is arduous to write a coherent, thoughtful, long letter of recommendation, so that writers will not write long letters except for very good candidates. In this view, the length of the letter is the best guide to the enthusiasm of the writer for the candidate.

Full Product Line

Many firms feel a need to offer a full product line, and a full product line is often seen as a significant competitive advantage. A basic reason that having a full product line is valuable is that customers prefer one-stop shopping because it minimizes their costs. One-stop shopping is important for goods like OSHA-approved safety equipment, and it provides 3M with a significant advantage. For a firm, a full product line can also offer the ability to create and exploit synergies between products. For example, most makers of televisions and stereo equipment have proprietary interconnections, so that different components of the stereo equipment are coordinated (e.g., turning on the CD turns on the stereo receiver, pushing the record button on the tape deck starts play on the CD, turning on the DVD player switches the TV to digital input), and all the units are controlled with the same remote. Such a system creates value and lock in simultaneously. For example, the purchase of a Sony receiver makes other Sony components offer better value.

A full product line also sends a signal. A firm that is not certain whether it can profitably compete on a group of products may test the waters with a single entry. A firm that has inadequate capital introduces one product to see if the market will sustain it, hoping to grow enough to offer additional products. Currently, many of the dot.coms are exiting, having failed to achieve profitability before running out of startup funds. (For example, Toysmart has failed, in spite of massive initial funding.) In each case, the firm has a significant probability of exit, either because the firm was not competitive, or because it could not get an adequate toehold before funding ran out. Consequently, single-product entry sends a signal of lack of commitment to a marketplace, because typically the firms that exit are the single-product entrants. Therefore, entry with a full product line signals a commitment to the market.[5]

Customers generally value a commitment to the market, because the customer wants future service, upgrades, and replacement parts that require the firm to remain in the industry. Software giant Computer Associates (CA) has been seriously injured by a perception that it does not support old products, ones that CA viewed as obsolete but some customers are still using. CA's aggressive acquisition strategy has left many customers injured by the lack of support for products that the customer bought from a firm later acquired by CA. The effect of such surprise obsolescence is that CA has relative difficulty selling many of its new products, because of customers' fears that the product will not be supported.*

A full product line signals a commitment to the industry, and often has value well beyond convenience factors like one-stop shopping. Moreover, failing to keep up with the advance of technology, by falling behind on the full product line, can be a signal that the firm is exiting the business using a "harvest" strategy. Therefore, it is often necessary not only to enter with a large product line, but to stay abreast of current technological developments. Flagship products, like the Chevrolet Corvette and the Philips flat-screen TV, perform a major role as signals of technological supremacy. These products build confidence in the more pedestrian, mass-market products where the serious money is made.

Indeed, much of the malaise of the American automobile industry has less to

*The problem of creating commitment is parodied by Groucho Marx: "Those are my principles. If you don't like them, well, I have others."

do with creating small, inexpensive cars than with technological superiority. The American companies have ceded technological superiority at the upper end to Mercedes (luxury), Porsche (performance), and BMW, and ceded superior reliability to Japan. The loss at the top end has cast a shadow on the rest of the product lines. The argument of some authors that environmental restrictions are the culprits is unconvincing, as imports have met these standards as well. Problems in creating small cars are a symptom of Detroit's failure to keep up technologically, not the cause. Even with all the problems, however, import penetration has remained modest, so that the perceived societal problem was overblown. What was lost was the premium American companies could earn on their cars, not the ability to sell cars.

Appearing Informed in an Auction

Information has value in an auction environment. By reducing the risk of overpaying, well-informed bidders can bid more aggressively and win the item at a good price with greater frequency. Moreover, information has value in softening the bidding of rational competitors. Even if you are poorly informed, it generally pays to appear well informed.

As noted in chapter 10, the optimal response in an auction to facing a well-informed bidder is generally to bid less. Facing an informed bidder means that winning can be very bad news—the informed bidder chose to lose! Consequently, it pays to appear well informed. This will cause rational opponents to weaken their bidding strategy, thus softening price competition.

There are a variety of ways of appearing well informed. Jump bids may proclaim, "I know a lot about the item for sale, so I am willing to bid a lot by myself." The method of inspecting items at antiques auctions can also signal expertise. Casual chat prior to the auction may signal expertise as well. If you are not well informed, you may want to stay out of the auction, or employ an agent to bid for you. An agent has the advantage of being unknown to other bidders, which is generally preferable to a bidder known to be poorly informed.

Tylenol Recall

In the fall of 1982, seven people died mysteriously on Chicago's West Side, three of them in the same home.[6] Two off-duty firemen, listening to police radios, realized that Johnson & Johnson's pain reliever Tylenol was mentioned in two of the incidents. After some discussion, they alerted authorities, who quickly found that the deaths occurred because of Extra Strength Tylenol laced with 65 milligrams of cyanide, approximately 10,000 times more than is necessary to kill a person.

Police in Chicago broadcast the news of the poisoned Tylenol over local television and, using loudspeakers attached to police cars, driving throughout Chicago. Johnson & Johnson, along with its McNeil subsidiary that manufactured Tylenol, advised that the tampering had not occurred at its plants, and authorities concluded that the tampering of the Tylenol, from four different batches and from five different stores, had occurred after the product reached Chicago. Nevertheless, reports of poisoned Tylenol created a nationwide hysteria. The hysteria also prompted copycats, with at least thirty-six cases of confirmed product tampering.

The view of the nation was that Tylenol was a dead product. According to advertising expert Jerry Della Femina, "There may be an advertising person who thinks he can solve this and if they find him, I want to hire him, because then I want him to turn our water cooler into a wine cooler" (Kaplan, "The Tylenol Crisis").

Johnson & Johnson's response to the crisis has become the benchmark by which all other business crisis responses are measured. Johnson & Johnson took action in two distinct phases. The first focused on customer safety. From the start of the crisis, Johnson & Johnson was very forthcoming with police, honest with the press, and never attempted to avoid blame.* It posted a $100,000 reward for information leading to the capture of the poisoner. A week after it became clear that Tylenol was the poisoned product, Johnson & Johnson recalled 31 million bottles of Tylenol products, at a cost of over $100 million. (Johnson & Johnson delayed the decision to recall all Tylenol products partly out of fears that the killer or killers might begin lacing other products instead.) Finally, Johnson & Johnson offered to exchange all purchased Tylenol capsules for Tylenol tablets.

Planning for the second phase, to restore Tylenol's previous 37% market share, began even as the first phase of protecting the customers was being implemented. Triple-seal, tamper-resistant containers were designed and introduced, along with discount coupons worth up to 25% of the purchase price. A critical role in the comeback of Tylenol was performed by the media, which provided a great deal of free publicity concerning the reintroduction of Tylenol, and praised the way the company acted during the crisis. The company's concern for its customers during the crisis, and the forthright way that it acted, signaled a high degree of care, which made it believable that the reintroduced product was, in fact, safe. Indeed, press coverage of the three security features of the new product container (glued box flaps that rip when opened, shrink-wrapped plastic seal over the bottle cap, and an inner foil seal over the mouth of the bottle) was much more persuasive to customers than claims by the company due to the perceived impartiality of the press. Moreover, the press coverage occurred without charge.

*In contrast, Perrier claimed that benzene found in some North American bottles of its water was the result of an isolated incident and recalled only a small portion of its stock. It was later embarrassed to have to institute a worldwide recall, after benzene was found in European bottles as well. Perrier was harshly criticized by the press.

Recovering from the Tylenol poisoning crisis was expensive, costing the company well over $100 million. However, the company came out of the crisis with the trust and respect of its customers, a critical asset of a company selling health-care products. Indeed, an alternative course of action not only would have cost the company the Tylenol brand but would have tainted their other products, such as baby shampoo. The signaling aspect of the hard decision to take responsibility, even when it was not clear where responsibility lay, mitigated the cost of the recovery substantially, by making the company's later claims credible with the press and the public.

Was it good business for Johnson & Johnson to expend so much money to save the Tylenol brand? An important implication of the signaling model was that the Tylenol brand was not the only product at risk: Johnson & Johnson's entire reputation for quality and safety was on the line during the crisis, and a misstep could have done tremendous damage to Johnson & Johnson's other products. Thus, even if saving Tylenol were not profitable by itself (although it almost certainly was profitable), the rest of the Johnson & Johnson line could have been seriously injured, had the company not acted in the fashion that it chose.

In contrast to Johnson & Johnson, computer processor manufacturer Intel's handling of the Pentium floating-point division problem, also known as the Pentium bug, is a model for how not to handle a crisis. In November 1994, mathematician Thomas Nicely asked colleagues to check some computer calculations he had made, which were coming out with errors.[7] The colleagues found that the new Pentium processors were consistently making division errors, and the problem quickly became public. Intel admitted that it had known about the problem since June 1994, but argued that the problem was rare, and that for most users the processor did not need to be replaced. Pentium owners concerned about the problem were encouraged to contact Intel and discuss the problem with them; Intel would agree to replace processors when it might matter, such as with complex scientific calculations. Sometime later, Intel admitted that it was "quietly" offering to replace the processors.

The Pentium bug was actually caused by a software problem. Processors have extensive software, which is embedded in the processor itself. The method by which the Pentium processor performed division had been inaccurately programmed. Essentially, a Pentium does long division by a means of successive approximations (getting successively close to the actual answer), and five of the 1,066 components of the methods were incorrectly specified. (In fact, these five were not specified at all, which meant they were set at zero when they should have all been two.) Because of the nature of the misspecified components, the problem could affect only the fourth significant digit—for example, in the number 123,456.789, the numbers after 3 could be erroneous. Intel said that such problems would arise only once in 27,000 years of constant spreadsheet calculations, partly because spreadsheets rarely employ high accuracy. IBM, which yanked Pentium processors from its personal computers the same day the problem was discovered, said the problem could arise as often as every twenty-four days.* IBM was by no means impartial in this debate, as it was a cosponsor of the PowerPC processor, which was intended to compete with the Intel Pentium, and thus IBM could well benefit from bad press for the Intel processor.

Intel clearly ignored the important confidence aspect of the calculation problem by not acknowledging the problem voluntarily. Customers naturally wondered what other calculation problems existed in the processors. Moreover, Intel indicated that it could not be trusted to admit flaws in its circuits, so that customers cannot fully believe Intel when it says there is no problem. While Intel's dominance of processors for personal computers was not destroyed by the poor handling of the Pentium bug, the bad publicity and loss of faith in Intel likely contributed to the success of the competing AMD Athlon processor. After all, if the Pentium has bugs, why pay more for it?

Fast-food retailer Jack in the Box illustrates how even a slight delay in taking responsibility can send a terrible signal to the market. In January 1993, a Jack in the Box restaurant in Seattle, Washington, had an *Escherichia coli* outbreak, leading to three children dying and hundreds of people being hospitalized. In the initial shock, the company failed to react quickly.

After a supplier was identified as the source of the tainted meat, it took Jack in the Box two days to remove meat from its stores. It then shut down the stores until the employees had been trained how to grill a hamburger properly and thoroughly. Moreover, there was some attempt to blame inadequate government inspection rather than to accept responsibility for the problem and take immediate action to solve the problem. The lack of public and media confidence in the company created by the relatively brief delay in responding to the crisis was nearly fatal to the company, which lost $138 million over two years, and saw its bonds downgraded to junk-bond status.

To remedy the problem, Jack in the Box started an extensive meat-handling training program and hired a world-class microbiologist, David Theno, to become vice president of quality assurance and product safety. Theno made a number of changes based on his hazard analysis critical control points (HACCP) system, which is considered the best safety analysis methodology in the fast-food industry. In particular, chimes ring hourly to remind employees to wash their hands, and cooks cut into every hamburger to check that it has been cooked properly. Simple devices like sanitized tongs for handling meat make a significant difference.

*A major difference arose out of the meaning of "constant use" and what a typical spreadsheet does, with Intel assuming 1,000 floating-point divisions per day to IBM's estimate of 4.2 million.

David Theno was a key instrument in Jack in the Box's recovery. He established his own personal credibility with the media. He was forthright with the media, and even helped various members of the media report on other issues in food safety. Moreover, Jack in the Box invested in food safety, equipment, and research, including the development of the HAACP system. Not surprisingly, the nature of media reporting became much more helpful to Jack in the Box. The reaction of the media has been similar to Johnson & Johnson's experience, although Johnson & Johnson established credibility much more quickly, while it took years for Jack in the Box, because of a two-day delay in responding appropriately to the crisis.

While the effects of a company's actions on consumers can have a major impact on profits, there are sometimes large and significant direct effects as well. When U.S. District Court judge Jed Rakoff found Internet music distributor MP3.com guilty of willful copyright infringement for providing copyrighted music on its Web site on 5 September 2000, he could have set a penalty as high as \$150,000 per illegally copied compact disc. Instead, Judge Rakoff chose a more moderate penalty of \$25,000, citing the responsible behavior of the company over the preceding four months and the character of MP3.com's CEO, Michael Robertson, who "shunned the kind of lawless piracy seemingly characteristic of some others operating in this area."

LEMONS

An economist I will call RJM had a twenty-year-old rusty Mercedes to sell, and advertised it in the local paper, asking \$1800. The Mercedes had obvious problems—the three-pointed star had fallen off the hood, and the gas pedal was missing. A potential buyer came by, inspected the car in some detail, pointed out the obvious flaws to RJM, and offered \$1200. After a modicum of dickering, they settled on \$1500, at which point the buyer said he would return for the car the next day. RJM said, "Why don't you take it now?" to which the buyer responded, "You mean it runs?"

Investment banks generally prohibit top company officials and venture capitalists from selling stock for 180 days after an initial public offering (IPO), although the number of days varies from 90 to over 1,000. This period, known as lockup, protects the stock from major selling by insiders early in the setting of the price. As a consequence, however, at the expiration of lockup the stock is watched intensively by investors. A major sell-off by company officials signals that the insiders think the company is overvalued, and such a signal can cause the stock price to plummet. WebMethods, an Internet stock, fell 50% over the three weeks prior to its lockup expiration. Many stocks fall 10% to 15% around the expiration of lockup. Major sales by insiders, of course, raise the fear that the insiders know

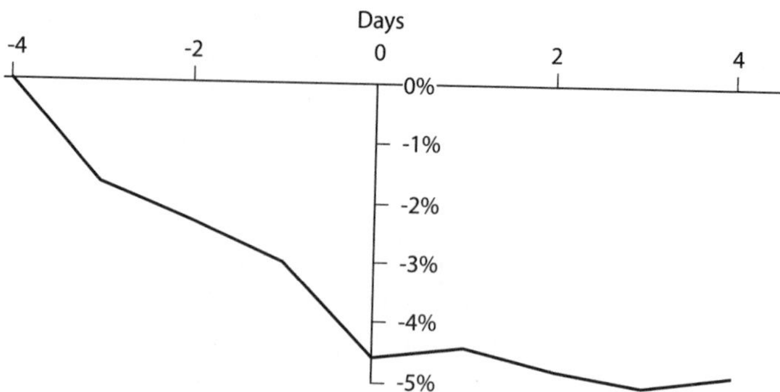

Figure 13.2. Stock performance before and after lockup expiration.

something relevant to the value of the stock, and that, moreover, what they know makes them want to sell at this price.

Prices tend to fall prior to lockup and continue to fall, although some rise. It is clear that unexpectedly large selling increases the fall. The market reacts to the signal that insiders are betting against the company. Figure 13.2 presents some data on lockup that was published in *The Standard*.[8] Prices fell around 5% in the few days prior to the lockup expiration, and remained at that level through the lockup expiration.

The fall in share prices as the lockup expires is a mystery not explained by the information revealed by insider sales. Indeed, as the date of the lockup expiration is public information, the market price should adjust to account for the average fall; what remains should be zero on average, with a larger fall or a smaller rise as more shares are or are not tendered by management. Someone is making a mistake. The evidence that larger sales by management create a larger fall in prices is weak. If larger sales significantly reduce stock prices, much of the effect is anticipated and does not occur in the days around the lockup expiration. As a practical matter, insiders rarely sell when the lockup expires, so there is scant data. That insiders rarely sell makes the negative returns even more mysterious—the market is reacting significantly to an event that does not even arise frequently.

In the case of RJM's car, and the case of insider sales, the willingness to trade signaled value. In both cases, buyers adjust their expectation of the value of the good for sale based on the owner's willingness to sell it.[9] This phenomenon is the same as the winner's curse, and might be called the buyer's curse: if the seller is willing to sell, obviously the seller values the good less than the offered price. When the seller has useful information about the actual value of the good, as arises with used cars and stock sold by insiders, the willingness to trade at a certain price can be a very negative signal about value.

Reverse Splits

A reverse split is the opposite of a stock split. In a typical example, ten shares are merged into one. For example, Musicmaker.com did a ten-to-one reverse split on 3 November 2000, and shareholders received one share for every ten they held. Reverse splits are used to keep share prices above $1, which is a NASDAQ requirement. After a company's share price trades below $1 for a thirty-day period, a company has ninety days to get its share price above $1 for at least ten consecutive days. If it fails to do so, it is delisted from the NASDAQ.

Reverse splits are generally treated by the market as bad news. For example, Musicmaker.com's share price was $.34 prior to its ten-to-one reverse split, and fell to $2.59 after the reverse split, a decline of over 25%.

According to Kenneth Yoon, a partner at Holland & Knight LLP, "Investors interpret a reverse stock split as a management expectation that their stock will go down, and that's why they are doing it, to avoid a delisting. A smart investor will then see it as not changing the value of the company. But, instead, it might be seen as saying something about the management."

It should be at least somewhat mysterious why a reverse split should depress share prices. After all, the fact that the price was near or below $1 is public information. A partial explanation for the phenomenon is that a reverse split shows that management has nothing "up its sleeve" to announce that would bring the price back up over $1. The announcement of a reverse split essentially proclaims, "We have no good news on the horizon," and no good news is, of course, bad news.

A second aspect of the reverse stock split is that firms with significant cash holdings might instead try to buy back shares as a way of boosting the price. Buybacks generally are treated as good news—management is making a statement that it thinks its shares are undervalued, and that a good use of firm investment funds is investing in the firm itself. Thus, the failure to buy back shares essentially says, "Either we lack the capital to buy back shares, or we don't think our shares are a good investment." Both of these explanations are bad news about future share value.

The ratchet effect (chapter 8) operates in the reverse split. Since investors see reverse splits as bad news, management avoids them if possible. Consequently, only very distressed firms will engage in reverse splits, so that on average the firms adopting a reverse split are in much more dire circumstances than firms who do not adopt it. This desire to avoid a reverse split exacerbates the bad-news component of such an announcement.[10]

Offers made in an attempt to settle lawsuits can have much the same problem as that arising in insider sales—a high offer may signal a high willingness to pay by a defendant. In this case, there is a partial solution known as a settlement escrow, discussed in chapter 14. In the case of used cars, used-car dealers use warranties and their reputations to mitigate the "lemons" problem. The sellers generally include most or all of the owners of lemons, while those with a good car hold on to the car a long time. Given the reputation of used-car dealers, providing warranties and reputations meets with mixed results.

There is an ass for every seat.
—Motto of a Gainesville, Florida, used-car dealer

In the case of repeat purchases, however, a variety of other tricks are available to mitigate or eliminate the problem that a willingness to sell signals poor quality. These tricks include introductory offers, trial use, and advertising blitzes.

INTRODUCTORY OFFERS AND ADVERTISING

You make a grown man cry.
—The Rolling Stones, singing on behalf of Microsoft's Windows 95 introduction[11]

An important way to signal product quality is to provide the product, temporarily, at negligible or low cost.

Around 20,000 Web sites advertise introductory offers on products and services, including some unexpected ones such as artery cleaner, Celtic sea salt, stolen Social Security numbers, frozen horse semen, group dance lessons, public relations work, rain-forest preservation, high-school reunion advertising, geese repellant, higher-education human resources management, bulk plankton, dental crowns and bridgework, Web-based banking policy statements, business ethics training, and mathematics home schooling. Introductory offers are a powerful means of removing the financial risk to the customer of trying a new product.

A low introductory price, first and foremost, subsidizes the customer's experimentation with the product. Thus, when customers are uncertain about the quality of the product and leery of risking the purchase price to try the product, an initial low price reduces the risk to the customer. From the firm's perspective, initial losses are recouped either by repeat purchases or by word-of-mouth advertising. Thus, the key to an introductory offer is enhanced future business.

Consequently, introductory offers also send a signal that shows the firm's belief in the quality of its product. A firm with a shoddy product will not find that offering a very low introductory price is profitable, because a product offering poor value will not attract repeat business nor will it obtain word-of-mouth endorsement. For example, a restaurant with bad food may get customers initially, and more of them by using initial-discount coupons, but it will find its business drying up shortly thereafter. Because introductory offers are profitable for the firm only when the firm has a good product, introductory offers signal a good product.

The logic of introductory-offer signaling applies to expenditures other than price cuts. In particular, any conspicuous large spending by the firm associated with a new-product launch sends the signal, "We're spending all this money and obviously expect to recoup it with your later purchases." Thus, a firm that hires the Rolling Stones to sing for its new product, shoots fireworks across North America, and drops parachuters into major sporting events is implicitly saying to its customers:

> These are extravagant expenditures, and we wouldn't be able to recoup such largesse unless we have a superior product. Thus, based on our willingness to spend freely, you should believe that our product is very good.

The key to the signaling use of advertisements is whether a firm with a poor product would also choose to invest in such extravagant advertisements; that is, whether the firm with a poor product could recoup the expenditure if its poor product was *believed* to be good. If customers start out being convinced initially that a product has high quality, will its low quality be discovered quickly enough to negate the value of the initial advertisements? With the opening of a restaurant, a media blitz might convince many people to try the restaurant, but if the restaurant's quality is inadequate, few will return. The only way to recoup major advertising expenses with a poor-quality restaurant is with one-time customers, which is a bad bet. Thus, typically only restaurants that believe themselves to be offering high value will run major advertising campaigns.

Internet companies provided some of the more entertaining examples of spending large sums of money to attract attention. For example, Carorder.com gave out 50,000 $3 metro cards for the New York subway and paid the tolls, 100 cars at a time, for all area bridges. Drivers going through the toll saw two people holding a banner that read: "Your commute brought to you by Carorder.com." Charitycounts.com scattered 10,000 wallets on the streets of New York and San Francisco. Each wallet had a note inside reading: "If you were looking to get some free cash, shame on you. Redeem yourself by visiting Charitycounts.com."[12]

Why not just use introductory discounts to signal quality, since introductory offers have the major advantage of subsidizing experimentation by customers? A problem with setting a low introductory price is that low prices tend to signal poor quality: You get what you pay for.

Thus, starting by offering a low introductory price risks sending the message that the unprofitably low price is the normal price of the product. This is an adverse inference by itself, but, in addition, customers may see the low introductory price as a signal that the quality is also pretty low, especially when compared to competitors with higher established prices. When the goal is to convince the high-end customers that the product was the highest quality in the market, starting with a low introductory price is likely worse than just charging a higher profitable price. Charging a profitable price, combined with a prominent advertising campaign illustrating the high quality of the product, sends the strong signal that the firm believes in the product sufficiently to risk the cost of a major advertising campaign.

Generally, such a major investment in marketing is necessary for the start of a product, to convince skeptical customers of the product's high quality. Continuing major investment in marketing, such as that employed by Coke and Pepsi, will not have an important signaling role. Instead, like most advertising, continuing advertisements are intended to associate the product with good feelings of one kind or another, and hence are primarily psychological in nature.

ENTRY DETERRENCE

An important use of signaling is to discourage entry. When a firm enjoys high profits, which usually would attract entry into the market, how can another firm be discouraged from entering? Firms will be discouraged if the incumbent's reaction to possible entry would be to significantly lower price, so low that the decision to enter would be unprofitable.[13] Generally, the idea of pricing to limit entry is to behave so that potential entrants could expect low postentry prices and would therefore be deterred from entering.

Charging a low price initially does not necessarily prevent entry. Just because a firm charges a low price to forestall entry, why should an entrant expect that the incumbent firms would not accommodate it? Once entry has occurred, the existing firms have a choice of accommodating an entrant and earning acceptable profits, or of setting new competitive prices, which would punish the entrant but mean lower profits for the existing firms. If entry has already occurred, the incumbent firms naturally should choose to accommodate. Once entry has occurred, the threat of having a price war is not credible.

If incumbent firms rationally would not start a price war in the event of entry, the price prior to entry is irrelevant. The pre-entry price does not signal anything about the postentry price and thus should be ignored by the entrant. An attempt to discourage the entrant by lowering prices should fail; if it enters, an entrant rationally can conclude that it will be accommodated. The entry decision is independent of the preentry price, which means an attempt to discourage entry fails.

There is a major problem with this logic, however. Existing prices are important signals about the profitability of the market. Why? Because prospective entrants are uncertain about the costs of incumbents, market demand, and the profitability of entry. A low pre-entry price signals either (1) that market conditions are unfavorable, (2) that the existing firm has very low costs, or (3) both. Either condition leads to lower profits for an entrant, discouraging entry.

There are two main conditions for low prices to work as a signal for entry deterrence. First, potential entrants must have significant uncertainty about the profitability of market entry, and be uncertain about the actions of incumbent firms. An incumbent firm's behavior can signal something about market conditions: the incumbent knows something the entrant does not know. Existing firms often know more about technology and the customer base than potential entrants, and either fact forms a basis for signaling. There is no reason, however, for existing firms to know more about macroeconomic fluctuations, interest rates, and the like than the entrant. The second condition is that there is some means of signaling the profitability, or lack thereof, of entry. The classic signal is price. If demand is weak, or if a firm has very low costs, the optimal price will be low. Thus a low price signals adverse market conditions, and a high price signals that the market is relatively attractive for entry.

Price is not the only signal of the attractiveness of market entry. If an incumbent company is building a new plant or distribution center, that signals that the market is growing and can likely hold more firms. If a company is investing heavily in R&D, that suggests that new products are on the horizon and that entering with a technologically superior product is a terrific way for a new firm to enter an industry. The extent of executive perks and compensation that an incumbent offers may also signal the degree of slack in the marketplace.

> If you cannot convince them, confuse them.
>
> **—Harry S. Truman**

Like the seller of a high-quality good, a low-cost firm wants to signal that it has low costs. The high-cost firm, in contrast, also wants to signal that it has low costs. The high-cost firm wants to mimic the behavior of a low-cost firm to create confusion in the mind of a potential entrant. To deter entry, the low-cost firm, in contrast, wants to demonstrate that it does have low costs. Thus, a high-cost firm wants to behave in the manner in which a low-cost firm would choose to behave. A firm that actually has low costs, however, wants to demonstrate that its costs really are low.

A convincing demonstration of having low costs is for a company to set a price so low that a high-cost firm would be better off with the new company's entry than with the low price. A low-cost firm demonstrates its low cost by setting a price below what a high-cost firm would ever offer. Notice that it may be necessary to set a price much lower than the profit-maximizing price to signal low cost. The price must be so low that a higher cost firm will not choose to mimic the low-cost firm's strategy, but will prefer to earn short-run profits and suffer entry instead. Such a low price may be substantially less than the level that maximizes a low-cost firm's profits.

LEADERSHIP

Almost everything a leader does is a signal. Any time they appeared in public, the leadership of the USSR was scrutinized by Western observers—for example, who was standing next to the premier during the May Day parade?—to deduce who was in favor and who was falling out of favor. Signaling plays a major role in leadership.

Signaling in leadership is exactly the opposite of signaling to deter entry—the leader wishes to encourage the followers to take action.[14] Conceptually, however, the two signals are closely related. Employees will work hard if the returns for working hard are very high. Unfortunately, the returns for hard work often come years in the future and are not easily observed. How could a young Michael Dell convince the first staff members of Dell Computer that they should work extraordinarily hard, so that their stock options would be worth millions of dollars and they would be "Dellionaires"?

The signaling approach suggests that Dell should behave as if it were true that the company would prosper. In particular, Dell himself should work very hard. Moreover, he should take most of his compensation in the form of stock. For the head of a company to give high base salaries would suggest skepticism about the future value of a company's stock. Most of the head's wealth should be in the form of company stock. Indeed, when insiders sell stock, the stock price often falls. Company heads who are confident about the company's future will not feel the need to diversity their portfolio, but instead will be comfortable holding a great deal of company stock.

Moreover, providing salary compensation in the form of stock options for employees is a way to find the right type of employee. Such risky means of compensation attracts those who believe in the firm and its products. They will value the options more highly than potential employees who do not believe in the future prosperity of the firm.

However, the problem of signaling is that even if the prospects of the company are only fair to poor, it may pay the company to fool employees into thinking that the company's prospects are good. The only way to signal this is for a head to work so hard to earn stock options that it would not make sense for a manager of a poor firm to imitate the strategy. (An extreme, yet not uncommon, example is the CEO who takes $1 in salary and the rest in options; this signals a very strong belief in the value of the options.) Working only moderately hard may send a signal that the company prospects are poor, since managers who believe in the company do work extremely hard.

ACTING TOUGH

There is a method in my madness.
—Hamlet

Entry deterrence is a matter of signaling that one is a strong competitor, and that entry will be unprofitable. Nuclear deterrence is a matter of signaling that aggressive acts will be met with retaliation. In both cases, the signalers are attempting to show that they will retaliate. In many situations, one wants to show that one is a tough type, one who does not yield. The chairman of the Federal Reserve Board of Governors wants to be perceived as staunchly anti-inflation, so that markets do not react to minor blips in the price level. A firm wishes to appear committed to an industry, so that customers do not fear future nonsupport. A bidder in an auction wishes to appear both very rich and very well informed. Firms attempt to convince the Environmental Protection Agency that certain proposed regulations will kill the industry. A kidnapper wants to convince a firm that he will kill the kidnapped executive if he does not receive the ransom. Those in bargaining situations want to convince the others that any reduction in their share will cause them to walk away from the deal. In all of these situations, people wish to appear tough, whether they are or not. Actual tough people have no difficulty in being tough, although they may still have difficulty appearing tough. How should a person who is not tough behave?[15]

Toughness depends on the situation. A firm negotiating with a labor union is toughest when it has high production costs, because increased labor costs will force its prices up, thereby decreasing demand for the firm's products. A firm with very low costs has room to absorb labor-union wage increases without significant price increases. In contrast, when negotiating with competitors (perhaps with implicit rather than explicit discussions) over market share, having low costs is an advantage, because the firm with low costs bears a smaller percentage of the cost of a price war than a firm with high costs. In either case, tough players are the ones that can insist on getting their own way. Negotiating with a labor union, a high-cost firm can credibly claim that it will be driven out of business if wages are not moderate. Thus, the labor union has little bargaining power with a high-cost firm. Negotiating with competitors, the low-cost firm is better off with a price war than with a small market share.

Generally, however, it is not clear to others whether one truly is tough, which is why signaling is important. Small things—not being available for a phone call, creating a plan to shut down a plant—may lead to major changes in beliefs in bargaining situations. For example, consider bargaining with a labor union. If the firm begins planning to shut down the factory, it signals that it cannot withstand a significant wage increase. The more that is expended in preparations to shut down, the stronger is the signal sent. If the firm has low costs, it is likely to reach agreement, and thus any expenditures on facility shut-down preparation are likely to create no direct benefit. Union leaders, understanding this logic, should get worried when they see extensive preparations to shut down the factory, although they will also understand that the preparations could be a bluff. Nevertheless, the preparations should make the leaders nervous and weaken their resolve to hold out for high wages.

The situation with the union versus the firm is symmetric—the union can signal its insistence on higher wages by preparing for a prolonged strike, by collecting a war chest (a very costly endeavor), and psychologically preparing the membership for a prolonged strike. The union leadership has an advantage in that it can to some extent remove the strike decision from its own hands. By requiring a majority of the membership to agree to a new contract, setting the stage for high demands, the union leadership can bind itself to rejecting low wages. Such a commitment can be very effective at forcing management to make concessions.

One common way of signaling toughness in negotiations is to be patient. Because a truly tough firm will not agree to anything but terms favorable to the firm, the tough firm will be patient; it would rather wait than accept a mediocre agreement. Negotiating with the union, a high-cost firm would rather be shut down than agree to raise wages. Thus, the high-cost firm can wait until the union concedes. In contrast, the low-cost firm loses a great deal of profit from delay, and would rather agree to raise wages than submit to a very long strike. Delay itself signals toughness. This phenomenon is familiar in the context of strikes and also in bargaining in other contexts. In the Middle East, sitting around drinking tea or coffee for hours may accompany the purchase of a rug. The seller's price will slowly fall, and the longer one is willing to wait, the lower the price.* Exactly the same phenomenon is very familiar in dating, where a person waits for the other to call, using patience and delay to say, implicitly, that he or she needs a good reason to make further interaction worthwhile.

Patience signals that one would rather have no bargain than an unfavorable bargain. The party that will not accept an unfavorable bargain finds it easy to reject unfavorable proposals. In many situations, this is tantamount to saying that one

*Of course, one has to say the right things, too. While delay is the primary signal, visible impatience is also a signal. Moreover, knowledge of reasonable prices is also a signal—the buyer who knows what the price ought to be is more likely to get that price than a buyer who obviously is guessing.

does not need the other party. The seller of fine carpets in Istanbul, by sitting and drinking coffee and not accepting your generous offer, says implicitly (although much more politely), "I will get a better offer from someone else. I don't need your offer, but I am happy to drink coffee with you." The buyer, by rejecting the seller's offer, says, "I don't want a carpet at that price, but I am enjoying your coffee."[16] The firm that rejects a supplier's offer says the same thing as the Istanbul rug dealer—that the firm can get an alternative supplier. (Having another source of supply provides a major advantage in the credibility of such statements.) These kind of signals are useful only if they are credible. Unions need the firms, but the only thing they can signal is the resolve to withstand a strike. Unionized firms typically need the workers, so they can signal the unprofitability of a wage increase. But often unions will have an excellent idea of just how profitable the firm is, from the firm's own annual reports. It might seem, then, that with good information, there is nothing to be signaled. But that is not right. One can signal irrationality.

When it is in your best interests to give in, should you give in? To be concrete, consider a simple division game known as the *ultimatum game*. In this game, the first person proposes dividing $1000; the second person can either accept or reject. If the second person rejects, the game ends and no one gets anything. If the second person accepts, each gets their assigned amount. The game is played only once, and the parties are anonymous—they do not know each other.

Put yourself in the first person's position. What should you offer? If you offer $1, most second parties will reject. With $1000 up for grabs, many will reject $100, and a few will reject anything less than $500. Rejection is not in the second party's interest—the second party gets nothing if the offer is rejected. But most people are willing to give up something to punish greediness, even when they will never see the person they are punishing.

Behavior in the ultimatum game provides a simple and intuitive example of irrational behavior. People who feel they were not treated fairly will usually punish, if the punishment is not too expensive. This is not in the punisher's self-interest, but is real nonetheless. People often do things that apparently are not in their self-interest, but a certain amount of craziness can be very productive, as the ultimatum games illustrates. The fact that many people will reject "unfair" divisions makes the first party offer more. Threats, such as "I'll reject if you don't give me half," need to be believed to be effective. A touch of irrationality can be very effective at making threats credible, especially when the irrationality concerns revenge.

Irrationality is relatively easy to imitate. However, the fact that it is easy to imitate makes the signal weak—irrational behavior could easily be imitated a rational person copying the behavior of irrational people in order to make an incredible threat seem credible. Nevertheless, leaders like Libya's Muzammar al-Qadhafi and Iraq's Saddam Hussein have very effectively convinced the world that they will pursue actions not in their self-interest, narrowly defined. There are several CEOs with useful reputations for a preference for revenge, which serves much the same effect: one would not undercut their firms, for fear of a massive punishment. Whether these reputations are calculated or genuine is difficult to ascertain.

VAPORWARE

It is always the best policy to speak the truth—unless, of course, you are an exceptionally good liar.
—Jerome K. Jerome

Vaporware is the preannouncement of a product that does not yet exist.[17] Generally, it is used to forestall customers from switching to rival products. For example, the recording industry is now very concerned about the ease with which music files in the MP3 format can be shared. MP3, which was the audio compression format of a video compression algorithm, takes CD-quality music and compresses it nine- to twentyfold without loss in audible quality. To combat MP3, the Recording Industry Association of America announced its own, competing music format standard, called SDMI (secure digital music initiative). At the time of this writing, it is years overdue. Many suspect that the goal of SDMI was to delay adoption of MP3 until a solution to the sharing problem could be found.

Microsoft is frequently accused of creating vaporware. What is now the Windows 2000 program, a complete rewrite of Windows, was originally promised in 1997. (Windows 98 was a revision of Windows 95, and was still, essentially, a DOS program, while Windows 2000 is, reportedly, free of DOS limitations and quirks, and thus as robust as Windows NT.) This new Windows operating system won the *Wired* news' "Vaporware of the year" award for three consecutive years. Caldera, a seller of competing operating systems, has sued Microsoft for monopolizing the field with DOS, and vaporware (of MS-DOS 4.0) is a centerpiece of its claims. Caldera alleges that Microsoft preannounced features that it could not yet deliver to discourage customers from switching to competing programs that already offered these features.

Vaporware need not succeed in discouraging switching. Netscape preannounced version 5.0 of its browser, nicknamed Mozilla, but never delivered it, jumping to version 6.0 nearly two years after 5.0 had been promised. While some users held on, waiting for Netscape to deliver, Microsoft was able to enhance the standards for Internet authoring, perhaps to a degree that shut Netscape out of the browser competition. Finally, vaporware need not be software. For example, according to *ZDNet*:[18]

> Varian Associates, a leading semiconductor equipment maker back in the early 1980s, was going to revolutionize lithography (the exposure of fine circuit lines) with highly-focused electron beams. At press conferences, the company rolled out a sleek new box, which it called a "direct-writer" machine. Problem was, there were no electronics in the box. Despite Varian's great hopes, e-beam lithography never caught on, and the company today is not a major industry player.
>
> At about the same time, a start-up called Insystems introduced a machine straight out of Star Wars, employing holographic images to inspect silicon wafers. The display at the annual Semicon West trade fair in San Mateo, Calif., featured a neat-looking hologram, supported by a huge machine. But, once again, the box was empty. The haunting image of that hologram is all that's left of Insystems.

Perhaps the most common example of vaporware is the airline that tells its patiently waiting customers that their aircraft is due in ten minutes, when in fact is has not left another city and cannot possibly arrive for two hours or more. Why do airlines engage in such dishonesty? One reason is to keep customers from exchanging their travel coupons for flights on another airline. Another reason is that they are truly hopeful of substituting an as-yet-unidentified aircraft, and want the customers close at hand. Such behavior, however, risks being disbelieved even when the truth is told.*

At best, vaporware is a gimmick to buy time, one that injures the firm's credibility. As firms may be injured if they rely on other firms' vaporware (especially common in database systems, for example), it pays to beware.

PRODUCT FAILURES

> If we don't succeed, we run the risk of failure.
>
> **—J. Danforth Quayle**

When products work together, it is generally difficult for customers to tell which product was at fault in case of failure. An extreme example is film and developing, where defects in either product are indistinguishable from each other. Replacement parts and servicing have the same feature—poor installation of good parts causes failures as rapidly as good installation of poor parts. Initially, compact-disc writers and blank CDs had compatibility problems. Some CD writers malfunctioned more than others, but some blank CDs failed more often than others. It has been

*Poor customer service reached such a point in 1998 that Congress began considering legislation to combat it. The airlines bought time with a "Customer First" plan, which now seems like vaporware to most air travelers.

alleged that Microsoft designed first DOS and then Windows so that Microsoft's competitors, including WordPerfect, Lotus, and Netscape, in the word-processing, spreadsheet, and, later, browser markets were disadvantaged—the competitors' products crashed because of an operating-system failure masquerading as a product failure. In such a common situation, customers are faced with the signal-extraction problem: Which product caused the failure? Because it will be difficult or impossible for customers to solve this signal-extraction problem, a fair portion of the blame will go to the innocent party.

The most important thing for a business to do is to fix the problem; otherwise, consumers will justifiably have low confidence in the product. If the fault is with a product, the producers needs to fix it. If the fault is with the complementary product, there are several ways to solve the problem. The firm could enter the industry and produce a higher quality complement. Kodak encouraged the use of Kodak-brand development, although the courts prevented Kodak from *requiring* Kodak development. Instead of entry, a firm can encourage the use of a high-quality complement, made by another firm, by offering a discount coupon or a bundling strategy. Makers of complementary products should cooperate to increase their quality—sometimes both products must be redesigned to work well together. A firm selling a product can provide a list of products that work well with it. Such a list sends the signal, "There are products that work well with our product, and products that don't." This can be a very useful signal to send, to discourage customers from using the low-quality complements.

SIGNALING PSYCHOSIS

The Federal Bureau of Investigation has released a report on how to assess the extent to which a school student presents a threat of violence. In assessing threats, the most serious threats are "direct, specific, and plausible," and offer "concrete steps for carrying [the threat] out." The more detailed the threat, the more serious it appears. In addition, the report provided a list of indicators that signal that a threat should be taken more seriously. These include:

- Low tolerance for frustration
- Poor coping skills
- Lack of resiliency
- Failed love relationship
- "Injustice collector"
- Depression
- Narcissism
- Alienation
- Externalizes blame
- Masks low self-esteem
- Anger management problems
- Intolerance
- Inappropriate humor
- Seeks to manipulate others
- Lack of trust
- Closed social group

- Dehumanizes others
- Lack of empathy
- Exaggerated sense of entitlement
- Attitude of superiority
- Exaggerated need for attention
- Fascination with violence-filled entertainment
- Negative role models
- Relevant behavior to carrying out threat
- Turbulent relationship with parents
- Family acceptance of pathology
- Access to weapons
- Lack of family intimacy
- Student "rules the roost"
- Change of behavior
- Few outside interests
- Rigid and opinionated
- Unusual interest in sensational violence
- No family limits (e.g., TV)
- Detached from school
- School tolerates disrespect
- Inequitable discipline
- Inflexible school culture
- Pecking order among students
- Code of silence
- Unsupervised computer access
- Drugs and alcohol prevalent
- Copycat potential

Most of these traits concern the individual and are bad signs generally, about students or employees. The last eight items concern the school. Such items like an inflexible culture, toleration of disrespect, a strong pecking order, and inequitable discipline are significant problems for firms as well as for schools.[19] There are three reasons for the strategist to be familiar with the signaling of psychosis. First, it sometimes pays to appear irrational. For example, in order to signal a commitment to a punishment that is not credible, a manager may want to appear excessively vengeful. Second, everyone should have a passing familiarity with the warning signs that an employee is about to "go postal," as common parlance describes a murderer of coworkers. Third, the same environmental traits that make schools foster dangerous students also make the workplace dangerous, and are to be avoided by a savvy management.

EXECUTIVE SUMMARY—SIGNALING

- People and firms signal their character by the choices they make.
- Usually the individual has no choice about the interpretation of his or her behavior, which is determined by the observer.
- Examples of signaling include
  - Expensive buildings and furnishings to signal a successful firm
  - Warranties to signal reliability
  - Expensive clothes and accessories to signal wealth
  - Education to signal ease of learning, ability to focus
  - A full product line to signal commitment to a product category

Behavior in a crisis signaling corporate responsibility or lack thereof
Introductory offers and advertising to signal product quality to consumers
Prices as a signal to potential entrants about the profitability of a market
Vaporware buys time but signals an untrustworthy firm.

- In many situations, such as a product safety crisis or with a warranty, the signaling value of behavior may outweigh direct costs and benefits.
- By acting responsibly and rehabilitating Tylenol at great cost after the poisonings, Johnson & Johnson avoided tainting its entire product line.

You can tell a lot about a fellow's character
by his way of eating jellybeans.
—Ronald Reagan

Bargaining

Many distinct skills are involved in bargaining. Foremost is the ability to "read" another person's intent, to sense the point at which he or she will walk away from the table, to pick up relatively subtle cues from behavior—a narrowing of the eyes, a slight flush, finger tapping, an involuntary tic—and understand the person's position better. Similarly, the poker face, the ability to hide a willingness to make concessions, and the ability to conceal desperation can have enormous value in bargaining. There appears to be little or no business strategy associated either with the psychological ability to read others or the acting ability that permits concealing one's own intentions. There are, however, strategic aspects to bargaining, which comprise the subject of this chapter. While such strategic aspects will never substitute for people sense, an understanding of the theory can be valuable, especially in deducing what other parties are signaling by their actions.

BASIC THEORY

An income tax return is a first offer to a party
that accepts 99% of all first offers.
—Anonymous

The simplest theory of bargaining arises when two people decide how to divide a fixed pool of money.[1] The money is available only if both parties agree to the division. Such a situation arises when two parties consider a joint venture that has a given expected value—the partners have to decide how to divide the proceeds. Similarly, when an investor and a manager form an enterprise, how much should the manager be compensated? To start the analysis, consider a situation where there is $1 to be divided between two parties, who get nothing if they do not agree.*

*These amounts don't matter. The parties consider the division of the amount over what they would

Moreover, consider the situation in which the parties make alternating offers. That is, the first player proposes a division; the second player can either accept or offer an alternative division. If the second player offers an alternative, then the first player can accept or reject, and so on. To fix ideas, we will let the players be Bob and Ann.

Both parties are impatient—an earlier agreement is better than a later agreement. Impatience could arise for a variety of reasons. Extended bargaining delays the initiation of a project, so there will be lost profits and increased discounting of future profits. There is a risk that a project will be preempted by others or will become infeasible due to a changed regulation, which is common with construction in environmentally sensitive areas. There is some probability that the other party loses interest in the project, because of another alternative arriving, or perhaps the other party dies in a plane crash. We can model this by shrinking the pie as time passes. Thus, the value of a pie that starts out as \$1.00 might fall to \$.90, then to \$.81, then to \$.729, and so on, decreasing by 10% per period, a discount factor of 90%.* This would be a large fall, one that arises when offers are complex to make and thus cannot be made quickly, or in a situation where time is of the essence, an opportunity that will likely disappear if not exploited immediately. Let Bob discount with the discount rate b, so that the delay of one stage of bargaining reduces the value of the pie by the factor $1 - b$. A full round of bargaining (offers rejected by both Bob and Ann) reduces the value to Bob by $(1 - b)^2$. Similarly, Ann discounts with the discount rate a.

Suppose it is Bob's turn to make an offer. To figure out Bob's best offer, we need to consider what Ann will accept. Let A denote the smallest amount Ann will accept. Then Bob offers Ann the amount A when it is Bob's turn to make an offer. Similarly, Ann offers Bob B when it is her turn to make an offer. Then:

$$A = (1 - a) \times (1 - B), \text{ and}$$
$$B = (1 - b) \times (1 - A).$$

The first equation arises because Bob must offer Ann at least as much as she would get from rejecting the offer—otherwise she just rejects. When Ann rejects, she gets $1 - B$, which is what is left over when she offers B to Bob, but she discounts that to $(1 - a) \times (1 - B)$, because it comes one period later. Thus, Bob's offer to Ann is $A = (1 - a) \times (1 - B)$. Similarly, Ann knows that if Bob rejects

get without agreement. Thus, if a joint venture is expected to earn \$62 million, but the investor has to put in \$15 million and the manager is leaving a job worth \$5 million, there is \$42 million to be divided. The division of \$1 can be interpreted as shares of the amount over the value of no agreement.

*The discount factor is the present value of \$1 delayed one period; it is \$1 minus the discount rate.

her offer, he will offer her A, keeping $1 - A$ for himself. Thus, Ann offers Bob $(1 - b) \times (1 - A)$, which is the least he will accept, and keeps the balance for herself. Substituting the second into the first yields

$$A = \frac{(1-a)b}{1-(1-a)(1-b)}, \quad B = \frac{(1-b)a}{1-(1-a)(1-b)}.$$

For example, if Bob discounts at a rate of 10% ($b = 0.10$) and Ann discounts at a rate of 5% ($a = 0.05$), Bob's offers to Ann should be approximately 0.655, keeping 34.5% for himself, while Ann's offer to Bob should be 0.31, keeping 69% for herself. These numbers represent a large amount of discounting, relative to ordinary bargaining situations in which offers can be made relatively quickly. If Bob discounts at the rate of 0.05% ($b = 0.995$) and Ann at the rate of 0.25% ($a = 0.9975$), then $A = 0.664$ and $1 - B = 0.668$, and there is almost no disagreement about Ann's share—around two-thirds of the total.

When offers can be made very quickly, it turns out that the proposals by Ann and Bob become the same, and depend only on the relative discount rates. In particular, the shares will be

$$A = \frac{b}{a+b}, \; B = \frac{a}{a+b}.$$

These shares are the relative impatience levels, since a is Ann's discount rate, and b is Bob's discount rate. In the previous example, with Bob's discount rate twice Ann's, Bob gets half as much as Ann, which implies that Bob gets one-third of the total, to Ann's two-thirds. If Bob discounts the future three times as much as Ann, his share will be one-third of Ann's—or one-quarter of the total, to Ann's three-quarters. Moreover, equally patient players can be expected to split the gains from their agreement. Thus, the "usual" outcome will be 50-50—each getting half the surplus.

Patience is strongly rewarded. In this simplest theory of bargaining, the relatively patient player gets the larger share, and the shares are proportional to the patience levels. As we saw in signaling theory, patience is a way of signaling that one is a strong player. In the abstract theory of bargaining, patience is directly translated into bargaining strength, even without signaling.

The basic theory of bargaining suggests not only that patience is rewarded, but also by how much—both parties share in the proceeds of the bargain proportional to their relative patience.

The prospect that a better deal may arrive for one of the parties is easily incorporated into the theory. The possibility of a better deal, from a third party, reduces the discount rate (increases the discount factor), because this possibility reduces the cost of waiting. Thus, the option value not settling gets incorporated into the discounting of each party. A player who is likely to get a good offer in the future will be relatively patient, and thus can expect to obtain the lion's share of the bargain.

The basic theory ignores many real-world aspects of bargaining and negotiation. Besides ignoring the already-mentioned ability to read people, the basic theory posits alternating offers—a rigid bargaining framework. Within this framework, there is a first-mover advantage that may be substantial. In real life, one often wants to let the other party make the first offer—there is an informational advantage to moving second.

DELAY

Usually, it is not obvious how patient someone else is. Consider the buyer and seller of a house. Does the buyer need to buy immediately, or does he or she have a rented apartment with six months remaining on the lease? Has the seller already bought in another city, or is he or she relatively well positioned to delay?* Consequently, both parties may engage in the attempt to convince the other party of their patience. The most direct means of signaling patience is delay—one signals patience by acting patient.

Firms and unions signal patience by enduring a strike. The firm shows that it will wait a long time, making the strike very costly to the union, by not settling. The union signals its patience, its unwillingness to settle, by striking.

There is a variety of means of signaling patience, but the most direct means is intentional delay. Intentional delay implicitly makes the statement, "I'm unwilling to accept this deal unless it is on very good terms; otherwise, I'm better off waiting." Delay signals a comparative advantage at outwaiting the other party. Delay also signals better alternative prospects—that the deal is not so great. In some cases, delay is the *only* signal available to the parties—delay is the means of showing strength.

Depending on the context, there are other activities and preparations helpful to strengthen the delaying signal. A firm should prepare for a long strike by building up inventory, arranging alternative sources of supply, and training management to fill some of the workers' positions. American Airlines has used these techniques very successfully in its stormy labor history. Unions also can build a war chest to

*As a practical matter, some of these issues are mitigated by having the closing date be months after the agreement is signed, but there is still significant and important uncertainty about the patience—the cost and risk of rejecting an offer—of buyer and seller.

mitigate the costs of a long strike. In a contentious lawsuit, the parties should prepare for trial. It is not uncommon for firms to attempt to appear to prepare for trial, but there can be leakage to the other side about the relative level of preparedness. For example, the failure to ask relevant questions of deposed witnesses or to bring useful motions signals a low level of preparation. Similarly, an expert witness may appear unprepared in a deposition, which signals an expectation of settlement.

Actually lowering the cost of patience by making investments, where practical, is better than signaling patience, for the same reason that real toughness is better than the appearance of toughness. Preparation for bargaining with a labor union can include arranging alternative sources of supply, so that customers are not left in the lurch and tempted to switch to other companies. Fierce competitors in the product market may be able to implicitly agree not to exploit the opportunity created by a labor strike, because over time the firms are in the same position. Indeed, one mechanism for creating such cooperation among firms is to arrange to supply each other during labor strikes.

In summary, the majority of the surplus of an agreement tends to go to the more patient bargainer. There are means of signaling patience, and means of creating patience; both will tend to be rewarded in bargaining.

THE WAR OF ATTRITION

The quickest way to end a war is to lose it.
—George Orwell

The war of attrition concerns a situation in which two or more parties struggle until all but one quit, concede, run out of money, or die. The elks that lock horns and fight for the right to be the dominant male fight a war of attrition, with both struggling until one gives up in exhaustion. The corporations that file suit, countersuit, and countercountersuit, each with document production, depositions, extended discovery, an army of attorneys, and a flurry of motions and pleas, fight a war of attrition, usually ended by a settlement. Two companies that struggle for customers by using price cuts and advertising in a market that can only support one company fight a war of attrition, fighting until one quits. Some commentators consider that Microsoft's battle with Netscape in the browser war was just such a war of attrition. Telephone companies that lobby the Federal Communications Commission for their wireless standards fight a war of attrition. Such wars of attrition are sufficiently common that the formal analysis of the war of attrition has some value in formulating business strategy.

The simplest, and hence least realistic, theory of the war of attrition arises when there are two players and expenditures per period are fixed.* Say there is a prize of \$1 million that goes to the firm that lasts the longest, and it costs an amount c to stay in the game each day. The per diem cost is less than \$500,000.† To simplify the analysis, we will ignore discounting—\$1 million delayed will be valued at \$1 million. Each morning, each firm decides whether it should stay in or exit. If you were the CEO of one of the firms, what should you do? Clearly, it matters what you believe about the other firm. If you think the other firm is likely to remain in for a long time, it clearly pays to quit immediately. If, in contrast, you think the other firm is likely to get out soon, you should stay in. Thus, having one firm quit immediately is an equilibrium,‡ and it is the right response to the strategy that dictates staying in for a long time. If one firm quits immediately, there is no war of attrition—the war is over before it has started. Such an equilibrium makes for an unsatisfactory theory of war—it is over before a shot is fired.

There is another equilibrium, where both firms decide randomly whether they should remain in the game or quit, flipping a coin in each period. In this equilibrium, each firm chooses the probability that it quits in the current period. Let p represent the probability of quitting in each period. We can find an equilibrium value of p by examining the incentives of one player, given that the other plays this randomized strategy. Consider the choice of quitting now or staying in for one more period and then exiting. By exiting now, the firm gets \$500,000 if the other firm also exits, which occurs with the hypothesized probability p. If the firm stays in, and then exits one period later, it gets \$1 million if the other firm exits (probability p), but pays the cost c (measured in millions of dollars). Moreover, if the other firm does not exit in this period, but exits in the subsequent period, the firm obtains $\$\frac{1}{2}$M = \$500,000; this happens with probability $p(1 - p)$.

In order for both of these strategies—exit now or wait to exit—to be sensible for each firm, the strategies must produce exactly the same expected profits. Since the equilibrium requires the firms to randomize, they must be indifferent about exiting now or not exiting now. If both quitting and staying in for one period produce the same profits, the firm is indifferent about the alternatives. Consequently, any strategy, including the randomized strategy, is optimal behavior. (One way of thinking about such a mixed strategy is that it cannot be exploited by a competitor.) The strategy of staying in produces the same profits as exiting if

*The war of attrition differs from the basic bargaining model in that there is no way to split the pie—one side gets it, and the other does not.

†If both firms choose the same period to exit, they each get half of the prize. If the cost exceeds \$500,000, both will exit immediately.

‡An equilibrium means that each firm is giving its best response to the strategy of the other firm, and thus neither firm has an incentive to change its strategy. Both firms are maximizing their profits, given the behavior of the other firm.

$$\tfrac{1}{2}p = p - c + (1-p)\tfrac{1}{2}p.$$

The left side represents the profits associated with an immediate exit, which produces positive profits only when the other party also exits (probability p), in which case the profits are one-half of the amount. The right side is the profit associated with staying in one period, and then exiting. This always costs c (recall it is measured in \$Ms), and produces a profit of \$1 million with probability p, giving the term $p - c$. In addition, if the other firm does not exit (probability $1 - p$), then exits in the next period (probability p), the firm obtains the value of one-half.

This equation can be simplified to read $\tfrac{1}{2}p^2 - p + c = 0$. The equation can be readily solved for p using the quadratic formula. The solution is

$$p = 1 - \sqrt{1 - 2c}.$$

The interpretation of p is the probability that one side concedes in each period. Thus, if c is near zero, this probability is also near zero. If c, the cost of remaining in the battle, is near one-half, the likelihood of exit approaches 1, which means a certain exit for both firms.

How long does such a war of attrition last? The cost of a loss in an antitrust battle can be \$100 million dollars and might cost \$10 million per year to fight, which makes c around 10%. This gives the probability of a concession, p, about 10.55% per year. At such a rate, the war will last five years on average.[2] This is not an unreasonable estimate of the duration of such battles. The theory seems to be in line with legal battles.

The profit obtained by firms in the simple war of attrition equals $\tfrac{1}{2}p$, which is approximately equal to the cost of staying in one more period. Period length is not arbitrary, but depends on the nature of the battle. The period length will be, at most, the amount of time that it takes to observe that the other party has given up. Alternatively, the period is the amount of time one can appear to be continuing to fight when one has stopped expending costs. Thus, in a legal battle, one may spend weeks in a delaying motion that is relatively inexpensive, but eventually it will become clear that one has quit taking depositions and filing motions and has essentially surrendered. In a market-share battle, it may become clear in a week or less that one opponent has given up. When the period is short, the cost of continuing to fight as a proportion of the value of winning is very low, perhaps less than 1% or even 0.10%. In such situations, the expected profits of the two firms are very, very low, and almost all the proceeds are frittered away in the war itself. For example, when the cost of the fight each period is 1% of the value of winning, the expected profits from the fight are also about 1.005% of the value of the prize!

While the firms fighting a war of attrition expect to make money, albeit a modest amount, on average, because of the randomness in strategies, it is easily possible for *both* firms to lose money. At least one firm will lose money, of course, but sometimes even the winner loses money. When c is 1% of the value of the prize, the probability of a concession, p, is about 2%. The probability that neither firm concedes for one hundred periods (in which case neither firm makes money) is $0.98^{100} = 13.3\%$. Thus, there is a significant probability that the war will last so long that it would have been better for the ultimate winner to concede. This is part of the nature of wars of attrition—the war has no fixed ending date, and can continue for a very long time. Indeed, the war may last so long that even the eventual winner would have quit if it had known what it would take to win.

An interesting aspect of the war of attrition is that a reduction in the cost of the war does not reduce the cost of effort expended in fighting the war. Indeed, the probability that the war does not end in a given period, which requires neither firm to drop out, is $(1 - p)^2$, which is equal to $1 - 2c$. Thus, the probability that the war will end in any given period is $2c$. It then turns out that the expected duration of the war is $1/(2c)$. Reduce the cost of war by half, and the war doubles in length!

In sum, most of the value of a war of attrition is expended in the attempt to win the war. A reduction in the cost of fighting the war increases its expected length, and generally reduces the expected profits from fighting the war.

Lawsuits

A common war of attrition fought by corporations involves suit and countersuit wars of litigation. For example BMC Software filed a patent infringement lawsuit against fledgling competitor Neon Systems and related corporate entities, which promptly responded with an antitrust suit against BMC. BMC filed a countersuit, and ultimately two more lawsuits were filed. Hundreds of depositions were taken, and millions of pages of documents were produced in the lawsuits, which lasted for more than a year. BMC's lawsuit-related expenses in the last quarter of the lawsuit were nearly $9 million.

Longhorn Partners, a consortium of energy firms including Exxon-Mobil, purchased a fifty-year-old Exxon pipeline that had brought crude oil from the Midland, Texas, area to Houston. Longhorn planned to extend the pipeline to El Paso, reverse its flow, and ship gasoline from Houston to El Paso. Months before the pipeline was to go into service, Longhorn was served with eight lawsuits by ranchers whose property was crossed by the pipeline. These lawsuits were paid for by Holly Corporation, owner of the Navajo Refinery, which supplies gasoline in El Paso. The lawsuits were eventually joined by the city of Austin, which was also concerned by the change from crude oil to gasoline passing over the environmentally sensitive Edwards aquifer. U.S. District Court judge Sam Sparks ordered an environmental impact study, based on the lawsuits. The companies spent around $5 million each for this part of the action. Shortly after the court ruling, Longhorn Partners sued Holly Corporation on antitrust grounds, alleging attempted monopolization of the El Paso gasoline market and requesting a billion dollars in trebled damages. The stock-market value of the Holly Corporation fell substantially after this lawsuit was announced. Both sides have hired high-profile lobbyists, public relations firms, and attorneys.

Drug Wars[3]

Abbott Laboratories makes a prescription drug, Hytrin, for high blood pressure and prostate enlargement. Several companies, including Zenith Goldline Pharmaceuticals, would like to sell a generic version of Hytrin under the name terazosin. Hytrin had revenues in 1998 of approximately $500 million. To protect its market, Abbott wanted to delay the sale of generic versions of the product. "Abbott makes a million dollars a day for every day it keeps us off the market," Bill Mentlik, Zenith's lawyer, argued in court. Without a cheaper generic, he warned, "the public is losing."

Zenith's desire to protect the public from high prices gave way to Abbott's cash. Abbott settled a patent lawsuit with Zenith by agreeing on 31 March 1998 to pay $2 million per month to Zenith in order to keep Zenith out of the market. Shortly thereafter, Abbott paid an undisclosed amount to keep Geneva Pharmaceuticals out of the market as well.

Abbott filed many patents to protect Hytrin. Abbott was accused of improperly listing a patent in the federal registry, a patent later struck down by the federal appeals courts in July 1999. Abbott filed patent infringement suits against five generic manufacturers, and countersued an additional firm.

It appears that Abbott successfully used the court system to delay entry of terazosin, thereby protecting its market. Because lawsuits take time to settle and tend to delay entry pending a decision, Abbott's strategy makes good business sense. Moreover, the law supports this strategy by granting a brand-name firm the right to sue for patent infringement, and by prohibiting the FDA from making a decision on the generic introduction for thirty months, while the courts consider the issue.

The deal with Geneva was dropped in August 1999 after attracting antitrust scrutiny by the FTC, which prompted Geneva's entry into the field with the first generic. In a similar case, the court found an antitrust violation in such agreements, in particular when pharmaceutical manufacturer Hoechst Marion Roussel paid

$90 million for Andrx Pharmaceuticals not to market a generic alternative to its heart medication Cardizem.

Differences between Litigation and the War of Attrition

Lawsuits often create a war-of-attrition situation. There are three important differences between a legal war of attrition and the theory discussed above. First, it is possible to impose costs on the opponent. Document requests are inexpensive to manufacture, but compliance is quite costly. Depositions are more costly for the deposed, since both sides provide attorneys but the deponent has to be prepared and will waste typically two days—one for preparation and document review, another in the deposition itself. In the BMC Software cases cited above, some executives were deposed for five full days. The ability to inflict costs on the other side at a relatively inexpensive rate makes legal wars of attrition particularly insidious. The temptation is to impose major costs, but the likely outcome is to have major costs imposed on you, in a tit-for-tat response.

Second, legal wars are generally fought with the aid of outside law firms, rather than by using the firm's general counsel, due to the relatively specialized nature of the litigation. This situation can easily create a moral hazard problem—the law firm, while ethically bound to represent the firm to the best of its abilities, of course has an incentive to prolong and even maximize the litigation.

Third, it is possible to settle a lawsuit without a clear winner, by using a payment. Thus, in a suit that asks for a billion dollars, a payment of $10,000 might be construed as a victory for either side. BMC apparently paid about $30 million to Neon and its corporate partners (according to its annual report), but also obtained withdrawal from the market of the products that BMC asserted infringed on its patents. As in this case, often both sides claim victory. Longhorn Partners thought the outcome of the environmental impact study was a victory, because it was permitted to operate the pipeline. Holly and the city of Austin also thought they had been victorious, because Longhorn was required by the impact study to increase the level of care and pipeline maintenance quite substantially.

Settlement offers are difficult, because they pass information on to opponents. For example, a defendant in a tort lawsuit might be willing to settle for up to $10 million, but fears that if it makes an offer, the offer itself will increase the demands of the plaintiff. In particular, a savvy plaintiff might demand $7 million, while an ignorant plaintiff might demand $300,000. The defendant wants to settle with both types of plaintiff. The standard bargaining method requires an initial offer of $300,000, and then a significant delay until the offer rises to $7 million or more, as a means of separating the two types of plaintiffs. Without that substantial delay, the ignorant plaintiff will manage to obtain the high payout. The problem of information leakage often means that a case that ought to settle instead lingers on, while the companies find a mutually acceptable price.

Amazon and Barnes & Nobles, the two largest Internet booksellers, have a long-running feud. Amazon won a restraining order preventing Barnes & Noble from offering its "Express Lane" checkout, which Amazon maintained infringed on its "one-click" checkout. As a consequence, shoppers on Barnes & Noble's Web site had to click twice to make an expedited purchase. This restraining order was later canceled. Barnes & Nobles sued to prevent Amazon from saying it offered the "earth's largest selection." These companies represent an all-too-common case of the use of the legal system to take potshots at a rival, usually accomplishing nothing.

Settlement Escrows

University of Chicago business school professors Robert Gertner and Geoffrey Miller[4] have introduced the concept of a "settlement escrow" as a means of preventing the leakage of information about an offer. A settlement escrow works as follows. First, a trusted third party, independent of both sides, is identified. This will generally be an attorney who does not represent either party. The major terms of a settlement, other than payments, are then established. These terms include secrecy of the settlement, the term structure of any payments, agreement not to appeal, and so on. At this point, both parties make secret offers to the third party. The third party compares the offers, and if the plaintiff asked for less than the defendant offered, the parties have an agreement at the average of the two offers. If the defendant offered less than the plaintiff requested, the parties go to trial.

It is generally better to try a settlement escrow than to proceed to trial. Moreover, settlement escrows are better than direct offers. The advantage of a settlement escrow is a one-time chance to settle the case at a price reasonable to both sides. Given that the chance only arises once, both parties have an incentive to make reasonable offers.

There are several strategic aspects to settlement escrows. First, the final price will reflect each party's offer, and thus the plaintiff should inflate the asking price above the minimum the parties would take, and the defendants should reduce their offer to below the most they would pay. Second, when the agreement fails to materialize, both parties learn something about the other party. This effect is something of an advantage, because when the settlement escrow fails, the plaintiff learns that the defendant is optimistic, and vice versa; such communication of optimism should make both parties more amenable to a future settlement. The final strategic aspect of a settlement escrow is problematic. If the agreement fails to materialize, there will be a tendency to try a settlement escrow again. However, the possibility of repeated attempts to have settlement escrows undermines the incentive for a firm to make a serious offer. If one can improve the offer later, why not see what the market will bear by trying a sequence of progressively better offers? Much of the advantage of settlement escrows is lost if the parties know that they can improve subsequent offers.

BSB versus Sky TV

A striking example of the war of attrition in action is reported by Pankaj Ghemawat in the battle to provide Britain's satellite television.[5] British Satellite Broadcasting (BSB) raised over £200 million by July 1987, which it earmarked for buying and launching two satellites, the second one for redundancy. BSB estimated that it would launch broadcasting in 1990 and reach break-even status, with three to four million subscribers, in 1993. Total costs were estimated at £500 million, and a second round of financing was planned for 1990.

In June 1988, BSB's plans were disrupted by the surprise announcement by Rupert Murdoch's News Corporation that it would offer a competing service named Sky Television. Sky Television planned to use smaller dishes, have substantially reduced costs of £100 million, and reach the market in 1989. In response to Sky's entry, BSB revised its sales projections upwards, due to accelerated promotions and advertising. By the end of 1988, the two companies entered a bidding war for Hollywood films, paying £670 million for Hollywood movie rights alone. Sky went on the air in January 1989, and BSB reached the market in April 1990. At that point, both companies experienced disappointing sales, due primarily to consumers waiting to see which technology would dominate. Over the two-year war, the two companies lost £1,250 million. In November 1990, they announced a merger.

HOLDUP

Oil refineries are designed to process a particular type of crude oil. Crude oil varies in sulfur content: oil with little sulfur is "sweet," while oil with high sulfur content is "sour." Sulfur must be removed in the refining process, and a refinery that was designed for sweet crude cannot handle a sour crude without the installation of additional desulfurization facilities. Crude oil also varies in the density or weight of the oil. A light crude contains a higher proportion of relatively valuable gasoline, jet fuel, and home-heating (diesel) oil, while a heavy crude has a larger proportion of heavy molecules. These molecules can be made into low-value asphalt, or cracked into lighter products. A plant designed to process light crude requires substantial investment in order to process heavy crude oils. Light oils have a high specific gravity (API), and sweet crude oils have a low percentage of sulfur.

Many California refineries were designed to process oil, known as ANS, from the North Slope of Alaska. ANS is a sweet crude, with around 0.1% sulfur, and a fairly light crude, with an API of 35. As the supplies of ANS began to decline in the 1990s, the price of ANS rose. Moreover, the prices charged by British Petroleum (BP), the largest seller of ANS, varied with the refinery; refineries able to run alternative crude oils received significantly lower prices than refineries designed specifically for ANS. This is an example of the *holdup problem:* firms that made investments in ANS uses specific to a particular partner (BP) were charged a higher price because they had no alternatives. The holdup problem arises because investments that are specific to another party are vulnerable in renegotiation—the other party can extract some or all of the value of the investments. The value of specific assets—those specific to a relationship with another party—are vulnerable to expropriation by that other party, because the assets have low or no value without the other party's participation.

In its extreme form, the holdup problem can render the investment unprofitable. Consider a company that makes hood latches for GM cars. It spends $5 million on a machine that stamps out these latches, which cost $5 each, and expects to sell GM one million of the latches at a price of $12 each, thereby earning a $2 million profit. If the price and quantity are set prior to the machine being purchased, then the company is reasonably protected from holdup. However, if either is not set in advance, GM can renegotiate the contract. Suppose, for example, that the price was not set before the machine was purchased, and suppose that GM can produce the latches itself for $13 each. Once the machine has been purchased, the negotiation is between a supplier with an incremental cost of $5 and a buyer with a value of $13; the standard theory described at the beginning of this chapter suggests splitting the difference, which leads to a price of $9. The sunk investment in the latch-making machine is not relevant to the bargain—it has already been purchased! Of course, a price of $9 renders the original investment in the machine unprofitable, because only $4 per unit is available for the investment.*

The hood-latch problem illustrates the general holdup problem. When specific investments are made prior to the setting of the terms of exchange, the terms will not reflect the costs of the investments, but instead will be the value of the investment to the exchange. Moreover, under the "split the difference" solution of the standard theory, each party recovers half the value of the exchange. In this circumstance, each party pays the entire cost of a specific investment, but receives half

*Not surprisingly, automobile manufacturers have found solutions to this problem. Often U.S. auto companies own the machine used by its supplier; when it tenders a contract for the supply of hood latches, the machines are supplied by the auto company and not by the latch maker. In contrast, Japanese companies generally depend on their reputation for not expropriating the investments of suppliers. Vertical integration was discussed in chapter 7.

the value of the investment. Unless the investment has an extraordinary return, the recovery is inadequate to cover the cost. For this reason, the holdup problem creates underinvestment.

There are a variety of solutions to the holdup problem. Firms could set the terms of exchange prior to the investments. Setting the terms of exchange for an investment with a long time horizon creates its own problems. The Churchill Falls agreement between Newfoundland and Quebec, in which Newfoundland would supply Quebec with a large amount of electricity, set a price without inflation adjustment. The agreement, signed in 1969, was to last for sixty-five years. By 1980, the agreed price was about 10% of the price Quebec received from power sales to the United States, and the price remains a modest fraction of average energy prices. This contract created a massive windfall gain to Quebec. Because it is difficult to forecast all the circumstances that might prevail far into the future, it is difficult to write a sensible contract that protects the parties from renegotiation.

Another solution to the holdup problem is vertical integration. In this solution, the two parties merge, which in principle aligns their incentives and reduces the problem of negotiating a contract to the problem of setting a transfer price. Vertical integration mitigates the problem, and in some circumstances eliminates it. However, vertical integration carries its own costs, including those for managing two disparate businesses. Some of the problems of vertical integration are discussed in chapter 7.

Vertical integration is an extreme form of a third solution, which involves the separation of ownership and operation of an asset. Thus, if the hood-latch supplier is worried that it will not receive an adequate price for its latches, one solution is for GM to own the latch machine. Then, GM can use competition among potential operators of the hood-latch machine to set the price for the operation of the machine. Because the operators make no significant specific investments, operators are protected from GM opportunism, GM is protected, provided that there is adequate competition by potential operators.*

CONTRACT DESIGN AND VERIFICATION

The basic theory of bargaining is one dimensional, focusing on bargaining over price or some other single attribute. Such a theory is applicable to buyers and sellers who are dickering over the price of an object, but it fails to cover many more

*The creation of adequate competition by potential operators is a thorny issue. One solution is to split the contract award among companies. The U.S. Department of Defense experimented with split awards in the 1980s, but the experiments were, by and large, a failure. The problem is that when firms know the award will be split, competition is less intense, so the goal of promoting competition is undermined by split awards.

complex bargaining situations. Often, there are many terms of the agreement to be decided simultaneously. Moreover, some of these terms may be subject to problems of verifiability later. Did the seller provide the product specified in the contract? What does a buyer do when the buyer needs only minor modifications of the contract and the seller wants to renegotiate all the terms? An important idea is that the design of breach penalties influences the desired contract design. Breach penalties play a crucial role is the creation and enforcement of contracts.

Verification and Observability

Contract terms that cannot be verified are not readily enforceable. Contracts that provide an actor, author, or other talented person with a percentage of the profits are rare because it is straightforward to hide profits in line items that appear to be costs, such as company planes and executive compensation. To solve this verification problem, contract terms are often a portion of revenues rather than of profits. Similarly, franchise contracts tend to provide the franchiser with a percentage of the gross revenues, which can be observed relatively easily, rather than a percentage of the profits.

The difficulty in observing or measuring important aspects of performance leads to contracts that are based on imperfect measures of performance. Using revenues or quantity, rather than profits, as a means of compensating the sales force skews incentives relative to using profits as a means of compensation.

In some cases, it may be difficult to measure how much of a behavior occurs, but it may be readily verifiable whether zero occurred or not; in such cases, specifying zero is an important option. This idea is familiar from two nonbusiness applications: taxes and nuclear weapons. With taxes, it is often difficult to determine whether taxes have been increased or not. The tax code is complex; an increase in some taxes with decreases in others may or may not represent an overall tax increase. On the other hand, it is simple to verify when no change has occurred. As a consequence, there is a tendency to choose "no change" as a means of implementing "no increase." Similarly, many voters oppose the introduction of a new form of taxation, however small, on the "thin edge of the wedge" principle. Once introduced, a tax can be increased in small increments until it is a large tax, as occurred with the U.S. income tax.

As Thomas Schelling so eloquently argues, most people view nuclear and nonnuclear conflict very differently.[6] The distinction is artificial in the sense that some nuclear weapons are purely defensive in nature, with the neutron bomb being the prime example. Why should the deployment of a defensive nuclear weapon be considered a step on the path toward a nuclear Armaggeddon? The distinction between nuclear and nonnuclear weapons is sensible in that it is readily verified whether any nuclear weapon is used, and there must be a first use of a nuclear weapon for a nuclear conflict to arise. Thus, the rule that says "no nuclear weapons, ever" is much easier to verify and enforce than the rule that says "no nondefensive nuclear weapons, ever," because it is much easier to disagree about what weapons are defensive than about what weapons are nuclear.

What is true for nations is often true for businesses. It is important that behavior specified in contracts, or required by tacit agreement, be readily verifiable. Contract design involves a trade-off. A more complex design permits a more detailed specification of activity or behavior, and the contract can condition this behavior on more relevant variables. The cost of more complexity is that enforcement becomes problematic and the likelihood of loopholes increases, either of which can lead to disastrous performance. Good contract design balances the overall performance goals against the likelihood of a major defect in the contract.

Until recently, the tobacco industry litigated every lawsuit with tremendous effort and took every action available to win each lawsuit. No cases were settled, even though it would have been cheaper to settle than to litigate. As a consequence of the behavior of the tobacco companies, bringing a suit against the tobacco industry was extraordinarily costly, and relatively few lawsuits were filed. The advantage to the industry of not settling, ever, was that it discouraged relatively weak cases from being filed. Only the strongest suits were filed, and the attorneys and plaintiff suing the industry had to prepare for a long, costly war and probable loss.

Wal-Mart litigates all harassment and discrimination lawsuits. Any attorney representing a client in such a suit against Wal-Mart must be prepared to go to trial, because the attorney can readily find out that Wal-Mart does not settle. For many cases, and perhaps most of the cases actually brought, this policy has been disadvantageous for Wal-Mart. Many of the cases actually brought will have significant merit, and the plaintiffs will likely win at trial. Losing at trial will almost invariably cost Wal-Mart much more than if it had offered a modest, acceptable settlement. Thus, on a case-by-case basis, it would be significantly cheaper for Wal-Mart to settle. However, the policy of "only settle the cases that have merit" is not verifiable. Thus, if Wal-Mart adopts a policy that settles any case, no matter how meritorious for the plaintiff, Wal-Mart will lose its very valuable reputation of not settling. The reputation is valuable because it eliminates those suits brought against it with a hope of a settlement rather than a significant probability of victory for the plaintiff. In particular, a case that will cost more to litigate than could possibly be awarded by a jury will not be filed against Wal-Mart, but might be filed against a firm that is known to settle some portion of its lawsuits. Any breach of the "litigate every suit" reputation is likely to encourage nuisance suits.[7]

Renegotiation Proofness

A second reason for a "zero tolerance," "always," or "never" in contracting is the difficulty of committing to a desirable alternative. Consider the difficulties in litigating only those matters in which Wal-Mart is, in fact, innocent. The problem with settling matters when Wal-Mart is guilty is that no one can see Wal-Mart's guilt in the matters it settles. Wal-Mart could settle matters when it is, in fact, innocent, and no one would be the wiser. Since Wal-Mart would have an incentive to settle such matters, especially where the issues are cloudy and Wal-Mart can avoid a costly trial, any possibility of settling would provide an encouragement to settle more and more lawsuits. Essentially, if Wal-Mart opens the door to settlement, it is difficult to avoid going through that door.

Contracts can offer a similar conundrum. An employer, to discourage the use of drugs and alcohol on the job, may announce a "zero tolerance" policy, with the requirement that anyone caught using these substances on the job would be summarily fired. This is a fine policy most of the time, but what happens when a key employee, one who is responsible for major contributions and who is expected to rise in the corporation, is depressed over the death of a spouse and comes to work slightly intoxicated? The tendency is to send the employee home and pretend the problem never arose, because the alternative is to lose an extraordinarily valued employee who is having a rough time. The problem, of course, is that this sets a new standard, which is that drinking on the job is not tolerated unless the employee is sufficiently valuable and has a good excuse; such a standard is no longer a verifiable one.*

When selling spectrum or assigning telecommunications licenses, the Mexican agency Secretaria de Communicaciones y Transportes (SCT) typically sets a deadline: applications must be received by 8 P.M. Friday. It is not uncommon, however, for many or most of the petitioners to appear in the subsequent two hours after 8 P.M. To combat this tardiness problem, SCT introduced a time stamp, and required a stamped time prior to 8 P.M. This procedure did not work at all, because employees of SCT knew how to reset the stamp by a couple of hours, and thus provide tardy firms with the requisite time. SCT employees would rather reset the time stamp than risk having the companies complain to the minister of SCT about the process; consequently, employees permit the tardiness to run unchecked.

In designing contracts, it is useful to consider what will happen when parties fail to live up to their agreement. A contract is described as "renegotiation proof"

*An interesting example of this was the airline pilot whose ex-wife, who temporarily lived in the same house, put drugs in the pilot's food in order to cause the pilot to lose his job. In spite of a police finding that the pilot had not known about the drugs, the pilot was fired under a zero-tolerance policy.

if there are no clauses that will be renegotiated rather than enforced. Without proof against renegotiation, contract provisions are unlikely to be enforced. The problem of renegotiation became apparent with the difficulties in enforcing "poison pill" provisions. A poison pill requires the destruction of some of a company's value, usually by selling divisions at fire-sale prices, in the event of a hostile takeover. Such provisions are intended to discourage hostile takeovers. The renegotiation problem is that when a takeover attempt occurs, the tendency is to renegotiate the clause, and try to break it. Management can be induced to try to undo the poison pill by providing golden parachutes (exceptionally generous severance packages) which the board of directors will authorize in order to obtain the higher share value associated with the takeover. The problem of renegotiation is that a poison pill is effective only if it is believed to be ironclad; once the possibility of renegotiation arises, the deterrent effect is reduced or lost.

Breach Penalties

There are three major kinds of penalties imposed for breach of contract:[8]

- *Expectation Damages,* which guarantee that the nonbreaching party gets something equivalent to what the contract specified absent the breach.
- *Reliance Damages,* which guarantee that the nonbreaching party gets something equivalent to what it would have had, absent the contract.
- *Specific Performance,* in which a court imposes a remedy, usually to force performance.

The form of the remedy matters, both to behavior and to investment. For example, breaching a contract is more costly under expectation damages than under reliance damages, so firms will tend to invest more to avoid a contract breach under expectation damages.

Suppose Dell Computer contracts for one million AMD Athlon computer processors, at a price of $250 each. Dell expects to sell the Athlon-equipped computers for $2000, at a profit of $250 each. If it could not get the Athlon chips, Dell could instead buy Cyrix chips for $200, but it would have to cut the price of the computer by $100, and so would net $200 instead. Suppose that a machine breakdown at the AMD plant prevents AMD from delivering the Athlon chips in a timely manner. Suppose as well that Dell has spent $100 million preparing to produce the Athlon-equipped chips. AMD would owe Dell $350 million under expectations damages, but only $300 million under reliance damages. Under expectation damages, AMD is responsible for the profit that Dell would have made under the contract plus the costs already incurred, which is $250 profit per computer plus $100 million in costs. Under reliance damages, AMD is responsible for the profit that Dell would have made had Dell not contracted with AMD. This amount is $200 per computer plus the $100 million in costs. The difference is whether the profit from the contract itself is used, versus the lower profit associated with the best alternative (Cyrix).

Expectation damages provide efficient incentives for contract breach. Under expectation damages, AMD will choose to breach the contract whenever it can sell the processors for more than $600 each. At any price above $600, AMD can pay the $350 in damages, plus lose the $250 in payments from Dell, and still make a profit. This is the efficient price, because the value of the processors to Dell (once $100 million is a sunk investment) is $600 each. Dell expected revenue of $2000 and profit of $250 each on a million computers. Of the $2 billion in revenue, $100 million, or $100 each, is a sunk cost of preparing the computer, and $250 million was the contract price of the processors; thus, there are $1.4 billion in other costs. Thus, once the $100 million is sunk, the processors are worth $600 to Dell—$2000 minus the $1400 in other costs. Consequently, expectation damages insure that the company with the highest value for the processors winds up owning the processors, and yet leaves Dell, the party injured by breach, unharmed.

Ex post efficiency is a general property of expectation damages. Expectation damages provide incentives to breach only when it is *jointly* better to do so. Because the breaching party has to make the other party as well off as if the contract were not breached, it is only profitable to breach under expectation damages when an integrated or merged firm would choose to breach. In contrast, reliance damages create too much breaching. AMD would like to breach when it can sell the Athlon for anything over $550, which is less than the value to Dell. In principle, it might be profitable under reliance damages for AMD to breach the contract, and then sell the Athlon processors to Dell for $575! (Courts are unlikely to permit such a breach.)

The choice of when to breach is not the only consideration relevant to the choice of damages, however. Consider investments in computer design made by Dell. Since Dell recovers these investments whether the contract is breached or not, Dell has an incentive to overinvest in computer design under expectation damages, because it captures the return on its investments even in circumstances (breach) that the investments have no value. Thus, there is a general tendency of the party that might be breached to invest too much under expectation damages. Reliance damages cure this problem, though at the cost of breaching the contract too frequently.

Specific performance may provide a compromise between the overinvestment of the expectation damage and the overbreaching of reliance damages by conditioning the payment on the reason for breach. Thus, a breach remedy that amends expectation damages to make investments of the other party partially unrecoverable may actually represent a preferable alternative to straight expectation or reliance damages.

In summary, expectation damages are preferred the less important early investment are; conversely, important early investments and a significant likelihood of efficient breach favor reliance damages. Specific performance may represent a useful compromise in some circumstances.

Strategic Ambiguity

Give me ambiguity, or give me something else.
—Source unknown

Many contracts are substantially incomplete.[9] Employment contracts for university professors tend to be single-page letters specifying little more than current salary, although mentioning university rules and regulations. Key aspects of the job are left to mutual understanding.

In some cases, ambiguity about the exact nature of a contract can have an important strategic value, especially in a repeated relationship. Consider, for example, an agreement by a firm to purchase architectural plans from an architect. If the contract specifies the price that the firm will pay, the architect has a weak incentive to produce good plans, since the architect gets paid either way. Consider an alternative contract that does not specify the price, but instead lets the architect propose a price once the plans are finished; the firm can either buy them or not. In this case, the architect will propose a reasonable price, given the quality of the plans, because if the price is unreasonably high, the firm can choose not to purchase. Moreover, the architect has strong incentives to produce a set of high-quality plans, because then the amount the firm will be willing to pay rises with the quality of the plans. Thus, contracting about price in advance may harm both parties—the buyer, because the architect has little incentive to work; and the architect, because the only price the buyer will agree to is low, given that the architect may not work very hard.

Often, it will be useful to leave key aspects of contracts incomplete, rather than try to specify what will transpire in every possible situation. The advantage of contractual incompleteness is that one can effectively condition the outcome on circumstances that are difficult to describe or predict in a contract. Such designs need to be handled with care, insuring that both parties can protect themselves satisfactorily. In circumstances where quality is difficult to describe or enforce, contracts that leave price and quantity to be negotiated may improve on contracts that specify price and quantity.

DELEGATION

With similar discount rates, the basic bargaining theory suggests that the parties will split the gains from an agreement. Bargainers would do better if they could make a take-it-or-leave-it offer, one that takes a large portion of the gains from trade. A key method of creating the power to make such offers is to delegate the bargaining to an agent who lacks the authority to negotiate.

Firms selling retail consumer goods typically use clerks for transactions, and do not give the clerks the authority to negotiate prices. Hotels provide a limited authority to negotiate prices, by creating corporate discounts and the like. As a practical matter, such discounts are usually available to anyone who asks for them and hence represent negotiated prices, although with limitations imposed by the hotel. Automobiles prices are usually negotiated, although there have been recent attempts to eliminate negotiation from the process.

Delegation of the negotiation to a party with limited or no authority to reduce prices can be a very effective means of making a take-it-or-leave-it offer. In essence, a department store says, "Go ahead, try and find someone with the authority to negotiate prices. It will not be worth your time." In this way, a commitment to an offer is created. It is common to see such a commitment process in consumer goods in developed countries, although much less common in the Third World.

Attorneys can often be employed to accomplish delegation. In order to commit to an offer, provide an attorney with the ability to make the offer and perhaps make some modifications that do not involve pricing; then, go on vacation to a remote location where you cannot be reached. This puts the other party in the position of accepting the offer or waiting a long time for your return. An alternative way of thinking about the value of delegation, highlighted by the vacation approach, is that delegation increases the discounting required to make a counteroffer, reducing the patience of an opponent. Delegation accomplishes this by delaying access to the decision maker.

EXPLODING OFFERS

An exploding offer is an offer that is good only for a limited time. Such offers have two main advantages. By limiting the amount of time devoted to bargaining, the party making the offer is free to seek other parties with whom to bargain. For example, an offer open for only a short time to a firm's first choice to fill an open position permits the firm to seek its second choice if it needs to, with an increased likelihood that that choice is still available. The main reason for an exploding offer, however, is to increase the likelihood that the first choice will say yes, by having the offer expire prior to the time that the candidate receives other offers. Consider an individual graduating with an M.B.A. This person would like to work for Dell most, and ranks Compaq a close second and Hewlett-Packard a distant third. If Compaq makes an early offer that expires quickly, the candidate might accept it, for fear that an offer from Dell might not come through.

Professors Alvin Roth and Xiaolin Xing[10] describe what may be the fastest kind of exploding offer. Traditionally, an exploding offer means that there is only a short time to accept or decline, usually less than a day, sometimes just an hour. For candidates for federal court judge clerkships, however, an exploding offer means that the candidate is expected to accept or decline immediately, while still on the telephone. The speedup of the decision process has prompted some candidates to become unavailable in real time, screening their calls with an answering machine and attempting to contact a preferred judge when a call comes from a less preferred judge.

Roth and Xing document a wide array of markets that "unravel," occasionally with perverse consequences.* The term "rush," associated with fraternities and sororities, documents the process of unraveling: it arose as membership in fraternities and sororities moved from being fourth-year honorary membership to first-year membership, and "rush" itself refers to the hurry to obtain members. The college football bowl assignments are generally set well before the end of the season, with the consequence of a poorer matching of teams than would arise if the bowl assignments were made later, after more information about team standing had become available. Judge clerkship offers are often made to students in the second year of law school, before the ranking of the student is known with much precision. Top M.B.A.'s have been the subject of both early offers and exploding offers, by consulting firms in the 1970s and investment banks in the 1980s. They have been subject also to an interesting variant of the exploding offer: the salary offer falls for each day the candidate waits before accepting. Internship offers for clinical psychology students originally were required to be open for five days, which was reduced to three days, then to one day, and finally centralized to the second Monday of February, from 8 A.M. that day until noon the following day. Residency assignments for physicians unraveled so much that offers were made in the second year of medical school. The inefficiency of this system led to the telephone-call-based matching system being replaced by a voluntary, centralized matching system, the National Residency Matching Program, which matches twenty thousand doctors to residencies each year.

MULTILATERAL BARGAINING

Consider a group of employees who work together as a team. The team might design aircraft, write computer programs, manage a project, or play basketball. If the

*Since Roth and Xing's article, the market for federal judge clerkships has itself unraveled.

TABLE 14.1
Stole-Zwiebel Illustration

Number of Workers	*Opportunity Cost*	*Value of Production*	*Net Profit*	*Wage*	*Firm Profits*
1	\$100	\$400	\$300	\$250	\$150
2	\$100	\$650	\$450	\$200	\$250
3	\$100	\$850	\$550	\$175	\$325
4	\$100	\$850	\$450	\$125	\$350
5	\$100	\$850	\$350	\$100	\$350

team members are readily replaceable, then they are just paid market wages, but in many important situations team members are difficult to replace. A well-designed team generally has some excess capacity—if one person is ill, the team can continue to operate, although at some handicap. How should bargaining over wages work with this team? An intriguing answer has been given by professors Lars Stole and Jeffrey Zwiebel.[11]

Stole and Zwiebel's basic bargaining theory suggests that, if they are equally patient, each team member should split the gains from agreement with the firm. To figure out what the gains from agreement are, we need to know the value to the firm of the complete team, the opportunity cost to the worker of employment, and the value to the firm of not having the employee. However, if one employee leaves, the bargaining power of the remaining employees changes! If everyone but one person has left, that person is in a two-person bargaining situation with the firm, and can be expected to split the gains from trade with the firm. If an employee quits, the bargaining power of the remaining employees is enhanced, and thus all the employees can expect to capture not only some of the value they bring to the firm, but also some of the reduction in bargaining power accorded to other employees that their employment brings.

An example makes the Stole-Zwiebel theory operational. This example is stylized and does not incorporate the unique role each member of a team would normally occupy. It is intended only to illustrate the logic of multilateral bargaining. The team can consist of one to five workers. We let the opportunity cost of workers be \$100; this is what each could earn in alternative employment, for example. The third column of table 14.1 lists that value of production of a team.

With one worker, the net gains from trade are \$300 (production of \$400 minus the direct cost of the worker at $100), which is split between the firm and the worker. This yields a wage of $250 ($100 in opportunity cost plus $150 from the split). To find the wage with two workers, note that if one quits, the firm expects to earn $150. The gross value of two workers is $650. Each worker has a cost of $100, and the firm now has a cost of $150. The firm would rather have one worker than have earnings below $150. This leaves $300 to be split three ways, or $100 each. Thus, in the second row, the firm gets the $150 it gets with one worker, plus another $100, and the workers get $100 each plus their opportunity cost of $100. With three workers, the workers create direct costs of $300 and the firm expects $250 (its profits with two workers), so there is $550 in costs. Thus, there is $300 ($850 in production minus $550) to be split among four parties, or $75 each. The firm gets $325 and the workers earn $175. With four workers, the firm expects a minimum of $325 and the workers cost $400, so there is $725 in costs, leaving $125 to be split among the five parties. The firm earns $350, and workers wages fall to $125. Note that the fourth worker added nothing to production—the value of the fourth worker to the firm is in reducing the bargaining power of the other workers. Five workers push the wage down to the opportunity cost—the firm has enough redundancy to eliminate the bargaining power of workers in this theory. A sixth worker would necessarily reduce firm profits—there would be no further enhancement of bargaining power.

The Stole-Zwiebel bargaining theory highlights three major ideas. First, a worker's production and the value of that worker to the firm are not the only relevant issues in a wage negotiation. The effect of a worker's departure on other workers, and the deals those other workers can strike with the firm, also matter. Second, the value of an extra worker to the firm includes the ability to improve negotiations with each worker. By hiring additional employees, the firm can resist wage increases demanded by many others. Third, it can easily be in the firm's interest to have more workers than are strictly necessary to do the job. Excess capacity can, with specialized workers, lower the total wage bill. In the example, an unproductive fourth worker increased the firm's profits by reducing the total wage bill. Sometimes redundancy has bargaining value.

CHEAP TALK

Talk is cheap. The entire basis of signaling theory is that actions, especially costly actions, speak louder than words, and can speak loudly even when words are unconvincing. In some situations, however, talk can matter. An important role for talking is coordination—getting firms to coordinate on activities beneficial to all. For example, suppose that there are sufficient supplies of wood to support a new paper mill in both Rome, Georgia, and Athens, Georgia, and that both International Paper and Georgia-Pacific are planning new paper mills. The outcome in which both build in Rome and neither in Athens is a bad outcome for both firms. That outcome can be avoided by the simple announcement that Georgia-Pacific is building in Rome. If International has not yet decided where to build, it would naturally choose Athens.

To think about the role of talking, it is important that the speaker place himself in the role of the listener. The two questions the listener must ask are (1) If the statement were true, would the speaker want me to believe it? and (2) If the statement were false, would the speaker want me to believe it?

If the answer to question one is yes, and the answer to question two is no, then the statement is credible; the only time it makes sense to make the statement is when it is true. With the paper mill example, when the statement that GP is planning to build in Rome is true, it is useful to say it because it helps deter International from building in the same spot. Would they say they were planning to build in Rome when they are not; that is, is the answer to question two true? Perhaps. Suppose that GP had ruled out Athens but had not decided whether to build a new paper mill in Rome, or to expand an existing mill near Savannah, Georgia. GP might reasonably make the statement trying to deter anyone else from building in Rome, thereby keeping the option alive. GP could corroborate the statement by expending some money—buying land, applying for environmental permits—to signal that its statement is in fact correct, that GP is building in Rome. Indeed, public announcements combined with costly signals are often much more convincing than either alone.

To make statements credible, a company should consider how it wants the listener to interpret the statement, and craft the statement to assist with that interpretation. Thus, in a press release, Georgia-Pacific might announce that it had decided to build in Rome because it has experience in the area, that the proximity to a GP sawmill provides an additional source of supply of wood chips for the new paper mill, and that the two plants can be run by the same management team at a considerable economy. GP could even reveal parts of a study showing that a paper mill was economic, but that strategy risks revealing valuable proprietary information and is rarely a good choice. By making the reasons for its choice clear, GP makes the claim that it is building in Rome more credible.

In most cases, there are several reasons firms might make a given statement. The problems of vaporware (discussed in chapter 13) are endemic to cheap talk. It can usually be the case that a firm that has not made a choice wants to deter other firms, or customers, from making choices or succeeding. However, signaling without talk is usually much less effective than a costly signal combined with an explanation.

EXECUTIVE SUMMARY—BARGAINING

- Bargaining theory suggests that the gains from agreement are split according to the relative patience of the parties.
- The party that least needs the agreement gets the majority of the proceeds.
- Consequently, it pays to be patient and to appear patient.
- The war of attrition is a bargaining situation in which only one party can win.
- In wars of attrition, most of the proceeds are lost in the battle.
- A war of attrition is often created by litigation.
- Litigation wars are worsened by the fact that settlement offers can signal important aspects of the case.
- The signaling aspect of settlement offers can be minimized by using settlement escrows, in which a third party sees the offers but does not report them to the litigating parties.
- Holdup is the ability of one party to extract most or all of the proceeds of another party's investment after the fact.
- Holdup can render investment unprofitable, and it typically has no bargaining solution, although it has other solutions, including vertical integration.
- Contract terms that cannot be verified cannot be enforced.
- It is useful to agree to readily observable terms even if these terms are not ideal.
- In many cases, it is better to have a bright-line standard that is not perfect than a gray-line standard that is in principle perfect.
- There are three major types of penalties for contract breach:
  Expectation (get something equivalent to the contract)
  Reliance (get what would have been gotten from another party)
  Specific performance (court-imposed remedy)
- Expectation damages create efficient contract breach but result in overinvestment. Reliance damages create efficient investment but too frequent breach. Specific performance may balance these conflicting incentives.
- Ambiguity or flexibility may be a valuable part of contracts, especially when both parties have countervailing power.
- Delegation is often an effective means of creating a take-it-or-leave-it commitment.
- When many employees are required for a project, it may be valuable to have additional replacement employees to mitigate the bargaining power of others.
- Well-crafted credible strategic announcements can serve a useful purpose.

15

Last Words

SUSTAINING COMPETITIVE ADVANTAGES

A great deal has been written about sustaining competitive advantages but little that has practical content. The problem with sustaining a competitive advantage is that a great deal of luck is necessary to sustain it for a long period of time. Sustaining an advantage requires a permanent entry barrier of some form, for otherwise competitors will chip away at the advantage until it has eroded completely.

Cost advantages tend to be overwhelmed by new technology, and generally give, at best, a ten- to twenty-year run of advantage. Ford's 1920 cost advantages lasted about fifteen years. Cost advantages are often easier to imitate than quality advantages, because a entrant can exploit new technology to provide comparable costs, and there is less of a barrier arising from reputation, branding, and quality issues. Thus, few cost strategies provide an advantage for more than ten years, while quality advantages and technological leadership may last more than a century. Technical prowess has persisted in rifles, elevators, and watches for a very long time. Therefore, when choosing a firm's position in quality space, the long-term better bet is often high-quality strategy. However, several factors reduce the attractiveness of high-quality strategies. First, there are usually more firms vying for the position of technological leader. Second, sustaining competitive advantages is not as important as having overall profits, and the low-cost firm may enjoy substantially higher profits over the near term, sufficient to outweigh the larger profits of high-quality rivals twenty years hence. Third, the low-cost firm, with its mass market positioning, may be in a better position to move up technologically, because of its greater scale, then boutique high-quality firms.

The key to sustaining any advantage is a solid barrier to entry and the expansion of rivals. Entry barriers limit the competition to a fixed number of firms, permitting firms to specialize in niche markets, or to cooperate, as a means of sustaining profits above competitive levels. There are two very important sources of entry barriers that should play a central role in the formulation of business strategy.

One source of entry barriers is a market with such ruthless price competition that only one firm can survive. Enterprise Rent-a-Car seems to be in this position. By locating a kiosk inside automobile dealerships, Enterprise insures that no other company can compete; to have two firms inside the same automobile dealership would invite such cut-throat competition that both firms would lose money. Provided that Enterprise's costs are low, no other firm can find it profitable to move into most of Enterprise's locations. Enterprise also delivers cars to those who need them. This is useful because a second firm in the rental-car-delivery business faces the problem of selling a very similar product as Enterprise's, again encouraging ruinous price competition. That is, the choice to deliver cars insures that there is only room for one firm in the market for delivered cars.

The second main source of entry barriers is complementarities, where the various elements of strategy reinforce each other. Complementarities make it difficult for rivals to imitate the success of the firm, because complementarities increase the costs of experimentation. Basically, a toe-in-the-water approach to finding a strategy will fail to uncover a profitable strategy when there are significant complementarities. Imitation requires a firm to get the strategy substantially right, which means getting a large number of complementary aspects to the strategy aligned; hence, complementarities penalize experimentation. Positioning the firm to exploit complementarities will make competitive entry difficult.

Probably the best chance to have a sustainable competitive advantage arises when a company finds a technology that is subject to strong complementarities and protects it by vigorous R&D. Otis has managed to remain the world's leading elevator company for a century, in part because it exploits synergies among divisions, and in part because it is committed to remaining on top.

How were the circus receipts in Madison Square Garden?

—Last words of P. T. Barnum

Leave the shower curtain on the inside of the tub.

—Last words of Conrad N. Hilton

Don't let it end like this. Tell them I said something.

—Last words of Pancho Villa

Endnotes: Sources and Caveats

PREFACE

1. Pankaj Ghemawat, *Games Businesses Play: Cases and Models* (Cambridge and London: MIT Press, 1977), is a partisan for game theory but summarizes both sides well.

2. This delightful insight was first presented, as far as I can tell, in Adam M. Brandenburger and Barry J. Nalebuff, *Co-opetition* (New York: Doubleday, 1996).

CHAPTER 1: INTRODUCTION

1. The source for this observation, as well as several below, is the entertaining book by Kara Swisher, *AOL.COM: How Steve Case Beat Bill Gates, Nailed the Netheads, and Made Millions* (New York: Times Books, 1999), p. 97.

2. See "This Is Not Your Father's Prodigy," *Wired*, December 1993.

CHAPTER 3: FIRM STRATEGIES

1. This surprising claim has an elementary proof. Suppose $v(q, t)$ is the value placed on quality q by customer type t, and that v is increasing in t. The marginal customer, say type t^*, that will buy the good is given by $v(q, t^*) = p$, where p is the price. The firm's profits are $(p - c(q))(1 - F(t^*)) = (v(q, t^*) - c(q))(1 - F(t^*))$, where F is the cumulative distribution of customer types. Consequently, maximizing profit entails maximizing $v(q, t^*) - c(q)$ for the marginal customer type t^*.

2. There is a formula that governs the design of the quality. The marginal value to the lowest purchasing type of increasing the low-quality good should exceed the marginal cost by an amount that is the difference between the marginal value of the highest purchasing type minus the marginal cost of quality, times the proportion of customers who buy the higher-quality good. This is because any increase in the quality of the low-quality good requires a price cut (or quality increase) of the high-quality good, to prevent defection to the low-quality good. Essentially, an improvement of a low-quality good carries two costs—the physical cost of improvement, and the need to cut the price of the high-quality good to maintain sales of that good. The price of the high-quality good must be cut by the value of the increase of the low-quality good to the marginal high-quality purchaser to maintain sales.

3. These ideas are taken from Professor Dale Stahl's "Evolution of Smart-*n* Players," *Games and Economics Behavior* 5, no. 4 (October 1993): 604–17.

4. Ultrasophisticated conjectures are ordinarily called Nash conjectures after Nobel laureate John Nash. When all players have Nash conjectures and play their best strategy, the resulting play is called a Nash equilibrium. The Nash equilibrium has the desirable property that everyone correctly anticipates the strategies of the other players, and thus no one is fooled. Thus, when all parties play the strategies associated with a Nash equilibrium, no one has an incentive to revise their strategy in light of what they learned from the previous play of the game. When a game is repeated with the same players again and again, they usually arrive at a Nash equilibrium.

5. "Pushing Deeper into Services," *Business Week,* 28 October 1996.

6. *Chicago Tribune,* 20 January 2001, section 2, p. 1.

CHAPTER 4: DIFFERENTIATION

1. Harold Hotelling, "Stability in Competition," *Economic Journal* 39, no. 15 (March 1929): 41–57. Interestingly, this paper contains a much more substantial theory than is usually credited to Hotelling. In particular, the "Hotelling line model" is usually meant to signify competition in location but not in prices; in fact, Hotelling analyzes price competition first.

2. There is no determinate solution to the location problem for three firms. With four firms, one obtains two next to each other one-fourth of the way down the line, and the other two next to each other three-quarters of the way down the line.

3. Poor-quality food combined with good ambiance coexist in some markets like hotels, because there is little opportunity for repeat business.

4. This seems to have been an important insight of Microsoft cofounder William Gates Jr., along with the observation that software could be more valuable than hardware. See, for example, the compelling article by John Heilemann, "The Truth, the Whole Truth, and Nothing but the Truth: The Untold Story of the Microsoft Case," *Wired,* November 2000.

5. Ghemawat, *Games Businesses Play,* chap. 5.

6. Quoted in the *New York Times,* 31 October 1971. Several sources suggest a slightly different quote.

7. The concept of hedonic pricing originates with Frederick Waugh, "Quality Factors Influencing Vegetable Prices," *Journal of Farm Economics,* but the term is due to Andrew Court, who analyzed automobile value. The modern theory of hedonic pricing is due to Zvi Griliches's 1961 report, "Hedonic Price Indexes for Automobiles: An Econometric Analysis of Quality Change," published in *The Price Statistics of the Federal Government,* which was chaired by Nobel laureate George Stigler. The economic interpretation of hedonic pricing was developed by Sherwin Rosen, "Hedonic Prices and Hedonic Markets: Product Differentiation in Pure Competition," *Journal of Political Economy* 82, no. 1 (January-February 1974): 34–55.

8. Nicole Shepler, "Developing a Hedonic Regression Model for Camcorders in the U.S. CPI," Bureau of Labor Statistics (Washington, D.C.: U.S. Government Printing Office,

2000). I have adjusted her numbers to express them in the percentage of base prices rather than logarithms, and I have not reported all categories.

CHAPTER 5: PRODUCT LIFE CYCLE

1. *Statistical Abstract of the United States,* 2000. See http://www.census.gov/statab/www/.

2. Steven Klepper, "Entry, Exit, Growth and Innovation over the Product Life Cycle," *American Economic Review* 86, no. 3 (June 1996): 562–83.

3. *Statistical Abstract of the United States,* 2000. The current boom in patent filings may not indicate increased technological development so much as an increased ability to patent software, business methods, and other formerly unpatentable discoveries.

4. The mathematical derivations are available in R. Preston McAfee, "Production Capacity for Durable Goods," in C. Holsapple, V. Jacob, and H. R. Rao (eds.), *Business Modeling: Multidisicplinary Approaches* (London: Kluewer Academic, 2002).

5. It is profitable to sell the good if $rc < 1$; if $rc \geq 1$, the good will not be sold.

CHAPTER 6: COOPERATION

1. Robert H. Porter, "A Study of Cartel Stability: The Joint Executive Committee, 1880–1886," *Bell Journal of Economics* 14, no. 2 (Autumn 1983): 301–14.

2. Robert H. Porter, "On the Incidence and Duration of Price Wars," *Journal of Industrial Economics* 33, no. 4 (June 1985): 415–26.

3. Timothy Bresnahan, "Competition and Collusion in the American Automobile Industry: The 1955 Price War," *Journal of Industrial Economics* 35, no. 4 (June 1987): 457–82.

4. Jon Joyce, "Effect of Firm Organizational Structure on Incentives to Engage in Price Fixing," *Contemporary Policy Issues* 7, no. 4 (October 1989): 19–35.

5. Peter Bryant and Woodrow Eckard estimate that the probability of a price-fixing cartel being charged is 15% per year. They study cartels that are eventually caught and acknowledge that there might be some cartels that disband prior to detection, and thus are never caught. Clearly we cannot observe the duration of cartels that are never detected. This is an entertaining example of sample selection bias, a topic discussed in chapter 10. Peter Bryant and Woodrow Eckard, "Price Fixing: The Probability of Being Caught," *Review of Economics and Statistics* 73, no. 3 (August 1991): 531–36.

6. This is the nature of cartel pricing—the prices are higher than the competitive prices. By definition, competitive prices are the prices at which each firm or country can sell all it wants to sell.

7. Martin Pesendorfer, "A Study of Collusion in First-Price Auctions," *Review of Economic Studies* 67, no. 3 (July 2000): 381–411.

8. This discussion is based on R. Preston McAfee and John McMillan, "Bidding Rings," *American Economic Review* 82, no. 3 (June 1992): 579–99.

9. Ghemawat, *Games Businesses Play,* table 2.4, p. 55.

10. W. Kip Viscusi, John M. Vernon, and Joseph E. Harrington Jr., *Economics of Regulation and Antitrust* (Cambridge and London: MIT Press, 1992); Nancy L. Rose, "The In-

cidence of Regulation Rents in the Motor Carrier Industry," *Rand Journal of Economics* 16, no. 3. (autumn 1985): 299–318.

11. A formal analysis of incrementalism is presented in Anat R. Admati and Motty Perry, "Joint Projects without Commitment," *Review of Economic Studies* 58, no. 2. (April 1991): 259–76.

12. Michael E. Porter, *Competitive Advantage: Creating and Sustaining Superior Performance* (New York: Free Press, 1985), p. 511.

CHAPTER 7: ORGANIZATIONAL SCOPE

1. Paul Milgrom and John Roberts, *Economics, Organization and Management* (Englewood Cliffs, N.J.: Prentice-Hall, 1992).

2. See Marius Schwartz and Earl A. Thompson, "Divisionalization and Entry Deterrence," *Quarterly Journal of Economics* 101, no. 2 (May 1986): 307–21; and Michael R. Baye, Keith J. Crocker, and Jiandong Ju, "Divisionalization, Franchising, and Divestiture Incentives in Oligopoly," *American Economic Review* 86, no. 1 (March 1996): 223–36.

3. R. H. Coase, "The Nature of the Firm," *Economica* (New Series) 4, no. 16 (November 1937): 386–405.

4. See, for example, Oliver Williamson *The Economic Institutions of Capitalism: Firms, Markets and Relational Contracting* (New York: Free Press, 1985).

5. Paul R. Milgrom, "Employment Contracts, Influence Activities, and Efficient Organizational Design," *Journal of Political Economy* 96, no. 1 (February 1988): 42–60.

6. Coase, "The Nature of the Firm," pp. 386–405.

7. Martin Weitzman, "Prices versus Quantities," *Review of Economic Studies* 41, no. 4 (October 1974): 477–91.

8. *Business Week,* 2 October 2000, p. 78. The numbers provided in this article conflict with *Business Week*'s M.B.A. calculator, described in its article of 22 October 2001, which puts the postgraduation salary increase at the more plausible figure of $40,000. Interestingly, the later article also makes the mistake of suggesting that the candidate maximize the return on investment rather than on the NPV—an error that suggests picking a less expensive school (Rutgers) over Wharton in spite of the latter's higher NPV.

9. William Sharpe, "Capital Asset Prices: A Theory of Market Equilibrium under Conditions of Risk," *Journal of Finance* 19, no. 3 (September 1964): 425–42; and John Lintner, "The Valuation of Risky Assets and the Selection of Risky Investment in Stock Portfolios and Capital Budgets," *Review of Economics and Statistics* 47, no. 1 (February 1965): 13–37.

CHAPTER 8: INCENTIVES

1. James A. Brander and Tracy R. Lewis, "Oligopoly and Financial Structure: The Limited Liability Effect," *American Economic Review* 76, no. 5 (December 1986): 956–70.

2. R. Preston McAfee and John McMillan, "Bidding for Contracts: A Principal-Agent Analysis," *Rand Journal of Economics* 17, no. 3 (autumn 1986): 326–38.

3. Bengt Holmstrom and Paul Milgrom, "Multi-Task Principal-Agent Analyses: Linear Contracts, Asset Ownership and Job Design," *Journal of Law, Economics and Organization* (1991): 24–52.

4. A striking example of the difficulty of providing incentives to maintain trucks arose with a particular Domino's Pizza franchise in Jacksonville, Florida, which had over thirty trucks, but never more than four that ran at any given time in the author's experience, well prior to the "thirty minutes or it's free" campaign.

5. B. Douglas Bernheim and Michael D. Whinston, "Common Agency," *Econometric* 54, no. 4 (July 1986): 423–42.

6. Edward R. Lazear and Sherwin Rosen, "Rank-Order Tournaments as Optimal Labor Contracts," *Journal of Political Economy* 89, no. 5 (October 1981): 841–64. See also Joel Sobel, "A Re-Examination of Yardstick Competition," *Journal of Economics and Management Strategy* 8, no. 1 (spring 1999): 33–60; and Richard Fullerton and R. Preston McAfee, "Auctioning Entry into Tournaments," *Journal of Political Economy* 107, no. 3 (June 1999): 573–605.

CHAPTER 9: ANTITRUST

1. These fines were instituted in 1974; the original fines were $5000, with a maximum imprisonment of one year.

2. *U.S.* v. *Grinnell Corporation,* 1966.

3. Malcolm R. Burns, "Predatory Pricing and the Acquisition Cost of Competitors," *Journal of Political Economy* 94, no. 2 (April 1986): 266–96.

4. Greg Sandoval, "FTC Says Toysmart Violated Net Privacy Law," *CNET Technology News,* 21 July 2000.

5. Baseball's exemption was enacted in 1922, and was ended by 1998 legislation. Other sports are not covered. The National Football League has repeatedly been found guilty of antitrust violations associated with restrictions on the free agency of players.

6. The major oil companies known as the "seven sisters" were prohibited from bidding jointly on off-shore oil for many years, but this restriction has been removed.

7. See Preston McAfee, Daniel Vincent, Michael Williams, and Melanie Havens, "Collusive Bidding in Hostile Takeovers," *Journal of Economics and Management Strategy* (winter 1993): 449–82, and "Collusive Bidding in the Market for Corporate Control," *Nebraska Law Review* 79 (2000).

8. *United States* v. *Terminal Railroad Association,* 224 US 383 (1912).

9. Generally, the guidelines call for the use of the shares of market capacity rather than of production or sales. Thus, potential entrants' capacities might be included, even if the firms had zero sales. McAfee et al., "Collusive Bidding."

10. A simplification exists: if the shares of the merging parties are x and y, the change is $(x + y)^2 - x^2 - y^2 = 2xy$.

11. Jerry Hausmann and Gregory Leonard, "Documents versus Econometrics in *Staples,*" see www.antitrust.org/cases/staples/hausleon.html; and Jonathan B. Baker, "Econometric Analysis in *FTC* v. *Staples,*" paper presented to the American Bar Association, Antitrust Section, Economies Committee, 18 July 1997.

12. Source: http://www.antitrust.org/cases/mergers.htm#pencase.

13. Commissioner Christine Varney, "Vertical Merger Enforcement Challenges at the FTC," speech presented before the 36th Annual Antitrust Institute, San Francisco, California, 17 July 1995.

14. This case was viewed as a pure vertical merger. However, it could have been viewed as a merger of firms selling complementary products. As we observed earlier, such mergers tend to decrease prices—the integrated firm accounts for the external effect of the pricing of the two products—and therefore would be procompetitive.

CHAPTER 10: ELEMENTARY STATISTICS

1. Apparently Mark Twain attributed this statement to Disraeli, but an alternate source says the original involved lies, damned lies, and *church* statistics.

2. The 0.48 can be calculated from $1 - 0.16 - 0.36$, but it also can be calculated because the probability of DR and the probability of RD are each $0.4 \times 0.6 = 0.24$, and either give one of each.

3. To compute the odds of two Rs and one D, note that there are three distinct ways to produce that outcome—RRD, RDR and DRR, each of which has probability $0.4 \times 0.6 \times 0.6 = 0.144$, or 14.4%.

4. To compute this number, first note that the probability of the first voter being an R, then the rest Ds, is 0.6×0.4^{24}. Each of the other ways of getting one R—an R sampled second, an R sampled third, etc.—has the same probability. Thus, the probability of one R is $25 \times 0.6 \times 0.4^{24}$.

5. The third measure of the typical outcome is the mode, which is the most frequent outcome. The mode, while being more frequent than other outcomes, need not be frequent, and for this reason is less common as a measure of the usual outcome.

6. There is a stronger version of Chebyshev's Inequality that applies to this problem and would reduce the upper bound to 24%, still a large overestimate of the true number. The stronger version is that the probability of observing a value greater than the mean plus $b\sigma$ is less than $1/(1 + b^2)$.

7. The mean is $0.0001 \times 100{,}000 + 0.9999 \times 0 = \$10$. The variance is, then, $0.0001 \times (99{,}990)^2 + 0.9999 \times 10^2$.

8. The exact number is $(4 \times 666.63)^2 = 7{,}110{,}393$.

9. This value arises from the formula σ^2/n, which is the variance. The square root of this formula, with $\sigma \leq \frac{1}{2}$, gives the result.

10. The data come from the Educational Testing Service by way of Professor P. B. Stark. Posted on the Web at http://www.stat.Berkeley. edu/users/stark/SticiGui/Text/index.htm.

11. These methods were introduced in 1979 in James Heckman, "Sample Selection Bias as a Specification Error," *Econometrica* 45 (1979): 153–61. Now, most statistical packages include methods for sample selection bias correction.

12. David Dranove, Daniel Kessler, Mark McClellan, and Mark Satterthwaite, "Information Is Good Except When It Is Not: The Effects of Health Quality Report Cards," Northwestern University, unpublished manuscript.

13. This line of research was initiated by T. R. Gilovich, R. Vallone, and A. Tversky, "The Hot Hand in Basketball: On the Misperception of Random Sequences," *Cognitive Psychology* 17 (1985): 295–314.

14. To compute the odds, note that a run of five or more Hs can arise in one of six ways: HHHHHxxxxx, THHHHHxxxx, xTHHHHHxxx, xxTHHHHHxx, xxxTHHHHHx,

and xxxxTHHHHH, where *x* can be either H or T. These six descriptions are mutually exclusive. The odds of the first is 1 in 2^5, or 1 in 32. The odds of the other five are 1 in 2^6, or 1 in 64. Thus, the odds of getting five or more heads in a row is seven in sixty-four. The analysis of runs of tails is symmetric. However, the outcomes HHHHHTTTTT and TTTTTHHHHH are counted twice, as they have both a run of heads and a run of tails.

15. I don't mean this to be an explanation—what superficially makes sense, doesn't. As a player improves, the likelihood of a string of successes increases, and the likelihood of a string of failures falls. Thus, if a player's success rate is increased from, say, 40% to 60%, the odds of a string occurring is unchanged. However, it may be that people perceive strings of successes more readily than strings of failures.

16. Judith Chevalier and Glenn Ellison, "Are Some Mutual Fund Managers Better than Others? Cross-sectional Patterns in Behavior and Performance, *Journal of Finance* 54, no. 3 (June 1999): 875–99.

17. If a stock is consistently riskier in a way that can't be diversified, the stock will have a higher average return, as compensation to the bearers of risk. This is a pattern that can be seen from past performance. However, future peaks and troughs cannot be detected from past behavior.

CHAPTER 11: PRICING

1. There are many other terms of the same two broad pricing strategies. Classically direct and indirect price discrimination were known as third- and second-degree price discrimination, respectively, a tortured nomenclature. Direct price discrimination is also known as characteristics based, while indirect is known as menu based or self-selection, terms that are informative concerning the method of price discrimination.

2. Raymond Deneckere and R. Preston McAfee, "Damaged Goods," *Journal of Economics and Management Strategy* 5 (summer 1996): 149–74.

3. George Stocking and M. Watkins, *Cartels in Action: Case Studies in International Diplomacy* (New York: Twentieth Century Fund, 1946), pp. 402–5.

4. Wolfgang Pesendorfer, "Design Innovation and Fashion Cycles," *American Economic Review* 85, no. 4 (September 1995): 771–92.

5. Deneckere and McAfee, "Damaged Goods."

6. Ibid.

7. Ronald Rudkin and David Sibley, "Optional Two-Part Tariffs: Toward More Effective Price Discounting," *Public Utilities Fortnightly*, 1 July 1997.

8. Copyright © 1998 Alan H. Hess. Originally printed in *Travel Weekly*, October 1998. Reproduced by permission of the author.

9. The logic is that each percentage of increase in the price reduces the quantity demanded by 2%, so a 10% increase will reduce the quantity by 20%. There are two sources of error in this approximation. First, a 10% increase in price is not ten 1% increases in price, a concept familiar from what small-town bankers used to call "the miracle of compound interest." Ten 1% increases in price, in fact, are a 10.462% increase in price. Similarly, ten 2% decreases in quantity give an 18.3% decrease in quantity. Thus, a 10% increase in price

would be associated with about a 17.5% change in quantity. This source of error arises from using multiple bases for percentage changes, the same way that a 10% increase, followed by 10% decrease, results in a 1% decrease. (1.1 × 0.9 = 0.99). This source of error is readily corrected with a calculator. It is much more difficult to account for the second source of error, which is "out-of-sample extrapolation." We might, through experience, know the elasticity of demand at a given price. After changing that price, however, the elasticity may be expected to change, and change more the larger the price change. Thus, the effect of the tenth 1% price change may be significantly different from the effect of the first. This source of error is likely to accumulate; that is, if the elasticity is rising as the price rises, the misestimation accumulates, rather than averaging out, when the size of the contemplated price change grows. Such "out of sample" problems have no compelling cure other than experimentation.

10. This is the per unit cost of the last few units. Thus, when an additional shift must be instituted to increase production, the marginal cost includes the wages of the additional workers, overtime pay required for existing workers, added wear and tear on equipment, and other charges that arise because of the added shift. The marginal cost would not include fixed costs like factory space unless that space had to be enhanced, and then the incremental cost would reflect the cost of enhancements.

11. The elasticity of demand gives the percentage decrease in quantity associated with a 1% price increase.

12. For example, a diabetes medicine that sells for $46.00 in the United States sells for $6.75 in Mexico. *Austin American-Statesman,* 19 June 2000, p. 1.

13. According to some recent work by the author, offering two options does quite well in many circumstances; diminishing returns are strong in relation to the number of items in the menu of options. In contrast, the full theory, as presented by Robert Wilson's 1993 classic, *Nonlinear Pricing* (Oxford: Oxford University Press; in association with the Electric Power Research Institute, 1993), requires massive computing effort.

14. There is a corresponding theory of optimal taxation—the theory seeks to minimize the distortion of taxation subject to a revenue constraint—that posits a menu of taxes with taxpayers choosing at the beginning of the year which category they fall into, and paying a fixed amount to reduce their marginal tax rate. Such schemes create problems of bankruptcy in a world with uncertainty and hence tend to be fatally flawed for taxation, while quite successful for pricing, where bankruptcy created by the pricing scheme is rarely an issue.

15. An interesting piece of evidence for the claim that brand-name drugs do not compete directly with generics is that when generics come into existence, the price of the branded drug rises on average. This makes sense from a price-discrimination perspective. Prior to the introduction of generics, the brand name served both the high-value and low-value markets, with a corresponding intermediate price. After the generic is introduced, the brand name serves only the highest-value, most inelastic customers, with a correspondingly high price.

16. Product branding has many functions other than price discrimination including signaling quality and commitment to uniformity.

17. ABC *Morning News* 11 July 2000.

18. In some cases, it is desirable to charge a premium for the bundle. Arbitrage is a major problem because consumers can simply make two independent purchases. Arbitrage may be preventable in services, where it is possible to observe who buys what products. However, charging more for the bundle is an invitation to competitors to skim off the best customers by offering lower single-good prices.

19. This logic was discovered by R. Preston McAfee, John McMillan, and Michael D. Whinston, "Multiproduct Monopoly, Commodity Bundling, and Correlation of Values," *Quarterly Journal of Economics* 104, no. 2 (May 1989): 371–83.

20. *Business Week,* 16 October 2000, p. 60.

21. This analysis is based on Philip Pfeifer, "The Airline Discount Fare Allocation Problem," *Decision Sciences* 20, no. 1 (1989): 149–57.

22. R. B. Childs, "Home Video," in J. E. Squire (ed.), *The Movie Business Book,* 2d Fireside ed. (New York: Simon and Schuster, 1992); reported by Ashutosh Prasad's Ph.D. dissertation, University of Texas, 1999, which is the source for other information about the timing of video release.

23. Indeed, as Adam Brandenburger and Barry Nalebuff eloquently argue, doing the opposite is the most desirable way to insure cooperation and soften price competition, a theme expanded above. See Brandenburger and Nalebuff, *Co-opetition.*

24. The current version of Microsoft Word is also cheaper for users of past versions of Word, for precisely the same reason—earlier versions of Microsoft Word are competitors to the current version.

25. *Daily Telegraph,* 27 June 1994.

26. This is based a true story. A court-mandated seal prohibits revealing the identities of the franchiser, so the numbers have been changed to disguise the company. The courts prohibited the company from decertifying the suppliers without a quality-based reason.

27. Paul Joskow presents a fascinating and comprehensive study of these solutions. See Paul L. Joskow, "Contract Duration and Relationship-specific Investments: Empirical Evidence from Coal Markets," *American Economic Review* 77, no. 1 (March 1987): 168–85.

28. The text oversimplifies a bit; in reality, the complementarities are more complex. Some capture cards are bundled with software products of three or more different firms and include software that coordinates all of the software products. Some software products are also designed to work together as well.

CHAPTER 12: AUCTIONS

1. Value refers to willingness to pay for the particular item. Thus, a bidder may have a use value of $10,000 for a computer, but be willing to pay only $2000 for a particular computer because of the existence of substitute computers. The value of the particular computer is $2000; at any price over $2000, the buyer will substitute another computer.

2. The price will not generally equal the second-highest value, because of bid increments—the minimum increase permitted by the auctioneer. It is a remarkable fact that bid increments have little substantive effect even at high levels. For example, a 10% bid incre-

ment, which seems like a lot, typically has less than a 1% effect on the efficiency of the process. The reason is that the likelihood the increment matters to the outcome is approximately the value of the increment, and the amount that it matters is, on average, half the increment. Thus, the effect of a 10% increment tends to be 10% of 5%, or 0.5%.

3. With major projects and significant variation in expected values, a deeper analysis is appropriate. In addition to adjusting for the winner's curse (discussed below), winning bids usually won't be proportional to value, and may depend on factors other than just the value estimate. These other factors can be handled by using a multivariate regression with a heteroskedasticity correction. While such an analysis requires a much more complex and detailed statistical and economic analysis, the logic of the analysis is the same as the present discussion.

4. The standard deviation can be indirectly estimated by the variation in the bids, using the formula for computing the standard deviation shown in chapter 10.

5. Other reasons for the winner's curse correction to vary include nonnormality or skewness in the distribution, compactness or a finite variance of the true value (the corrections sent the variance of the true value to infinity), and a mixture of common and private value aspects of the auction environment. The model presented sets the estimates to be $v + \epsilon$, where the true value is v and errors are independently distributed.

6. The statistical mechanics of updating projections is akin to updating actuarial tables for new information. Imagine calculating life expectancy for a forty-year-old male, and finding it is seventy-five years. When you learn the male is not a smoker, life expectancy rises to eighty years. Add a history of heart trouble, and it falls. Updating bids is analogous—high bids by others reflect high estimates, which can be deduced approximately by removing winner's curse corrections, which leads to recovery of a floor for their underlying estimates. That floor can be folded into one's own estimates.

7. See, for example, the references in R. Preston McAfee and John McMillan, "Auctions and Bidding," *Journal of Economic Literature* 25, no. 2 (June 1987): 699–738.

8. This result and several others used in this section were developed in the remarkable paper by Paul R. Milgrom and Robert J. Weber, "A General Theory of Auctions and Bidding," *Econometrica* 50, no. 5 (September 1982): 1089–1122.

9. R. Preston McAfee and John McMillan, *Incentives in Government Contracting* (Toronto: University of Toronto Press, 1988).

10. R. Preston McAfee and Daniel Vincent, "The Declining Price Anomaly," *Journal of Economic Theory* 60, no. 1 (June 1993): 191–212.

11. This auction was developed by Paul Milgrom, Robert Wilson, and R. Preston McAfee. See John McMillan, "Selling Spectrum Rights," *Journal of Economic Perspectives* 8, no. 3 (summer 1994): 145–62.

12. Ibid.

13. See Jeremy Bulow and Paul Klemperer's intriguing article, "Auctions vs. Negotiations," *American Economic Review* 86, no. 1 (March 1996): 180–94.

14. This feature of auctions is emphasized by Alejandro M. Manelli and Daniel R. Vincent, "Optimal Procurement Mechanisms," *Econometrica* 63, no. 3 (May 1995): 591–620.

15. Ralph Blumenthal, *New York Times,* 22 April 2000.

CHAPTER 13: SIGNALING

1. The theory of signaling was pioneered by Michael Spence in his Harvard dissertation, with a portion published as "Job Market Signaling" (*Quarterly Journal of Economics* 87, no. 3 [August 1973]: 355–74), with the education application.

2. Cited in the *Journal of the American Bar Association* (August 2000): 70.

3. *Business Week,* 26 February 2001, p. 33.

4. *Business Week,* 19 March 2001.

5. This is an example of a more general phenomenon of signaling commitment by investing in "specific assets," which are assets that are useful only in a particular relationship. Thus, by investing in assets useful for one business but not for others, one signals a commitment to that business.

6. See the wonderful survey by Tamara Kaplan, "The Tylenol Crisis: How Effective Public Relations Saved Johnson & Johnson," on which this section is based, in Scott Cutlip, Allen Center, and Glen Broom, *Effective Public Relations* (Englewood Cliffs, N.J.: Prentice-Hall, 1994).

7. "Circuit Flaw Causes Pentium Chip to Miscalculate, Intel Admits," *New York Times,* 24 November 1994.

8. Mark Mowrey, "Do Expiries Matter?" *The Standard,* 10 April 2000.

9. The issue of the informational content of willingness to trade was pioneered by George Akerlof, "The Market for 'Lemons': Quality Uncertainty and the Market Mechanism," *Quarterly Journal of Economics* 84, no. 3 (August 1970): 488–500. The ultimate expression of this work is presented in Paul Milgrom and Nancy Stokey, "Information, Trade and Common Knowledge," *Journal of Economic Theory* 26, no. 1 (February 1982): 17–27.

10. Further Reading: *Upside Magazine,* May 2001.

11. To be fair, this is a line in the Rolling Stones's song, "Start Me Up," used to introduce Windows 95.

12. Stefanie Olsen, Staff Writer, CNET News.com 8 April 2000.

13. This issue has a long confused history in the economics literature. The main source of the confusion will become clear in the analysis—signaling doesn't work in all circumstances. The confusion was resolved by Paul Milgrom and John Roberts, "Limit Pricing and Entry under Incomplete Information: An Equilibrium Analysis," *Econometrica* 50, no. 2 (March 1982): 443–60.

14. See Benjamin Hermalin, "Toward an Economic Theory of Leadership: Leading by Example," *American Economic Review* 85, no. 5 (December 1998): 1188–1206.

15. David Kreps and Robert Wilson, "Reputation and Imperfect Information," *Journal of Economic Theory* 27 (1982): 253–79.

16. In the author's experience, the coffee itself provided a means of price discrimination. The coffee was enjoyable for locals and vile to Westerners, so it is a major accomplishment for a Westerner to sit and drink the coffee for hours on end.

17. Vaporware is also the name of a real company that sells real software for Amiga computers.

18. Mark Mehler, "From the Vaporware Hall of Fame," *ZDNet,* 18 May 1998, 8:30 A.M., EST.

19. Mary Ellen O'Toole, "The School Shooter: A Threat Assessment," Federal Bureau of Investigation, September 2000 (Washington, D.C.: U. S. Government Printing Office).

CHAPTER 14: BARGAINING

1. This analysis is based wholly on the much deeper analysis of Ariel Rubinstein, "Perfect Equilibrium in a Bargaining Model," *Econometrica* 50, No. 1 (January 1982): 97–110.

2. The war ends when either party concedes. If each party conceded with probability p, the probability that at least one concedes is $1 - (1 - p)^2 = 2c$, which is 20% for $c = 10\%$. This gives an expected duration of five years. For any event that happens with probability x per period, the expected time until the event happens is $1/x$ periods.

3. *New York Times,* 23 July 2000.

4. "Settlement Escrows," *Journal of Legal Studies* 24, no. 1 (January 1995): 87–122.

5. Ghemewat, *Games Businesses Play.*

6. Thomas Schelling, *The Strategy of Conflict* (Cambridge: Harvard University Press, 1960).

7. The downside of Wal-Mart's legal tactics, besides litigating cases it is likely to lose, is that it angers judges. See *Business Week,* 16 July 2001, pp. 58–59.

8. See Aaron Edlin and Stefan Reichelstein, "Holdups, Standard Breach Remedies, and Optimal Investment," *American Economic Review* 86, no. 3 (June 1996): 478–501; and Aaron Edlin, "Breach Remedies," National Bureau of Economic Research, October 1997. Expectation damages include two forms: compensatory damages, which reimburse the breached party for its loss, and consequential damages, which reimburse the breached party for its added costs of carrying out the contract with another party.

9. The concept of strategic ambiguity of contracts was pioneered by Douglas Bernheim and Michael Whinston, "Incomplete Contracts and Strategic Ambiguity," *American Economic Review* 88, no. 4 (September 1998): 902–32.

10. Alvin Roth and Xiaolin Xing, "Jumping the Gun: Imperfections and Institutions Related to the Timing of Market Transactions," *American Economic Review* 84, no. 4 (September 1994): 992–1044. This fascinating paper documents the phenomenon of offers made and accepted earlier than optimal, largely for the reason given—a less desirable partner makes an early offer to obtain agreement of a more desirable partner. What is perhaps the earliest example of an offer made and accepted occurs in the Arunta, a Stone Age aborginal tribe of Australia. Shortly after the births of a girl and a boy, the infant girl's prospective *daughter* is betrothed to the infant boy. That is, an infant girl becomes the planned mother-in-law of the infant boy.

11. Lars Stole and Jeffrey Zwiebel, "Organizational Design and Technology Choice under Intrafirm Bargaining," *American Economic Review* 86, no. 1 (March 1996): 195–222.

Index